Salamone Rossi

Jewish Musician in
Late Renaissance Mantua

❦ ❧

DON HARRÁN

Donated by

Barbara & Sidney Marks

OXFORD
UNIVERSITY PRESS

OXFORD

UNIVERSITY PRESS

Great Clarendon Street, Oxford OX2 6DP

Oxford University Press is a department of the University of Oxford
and furthers the University's aim of excellence in research, scholarship,
and education by publishing worldwide in

Oxford New York

Athens Auckland Bangkok Bogotá Buenos Aires Calcutta
Cape Town Chennai Dar es Salaam Delhi Florence Hong Kong Istanbul
Karachi Kuala Lumpur Madrid Melbourne Mexico City Mumbai
Nairobi Paris São Paulo Shanghai Singapore Taipei Tokyo Toronto Warsaw
and associated companies in Berlin Ibadan

Oxford is a registered trade mark of Oxford University Press

Published in the United States
by Oxford University Press Inc., New York

© Don Harrán 1999

The moral rights of the author have been asserted

First published 1999

All rights reserved. No part of this publication may be reproduced,
stored in a retrieval system, or transmitted, in any form or by any means,
without the prior permission in writing of Oxford University Press.
Within the UK, exceptions are allowed in respect of any fair dealing for the
purpose of research or private study, or criticism or review, as permitted
under the Copyright, Designs and Patents Act, 1988, or in the case of
reprographic reproduction in accordance with the terms of the licences
issued by the Copyright Licensing Agency. Enquiries concerning
reproduction outside these terms and in other countries should be
sent to the Rights Department, Oxford University Press,
at the address above

This book is sold subject to the condition that it shall not, by way
of trade or otherwise, be lent, re-sold, hired out or otherwise circulated
without the publisher's prior consent in any form of binding or cover
other than that in which it is published and without a similar condition
including this condition being imposed on the subsequent purchaser

British Library Cataloguing in Publication Data
Data available

Harrán, Don.
Salamone Rossi, Jewish musician in late Renaissance Mantua / Don Harrán.
p. cm.—(Oxford monographs on music)
Includes bibliographical references and index.
1. Rossi, Salamone, 1570?–1628? 2. Composers—Italy—Mantua—Biography.
3. Composers, Jewish—Italy—Mantua—Biography.
I. Title. II. Series.
ML410.R78H37 1999 780'.92—dc21 [b] 98—7974
ISBN 0–19–816271–5

3 5 7 9 10 8 6 4 2

Music examples set by Tempo Music Publications, Inc.
Leawood, Kansas 66206, USA

Typeset by Kolam Information Services Pvt. Ltd, Pondicherry, India
Printed in Great Britain
on acid-free paper by
Bookcraft Ltd,
Midsomer Norton, Somerset

To the memory of my father

ACKNOWLEDGEMENTS

The illustrations are reproduced by permission of the Fondazione D'Arco, Mantua (Plate 1); Biblioteca Comunale, Mantua (Plates 2–3, 14); Archivio Storico, Archivio Gonzaga, Mantua (Plate 4); Jewish Community Archive, Mantua (Plate 5); Bibliothèque Nationale de France, Paris (Plates 7, 11); Gesamthochschulbibliothek, Kassel (Plate 8); Bologna, Civico Museo Bibliografico Musicale (Plate 10); Giovetti Fotografia, Mantua (Plates 12–13).

Plates and music examples are published with the assistance of the Authority for Research and Development, Hebrew University, Jerusalem.

CONTENTS

LIST OF ILLUSTRATIONS

(between pp. 182 and 183)

LIST OF MUSIC EXAMPLES

ABBREVIATIONS

ASAG	Mantua, Archivio Storico, Archivio Gonzaga
ASFD	Mantua, Archivio Storico, Fondo Davari
Bc	*Basso continuo*
Bk 1	First book of madrigals *a 5* (1600)
Bk 2	Second book of madrigals *a 5* (1602)
Bk 3	Third book of madrigals *a 5* (1603)
Bk 4	Fourth book of madrigals *a 5* (1610)
Bk 5	Fifth book of madrigals *a 5* (1622)
BL	London, British Library
Br.	*brando*
chit.	chitarrone
Corr.	*corrente*
Cte	*Canzonette* (1589)
CW	Rossi, *Complete Works*, ed. D. Harrán (see Bibliography)
Gagl.	*gagliarda*
JCA	Mantua, Jewish Community Archive
M4	Madrigals *a 4* (1614)
Mti	*Madrigaletti* (1628)
RISM	*Répertoire International des Sources Musicales*
rit.	*ritornello*
S1	First book of instrumental works (S referring to *sinfonie* or, from third book on, to sonatas as well; 1607)
S2	Second book of instrumental works (1608)
S3	Third book of instrumental works (1613)
S4	Fourth book of instrumental works (1622)
Sgs	'Songs of Solomon' (*Hashirim asher lishlomo*; 1622/3)
Sinf.	*sinfonia*
Son.	sonata
v.	voice or voices (1 v., 2 v., elsewhere *a 1*, *a 2*, etc.)

For other abbreviations, in Appendix only, see there.

INTRODUCTION

T HERE were Jewish musicians before Salamone Rossi, but Rossi was the first of them to leave an indelible imprint on European music history as a composer. We know little of his predecessors: most appear to have been instrumentalists, perhaps accompanying themselves while they sang—Abramo dall'Arpa, active in Mantua around the mid-sixteenth century, comes to mind.[1] Of early Jewish composers we know even less. It stands to reason that some may have written one or more works, probably for a single voice, as, for example, Obadiah the Proselyte, thought to be the author of music to a prayer and part of a hymn in the twelfth century.[2] The larger part of the instrumentalists and composers are likely to have yielded to external pressures by converting to Christianity, as did Mahieu *le juif,* a trouvère from the thirteenth century,[3] or the lutenist Giovanni Maria *ebreo,* active in Rome, until 1523, under Leo X, Adrian VI, and Clement VII.[4] Only once does one encounter a bona fide Jewish composer of part music before Rossi: in 1575 David Sacerdote, Italian for Cohen, published a collection of madrigals for six voices, of which the quinto alone survives.[5] Moving on to Rossi's contemporaries, one finds David Civita and Allegro Porto,[6] yet again their collections are incomplete, so much so that not a single work can be reconstructed in its entirety. Said otherwise, there is no fully preserved polyphonic music by a Jewish composer until Rossi; though as a word of caution one might add: to judge from the sources at hand.

Rossi differs from his Jewish predecessors and contemporaries in having a somewhat less than totally fragmentary biography; in utilizing his talents as a vehicle for renewal, with results that if not irrevocably, at least temporarily changed the face of Mantuan instrumental and Jewish sacred music in the early seventeenth century; in leaving behind an impressive legacy of thirteen printed collections, some of them in one or more reprints and, but

---

[1] For Abramo (and his grandson), see under Ch. 1; for a general survey, see Nettl, 'Musicisti ebrei del Rinascimento italiano'.

[2] Cf. Werner, 'The Oldest Sources of Synagogal Chants'; and Adler, 'Les Chants synagogaux notés au XIIe siècle par Abdias, le prosélyte normand'.

[3] Two songs are extant ('Par grant franchise', in twelve sources, and 'Pour autrui movrai').

[4] See Slim, 'Gian and Gian Maria', esp. 563–8.

[5] Cf. Foa, *Gli ebrei nel Monferrato nei secoli XVI e XVII,* 47, 73–5, 77; also various references in Segre, *The Jews in Piedmont* (see Ch. 1 below). Other details of a biographical order may be gleaned from the dedication to the collection (Sacerdote's patron was the marquis of Vasto) and its poetry. (The quinto, along with the various remaining parts of works by Civita and Porto, will be published in Harrán (ed.), *Fragmenta polyphonica judaica;* in preparation.)

[6] On David (or Davit) Civita (or da Civita), see Birnbaum, *Jüdische Musiker am Hofe von Mantua,* in Italian tr. Colorni as 'Musici ebrei', etc., 192; and on Allegro Porto, Harrán, 'Allegro Porto, an Early Jewish Composer on the Verge of Christianity'.

for one, complete in all their parts; in writing vocal music to verses by poets who were particularly fashionable in his day; and, last but not least, in establishing himself not only as a serious composer of art music, but, via his Hebrew works for the synagogue, as a specifically Jewish art music composer. Rossi thus made a double statement, writing and performing music for his Gentile patrons and serving his people as an indigenous Jewish musician. In the quantity and quality of his works he is unique among *musici ebrei*, as he is in his twofold abilities as performer and composer. No other Jewish musician of his stature and accomplishments is known from ancient times to the early seventeenth century; he was described, in fact, as the first to have restored music to its splendour in the Ancient Temple and as having David the psalmist as his forebear.[7] Nor can any later Jewish composer, of the same calibre, be found until the nineteenth and twentieth centuries. True, Mendelssohn and Mahler were Jewish-born, but by converting they masked their origins. Other composers, who were, in fact, preoccupied with their Jewish heritage, better qualify as Rossi's spiritual descendants, among them Ernest Bloch, Darius Milhaud, and Leonard Bernstein.

As a Jewish composer who identified with the community, yet plied his trade for a largely Christian audience, Rossi moved between two worlds. Their bounds were demarcated for him, at the one end, by musical life, in Mantua, at the court and in the houses of the nobility; and at the other, by the uses of music in the religious and social activities of the Jewish community. The distance between them was as that between Christians and Jews, in Mantua and its domains, in the later sixteenth and early seventeenth centuries. As elsewhere in Northern Italy, though sometimes less severely in Mantua, the Jews were a victimized minority, removed from their neighbours socially and, with the establishment of ghettos, physically. The Jews served the Christians in many capacities, as business entrepreneurs, loan bankers, doctors, actors, dancers, musicians; but they remained *ebrei*, hence alien. In the wake of the Counter Reformation more stringent measures were taken to restrict their movements, leading to increased repression.[8]

Rossi thus catered to two audiences, each with its own demands and customs. For the Christians, he performed or composed music as requested or after having offered his services. For the Jews, it is less clear what he did: madrigals and instrumental music, including dances, might have been heard in private gatherings, but music was clearly an indulgence that only the more prosperous Jews could allow themselves. Nor was art music

---

[7] In the introductory matter to his Hebrew collection (to be discussed in Ch. 7).

[8] On the worsening situation of the Jews in the later 16th c., see Milano, *Storia degli ebrei in Italia*, 244–85; Bonfil, *Jewish Life in Renaissance Italy*, 63–77; and for Mantua, Simonsohn, *History of the Jews in the Duchy of Mantua*, 113–43. In a separate study, Bonfil considered Italian Jewry of the outgoing 16th c. under the profile of 'Change in the Cultural Patterns of a Jewish Society in Crisis'.

regularly included in the synagogue ritual, which, by tradition, relied on monophony for intoning prayers, scriptural readings, and hymns. That Rossi tried to alter this tradition is another matter, to be discussed in a separate chapter. It is only natural for the introduction of art music into the synagogue to have met with resistance from certain rabbinical authorities, who preferred continuity to change;[9] and until such time as Rossi tried out his Hebrew works in one or more synagogues, in preparation for their publication, his services, as a composer of sacred music, would seem not to have been solicited. What he did probably do for the Jewish community was write pieces and rehearse the Jewish musicians for various performances, by ducal command, of the Jewish theatrical troupe. His services may also have been sought for Jewish weddings and other family or community celebrations.

The problem of being a Jewish artist in a non-Jewish society is not new, but it is the more acute when the Jew works for Christian patrons and hopes to succeed by pleasing them. Ambitious as he was, Rossi was probably the first musician to confront the problem in all its complexity. His 'case' might be tested against the analogous ones of later Jewish musicians employed or commissioned by non-Jewish patrons and determined to earn recognition from them. It was much easier for leading Jews who remained within the fold, serving their people as rabbis and talmudic scholars or as craftsmen and small businessmen; though they occasionally came into contact with Christians, their activity was circumscribed by the spiritual and material needs of the community. As soon as the Jew ventured outside, to gain his reputation in the Christian world, his experience became dichotomized into two uneasily compatible varieties. Consequently, his biography was often an exercise in accommodating to conflicting demands: for his patrons, he disguised his Judaism, hoping to be accepted for what he did and not who he was; for his co-religionists, he reasserted his Judaism, lest it be thought that his outside activities weakened his allegiance to the community.[10]

Thus Rossi, for his Christian patrons, exhibited his skills as a performer and composer of the then fashionable modes of vocal and instrumental chamber music: madrigals, *canzonette, sinfonie*, sonatas, *gagliarde*, and *correnti*. For the Jews, he prepared the 'Songs of Solomon', meant to demonstrate his commitment to the Hebrew tradition.

The situation of the Jews became increasingly difficult as time progressed. Duke Vincenzo tried to withstand the pressure exerted from papal circles to place further limitations on the Jews, if not fully to abrogate their rights.[11] With the institution of the ghetto, walls were erected around the community

---

[9] On the powers of the Italian rabbinate, see Bonfil, *Rabbis and Jewish Communities in Renaissance Italy*.

[10] On the processes of accommodation, see Harrán, 'Jewish Dramatists and Musicians in the Renaissance'.

[11] See Stow, *Catholic Thought and Papal Jewry Policy, 1553–1593.*

that, for years, had already been separated by ethnic and economic barriers.[12] Life continued as before, though with increasing hardship; the ghetto offered protection against the hostility of the populace, but beyond its walls—and there was considerable movement beyond them in daytime—the Jews were prey to acts of violence. After the death, in 1627, of Vincenzo II, who left no heir, there was a struggle for the Mantuan succession; rumbles of warfare could be heard from the conflicting parties.[13] The end came in 1630, with the invasion of the imperial armies. They looted and ravaged the ghetto. Its inhabitants fled Mantua by the hundreds, only, in many cases, to be marauded or to expire from hunger and exhaustion in the countryside. That is where the story of Rossi ends, for after 1628, when the clouds of the impending disaster settled upon Mantua, nothing is known of him.[14]

This book then is not about an Italian composer, but about an Italian Jewish composer: there is a difference. True, one would not expect to find a study on Giaches de Wert, Pallavicino, or Monteverdi, Rossi's contemporaries at the Mantuan court, to describe them, in the title, as Christian composers; but that is because it is obvious they were, as almost all other musicians in the Italian courts. Rossi's Jewish faith set him apart, with serious consequences for his biography and works: in his publications Rossi was identified as a 'Jewish musician', which is reason enough to retain the qualifier in any modern critique.

Other terms in the title—*musician*, for one—likewise call for explanation. Musician, because Rossi was active not only as a composer, but as a performer; in its Boethian sense, *musicus* also implies exercising powers of musical discrimination,[15] and Rossi revealed his critical acumen in the dedication to his Hebrew songs.[16] More problematical are the terms *late Renaissance* and *Mantua*.

Late Renaissance has the advantage of being a compact formulation for what otherwise could, and will, be referred to, in the context of Rossi's activity, as the rather cumbersome 'later sixteenth and early seventeenth centuries'. Its disadvantages are its chronological ambiguity; its suggestion of a pervading *Zeitgeist*; and, more seriously, its inapplicability to certain compositions within Rossi's repertory, particularly his sonatas, usually

---

[12] About 1,500 persons were living in the area of the ghetto, mainly in the Contrada degli Ebrei, prior to its establishment (another 835, eventually to join them, were scattered about the city; cf. Simonsohn, *History of the Jews in the Duchy of Mantua*, 191). On the ghetto, see Carnevale, *Il ghetto di Mantova*.

[13] On the origins of the struggle, see Quazza, *Mantova e Monferrato nella politica europea alla vigilia della guerra per la successione (1624–7)*; and specifically on the years of warfare, id., *La guerra per la successione di Mantova e del Monferrato (1628–31)*.

[14] The Jewish sufferings belong to a larger cadre of historical upheaval: cf. Parker and Smith (eds.), *The General Crisis of the Seventeenth Century*; Kamen, *The Iron Century*; and Parker, *Europe in Crisis, 1598–1648*.

[15] I am referring to the well-known passage, at the end of the first book, in Boethius' treatise *De institutione musica*.

[16] Assuming he wrote the dedication; on this more in Ch. 7.

treated as characteristically Baroque. As a terminal figure, though, Rossi looks in both directions; in this he can be compared to Monteverdi. It is symptomatic that Monteverdi, in an important early monograph on his life and works, was designated 'creator of modern music'; yet in a more recent one, he figures, in the title, at 'the end of the Renaissance'.[17]

The later Renaissance did obviously include the changes that led to *musica moderna*. Though Rossi conspicuously leaned towards the *moderna* in his last two books of instrumental music, and possibly in his fifth book of madrigals, to judge from the one part extant, the *continuo*, he seems to have been more oriented towards the *antica*, that is, the sixteenth century, in everything else. But the Renaissance was perpetuated, on a continuum, into the Baroque, through the madrigal, the *canzonetta*, short instrumental works (*preludia, intonazioni*, etc.) prototypical of Rossi's *sinfonie*, the *canzona* as a structural precedent for many of his sonatas, and even the motet as a model for his Hebrew 'Songs of Solomon'. By training and inclination, Rossi belonged to old and new, Renaissance and Baroque. Yet, for all that, the crux of his activity lay, stylistically, in the *prima pratica*. Historically, the Renaissance did seem to continue in Mantua, only to come to an abrupt end with the turbulence of the later 1620s; and as far as the Jews are concerned, whatever 'Renaissance' they enjoyed before then ceased to exist thereafter. Indeed, Jewish history has often been characterized as 'medieval' until the Emancipation. It is clear, then, that the term *Renaissance*, however serviceable as a cultural and temporal point of reference, must be redefined in its various contexts, historical, social, religious, and musical.

It was in Mantua that Rossi lived and was active for as much as we know of his career; and though one cannot be sure of it, it was in Mantua that he was probably born and may have died. Late Renaissance Mantua refers, historically, to courtly and public affairs under the late Gonzaga dukes. Musically, it implies a regional style, which is not easily pinpointed. Granted, there is a certain resemblance between Rossi's and Gastoldi's madrigals, or between his and Monteverdi's early ones, or between all three composers' *canzonette*. But it is questionable whether the resemblance can be defined as an equation with the coefficient of a specifically Mantuan mode of expression. It might be remembered that Monteverdi's opera *Orfeo* was likewise written for Mantua, as were Giaches de Wert's dramatic, often recitative-like madrigals, which of course abnegates the notion of a unified Mantuan style. Mantua serves, for Rossi, as a geographical designation for his connections more with the Gonzaga court and the Jewish community under its jurisdiction than with an explicit stylistic orientation.

The affiliation with the court and Jewish community as the locus of Rossi's activity delimits the socio-historical sources on which any study of

---

[17] Schrade, *Monteverdi, Creator of Modern Music*; Tomlinson, *Monteverdi and the End of the Renaissance*. For a mediating appraisal, with Monteverdi now as partner to 'music in transition', see Leopold, *Monteverdi*; thus Rossi might also be perceived.

Rossi as a 'Jewish musician in late Renaissance Mantua' must rely. They are, first, the body of documents held in the Archivio di Stato, Mantua, mainly in the Gonzaga archive, with its various *Libri dei Decreti* and *Mandati*, its extensive files of letters, and three copious folders on *ebrei*.[18] These documents were originally investigated for their musical contents by one of the archive's former librarians, Stefano Davari, who transcribed many of them, adding his own comments and annotations;[19] then by Antonio Bertolotti, who summarized his findings in *Musici alla corte dei Gonzaga*; and most recently, for the sixteenth century, by Iain Fenlon, in *Music and Patronage in Sixteenth-Century Mantua*, and, for the succession of four dukes from Vincenzo I to Vincenzo II, by Susan Parisi, in considerable detail, in 'Ducal Patronage of Music in Mantua, 1587–1627'. Obviously, the archives have already been well combed for their musical material. Still, with my own research in the Archivio di Stato, I was able, in the end, to add a few more documents to the rather sparse number of those that relate specifically to Rossi and his family and, more generally, to Jews as musicians. By the nature of things, however, it was clear that without major biographical or musical discoveries, and there were none, the thrust of my efforts was to be directed toward adding, where I could, new shades of meaning and new contextual situations to the already existing documents.

The second body of documents is held in the Mantuan Jewish Community Archive.[20] It consists of three hundred portfolios plus sixty bound volumes, including the community's minute books, from the years 1522 to 1810. They were thoroughly scoured for their historical matter by Shlomo Simonsohn in his magisterial *History of the Jews in the Duchy of Mantua*. In my own research on the Hebrew documents I re-examined the larger part of those that concern Rossi and Jewish musicians and actors, without coming upon anything strikingly new in them. Yet, again, the existing documents may be read in diverse ways, and I, too, tried to form my own opinions on their content.

A third body of documents, relating to the composer's biography and works, is the series of dedications in his various Italian collections and, for his Hebrew songs, the extensive prefatory material by various contributors, including the composer and one of his staunch admirers, Leon Modena. The Hebrew texts have been studied by several authors (Simonsohn, Gradenwitz, Rikko, and most innovatively Israel Adler, in his *Pratique musicale savante* and his anthology of *Hebrew Writings Concerning Music*). I endeavoured to give the Italian and Hebrew texts fresh readings in various earlier studies, among them 'Salamone Rossi, Jewish Musician in Renaissance Italy' for the Italian dedications and 'Tradition and Innovation in Jewish Music of the Later

---

[18] Cf. Luzio and Torelli, *L'archivio Gonzaga di Mantova*.

[19] Part of his material was published in Davari, *La musica a Mantova*.

[20] Cf. B. I. Levi, *Indice-repertorio dell'Archivio della Comunità israelitica di Mantova*; also Mortara, *Catalogo dei manoscritti della biblioteca della Comunità israelitica di Mantova*.

Renaissance' for the Hebrew texts. The dedications are included in the respective volumes of Rossi's *Complete Works*; and the Hebrew texts will appear, in a
new edition and translation, in Volume xiii (forthcoming). These documents
are essential to our understanding of Rossi as he saw himself and was seen, in
his time, by others. They allow us to tie him to conceptual trends in Jewish and
Renaissance music and to place him in the different socio-historical contexts to
which he properly relates in his ideas and their execution.

By far the most impressive series of documents is contained in the more
than three hundred musical works of the composer's thirteen collections
and other sources: for a complete listing see the Appendix. They enable a
reconstruction of Rossi's tastes and generic choices in poetry and music and
his formal and stylistic procedures in composition. The various collections
may be subsumed under the larger headings of vocal music, instrumental
music, and Hebrew songs, to be covered, below, in their respective chapters.
It is through his works that Rossi makes his most eloquent historical and
artistic statement; and it is on the basis of his works that he can truly be
considered the first and foremost early Jewish art music composer.

There is a small, but significant literature on Rossi, in various contexts, by
the authors already mentioned, as well as others, most notably, in chronological order, Eduard Birnbaum, in his pioneering study on Jewish musicians in Mantua;[21] Joel Newman, in his dissertation on the composer's
madrigals; Franco Piperno, in two articles on Rossi's instrumental music;
Massimo Torrefranca, in a thesis on his sacred music; and Judith Cohen, in
studies on Rossi's madrigal style and his *canzonette*. For a full listing,
including my own writings on Rossi, see the Bibliography. Despite the
interest that Rossi awakens historically and musically, there has, until
now, been no inclusive study on the man and his works, a deficiency
which, it is hoped, the present book will remedy.

The book began in the late 1970s, at least in idea. Yet it soon became
apparent that without a detailed investigation of the composer's works, of
which only a small selection was then available in modern edition, there
could be no book. I thus directed my efforts, in the 1980s, towards assem-
bling, transcribing, and preparing them for publication. The work on a
collective edition, in thirteen volumes, of which twelve have recently been
published, while delaying the present monograph, at the same time allowed
me to exercise a measure of control over its contents. It was especially
advantageous in giving me a fuller picture of Rossi's contribution and in
permitting me to repair or revise a number of conclusions I had drawn in
earlier studies.[22] Horace was right in hailing the benefits of later publication
('Nonumque prematur in annum'), though I may have exaggerated in
doubling his nine-year limit to eighteen.

---

[21] To whom reference was made in connection with Civita (see above).

[22] Of these earlier studies, the only one incorporated, though revised, in the present monograph is that on 'Rossi as a Composer of Theatre Music', here Ch. 6.

Rossi's name has variously been spelled in the literature (Salomone, Solomone, Salamone, de' Rossi). In this book, as in the *Complete Works* edition, I have chosen the spelling to be found in the documents prepared under and signed by the composer, namely his publications. There, with no exception, his name appears in the title or in the signature as Salamone or Salamon Rossi, as it does, moreover, in a new letter whose signature is in the composer's hand.

Hebrew words are quoted in transliteration. Of the various procedures for romanizing Hebrew script, I have chosen the simplest possible, using, however, a diacritic for the consonant *het* (similar, in pronunciation, to *ch* in the German *doch*), e.g. *eftaḥ*; a regular apostrophe for the silent *aleph* in medial position, e.g. *she'ela*; and a turned comma for the mute, but slightly guttural *ayin*, e.g. *'al*. The letter *h* is omitted when silent, though included when marked, in vocalization, with the special sign known as *mapik* (thus the *h* at the end of *todah* is dropped to read *toda*, but the *h* at the end of *haleluyah* is retained). Single years in the Jewish calendar, when they span two years in the Gregorian one, are designated with a virgule (for example, the 'Songs of Solomon', 1622/3), to be contrasted with the indication for publications that extend over two or more years, now with a dash (for example, Chiabrera's *Opere*, in four volumes, 1730–1).

In a book with a gestation span of nearly two decades, it is clear that my indebtedness to persons and institutions is greater than could ever be satisfactorily acknowledged. Nor can I, in retrospect, distinguish between the many colleagues whose assistance or advice was vital to the *Complete Works* edition or, on the other hand, to the book; the termination of the one permitted the completion of the other. The trajectory is too long to be mapped out in detail: I shall only signal some landmarks. I am particularly grateful to my long-term friend and colleague Professor Israel Adler, who introduced me to Rossi as a research topic and with whom I have had the opportunity, over the years, to sharpen swords over our sometimes conflicting interpretations; to Dr Armen Carapetyan, of blessed memory, a man who, in the sweep of his vision, recognized the need for an edition of Rossi's music and its import as a socio-cultural statement, urging me to go ahead with it despite the many obstacles that marked the way to its completion; to my students at Hebrew University, providing me with a critical sound-board, in various courses on Italian and Jewish music in the Renaissance or, more specifically, on Rossi himself, for discussing and refining my ideas; to my institution, the Hebrew University of Jerusalem, for numerous grants; to the Israel National Academy of Sciences, for subsidizing basic research, over the course of six years, on the edition; to the Memorial Foundation for Jewish Research, for two fellowships, one in 1980, permitting me to lay the foundations of a future book, and another in 1994, permitting me to add and complete its upper storeys; and to the wise readers of the manuscript, Professors Benjamin Ravid (Brandeis University) and Eliyahu Schleifer

(Hebrew Union College, Jerusalem) and Dr Graham Dixon (BBC), from whose counsel and comments I benefited in preparing the final draft. Most important is the debt I owe my wife and children: they understood and encouraged, always ready to take Salamone Rossi into the household as a guest, despite the inconvenience of his protracted stay.

A word on externals: Rossi proclaims his 'colour'. If the jacket of this book is noticeably *rosso*, it is because the Press adjudged Rossi ' " il rabbino" rosso',[23] Mantuan Jewry's answer, perhaps, to Vivaldi, 'il prete rosso', worthy of receiving the 'red-jacket' treatment. For this and many other Oxfordian favours I am 'blushfully' grateful.

This book is a summing-up. Where the edition and my separate writings on Rossi were laden, sometimes excessively, with critical annotations, I decided, in the interest of legibility, to cut down on the footnote matter, referring instead to relevant data by more modest annotations. Quotations in the original language will be included only when the sources are new documents essential to the main argument or unavailable in the secondary literature. The poetry and music of Rossi's works are accessible in the edition, as are the various dedications to his collections: they should be consulted as a control for the statements made about the man and the readings suggested for his music. Footnote references to the works are according to their numerical listing in the Appendix. The book ends with a Bibliography: it sprawls over a wide area, for Rossi, in his life and works, invites treatment from varied cultural and historical perspectives; indeed, that is why, in compliance with the request of colleagues from other disciplines, I included a 'glossary of musical terms for the general reader'.[24]

---

[23] For 'rabbi' in the general sense of 'master' or 'teacher' (Hebrew *rav* or, when inflected, *rabbi*, 'my *rav*'), see Ch. 1, two sentences before fn. 95. Rossi was thus addressed in his collection of Hebrew songs, in both the title and the statement of copyright ('his honoured eminence, *rav* Salamone Rossi').

[24] Though not, at the beginning, without a certain reluctance. Since the appearance of such a 'glossary' is rather unaccustomed in books with a strongly musicological core, I should explain. True, a general reader in philosophy would not expect to be told what teleology and dialectical materialism are. If so, why would a general one in music expect to find definitions of modality and homophony? For the simple reason that musical locutions do, in many ways, constitute a professional jargon unfamiliar to all but the initiated. Even the dictionaries and basic textbooks are largely silent or obscure on a hexachord, a cautionary accidental, *falso bordone*, a melisma, an incipit, or a madrigalism. Still other expressions that the music historians bandy about in everyday discourse on the late Renaissance and early Baroque, among them *prima* and *seconda pratica*, the *concertato* madrigal, and *stile rappresentativo*, can only bewilder persons unable to place them in their proper context. My intention, in writing on Rossi, was to open doors, hence the decision to draw up a list of specifically musical terms, including American equivalents of standard British ones (quarter for *crotchet*, measure for *bar*, etc.), plus a few poetic terms of relevance to music (*ballata*, proparoxytone, *verso sdrucciolo*, etc.). By consulting the 'glossary' the diligent non-musical reader should have little difficulty in following discussions of characteristically 'musical' matters, as they relate to structure, style, and performance. I have written in various places on the obligations of the musicologist to an informed general readership, most recently in Harrán, 'Research into Music of the Renaissance: New Perspectives, New Objectives', esp. 97–8.

No one book can do justice to Rossi in all his dimensions. His main contribution is clearly his music, but the meanings of the music emerge only when it is considered in the full panoply of its musical and extra-musical associations. It is hoped that others will be prodded to correlate the biographical and musical material presented between these covers with as many fields of investigation as assure its further illumination. Thus Rossi lives on, as expressed in the acrostic, in the table of contents, to his first collection, *VIVAT S R*.[25]

[25] See Ch. 1 below.

1

The Man

W HAT is known about Salamone Rossi the man is considerably less than what is not. The sources are too fragmentary and their reading often too uncertain to allow one to construct a running biography. Where blanks exist, and there are many, the only way to fill them in is by relying on circumstantial evidence and, for all its inadequacy, on imagination, stirred by probability. The documentation on early music composers is habitually riddled with difficulties, and here Rossi fares no worse perhaps than his esteemed Mantuan colleagues Giaches de Wert, Benedetto Pallavicino, and Giovanni Gastoldi. Even the biography of the illustrious Monteverdi, in its Mantuan phase, leaves much to be desired; and if there is any consolation from a scholarly standpoint, leaves much to be explored. Rossi, like Monteverdi, has ever been, and will no doubt remain, a promising subject for research.

Archival documents usually reveal only a small part of what constitutes an early composer's life history, to be completed by music criticism. On the basis of Rossi's works one might stake out a claim for his importance: he innovated in his Italian poetic choices, in his *sinfonie* and sonatas, and, most notably, in his Hebrew songs. Rossi creates, in his life and works, his own storico-musical frame of reference. In Chapters 1 and, in part, 2 an attempt will be made, then, to reconstruct his rather shapeless biography as a prelude, in later chapters, to a consideration of his works. The difference between the two chapters is that, in the first, the reconstruction follows mainly from archival data and, in the second, from information within the composer's publications.

Like other Jews of his time, Salamone Rossi was designated *ebreo*. Thus he appears, for example, in the titles to his collections. The qualifier had a double meaning, referring to Rossi's people and his faith. It was attached to Jews to indicate their subordinate status as a minority, but since anti-Semitic sentiments ran high in Italian society, the Jews were a very conspicuous minority (around the time the ghetto was erected—1612—they numbered 2,325 in the capital, in a total population of 50,000).[1] Efforts were deployed to make them even more conspicuous by requiring that they wear some mark of identification. Thus the Jews were, despite themselves, 'important'. Yet other Jews were noted not because they were singled out for social discrimination,

---

[1] After Simonsohn, *History of the Jews in the Duchy of Mantua*, 192.

but, more substantially, because of their achievements. Salamone Rossi was one of them: he made a name for himself, in wider circles, as a musician.

Birth, Death, and Intermediate Years

Rossi might have been born in or around 1570. As much may be inferred from a collection of *canzonette*, published as his *primum opus*. It contains numerical allusions that could be meaningful: beyond having nineteen items (as do most other secular vocal collections), it is signed 19 August 1589. From the table of contents items 1–7 are seen to form the acrostic *VIVAT S R*, or 'Long live S. R.' Salamone could have been 19 at the time of publication, hence was referring to his own birthday.[2] It might seem rather presumptuous of a fledgling composer to hail himself in a collection that he dedicated to his patron, Duke Vincenzo, all the more so since, in the first number, he openly sings the duke's praises. Still, Rossi's birth in 1570 is a possibility, or at least the only reasonable one to date.

Similar uncertainty surrounds the time of death. Rossi is no longer heard of after 1628, a period of turmoil in Mantuan history and, more particularly, in the annals of the Mantuan Jewish community: in 1630 the ghetto was sacked and plundered, its residents were expelled (for the ghetto in 1628, see Plates 14*a* and *b*; and for a typical street scene, Plate 12). The Jewish records are sparse for these stormy years.[3] What we do know is that Rossi's last collection was published in 1628 and that, at the time, its composer was alive: it carries a dedication signed by him from Venice on 3 January 1628. Rossi probably repaired to Venice to supervise the publication. In the same year an 'academy' of musicians, many of them earlier Mantuan exiles, formed there under Rabbi Leon Modena's leadership. Whether Rossi stayed on and joined the 'academy' cannot be established.[4] It seems unlikely though, for Modena would doubtless have deferred to his musician friend Rossi as more qualified to be its *maestro di cappella*. Whether, further, Rossi was, as has been conjectured,[5] still alive in 1645, because in that year he was referred to by name, though without the traditional Hebrew formula for the deceased 'May his memory be blessed!',[6] likewise cannot be established. Yet it clearly defies credibility. All that can be said is that Rossi probably died in or shortly after 1628 (the year 1630 seems a plausible *terminus ad quem*).

---

[2] After Newman, 'The Madrigals of Salamon de' Rossi', 109.

[3] Except for a general account by Massarano, *Sefer hagalut vehapedut* (1634). For the War of Succession, see Quazza, *La guerra per la successione di Mantova e del Monferrato* (1628–31).

[4] For details, see Roth, 'L'accademia musicale del ghetto veneziano', and variously in Harrán, '"Dum recordaremur Sion"' and 'Jewish Musical Culture in Early Modern Venice'.

[5] See Adler, *La Pratique musicale savante dans quelques communautés juives en Europe aux XVIIe–XVIIIe siècles*, i. 57.

[6] 'Zikhrono livrakha' (Babylonian Talmud, Kiddushin 31, with explanation of formula). The document for 1645 will be discussed below.

Rossi appears on three payrolls of the Mantuan court, the first two with his sister Madama Europa from 1589 and 1592, the third from 1622.[7] He is not the first Jewish musician to have been employed by the Gonzaga dukes. Others from the same period or slightly earlier are Isacchino Massarano, who played the lute and sang, though is better remembered as a dancer, choreographer, and dance teacher;[8] and Abramino, who, like his grandfather Abramo dall'Arpa, played the harp.[9] There may have been many others, but their Jewish origins are either disguised by their having converted or implied by their having Jewish-sounding names.[10] Yet Rossi differs from these other, still unidentified Jewish musicians, so far as known, in being not just a performer of music, but a composer of works for two or more voices.

In his first publication (1589), Rossi referred to Duke Vincenzo[11] as his 'most revered patron' and to himself as the duke's 'most humble and devoted servant'. In his second one (1600), to the same dedicatee, he supplemented the phrase 'most revered patron' with 'my natural lord', to whom he was indebted, we are told, for everything he knows.[12] Vincenzo thus encouraged Rossi as a composer, giving him commissions, or letting

---

[7] ASAG 395, fos. 156^v–159^v, and 3146, fo. 64. For their most recent discussion, see Parisi, 'Musicians at the Court of Mantua during Monteverdi's Time'.

[8] On Massarano, see Birnbaum, *Jüdische Musiker am Hofe von Mantua*, in Italian tr. Colorni as 'Musici ebrei alla corte di Mantova', 191; Simonsohn, *History of the Jews in the Duchy of Mantua*, 663–5; and Parisi, 'Ducal Patronage of Music in Mantua, 1587–1627', 459–60, 602.

[9] Abramo (d. 1566) was connected with the court under Ercole's regency (he was already active in 1542). Cf. Canal, 'Della musica in Mantova', 701; Birnbaum, *Jüdische Musiker am Hofe von Mantua*, in Italian tr. Colorni, 191; and Fenlon, *Music and Patronage in Sixteenth-Century Mantua*, i. 43, 67–8. His grandson Abramino, by his son Daniel, appears in several documents from the later decades of the 16th c., including a court payroll from 1577 and on from the early 1580s (cf. Parisi, 'Musicians at the Court of Mantua during Monteverdi's Time', 185–6).

[10] Consulting the standard works on music in Mantua (by Canal, Bertolotti, Fenlon, etc.), one comes across persons with names indicating their place of origin, as often occurs with Jews (see, below, under Madama Europa): thus, for Germany, Augustino Alemanno, Michele d'Alemagna, Rodolfo d'Alemagna, and Simone d'Alemagna; and, for other localities, Aaron fiorentino, D. Matteo de Carpi, Giovan Battista Casali, various members of the Bassano family, Tassino Gallo (the 'Frenchman'?), and Daniele Nys (from Nice or the Serbian town Nis?). Aaron and Daniele are definitely Hebrew names, at least in origin, as are others: Giovanni Brith (*brit*, 'covenant'), Muzio Effrem (Ephraim, second son of Joseph), Geremia (Jeremiah), and Gabriele Symeoni (Simeon, second son of Jacob, by his first wife Leah). What is one to make of a certain Mendel (the family is known in Eastern European communities from the 15th c. on), or musicians with the namesake Mayr or Meyer (Jacopo, Lodovico, Massimiliano)? Even the two Rubini brothers from Casale, with whom Rossi seems to have entertained close relations, could have been of previously Jewish stock (see below), not to speak of the famous singer Francesco Rasi, whose name recalls the 12th-c. rabbinical commentator Rashi, and various individuals with the cognomen Vecchi or de' Vecchi, shared by Jews and Christians (the Jewish Vecchis, like the Jewish Rossis, appear to have been of ancient lineage). There is much work to be done on sorting out the religious affiliation, past and present, of these and other musicians. On Jewish family names, see Schaerf, *I cognomi degli ebrei d'Italia*, and more recently, Colorni, 'Cognomi ebraici italiani' and 'La corrispondenza fra nomi ebraici e nomi locali'.

[11] Fourth in the line of Gonzaga dukes, starting in 1530 with Federico I. The dukes were preceded, from 1328 on, by four captains and, from 1433 on, by four marquis. On the Gonzagas, cf. Bellonci, *Segreti dei Gonzaga*; Brinton, *The Gonzaga—Lords of Mantua*; and Coniglio, *I Gonzaga*.

[12] The expression was a commonplace: thus Leone Leoni, in dedicating his Bk 1 *a* 5 (1588) to Count Mario Bevilacqua (Verona), wrote of 'having learned, in his celebrated *ridotto*, that little

his works be heard, or providing him with teachers; not to speak of the services he expected of Rossi as an instrumentalist. The relations between the two are not clear, but the description 'my natural lord' would seem to indicate the duke's benevolence.

Rossi's affiliation with the court appears to have extended over the full length of his career, from the late 1580s to late 1620s, with the usual ups and downs to be expected in his relations with the dukes, depending on personal and budgetary factors. Where Vincenzo was liberal and intent on arranging splendid court festivities, with his death in 1612 his successors Francesco, Vincenzo's eldest son, and Ferdinando, his second son, were less sympathetic towards Jews and, operating under a worsening economy, tightened the purse strings (for the three dukes, see Plates 1–3). The years after 1612 were difficult ones for the Jewish community, and it is then that Rossi may have turned to the preparation of his Hebrew works, perhaps to compensate for what he hoped to gain, but did not, in court circles. True, his fourth book of *sinfonie* (1622) was dedicated to Prince Vincenzo, who, in 1626, succeeded his brother Ferdinando as the last duke in the line (Vincenzo II).[13] Yet Vincenzo died in 1627, and in the ensuing confusion Rossi was probably left without a benefactor at the court.

Evidence for Service in the Mantuan Court

Music-making in Mantua centred principally about the institutions of the court and, of the various churches, the ducal church Santa Barbara and the Cathedral (San Pietro). Rossi's connections with the Gonzagas and other nobles were limited to the court and their private residences. For the court one has the documentation of the payrolls and sporadic references in decrees and letters. For the private residences one has the evidence of the dedications, where the composer, under commission by patrons or in search of them, acknowledged them for their virtues. He seems also to have been loaned out, upon request and with ducal consent, to neighbouring courts or private households, to judge from various petitions.

Rossi knew the Mantuan court *cappella* in its heyday. Giaches de Wert was chapel master from 1565 to his death in 1596, when he was succeeded by Benedetto Pallavicino, to the chagrin of Monteverdi who had hoped for the appointment. Only upon Pallavicino's death in 1601 did Monteverdi win the post, though he was peremptorily discharged in 1612. The post then fell to Santi Orlandi, who had worked for Ferdinando during his five years as cardinal in Rome and quite naturally was appointed chapel master when Ferdinando was called to Mantua to succeed Francesco. With Orlandi's

---

of music that my weak brain was able to understand' (signed Vicenza, where Leoni was *maestro di cappella* at the Cathedral).

[13] Cf. Fochessati, *I Gonzaga di Mantova e l'ultima duca*.

death in 1619, the post devolved upon Francesco Dognazzi, who served as *maestro* until the early 1640s. These, then, were the persons under whom Rossi worked and to whom he was ultimately responsible for fulfilling his duties as court musician.

Beyond its chapel masters, the court had other, often notable composers on its rosters. Gastoldi served the Gonzaga family uninterruptedly from 1571 to his death in 1609, mainly at Santa Barbara, though also, as needed, at court; Frescobaldi spent three months there, in 1614–15, but could not become acclimatized and thus returned to Rome; the composer and viol and lirone player Alessandro Striggio the elder, after protracted service in Florence, settled in Mantua, where he spent his last years (1584–92) in affiliation, in one or another capacity, with the court; and the renowned singer Francesco Rasi, whose talents extended to composition and playing the chitarrone and keyboard instruments, regularly appeared there after 1598. Still other composers, associated for shorter or longer periods with Santa Barbara, the Cathedral, or the court, were Ippolito Baccusi, Giovanni Battista Buonamente, Muzio Effrem, Amante Franzoni, Alessandro Ghivizzani (husband of the singer Settimia Caccini), Monteverdi's brother Giulio Cesare, Stefano Nascimbeni, Francesco Rovigo, Antonio Taroni, Lodovico Viadana, and Paolo Virchi. Like Rossi, they variously wrote madrigals, *canzonette*, instrumental and sacred works; and like him, they served, sometimes, as both instrumentalists and composers (e.g. Frescobaldi, the two Monteverdis). Unlike Rossi, though, they were Christians, which meant that Rossi was competing for favours with the favoured: his chances of earning recognition as a composer, through commissions or monetary reward, were inevitably limited. For all that, he was not deterred from soliciting new patrons, sometimes beyond Mantua, as clear from his dedications.

Seven payrolls are known for the period 1577–1637, and of these only three are dated. While dates can be reconstructed for the others,[14] it is uncertain how many years each payroll covered. There was a gradual increase in musicians (composers, singers, instrumentalists) from the 1580s, when they were about fifteen, to more than double that number in the first and second decades of the seventeenth century, with a minor tapering off in the early 1620s and the near extinction of the *cappella* in 1628. With its re-establishment in the early 1630s, the personnel had dwindled to six.

Rossi figures, as said, on three of the payrolls. For the more than three decades that intervened between the second and third (1592, 1622) there is notice of three payments to Rossi in connection with productions of the

---

[14] The main work of reconstruction has been done by Parisi ('Musicians at the Court of Mantua during Monteverdi's Time'; also 'Ducal Patronage of Music in Mantua, 1587–1627', 21–36); yet see Fenlon, *Music and Patronage in Sixteenth-Century Mantua*, as well as Stefano Davari's useful annotations to his own files (ASFD xv).

Jewish theatrical troupe in 1611[15] and three other payments, made to him by ducal order, in 1615.[16] Whether, on the basis of these separate remittances for 1611 and 1615, Rossi served the court uninterruptedly from the later 1580s to the mid- or later 1620s cannot be determined, though it appears likely.

In a ducal decree from 1606, exempting Rossi from wearing the customary badge for identifying Jews, mention is made of the composer's having attended the duke (Vincenzo) 'for many years'; in renewing the dispensation in 1612, Francesco added that he does so for Rossi's years of service not only to his father, but 'at the same time to us'.[17] Since Francesco reigned only six months, he appears to be referring to music composed or performed by Rossi, in earlier years, at the family's request. Long service was essential to receiving favours, such as salary increases, letters of recommendation, or retirement pensions. But the definition of 'long' varies. In this respect another document might be taken into account: dating from 1602, it is a business permit granted to Emanuele Rossi in recognition of his brother Salamone's 'many years of service'.[18] The word *many* probably takes us back to the time of the first payroll (the late 1580s), if not earlier.

For Rossi's later service under Ferdinando one might refer to a comment in the prefatory matter to his Hebrew collection: there the composer is said to have 'served before the brightness and majesty of the duke of Mantua now as before', hence, presumably, from 1613, when Ferdinando took over as duke, to at least 1622/3, when the collection was printed. Ferdinando is hailed in the words 'May he, who is alive today, live forever after; and may his glory and splendour be lifted and raised, amen!'[19] Rossi probably attended Ferdinando for as long as he was duke, continuing on, in 1626, into the service of Vincenzo II. All told, then, Rossi was attached to the Gonzagas for almost forty years.

It is not always clear how Rossi fitted into the musical establishment. The salary rolls raise more questions than can be answered. In the first of them Rossi is listed, along with his sister, under the 'extraordinarij'. The locution appears to designate persons not on the regular payroll, but assumed for one or another activity at an additional expense. Rossi's services, like his sister's, may not have been put on a solid footing until one or two years later; on the second payroll the two are named together with, and not apart from, those receiving monthly allocations.

Among the 'extraordinarij' on the first payroll one finds, beyond the Rossis, Alessandro Striggio; Isacchino della Profeta, probably to be

---

[15] JCA, file 12, a list of expenses incurred by the Jewish community in mounting a 'comedia fata 1611', plus a 'sechonda comedia'; cf. Parisi, 'The Jewish Community and Carnival Entertainment', 302 n. 40.

[16] ASAG 3144, dated 31 Oct. 1615 (cf. Parisi, 'Ducal Patronage of Music in Mantua, 1587–1627', 590; also ead., 'The Jewish Community and Carnival Entertainment', 301 n. 30).

[17] ASAG, Mandati 97, fo. 62 (2 Aug. 1606); 98, fo. 2 (27 Feb. 1612).

[18] ASAG, Decreti 52, fos. 245ᵛ–246ᵛ (2 Oct. 1602).

[19] Quotations are from Leon Modena's foreword.

identified as Isacchino Massarano;[20] and Girolamo Galarza, court jester, it would seem, and because of his placement among musicians a musician, perhaps, in his own right.[21] Striggio's name catches our eye: not much is known of his connections with the Gonzaga family. As a supernumerary, Striggio may have been reimbursed for special services as composer or instrumentalist; but whatever he did, it earned him, monthly, 129 lire. His salary differs strikingly from that of the two Rossis, who each received 13.19 (i.e. 13 lire and 19 soldi, there being 20 soldi to a lira). Striggio was also the recipient of payments from the Florentine court, for which he composed *intermedi* in the 1580s.[22]

It is hard to know how to relate to Salamone's seemingly meagre 13.19 salary. The sum remained the same in the second payroll, as it did in three payments made to Salamone in 1615. (I dismiss the various sums of money he received in 1611, for they were paid to him by the Jewish community as disbursements for covering the cost of comedies for Carnival or other occasions: 93 lire; 18 'for a box to store the shoes for the comedy'; and 36 'for rental expenses [incurred] for the second comedy'.)[23] That there was no increase over the course of twenty-five years is surprising, but we will need to have more information before deciding whether he was so paid because, in the eyes of the Gonzaga, as a musician or Jew or both he deserved no more; or because he received support from the Jewish community (as he might have from his patron Moses Sullam, who perhaps subsidized one or more of his publications, if not helped the composer meet other expenses); or because he had an independent source of income, on which more below; or because he was without a family, hence could get by on a smaller salary. One or two mouths are easier to feed than the three for which Francesco Rasi received his salary or the four for which Lucrezia Urbana received hers around 1603.

A change occurred in the payroll for 1622: there Salamone is listed among string players as receiving an annual salary of 383.8 lire, or a little less than 32 lire monthly, an increase of almost two and a half times his previous earnings. Various questions come to the fore, all having as their common denominator the interrogative 'why'. Was Rossi performing additional services? Were his talents more widely appreciated? Were his personal expenses greater, leading him to request and be granted a salary increase? Was the rise due to inflationary adjustments? The year 1622 is one out of a number of years in a seemingly continuous period of service that runs from 1615, the last mention of payments to the composer, to at least the early, if

---

[20] On the basis of a ducal decree (from 1610), to be discussed below.

[21] On Galarza, see Parisi, 'Ducal Patronage of Music in Mantua, 1587–1627', 443, 584.

[22] On Striggio in Florence, see Kirkendale, 'Alessandro Striggio und die Medici', and variously in id., *The Court Musicians in Florence during the Principate of the Medici*.

[23] JCA, file 12, as above: 'dati al Signor Salamon Rosi L 93'; 'dati a Messer Salamon per una casseta per riponder le scarpi della comedia L 18'; 'a Salamon per il fito della sechonda comedia L 36'.

not later 1620s. One wonders, then, when the salary increase took effect: before 1622, and if so, how long before? In 1622 only, and why then in particular? Was there a further increment in later years?

One way of assessing how Rossi stood on the pay scale is by comparing his earnings with those of other musicians on the rosters. In the early 1590s, Wert, as *maestro di cappella*, received a monthly provision of 84 lire; Monteverdi's was set at 75 and Pallavicino's at 39. On a payroll from the early 1580s,[24] the Jewish instrumentalist Abramo [Abramino] dall'Arpa is recorded as receiving 16 lire, though all but five of the fourteen remaining Christian musicians earned no more than Rossi did in 1589. On the 1589 payroll three Christians were paid what Rossi was (13.19) and one other less than half. Rossi was, therefore, not the least reimbursed of musicians.[25] Yet his earnings seem not to have increased, through 1615 and perhaps as far as, though not including, the payroll notice from 1622. Then, however, except for the singers Giulio Cardi and Domenico Aglio, who earned about one hundred less than Rossi's annual 383 lire, Rossi was definitely at the bottom of the list. At its top was the famous soprano Adriana Basile, who, with an annual 3,600, earned nearly three times as much as the *maestro di cappella* Francesco Dognazzi;[26] the bass Matteo Rossi, in this case a Christian, who is listed as receiving 782; and almost all the string players, who earned twice, if not three times as much as Rossi.[27] By 1622, Rossi was at the height of his career, but his earnings were incommensurate with his achievements. Discrimination may have played a part in determining wage policies, though with no documents to clarify Rossi's standing at the court under Ferdinando one can never know; or perhaps the very lack of information is itself a document.

Duties as Musician

There remains the question of what Rossi was being paid for: his services as a composer and instrumentalist, yes, but was he also a singer? Two references raise this possibility. One occurs in a pragmatic published by the Jewish community in 1619, exempting Rossi and the physician David Portaleone from observing the decrees on clothing that otherwise were binding on the Jews: in the Hebrew version, Rossi is described as a 'singer (*meshorer*) of His Highness', though in the Italian translation submitted to the authorities the word *singer* was replaced by the more general one *musician*

---

[24] ASAG 3146, fos. 47–53.

[25] Parisi notes, moreover, that the salary was about the same as that earned by singers in Santa Barbara ('The Jewish Community and Carnival Entertainment', 301).

[26] As a supplement, however, to his yearly L. 1,262, Dognazzi received 600 'per altra provisione'.

[27] The highest paid were Luigi Farina and Cavagliere Luchesino (L. 1,080), with the Rubini brothers and Francesco Barberoli receiving 816, Fabrizio Trolandi 722, Giacomo Cattaneo 566, and Giovanni Battista Barberoli 432.

('musico').[28] The other occurs in a dedicatory poem within the prefatory material to Rossi's Hebrew collection: there the composer is said to be 'accustomed . . . to sing before princes, dukes, and nobles'.[29] There are no records of his having sung at court, or anywhere else, but as a 'musician' he could very well have done so in performances of his own and others' works. The word *singer* need not be understood as a vocalist with professional skills, like those, for example, with which Francesco Rasi, who played the title role in the Mantuan première of Monteverdi's *Orfeo*, was endowed. Rather, it probably denoted a musician capable of holding his own with others in performing a secular or sacred part song.

The Jewish community had its musicians: they took part in *intermedi* presented at court or in public festivities, often within plays prepared by the Jewish theatrical troupe.[30] Few Mantuan Jewish singers are known by name, except for the two already mentioned: Isacchino Massarano and Madama Europa. There may have been relatively few to start with: in a letter from 1610 we read of an *intermedio* to be entrusted, in its production, to the 'Jews, who do not have many singers',[31] though how many is 'many' is unclear. It might be noted that Rossi, in his Hebrew works, published in 1622/3, but tried out earlier, never wrote for more than eight singers and usually settled for four or five. He coached them, we are told, 'with much delight'.[32] They were urged, in particular, to observe proper diction,[33] either as a general instruction or possibly because they were unaccustomed to singing, polyphonically, in Hebrew. To supplement the modest forces, Rossi could himself have sung one of the parts.

Nor were singers always separate from instrumentalists, as we tend to think of them today. There were many persons in Mantua who performed in both capacities. Take Francesco Rasi and Isacchino Massarano, for example; or the female singers Adriana Basile, who played the harp, lira, and Spanish guitar; her daughter Leonora, who played the lute and chitarrone; Lucia and Isabetta Pelizzari, who played wind instruments (cornett, trombone); and Lucrezia Urbana, who played the harp.

We are on firmer ground when describing Rossi as an instrumentalist. For one thing, there is the evidence of his instrumental music collections.

[28] JCA, file 15, docs. 21–2. On this and the first pragmatic from 1599, cf. Simonsohn, *History of the Jews in the Duchy of Mantua*, 530–5; for the Italian tr., see copy in ASAG, Mandati 100, fos. 46ᵛ–48 (22 June 1619), esp. item 14: 'Nelle prohibitioni del vestire contenute nelli soddetti Capitoli non saranno compresi il Medico David Portaleone, nè Salamon de Rossi musico di Sua Altezza chè essi potranno usar nel vestir delle persone loro quello le piacerà'.

[29] Third dedicatory poem, by Modena (also in his *Divan*, ed. Bernstein, 82–3).

[30] On the problems of sorting out Jewish musicians, see n. 10.

[31] 'e sarà fatta al dosso degli hebrei che non hanno molti cantori' (in reference to one of the *intermedi* from *Le quattro età del mondo*); dated 17 Nov. 1610, the letter was written by Federico Follino to Duke Vincenzo (ASAG 2718).

[32] From second dedicatory poem, probably by Modena.

[33] 'It behoves the singers to pronounce the words carefully, observing the vowels, accents, and whatever other details enhance their delivery': from Modena's foreword.

For another, as said, Rossi appears in the salary roll for 1622 as a 'viola', i.e. string, player. Reference is made, in a letter from 1612, to his 'concerto', which, on the surface, would seem to indicate an instrumental ensemble. Written by Alessandro Pico, prince of neighbouring Mirandola, the letter was a request that Duke Vincenzo release 'Salamone the Jew and his company or *concerto*' to come to Mirandola 'for a couple of days' and entertain Alessandro's guests.[34] Salamone must have had his own group of musicians with whom he played at court and, with the duke's permission, elsewhere.

Perhaps it is to the same group that a document from 1609 refers: Francesco Gonzaga wrote, from Casale, to Monteverdi, then *maestro di cappella*, asking that he intercede with the duke to obtain a certain Orazio Casalasco, who was ordinarily employed as a violinist in performing Rossi's *sinfonie* or otherwise as an alto violist (violinist?) in a '*concerto* of viols' (strings?) used for dancing.[35] Francesco, who had just been named governor of Monferrato, wanted him as the bass player in his own dance band. Orazio may be identified as Orazio Rubini, originally from Casale; he appears in the salary rolls along with his brother Giovanni Battista, who, in fact, is named in the same passage as another member of the group that played Rossi's *sinfonie*. Two ensembles are specified then, the first for Rossi's *sinfonie* and consisting of violins, the second for dancing, this time perhaps, though not necessarily, a viol consort.

That Rossi led the group playing his own *sinfonie* seems rather obvious. Yet he could, for that matter, have also led the second group. Here the wording of Francesco's request might be of some help. It differentiates between *sinfonie* and dances. Rossi's *sinfonie* first appeared in 1607, in his *Libro primo* of instrumental works; another set of them was included in his second book, from 1608. Both books, though, include a number of *gagliarde*, which in style were more relaxed and clearly intended for dancing. These books must have set a standard for instrumental music at the court, and their built-in differentiation between *sinfonie* and *gagliarde* could easily have extended to actual performance: a *concerto* of violins for the one, a *concerto* of viols (or again violins?) for the other, both under the direction of Salamone.[36] On the terminological problem of violins as against viols, more will be said in Chapter 2.

---

[34] Alessandro directed the letter to Vincenzo's counsellor Annibale Chieppio (ASAG 1337; 29 Sept. 1612). The occasion was a visit of the duke of Modena and his daughter Giulia (see below). Cf. Birnbaum, *Jüdische Musiker am Hofe von Mantua*, in Italian tr. Colorni as 'Musici ebrei alla corte di Mantova', etc., 195–6.

[35] ASAG 2271 (18 Nov. 1609): see Parisi, 'Ducal Patronage of Music in Mantua, 1587–1627', 654–5, with quotation of relevant passage.

[36] The only problem is that the first group was not called a *concerto*, although it may be understood as such. For the expression 'il concerto della sinfonia', see a report by Malvezzi on various *intermedi* presented in Florence, 1589, namely that, 'in the fourth *intermedio*, the *concerto della sinfonia* consisted of a harp played by Giulio Caccini, a chitarrone, two small lutes, two lire,

But it is not as simple as that: who participated in the *sinfonie* and *gagliarde* and how were the parts assigned? Most of the works call for three parts, though, in the first two books, several are provided with one or two extra ones, leaving the musicians the option of different-sized ensembles. If Orazio Rubini played the violin, as did his brother Giovanni Battista, in the *sinfonie* for three voices, then what did Salamone play? Did he join the ensemble only in the versions for four or five voices? Who played the bass part, designated for a chitarrone or 'similar' instrument? Rossi might have, though beyond the assumption that he played both the violin and the viol there is no indication that he did.

On the other hand, it is not clear, from the wording of Francesco's request, whether Giovanni Battista played the violin: all that was said is that in the *sinfonie* Orazio, as violinist, appeared 'in the company of his brother'. Since, in fact, Orazio played the violin in the one group and the alto viol (viola?) in the other, yet was being sought by Francesco to play the bass (gamba?) in his own viol (or string?) consort, it could well be that Giovanni Battista also played the bass, in this case a chitarrone or archlute, in Salamone's violin ensemble, whereby Salamone would have assumed one of the violin parts. Or perhaps there was no fixed membership in the ensembles, meaning that the Rubini brothers might have participated at one stage, yet were replaced by others, among them Franceschino, i.e. Francesco Barberoli (whom Francesco, in the same passage, suggested as a substitute), at another.

In the light of these uncertainties, it is impossible to determine which ensemble Salamone took to Mirandola, in 1612, as 'his company or *concerto*'. Nor could one ever know how the parts were distributed. That the Rubini brothers may have been skilled in playing the chitarrone, as already suggested, is confirmed by a passage in a letter, from 1611, by Monteverdi, who recommended that they perform the two chitarrone parts in a madrigal by Ferdinando Gonzaga.[37] Another possibility is that the chitarrone was played, until 1610 at least, by Isacchino Massarano, Salamone's partner in various productions of the Jewish theatrical troupe, as he was on other occasions, among them a performance in Padua, on which more below.

In 1609 there is mention of a concert on Lake Garda at Goito, where the Gonzagas had a country residence. Participation of the Rubini brothers, Salamone, Monteverdi's brother Giulio Cesare, two boy singers, and three or four adult ones was requested.[38] Yet Salamone was not alone in assuming responsibility for instrumental entertainments at Goito or elsewhere. In 1608 all the 'violinists', presumably string players, appear to have been

and a psaltery' (after Solerti, *Gli albori del melodramma*, ii. 29). But here *concerto* seems to be synonymous with 'music'.

[37] The letter, dated 22 June 1611, was written to Ferdinando, then in Rome. See *The Letters of Claudio Monteverdi*, tr. Stevens, 85 (the madrigal, 'Ah che morir mi sento', was sung by Adriana [Basile] and Giovanni [Sacchi]).

[38] Letter by Alessandro Striggio (ASAG, 28 June 1609; and its sequel from 29 June).

summoned to Gazzolo, where they worked under the direction of Giovanni Battista Rubini.[39] Some of those known to be at the court then and later, though not always on the salary lists, are, in addition to Francesco Barberoli, just mentioned, the 'violinists' Giacomo Cattaneo (Monteverdi's father-in-law), Luigi Farina, Ottavio Trivoli, and Fabrizio Trolandi.[40] They could, at one or another time, have alternated in directing the players.

Like Salamone, the Rubini brothers were also composers, but not on a large scale. Two motets by Giovanni Battista and one by Orazio appeared, in 1618, in a collection of sacred works 'by various musicians serving His Most Serene Lord, the duke of Mantua' (Ferdinando).[41] Salamone paid homage to Giovanni Battista, in his third book of instrumental works, by borrowing a tune of his for a *corrente*. In the same book there is a sonata entitled 'la Casalasca' and two *brandi* based on tunes by Giovanni Francesco Rubini, who may have been Giovanni Battista's son.[42] It is my suspicion that the Rubinis or their ancestors were originally Jewish; the brothers could have apostatized before joining the Gonzaga court in the early 1600s. The name turns up often enough in different Jewish community records. In those for Milan, a physician by the name of Sancto Rubini appears four times during the years 1465–73 while there are thirty references to an Amadeo, son of Simone Urbino (Rubini), after 1581.[43] In those for Piedmont, one encounters Rubino Azezo in the early 1590s and Rubino Pescarolo from 1593 to 1620.[44] Rubino or Rubini derives either from Urbino or from the biblical Reuben, or again from *rubino* (Latin *rubenus*), whereby it connects with *rosso*. Thus Rubini and Rossi seem to have vague etymological, if not familial ties.[45]

As to the Jews as violinists, there is evidence that many of them, in the sixteenth century, may have been of Judeo-Spanish origins. Except for those who submitted to forced conversion, the Jews were expelled from the Iberian peninsula in 1492. As New Christians, though often secretly retaining their Judaism, large numbers left the peninsula in the sixteenth century, making their way not only to the East, particularly Turkey, but to different northern destinations. It has been shown that Jewish stringed-instrument

[39] Thus Giovan Battista Gutti in a letter dated 4 Sept. 1608, as copied by Davari (ASFD xvi).

[40] See Parisi, 'Ducal Patronage of Music in Mantua, 1587–1627', 125 (and separate listings in alphabetical section). Barberoli, for example, was in Mantua from c.1603 to 1632, though appears only on later salary rolls (1621–2, 1632).

[41] Fourteen 'musicians' in all (*Motetti* 1–4 v., *RISM* 1618⁴). Salamone was obviously absent from the collection, though for another Rossi there, Anselmo, see below.

[42] CW xi. 33 (*corrente*), 2 (sonata), and 25–6 (*brandi*). Giovanni Battista refers to his 'sons', e.g. in a letter dated 8 Sept. 1623 (ASAG 2761). Other Rubinis are known from the literature, particularly Nicolo, who had 25 motets published in a collection from 1606, yet does not seem to have worked in Mantua.

[43] Simonsohn, *The Jews in the Duchy of Milan*, i. 389–90, 490, 585–6, 602 (for Sancto Rubini); iii. 1693, 1712, etc. (for Amadeo; see iv, various references in index).

[44] Segre, *The Jews in Piedmont*, ii. 718, 803 (for Azezo); 774, 904, 918, 976 (for Pescarolo).

[45] On Reuben as Rubino, Rosso, or Rossino, see Colorni, 'La corrispondenza fra nomi ebraici e nomi locali', 813.

builders and musicians eventually came, via Northern Italy, to the Nether-lands, where they were responsible for the 'birth' of violin music.[46] Recent studies have also emphasized the Jewish presence in Germany[47] and Eng-land.[48] How these Crypto-Jewish musicians in Northern Italy, especially Milan, Brescia, Cremona, and Venice, relate to the violinists in Mantua still remains to be determined.

Obviously, the meaning of *concerto* is crucial to understanding 'Rossi et...suo concerto'. The term[49] may be defined in various ways, of which one has already been noted (Orazio Rubini playing 'alto' in a *concerto* of 'viols'). Specific instrumental works were often called 'concerti', and it is in this sense that Rossi referred, in the dedication to his fourth book of sonatas, *sinfonie*, etc., to his 'musical *concerti*'. Yet the term could just as well have denoted a vocal or mixed vocal-instrumental ensemble and its music. Thus we know of the 'concerto delle donne' in Ferrara; and there is a vast literature of vocal 'concerti', sacred and secular, with some sort of instru-mental support, from Viadana's three books of *Concerti ecclesiastici* (1602, 1607, 1609) to Stefano Bernardi's *Concerti accademici* (1615) and beyond.[50] Certain collections contain 'madrigali concertati' or 'madrigali da concer-tarsi'; others have madrigals to be performed 'in concerto' or are designated 'concerti musicali, voci o stromenti'.[51] One could go on, mentioning works for 'voci concertate' or collections entitled 'canti concertati', or 'musiche concertate', or 'trastulli estivi concertati'.[52] Were one to add to them still other collections having not 'concerti', but 'concenti musicali', or, from the mid-sixteenth century on, specifying that the contents were 'per (*or* da) cantare et sonare', then the meaning and application of *concerto* broadens. In its inclusive sense, it is even possible, and this is the main point, that Rossi directed, at one time or another, not just an instrumental ensemble, but a vocal or mixed vocal-instrumental one. *Concerto*, in short, denotes a

[46] Moens, 'La "nascita" del violino nei Paesi Bassi del sud'.

[47] Salmen, '...*denn die Fiedel macht das Fest': Jüdische Musikanten*, etc.

[48] Prior, 'Jewish Musicians at the Tudor Court'; Holman, *Four and Twenty Fiddlers*; Lasocki and Prior, *The Bassanos*.

[49] To date, its most exhaustive study is Piperno, ' "Concerto" e "concertato" nella musica strumentale italiana del secolo decimo settimo'.

[50] Similarly, the 'concerti ecclesiastici' by Franzoni (1611) and the 'concerti accademici' by Bellante (1629) and Bettino (1643). See, also, the *Concerti* 2–4 v. by Marastoni (1624), the *Concerti di camera* 2–9 v. by Arrigoni (1635), the *Concerti musicali* 1–5 v. by Banchieri (1626), the *Madrigali...et altri varii concerti* 2, 4–6, 8 v. by Mazzocchi (1638), not to speak of Monteverdi's Bk 7 of madrigals entitled *Concerto* 1–6 v. (1619).

[51] 'Madrigali concertati': Anglesio (1617); Bonaffino (1623); Ceresini (1627); Colombi (1621); Colombini (1640); Cremonese (1636); Delipari (1630); Grandi (1622); Lamoretti (1621); Marastoni (1619, 1628); Merula (1624); Modiana (1625); Piochi (1626); Quagliati (1608); Rinoldi (1627); Sabbatini (1625–7, 1630, 1636); Sabbatini (1629); Scacchi (1634); and Vivarino (1624). 'Madrigali da concertarsi': Guelfi (1631). 'In concerto': Grancino (1646); Pasta (1626); and Tarditi (1633). 'Concerti musicali 1–5 v. o stromenti': Banchieri (1626).

[52] 'Voci concertate': Todeschi (1627). 'Canti concertati': del Negro (1620). 'Musiche concer-tate': Priuli (1622); Rigatti (1636). 'Trastulli estivi concertati': Bizzarro Accademico Capriccioso (1620–1).

consort of voices or instruments, or both, and the works performed by it were often designated 'concerti'.

Evidence for Rossi's having conducted a vocal group may be culled from other sources, for example, his Hebrew songs, where, in the introduction, as has already been mentioned, Rossi is said to have trained the singers; or a rabbinical response from 1645, where the author, to strengthen his point that repeating the name of God in sacred songs is prohibited, refers, for proof, to the practices, some twenty or more years earlier, of 'the learned Rossi and his company'.[53] The Hebrew for 'his company' is 'si'ato', which could reasonably have been a translation of 'sua compagnia, o suo concerto'.[54] Thus the singers that Rossi trained might have constituted 'his company'.

Whether on other occasions instruments were added to voices cannot be said. Remember that the context, in the Hebrew songs, is sacred music, and instruments were generally banned from prayer services in the synagogue. But that does not rule out the possibility, first, of sacred music performed by singers on festive occasions in schools or in homes, or even in synagogues, though not in regular services; and, second, of instruments, on such occasions, being admitted to the ensemble. Such an assumption might be strengthened by the continuation of the rabbinical document just noted. There the author, for further proof of his argument, cites the example of his late wife, 'learned and skilled in playing the lute and viol and in singing the Kedusha'.[55] The passage is full of surprises: for one thing, the mention of instruments and sacred music in one breath; for another, the fact that a woman was singing sacred music, which was forbidden.

But what if these sacred songs were *not* performed in prayer services? And what if, outside the synagogue, they sometimes did have an instrumental complement? Rossi could well have been the leader of such a *concerto*, which served the needs of the Jewish community in its collective and private festivities; or appeared in performances of the Jewish theatrical troupe; or, with male singers and without instruments, sang at times in the synagogue services; or, with varying numbers of performers, male or female, vocal or instrumental, was called upon to entertain members of the Gonzaga and other noble families, in Mantua and elsewhere. Was this mixed ensemble the *concerto* that Rossi took to Mirandola in 1612?[56]

---

[53] Nathaniel Trabotto (9 Nov. 1645); see Adler, 'The Rise of Art Music in the Italian Ghetto', 357.

[54] That 'compagnia' was used here as a synonym for 'concerto' is clear not only from the present document but also from one dated 29 Feb. 1620, which refers to the duke's 'compagnia dei violini' (after the annotations in ASFD xvi. 896).

[55] The prayer Kedusha, which Rossi also set to music (see App.) after the version in the Italian rite, begins with the word *keter*, or 'crown' (the angels above, in concert with Israel below, 'crown' the Lord). See Idelsohn, *Jewish Liturgy*, 144.

[56] In 1604, the prince of Mirandola asked Duke Vincenzo to release Monteverdi so that he, together with 'his ladies', might come to Mirandola 'for composing and for acting and singing various things at the festivities in preparation' (see, for orig., Parisi, 'Ducal Patronage of Music in Mantua, 1587–1627', 603). By 'his ladies', another 'concerto delle donne' appears to be meant,

Special Privileges

For his many years of service to his rulers, Rossi was exempted, by decree, from wearing a badge. Introduced into Europe in the early thirteenth century, the badge marked the Jews as socially and religiously inferior. The result was that being immediately noticeable, Jews were ever the victims of baiting and aggression, as encouraged, moreover, by accusations of treachery levelled at them by the Church. In Mantua, after years of laxity in enforcing the requirement to wear the badge, Duke Guglielmo reinstated it in 1577, specifying, with maddening exactitude, not one, but 'two badges of orange colour, half an arm long and a finger wide, to be set in a visible place, that is, one of them on the frock or coat, two fingers away from its buttons, the other on the hat or other head garment and removed by the same space [two fingers] from its front border'. He then remarked that

he who wears a coat or frock is required to wear the badge only on his coat or frock and not [to wear] the other one on his cap or other head garment if he does not have one on. But when he does have a cap or other head garment on, even if it is made of felt, he is obliged, under penalty of 10 scudi on the first infraction, of 20 on the second, and of 30 on the third, to wear it in such a way as to be visible even from a distance. It should therefore not be hidden under a pleat or anything else. If someone is found to have violated this ordinance beyond a third time, he shall, at our command, be required to wear the orange beret uninterruptedly, according to the custom in Venice and other places.[57]

Naturally, the badge was shameful to those Jews who, in their activities, were in close touch with Christians, as was the case with Rossi and others serving them as musicians, actors, physicians, middlemen, and loan bankers. Dispensation, on merit, was sometimes granted; the custom may be traced back, in Mantua, to the late fifteenth century.[58] Under the heading of special favours, it included permission, to some deserving Jews, to carry weapons; or study medicine at the universities; or dwell outside the ghetto. Usually a request was submitted to the authorities, with the backing of an influential patron. The example of Leone de' Sommi, famed actor and stage director in later sixteenth-century Mantua, is typical. Fernando Gonzaga interceded on his behalf with Duke Guglielmo, describing him as 'so talented and having earned such distinction in the Mantuan Accademia [degli Invaghiti] for the long service he performed as a writer that I, as patron of the academy and well informed of Sommi's service, am obliged to entreat Your Highness to be so kind as to favour him with the privilege that

now including Monteverdi's wife Claudia Cattaneo; the young and promising singer, living in their house, Caterina Martinelli; and possibly a third singer drawn from those at the court.

[57] For orig., see D'Ancona, *Origini del teatro italiano*, ii. 408–9. On the yellow badge, see Kisch, 'The Yellow Badge in History', and Ravid, 'From Yellow to Red'.

[58] Isabella d'Este referred, in a letter, to various Jews exempted from wearing the badge (see D'Ancona, loc. cit.).

he himself will ask of you, concerning an exemption from wearing the customary badge'.[59]

On the social effects of the privilege[60] one reads, in the continuation, that though 'the badge now separates [Sommi] from Christians, without it he will be separated from the mass of other Jews'. Thus where the exemption eased the way for Jews who consorted with Christians, it must, conversely, have created tensions within the Jewish community, whose members were summarily divided, by the rulers, into the favoured few and the masses. How Sommi, or Rossi, or anyone else who received the privilege dealt with the problem can only be imagined. Elsewhere I suggested that Sommi's Hebrew play, his Hebrew translations of psalms, his interventions with the authorities on behalf of the Jews, and, similarly, Rossi's composition of Hebrew songs were ways of demonstrating that though the two were recipients of privileges, they remained faithful to the community.[61]

Rossi might have requested an exemption in the 1590s, but the first notice of his having received one comes in Duke Vincenzo's decree from 1606. From the wording we learn that in recognition of 'his musical talents and his playing' Rossi was conceded 'the free and unrestricted privilege to move through the city and its outer domains without wearing the customary orange badge around his hat or beret'.[62] The exemption, as pointed out earlier, was renewed by Francesco in 1612, upon acceding to the dukedom. Lest it be thought that the privileges conferred on various Jews owed to the genuine gratitude of their rulers, it should be remembered that the recipients paid for them: either Rossi or one of his Jewish patrons duly acknowledged the duke's magnanimity, on this and other occasions, by filling his coffers.

Outside Earnings

Salamone was involved in certain of his brother Emanuele's business affairs. In 1602 he appears to have asked Vincenzo to grant Emanuele the right to exact income on registering, for the ducal records, the formation or dissolution of commercial partnerships. Until then the job had been rather indifferently performed by Lazzaro d'Italia, and Salamone seized the opportunity to wrest it from him to his brother's advantage. Thus we read, in a decree concerning the 'exaction, by Emanuele Rossi, of moneys for partnerships', that inasmuch as the duke wished 'to show Salamone Rossi *ebreo* some sign of gratitude for services that he, with utmost diligence, rendered for many years and continues to render us, we have resolved to confer the duties once assigned to Lazzarino d'Italia, likewise *ebreo*, who,

---

[59] From a letter dated 7 May 1580 (after D'Ancona, *Origini del teatro italiano*, ii. 410).

[60] For a general study, see Hughes, 'Sumptuary Law and Social Relations in Renaissance Italy'.

[61] Cf. Harrán, 'Jewish Dramatists and Musicians in the Renaissance', 298–9.

[62] This and the next document were already mentioned under the section 'Evidence for Service in the Mantuan Court'.

because of his delinquencies, has proved unworthy of their execution, on the person of Emanuele, the said Salamone's brother, in whose faith and diligence we are confident'.[63] Lazzaro tried to regain his position, which led Salamone, in 1606, to write the duke a letter of admonition:

I am sending my brother to Your Most Serene Highness; through him will Your Highness be served. May you be so kind to me as to favour him, upon His Most Serene Highness's discretion, by [allowing] the fulfilment of our office. Lazzaro d'Italia endeavours to remove it from us and involve himself in it without any cause, as you will better be informed by my brother. He will bring to your attention that the service I have rendered over the course of so many years does not include having such an office removed from us for the benefit of a Lazzarino d'Italia whose qualities are so well known to everyone. Relying on your customary kindness I rest assured that you will see to it that no such displeasure be caused without reason. To this end, I pray our Lord for your every happiness and content. Mantua, 21 February 1606. Your Highness's most faithful servant.[64]

The request was submitted in a fair copy, but Rossi added, in his own hand, a personal closure and signature: 'Your Most Serene Highness's most humble and indebted servant, Salamon Rossi'[65] (see Plate 4).

From the reference to 'our office' and its being removed 'from us' it is clear that Salamone acted as partner in his brother's dealings, hence gained a percentage of the profits.

Salamone appears to have made further money on the side from a small tax-collecting franchise. In 1621 the dancer Giovanni Battista Perfetti leased him the right to certain earnings from the sale of pledges, that is, items pawned in exchange for loans from Jewish banks.[66] If the recipients of these loans did not repay them with interest at the specified time (usually a year

[63] ASAG, Decreti 52, fos. 245^v–246^v: 'Per dimostrare a Salamone Rossi hebreo qualche segno di gratitudine per la servitù fattaci da lui molt'anni, et che tuttavia ci fa con ogni assiduità habbiamo risoluto di conferire gli carichi che havevamo dati a Lazarino d'Italia parimente hebreo quale per suoi demeriti se n'è reso indegno nella persona di Emanuele fratello d'esso Salamone così confidati nella fede, et diligentia sua, et...deputiamo il sudetto Emanuele a poter oltre ad ogni altro, a chi secondo l'occorenze ci piacerà di dare qualche ordine circa ciò, trattare, et riscuotere le compositioni peccuniarie, che giornalmente occoreranno in questa nostra Città di Mantova et suo Dominio, prohibendo che alcun'altro non possa ingerirsi in esse senza nostra particolare Commissione', with a detailed description, in the continuation, of tax rates and the procedure for transferring monies to the treasury (the document is signed by the duke's counsellor Annibale Chieppio).

[64] ASAG 2705 (21 Feb. 1606): 'Mando da Vostra Altezza Serenissima mio frattello al qual Vostra Altezza restarà servita farmi gratia favorirlo appresso Sua Altezza Serenissima nel negotio del nostro Uffitio che Lazzaro d'Italia procura di levarlo a noi et inplicarlo in lui senza niuna Causa come meglio da mio frattello ne sarà informato facendoli sapere che la mia servitù fatta tanti anni sono non comporta che ci sia levato un tal Uffitio senza Caggione per benefetiare un Lazzarino d'Italia tanto noto al mondo della qualità sua, et assicurandomi nella solita sua benignità starò sicuro che quella producerà che non ci sia fatto un tal Dispiacere senza causa, con che fine restarò pregando nostro signore per ogni sua felicità et contento. Da Mantova alli 21 febbraio 1606. Di Vostra Signoria fidelissimo Servitore.'

[65] 'Humilissimo et dovutissimo servitore di Vostra Altezza Serenissima Salamon Rossi'.

[66] For relevant documents, cf. ASAG, Filze ebrei 3010: 1 Dec. 1621 (date of agreement), 5 Dec. 1621 (date of duke's approval); also 3391, fos. 172–177^v, including the original privilege granted

later), the bankers were free to sell the pledges at auction for their value plus accumulated interest, though they had to pay an excise tax.[67] It is with regard to the excise tax that Perfetti enters the picture. In 1614 he was granted a life warrant to exact 2 quattrini, i.e. 8 denari, from the loan banks on every lira gained from the trade in pledges.[68] With the lira valued at 240 denari in the early seventeenth century, 8 denari amounted to about 3 per cent of a lira.[69] The terms of the agreement for leasing the privilege to Rossi stipulated that the latter would provide Perfetti in return, over the next six years, an annuity of 200 scudi and twelve fat geese, which Perfetti was to buy from him.[70] Since the scudo came to about six times the lira, Rossi, from 1622, was paying Perfetti, yearly, some 1,200 lire.

The arrangement raises questions. First, what kind of profits was Rossi making to enable him to reimburse Perfetti for his due? Second, who is Perfetti and what bound him to Rossi?

Twelve hundred lire is a considerable sum of money to be paid by a musician whose annual salary from the court was set at 156 and, starting

to Perfetti on 20 Jan. 1614 and the contract drawn up between Perfetti and Rossi on 15 Nov. 1621.

[67] The interest rate on loans, in the 17th c., was $17\frac{1}{2}$%. On the contractual obligations of the Jewish loan bankers, see the various ducal decrees by Guglielmo (1577), Vincenzo (1587, 1594, 1602), and Ferdinando (1626) as reproduced in Simonsohn, *History of the Jews in the Duchy of Mantua*, 221–3, 229, 232–5.

[68] ASAG 3391, esp. fos. 176–176^v (20 Jan. 1614); the document, which Simonsohn reported (ibid. 231), but did not quote, reads thus: 'gli concediamo di poter conseguire in vita sua due quatrini per lira di soldi venti de picioli di tutti quei dinari, che si cavaranno da qui inanti dei pegni perduti, che gli hebrei Banchieri di questa Città sogliono vendere, o far vendere a certi tempi, et al pubblico incanto conforme al contenuto de luoro Privileggi, a quali in tutto ci riportiamo', etc. There is a decree stating that loans of 7 lire or less are not subject to the added taxation that accrued to Perfetti: ASAG, Decreti, 27 Feb. 1626 (for orig., see ibid. 789–98).

[69] For these and following rates, cf. 'Exchange Rates in Mantua', in Simonsohn, *History of the Jews in the Duchy of Mantua*, 742–4; and more generally, Cipolla, *Money, Prices, and Civilization in the Mediterranean World*.

[70] 'Il signor Giovanni Battista Prefetto affitta al Magnifico Messer Salomone Rossi hebreo il Decreto, che tiene da Sua Altezza Serenissima di poter conseguire dalli Banchieri hebrei un sesino per lira di capitale, et interesse delli pegni, che si vendeno all'incanto, che fanno li detti Banchieri, per scudi doi cento da lire sei l'uno ogn'anno, cominciando il primo di Gennaro prossimo 1622, con pagarli al detto Signor Giovanni Battista scudi cento anticipatamente per mesi sei avenire, e così conseguentemente di sei mesi in sei mesi, qual Decreto esso signor Giovanni Battista cede, e rinoncia al detto messer Salomone nel medemo modo, et con l'istessa auttorità, che possiede, et gode da Sua Altezza Serenissima, come dal Decreto sudetto si vede; Dovrà il signor Giovanni Battista dare il sudetto Decreto in mano al sudetto messer Salomone, affine che sij registrato nel'Instromento, che si doverà fare tra essi. Il detto affitto dovrà durare per anni sei prossimi avenire, che incominciaranno il primo di Genaro sodetto. Si obliga il sudetto Magnifico Salomone dar sicurtà a esso Signor Giovanni Battista per il mantenimento del detto affitto.... In fede di che la presente sarà affermata di propria mano dalle dette parti con obligatione di più del detto messer Salomone di dar'ogn'anno il primo dell'anno, et antecipat- amente durando detta locatione dodeci ocche grasse, quali esso signor Giovanni Battista si possa comperare a sua sodisfattione, et far pagar il prezzo d'esse al detto messer Salomone', etc. (again from ASAG 3391, as cited above [fos. 176–176^v, 20 Jan. 1614]). In 1627 the terms of the arrangement were changed: 150 scudi were to be paid by the bankers to the holder of the patent (Perfetti) and 50 to the treasury (ASAG, Filze ebrei 3010: 1 Dec. 1627; cf. Simonsohn, *History of the Jews in the Duchy of Mantua*, 231).

around 1622, at 383; and who, on at least one occasion, is known to have owed money.[71] The revenues on the privilege must have been sufficient to leave him enough, after compensating Perfetti, to score a profit. For Rossi just to meet his annual commitment to Perfetti, the bankers' earnings on the excise tax would have to have been 192,000 denari (or one third that amount in quattrini). Yet to make a reasonable profit, and it would have been senseless for Rossi to enter into such an arrangement unless there were one, the yield must have been larger.

Perfetti, or as otherwise designated in the documents, Perfetto or Prefetto, seems to have been the son of the dancer and musician Isacchino Massarano, also known as Isacchino della Proffeta.[72] A convert to Christianity, Perfetti was renamed Giovanni Battista Renato, or 'reborn', an epithet often shared by Jewish apostates.[73] The connection between father and son comes out in a ducal decree from 1610. There we learn that Isacchino had been the proprietor of a butcher's stand for fourteen years, according to a privilege that dates back, therefore, to 1596 (it may have been a renewal of an earlier one); that he was still alive in 1610; that the proceeds from sales were meant, among other things, to guarantee a suitable dowry for his daughter; and that, in recognition of his services to the court, the authorities had decided to let the stand pass, after his death, into the hands of his 'former' son, Giovanni Battista Renato.[74] Why 'former'? Because, with his conversion, he probably had been disowned by Massarano; and Renato must have acted with the authorities to ensure that he be recognized as a rightful heir to his father's estate.[75]

---

[71] JCA, file 14, doc. 1 (1615), with a notation to the effect that Rossi borrowed 11 lire, of which he paid back 6 on 29 Aug.

[72] The name may be traced to Spanish Jewish origins, as either Perfet (Isaac ben Sheshet Perfet, d. 1408) or Profiat (Profiat Duran, d. 1414).

[73] A certain harpist by the name of Bernardino S. Benedetto Renato appears in court records (including the salary roll) from the years 1588–9 (see Parisi, 'Ducal Patronage of Music in Mantua, 1587–1627', 28, 650). Another convert, Giovanni Paulo Eustachio Renato, put his knowledge of Hebrew to the service of the authorities, in the 1580s, by censoring Hebrew books (after Simonsohn, *History of the Jews in the Duchy of Mantua*, 687).

[74] ASAG, Mandati 97, fo. 240: 'Havendo Noi concesso ad Isacchino della Proffetta per quatordici anni scorsi, et hora in vita sua, per la buona servitù che tutto dì riceviamo da lui, et acciò possa più commodamente maritare una sua figliuola, di poter far una banca da beccaio tra gli Hebrei di questa nostra Città, et volendo ch'essa banca dopo la morte del detto Isachino passi nella persona di Giovanni Battista Renato già suo figliuolo durante parimente la vita sua' (dated 29 July 1610). The words *banca da beccaio* refer not to a butcher's bank, but, as translated above, to a butcher's stand. Cf. *Grande dizionario della lingua italiana*, ii. 32, for 'banca' ('bench, counter, stand for sitting, writing, selling or rowing'), and 135, for 'beccaio' or 'beccaro' ('butcher who sells butchered meats'), with references to passages in Vasari ('Fra le due colonne di piazza [si trovavano] alcuni *banchi di beccari*') and Garzoni ('A' *beccari* poi s'appartiene essere esperti nel comprare gli animali, saperli pesar con l'occhio, sapergli ingrassare . . . e tagliando alla *banca*, saper fare i tagli come vanno giusti, e netti'). In the inventory of books submitted to the censor in 1595, there is a listing for Isaac Profeta (362 items), assumedly Massarano; cf. Simonsohn, 'Sefarim vesifriyot shel yehudei mantova, 1595', 115.

[75] Still another son, though not a *ballerino*, was Abraham, remembered for his account of the tragic years 1627–31 (*Sefer hagalut vehapedut*).

Why did Perfetti lease the warrant to, of all persons, Rossi? Out of friendship, perhaps: Perfetti knew Rossi from his former affiliation with the Jewish community; he doubtless participated with him, at court or elsewhere, in various festivities. Or out of respect for his father Isacchino, who must have been on amicable terms with Rossi: the two appeared together in productions of the Jewish theatrical troupe[76] and collaborated in other entertainments; Rossi seems to have honoured Massarano, moreover, in a *gagliarda* entitled 'la Massara' (1607).[77] Or, more pragmatically, because Rossi, or one of his backers, paid the authorities a handsome sum for the privilege. Perfetti may not have had the time to execute his duties as diligently as required, hence was obliged to 'lease' them to another.[78]

The connection between Isacchino Massarano and the name Proffeta (alias Perfetto or Perfetti?) remains to be clarified. It could be that Massarano was so called because of an *intermedio* in which he impersonated a prophet, or if not that, then played some other part so well that he earned the plaudit 'perfetto'. One piece by Rossi could be of help, though its date of publication (1613) makes it applicable to the son Giovanni Battista: the fifth *gagliarda* in Book 3 of the instrumental works is entitled 'Amor perfetto', i.e. the Perfect Cupid,[79] perhaps in reference to a Cupid played and danced 'to perfection' by Perfetti. Another possibility, most convincing of all, is that the name Proffeta derives from Isacchino's mother.[80]

That Isacchino was a man of means is suggested by an event that, ever since Canal's report, has been noted in the literature, yet is not easily explained.[81] It concerns a banquet or rather 'masked ball' to which Isacchino invited the nobility in 1594, only to end with one of the Gonzagas getting into a brawl.[82] It is hardly likely for a Jewish dancer and singer, or, as he is described in the report, 'Isacchino who sings soprano', as respected as he

---

[76] Two documents list their names, one after the other, in conjunction with theatrical events for 1605 (JCA, file 9, doc. 1: 10, and file 10, doc. 1: 19).

[77] CW ix. 26.

[78] 'non potendo esso Prefetti così assiduamente attendere a questo officio, come converrebbe, egli habbia libera facultà, et licenza di sublocare, et contrattare il detto Decreto nella maniera, che più gli tornerà a conto con la persona di Salomone Rossi hebreo, passandone quelle conventioni, che tra essi s'accorderanno, et che ciò seguito il detto Salomone habbia a godere dell'istesso Decreto, come se a lui medesimo fosse conceduto' (from contract drawn up on 15 Nov. 1621; ASAG 3391 [see above], esp. fo. 177).

[79] CW xi. 20.

[80] I consulted with Vittore Colorni on the 'authenticity' of Perfetti/Proffeta/Prefetto, etc. If anyone, Colorni is familiar with Italian Jewish names, having written two major pieces on them ('Cognomi ebraici italiani' and 'La corrispondenza fra nomi ebraici e nomi locali'; see above). He told me the following charming story: 'When I was a boy in Mantua [Colorni was born in 1912—D.H.], there was a Jewish woman with the name Perfetta, and my father, I remember, used to joke, saying: "How could such an ugly woman be called *perfetta*?"'; and, more seriously, expressed the opinion that Perfetta and variant forms refer to the mother's given name, hence Isacchino della Proffeta might be construed as Isacchino, son, probably, of Isacco, his father, and of Perfetta (or Proffeta), his mother (letter dated 3 Oct. 1996).

[81] Canal, 'Della musica in Mantova', 701.

[82] ASAG 2665 (letter of Alfonso Gonzaga, 15 Jan. 1594).

was,[83] to have had the standing, let alone finances, to play host, in his house, to Christian notables. True, selling kosher meat, which was always in demand by the Jewish community, might have been a lucrative business. Yet any assumption that Massarano's fortune lay therein is contingent on his having been awarded a privilege to run a butcher's stand before 1596. Or was Massarano involved in loan banking, as was an early member of his family?[84]

Visits to Other Courts and Cities

So far Rossi has been treated in association with the Mantuan court, but the word *court* has neither been defined nor has the panoply of its activities been described. Where did the court assemble and which of its events might have involved Rossi as composer, instrumentalist, and possibly singer?

The court was officially located in the Ducal Palace, but the palace was only one of several places where the duke or other members of his family and guests resided. In the palace itself, different rooms were used for musical and theatrical diversions. The Sala degli Specchi was particularly suitable for chamber music, though if, as Monteverdi indicated, music was performed there on Friday evenings, then Rossi, who observed the Sabbath, would not have been among the participants.[85] Scenic entertainments usually took place in the ducal theatre. Music could also be heard in the private apartments. Outside the palace the riding yard and the Piazza Sordello were used for jousts and tournaments, often accompanied by music. Mock naval battles were staged on the lake, with music, again, as a supplement.

During Carnival time plays and processions, meant for the public, but sponsored by the court, were held outdoors or, for plays of the Jewish acting troupe, sometimes under the *loggia*, or covered porch, of the synagogue.[86] Music was executed in private residences of the nobles as it was in the public theatre, reserved for plays of visiting acting companies (among them the 'Fedeli'). A special theatre (seating 4,000) was constructed on the palace grounds for the première of Monteverdi's opera *Arianna* (1608). But performances of chamber music and theatrical works were also scheduled in the academies, as in the case of Monteverdi's *Orfeo*, presented, at least

---

[83] For his faithful service as instrumentalist and dancer, Massarano was, like Rossi, exempted from wearing 'the customary badge' ('concediamo a nostro beneplacito la licenza ad Isac dalla Profeta hebreo, attesa la servitù da lui fatta alla Casa nostra nell'essercitio suo di sonare, et ballare, di poter liberamente andare senza il solito segno per questa nostra Città, et suo Dominio'); ASAG, Mandati 97, fo. 108ᵛ, 2 Apr. 1607.

[84] On the loan banker Isaac Massarano, see Simonsohn, *History of the Jews in the Duchy of Mantua*, 218–20 (with reference to various documents, among them one where Massarano is authorized, in 1542, to lend money at interest).

[85] After *The Letters of Claudio Monteverdi*, tr. Stevens, 83–6 (letter from 1611; see above).

[86] Cf. Simonsohn, *History of the Jews in the Duchy of Mantua*, 667 n. 316.

once, before the Accademia degli Invaghiti, though where, exactly, remains to be said (one scholar has suggested that Rossi might have led the orchestra).[87]

Apart from music for the Church or for private devotions, Rossi could have been employed in a wide variety of private and public entertainments, some of them to mark special events (birthdays, weddings, anniversaries, visits of state, military successes, coronations) and others simply to add lustre to the name and house of their sponsor.

But the musical activities in Mantua, be they in the Ducal Palace, the Palazzo del Te, the Villa 'La Favorita', or private households, spilled over into the Mantovano, where the court had its country residences. Thus when the court retired, in whole or in part, to Goito, Porto, Gazzolo, Maderno, Marmirolo, Bozzolo, Casale, Poggio Reale, Belfiore, or Revere, the services of Rossi as of other musicians were occasionally, if not often required. The Mantovano was divided into principalities under the rule of different branches of the Gonzaga family, for whose members Rossi must also have performed.

The evidence for appearances outside the Mantovano is scanty, yet enough to suggest that Rossi might have travelled to various courts or households, either in the entourage of the duke or members of his family or, upon invitation, alone or with one or more musicians. Rossi is known to have gone to Padua in 1606 and, as has already been mentioned, to Mirandola in 1612. He also sojourned on at least three different occasions in Venice.

The trip to Padua was at the instigation of Pietro Priuli, a Paduan noble, who wrote to Duke Vincenzo asking him to send the singer Francesco Rasi or, if he was unavailable, the two Jews Isacco and Salamone, who, as it turned out, were the ones who came.[88] Isacco is to be identified, to all appearances, as Isacchino Massarano, who may have been Rossi's associate on his other 'tours'. The question is: were they joined by one or more local performers or did they play alone? If a group of three or more players and singers was formed, at least one collection of Rossi's instrumental works for three to five voices was available, as were his *canzonette* for three voices and, with optional instrumental accompaniment, at least three collections of madrigals for five. If, however, Isacco and Salamone appeared as a duo only, the repertory is less easily determined. They might have performed pseudo-madrigals, that is, madrigals scaled down to a version for voice and lute or chitarrone; or instrumental works, written or improvised, in two parts, of which no evidence remains in Rossi's repertory; or pieces for two voices and *continuo, madrigaletti* as it were, anticipating Rossi's last publication, though clearly the singers would have had to

---

[87] Denis Stevens, in his edition of *L'Orfeo*, p. ii.
[88] ASAG 1534: Priuli's letter to Vincenzo (14 Apr. 1602); 2255: Vincenzo's answer (17 Apr. 1602); and Priuli's note of thanks after the visit (7 May 1602).

supply their own accompaniment; or solo pieces, perhaps improvised, on the lute or the violin.[89]

The trip to Mirandola raises questions of its own, beyond those already considered in connection with Rossi's 'concerto'. Why, of all persons, was Rossi invited? Were there earlier trips to Mirandola? Did the trip lead to further invitations or commissions?

It should be remembered that Alessandro Pico, prince of Mirandola, was married to Laura, daughter of Cesare d'Este, duke of Modena, and that the duke and Laura's sister Giulia were the honoured guests at the festivities in which Rossi and his 'concerto' were invited to participate in 1612.[90] That Rossi knew Alessandro Pico before then, perhaps from an earlier visit to his court, is suggested by his having dedicated to him his third book of madrigals (1603, a year before Alessandro's wedding). It is in Mirandola that he may have met the duke of Modena and members of his family; or if not there, then in Mantua, on a visit of theirs, or elsewhere.[91] As much may be conjectured from his second book of *sinfonie*, offered to the Este duke, in 1608, as a token of gratitude for earlier favours ('your kindness, with which I, at other times, found myself favoured beyond anything I deserve'). The duke appears to have been taken by Rossi's works, which is why Rossi dedicated the present set to him ('for you showed that you were pleased, in days gone by, with my compositions.... [I offer you these new ones] more to satisfy the taste of Your Highness than for their deserving such protection'). Duke Cesare could well have asked his son-in-law Alessandro, as a special favour, to arrange for Rossi to visit Mirandola.

Or still another scenario is possible: Prince Alessandro, knowing Cesare's inclination to Rossi's music or his 'concerto', may, as a surprise to his father-in-law, have seen to it that Rossi be given leave to come and entertain him. In requesting Duke Vincenzo's permission, Alessandro asked 'to be honoured' by the composer and his ensemble, which, unless rhetorical, says something of their repute. That the relations with the Este family continued beyond 1612 is clear from Rossi's dedication of his four-voice madrigals, in 1614, to Prince Alfonso, the duke's son, in acknowledgement of his 'infinite kindness'. Rossi speaks, moreover, of his 'reverent devotion' to him and his 'immense desire' to serve him.

For Venice there is the evidence of the dedications. The word *Venice* appears in the composer's signature to three of them: the first book of five-voice madrigals, from 1600; the fourth book of instrumental works, from 1622; and, as has been mentioned, the *Madrigaletti*, Rossi's last

---

[89] For the relevant literature, cf. Mangsen, 'Instrumental Duos and Trios in Printed Italian Sources, 1600–1675'.

[90] For Alessandro's letter of invitation (ASAG 1337), see above.

[91] Before the Este court transferred to Modena in 1597, Rossi might have visited it in neighbouring Ferrara. Yet as plausible as such visits may seem, we know nothing of Rossi's connections with Ferrara or its Jewish community.

collection, from 1628. Whether Rossi paid additional visits to Venice for overseeing the printing of his other collections cannot be determined: the rest are signed Mantua, which is inconclusive. It means either that he was not in Venice at the time or, if he were, that the dedication was prepared after his return to Mantua.

Nor is it clear what else Rossi did in Venice beyond supervising his publications. He might have stayed in the house of Sara Copio, the daughter-in-law of his Jewish patron Moses Sullam and herself a patron of writers—she ran a literary salon in her home.[92] Through Sara he could, at some stage, have come to know Leon Modena, who, to all appearances, played a major role in the planning and realization of Rossi's Hebrew songs (see Plates 9–10); after settling in Venice in 1607–8, Modena, related to Sara's family on his wife's side, became her close friend and adviser. The idea of the Hebrew songs may have started from a meeting with Modena, in Venice, perhaps, sometime in the years 1610–12 or shortly thereafter, provided, of course, Rossi was there at the time.

In 1622, when Rossi did in fact turn up in Venice, it stands to reason that, beyond the publication of Book 4 of his instrumental works, he discussed with Modena the problems connected with the forthcoming edition of the Hebrew songs: Modena had been entrusted with preparing them for publication. He might even have tried out some of the songs in Sara's house or in one of the Venetian synagogues, which, if he did, was probably the Scuola Italiana where Modena officiated as cantor. On the same visit Rossi might also have looked into the publication of Book 3 of his instrumental works, in its third edition (1623). Further visits to Venice could have followed, though only the last one from 1628 is known. It is not clear whether Rossi went back to Mantua or, aware of the dangers at home, stayed on.[93]

There is a vague reference to a 'Salamon m[aestro] di musica' in the community of Savigliano, not far from Turin, in a document for 1596.[94] With the spelling Salamon and the appellation 'teacher of music', which could be construed, alternatively, as 'skilled in music', it is tempting to identify the designee as Salamone Rossi. Without further evidence, however, there is no way the identification can be ascertained. Nor can one know who the person was behind the equally vague reference, in a document from Turin for the year 1609, to a 'Salamon [thus spelled] Rabenu of

[92] On Sara Copio in relation to the poet Ansaldo Cebà, see Boccato, 'Lettere di Ansaldo Cebà, genovese, a Sara Copio Sullam, poetessa del ghetto di Venezia', 169–91; and in relation to Modena, Adelman, 'Success and Failure in the Seventeenth-Century Ghetto of Venice', 608–21. On Sara as a singer, see Harrán, 'Doubly Tainted, Doubly Talented'.

[93] See section above: 'Birth, Death, and Intermediate Years', where the possibility of an affiliation with Modena's music academy was raised. Why the academy was formed may in fact have to do with Rossi's presence in Venice: certainly Modena was busy enough in the late 1620s, as is clear from his autobiography (see Ḥayei yehuda, in English tr. M. Cohen, 131 ff.), without taking on the additional responsibility of running an academy, unless he did so to accommodate Rossi and other Mantuan musicians.

[94] Segre, The Jews in Piedmont, ii. 804.

Mantua', *rabenu* meaning anything from 'our rabbi' to 'our master' or 'our teacher'. The duke of Savoy (Carlo Emanuele) is said to have ordered the treasurer general to pay him 125 ducatoni as proceeds—one might assume—from the 'sale of several books copied by hand that were effectively transmitted to us' (music manuscripts?).[95] Since other members of Rossi's family were active in Turin (see below), it is not impossible for Rossi to have travelled to Piedmont on various commissions. If so, another chapter in Rossi's biography remains to be written.[96]

Other Members of the Family

The family name Rossi was well known in the Jewish community—one of its most distinguished representatives was the scholar Azaria de' Rossi (d. 1578). Yet Christians also bore the name: scrutiny of the extensive correspondence held in the Gonzaga archive reveals any number of them from the later sixteenth and early seventeenth centuries. The Jewish Rossis were referred to, in Hebrew, as 'min ha'adumim', which translates as 'de' Rossi', or 'of the red', possibly in reference to the ruddy complexion of the youthful David (1 Samuel 16: 12). In the introduction to the 'Songs of Solomon' the composer's pedigree is traced to King David; the family, along with three others, was said by legend to have been led back in captivity to Rome, by the emperor Titus, after the destruction of the Second Temple.[97] In Jewish documents written in Italian, most Rossis appeared not as 'de' Rossi', but simply as 'Rossi' (see Plate 5, one of various lists of participants in Mantuan Jewish theatrical productions); the prefix *de'*, or in Hebrew *min ha-*, would seem to have been added after the example of Italian nobles.

Rossi's father was a certain Bonaiuto, in Hebrew Azaria, as is evident from a document, dated 1621, with mention of 'Mr Salamone, the son of Mr Bonaiuto Rossi *ebreo*, in Mantua',[98] not to be confused with the aforementioned Azaria, again Bonaiuto, Rossi, whose wife bore him only daughters. Since nothing is known of Rossi's father, it is not clear whether Bonaiuto, which shows up in other documents, refers to the father or, as is usually assumed, to one of Madama Europa's sons, also Bonaiuto, named, it is likely, after his grandfather. The younger Bonaiuto, on whom more below,

[95] Ibid. ii. 902 ('...per vendita di tanti libri scritti a mano a noi effettualmente rimessi').

[96] Other references in the literature can easily be discarded, as for example the one to a certain Marco, son of Salomone of Mantua. Marco, it turns out, is Marco de Levi, son of the late Salomone di Leonello of Mantua (the document in question dates from 1575). See Simonsohn, *The Jews in the Duchy of Milan*, iii. 1611–12.

[97] The legend is recounted in various genealogical enquiries, among them the portion 'Yemei 'olam', or 'Olden Times', in Azaria de' Rossi's tract *Me'or 'einayim* ('Light of One's Eyes', 1574).

[98] 'concessit Domino Salomoni fili Domini Bonaiuti de Rossis hebreo Mantue': ASAG 3391, dated 15 Nov. 1621 (the document concerns Salamone's right to revenues from the sale of pledges; see above).

appears to have counted among the wealthier Jews in early seventeenth-century Mantua.[99] Yet there is a possibility that the elder of them was also a man of means, in which case the story of Salamone's finances, from his paltry earnings in the court—did he need them to start with?—to how he covered the expenses of his publications, would have to be rewritten. The lack of adequate documentation on the various members of the Rossi family frustrates efforts to separate them.

Emanuele (or, in Hebrew, Menahem) Rossi, brother to Salamone, has already been mentioned as having received certain privileges after Salamone's intervention, on at least two occasions (1602, 1606), with the authorities. Emanuele himself wrote to the duke, in 1606, informing him that some persons from Viadana had tried to smuggle goods and that, at his instigation, they were to be brought to trial.[100] His name appears along with his brother's, in 1605, on two lists of participants in the Jewish theatrical troupe[101] and alone, ten years earlier, on the register of those submitting an inventory of their books to the censor.[102]

Europa Rossi is not to be confused with Europa Rossa, a Christian noble-woman from Ferrara.[103] The Jewish Europa figures alongside her brother Salamone, as said, on two salary rolls of the court: on the first, as 'Madama Europa sua sorella' (1589, under 'extraordinarij'); on the second, as 'Europa di Rossi' (1592). In a letter from 1607, she is mentioned, now as Europa, in reference to her sons Angelo and Bonaiuto.[104] Her name is unusual,[105] though less so the designation 'Madama'[106] (there is mention, in a document from 1596 relating to the Jewish community of Piedmont, of a Madama Rachel and a Madama Susanna, both widows).[107] Europa appears to have been her real name or, if not that, was, for some reason, attached to her as a sobriquet. Whatever the reason, it was definitely not the one usually suggested, which is that the name has to do with her having played Europa in the *intermedio*, by Chiabrera, *Il ratto di Europa*, set to music by Gastoldi and performed as part of the festivities for the marriage of Francesco Gonzaga

[99] Cf. Simonsohn, *History of the Jews in the Duchy of Mantua*, 317 (with reference to his inheritance).

[100] ASAG 2705, fasc. 14, no. 57 (4 Apr. 1606).

[101] JCA, file 9, doc. 1: 10 (17 Feb. 1605); file 10, doc. 1: 164 (31 Mar. 1605).

[102] Cf. Simonsohn, 'Sefarim vesifriyot shel yehudei mantova, 1595', 108.

[103] She moved to Viadana in the 1590s, first living in her brother's house, only to submit a request, in 1597, to purchase her own property (ASAG, Decreti 52, fo. 45; 15 Oct. 1597); for details, see Harrán, 'Madama Europa, Jewish Singer in Late Renaissance Mantua', 205–7.

[104] 'Messer Angelo figliolo della Europpa [*sic*]...Messer Buonaiuto de Rossi pur ancor lui figliolo della europpa [*sic*]': ASAG 734 (18 Dec. 1607; a letter written in Turin by the Confaloniero di Valeriano to the Mantuan court official Alessandro Chieppio).

[105] On other 'geographical' names among Mantuan Jewry, see Harrán, 'Madama Europa, Jewish Singer in Late Renaissance Mantua', 205 (and n. 25).

[106] Lest it be thought otherwise, there is nothing pejorative about 'Madama': it was used, in Europa's time, as a variant of Madonna. Cf. ibid. 205 n. 24, referring to Girolamo Ruscelli (*Lettura...*, 1552) on its etymology.

[107] See Segre, *The Jews in Piedmont*, ii. 803–4 (doc. 1645).

and Margherita of Savoy in 1608.[108] Still, her name may have been the reason why she was chosen for the part, if indeed she was, which seems likely.

Many women were among the singers who, according to the court chronicler's report, participated in the *intermedi* and other entertainments on the same occasion.[109] They are said to be in the duke's service and to have few peers in Italy.[110] None, though, seems to have been as effective in the *intermedi* as the singer in the role of Europa. 'A woman understanding music to perfection, she sang to the listeners' great delight and their greater wonder, in a most delicate and sweet-sounding voice...delightfully modulating her mournful tones that caused the listeners to shed tears of compassion'.[111] If, as has been assumed, the description applies to Madama Europa,[112] she must have been a first-rate singer.

Europa's husband was her cousin David, son of Elisha de' Rossi, which explains why Rossi remained her family name after marriage. A list of his books was presented to the censor in 1595.[113] Their children, as said, were Bonaiuto (Azaria) and Angelo (Mordecai). Bonaiuto occurs several times in the Jewish and Gonzaga archives: he married Lipona, daughter of Gabriel Orefice (Zoref), in 1597;[114] he was involved in a business transaction, along with his brother Angelo, in 1607;[115] he served on a committee, formed in 1610, for solving problems of housing in establishing the ghetto[116] (another person on the committee was Salamone Rossi's benefactor Moses Sullam); he was responsible, in 1611, for executing a decree that stipulated that boys and girls in the community be instructed in arts and crafts 'lest they be idle';[117] he represented the community in its protest to the authorities, in 1625, against a libellous painting (it showed the hanging of seven Jews);[118] and he handled a commercial matter in 1620, again with his brother.[119]

While Bonaiuto seems to have stayed on in Mantua, Angelo, sometime in the early seventeenth century, was hired as musician at the court of Savoy.

---

[108] From the dating of the payrolls it is clear she was known as Europa in the later 1580s. Canal was the first to conjecture the name as derivative, 'after the custom of the time', from her performance in the *intermedio* ('Della musica in Mantova', 736–7).

[109] The chronicler was Follino, who provided a full description of the festivities, including the various *intermedi*: *Compendio delle sontuose feste fatte l'anno M.DC.VIII*, etc., 72–99.

[110] Follino, quoted by Solerti, *Gli albori del melodramma*, iii. 208.

[111] Ibid. 218–19.

[112] Cf. Harrán, 'Madama Europa, Jewish Singer in Late Renaissance Mantua', 207–12.

[113] See Simonsohn, 'Sefarim vesifriyot shel yehudei mantova, 1595', 108.

[114] JCA, file 17, doc. 22, and file 18, doc. 19 (after Simonsohn, *History of the Jews in the Duchy of Mantua*, 533 n. 83).

[115] The document in which they are identified as sons of Europa (see above).

[116] JCA, Minute Books C 37a (after Simonsohn, *History of the Jews in the Duchy of Mantua*, 41).

[117] JCA, Minute Books C 40b (5 Oct. 1611; cf. Simonsohn, *History of the Jews in the Duchy of Mantua*, 588).

[118] JCA, file 19, doc. 7 (cf. Simonsohn, *History of the Jews in the Duchy of Mantua*, 38).

[119] JCA, file 16, docs. 17–20 (from 1620; cf. Simonsohn, *History of the Jews in the Duchy of Mantua*, 676 n. 352).

He may have returned, on various occasions, to Mantua. In 1605, for example, his name appears, once as Agnolino, then as Angelo, among the participants, in Mantua, in productions of the Jewish theatrical troupe.[120] A year later he received a permit, from Carlo Emanuele I, duke of Savoy, to run a loan bank in Rocconigi, near the ducal family's country residence; the same bank was still operating in 1624, if not later.[121] He was active at the court, variously as composer, lute and guitar player, and teacher of music, between the years 1608 and 1649 (and died in 1651). Angelo's sons were Giuseppe (Josef) and Bonaiuto (Azaria), who, like their father, served the dukes of Savoy as musicians.[122] Perhaps the Isep de' Rossi, listed as participant, along with Angelo, in one of the theatrical productions for 1605, was in fact Giuseppe.[123]

Other persons with the name Rossi on inventories of their libraries or on the rolls of Jewish theatrical productions have still not been identified. It would be useful, to say the least, to know how Benedetto di Rossi, Eleazar Rossi, Isaac de Rossi, Lazzaro Rossi, Miriam Rossi, Judah Rossi, and Zacharia Rossi related to Salamone.[124] Additional members of the Rossi clan, outside Mantua, await identification: the Venetian Joshua Rossi, to whom a wedding ode, undated, was dedicated;[125] and Benjamin Saul Rossi, a cantor in Ferrara before 1612.[126]

As to Anselmo Rossi and Matteo Rossi, who turn up in the Mantuan archives, they were musicians, true, but not Jews. Anselmo, until recently thought to be another of Europa's sons, composed a motet ('Aperi oculos

---

[120] JCA, file 9, doc. 1: 10 (17 Feb. 1605); file 10, doc. 1: 164 (31 Mar. 1605); file 10, doc. 1: 19 (31 Dec. 1605; Tasso's *Intrighi d'amore*).

[121] The permit is dated from Asti, 7 Nov. 1606. For Angelo in Turin, see Roth, *The Jews in the Renaissance*, 287–8; and Segre, *The Jews in Piedmont*, ii. docs. 1867, 1909, 1944, 2030, 2077, etc., altogether twenty documents (covering the years 1610–51). On music at the court, see Cordero di Pamparato, 'I musici alla corte di Carlo Emanuele I di Savoia'; and Solerti, 'Feste musicali alla corte di Savoia nella prima metà del secolo XVII'. On Jewish loan bankers in Savoy, see variously in Foa, *La politica economica della casa savoia*.

[122] For Giuseppe, see Segre, *The Jews in Piedmont*, ii. 1043, 1080, 1087, 1092, 1133, 1139 (for the years 1629–58, the latter marking his decease). For Bonaiuto, or as he figures in the documents Buonaggiunto, see ibid. ii. 1090, 1099 (for the years, respectively, 1646, 1648). One can follow the Rossi family in Turin until at least the end of the century (Alessandro de Rossi, Giuseppe's son; Ferdinando Rosso; Jacob Rossi). Another Jewish musician at the court of Savoy is Benedetto Senigli (cf. Segre, *The Jews in Piedmont*, ii. 943, 964, 992, 1030, for the years 1615–28). The composer David Sacerdote is also mentioned in at least ten documents for Piedmont, though not in a musical connection (cf. ibid. ii. 705, 708, etc., for the years 1590–1606); in two others for the duchy of Milan (dated, respectively, 1594, 1613), again non-musical in their content, he appears in the first, however, as 'a musician from Monferrato' (see Simonsohn, *The Jews in the Duchy of Milan*, iii. 1906–7; for the second, see ibid. 2075).

[123] JCA, file 10, doc. 1: 164, for 31 Mar. 1605 (as above).

[124] JCA, file 5, docs. 1–432 for 1595 censorship (see Simonsohn, 'Sefarim vesifriyot shel yehudei mantova, 1595'; and in greater detail, Baruchson, 'Hasifriyot haperatiyot shel yehudei tsefon italya beshilhei harenesans'); same archive, file 9, docs. 2–431 for 1605 censorship; and for theatrical participation, various documents cited above.

[125] See Modena, *Divan*, ed. Bernstein, 186 (no. 184, in celebration of Joshua's marriage to a daughter of the Butari family).

[126] See *Encyclopaedia judaica*, xii. 620.

meos') for an anthology in honour of Duke Ferdinando.[127] Matteo Rossi was a bass singer at the court between the years 1613 and 1622, after which he joined the imperial chapel in Innsbruck.[128]

To continue with the Christian Rossis, one might mention Giovanni Maria de' Rossi, curator, during 1553–9, of the ducal instrument collection and chapel master, during 1563–76, at the Cathedral; a collection of his motets and another of his madrigals was published in 1567.[129]

One wonders who Sebastiano di Rossi was: he is listed, in 1589, as having lodged viol (string?) players come to serve the duke, for which he received a payment of 240 lire. Could Sebastiano have been a scribal error for Salamone, who, if anyone, might have been entrusted with arrangements for a viol (string?) consort?[130] Since the sum was nearly one and a half times more than what Salamone earned in a year, it seems unlikely.

Two non-musicians, already cited, with the family name Rossi were well known to Salamone: Carlo Rossi, chief of the Mantuan militia and, among other things, responsible in 1608 for the *intermedi* for Guarini's *L'Idropica*; and Federico Rossi, who may well have been Carlo's son, to whom Salamone dedicated his fourth book of madrigals *a 5* in 1610.[131] For the years 1604–12 the archives preserve letters by still other Christian Rossis, among them Alessandro, Antonio, Ferrante, and Giovanni. More needs to be done on the genealogy of the Jewish and Christian Rossis.

Slightly later than Salamone there are, of course, the renowned Christian musicians, though not from Mantua, Luigi Rossi and Michelangelo Rossi, not to speak of various lesser ones from the seventeenth century: Francesco Rossi, a name shared by at least three different figures; Giovan Carlo Rossi; Giovanni Battista Rossi; and Giuseppe de Rossi.

What of Salamone Rossi's own immediate family? Of his wife or children we know nothing. He could well have been childless, or so one might conclude from Leon Modena's remark that the composer, by publishing his Hebrew songs, 'left to posterity a name better than sons'.[132] Yet the remark should be qualified by the reference, in the copyright to the same collection, to Rossi's 'heirs', who, if not 'sons', may have included daughters, unable to perpetuate his 'name'.

---

[127] It has already been mentioned in connection with the two Rubinis, who also contributed to it. On Anselmo's identity, see Ghirardini, 'Salamone Rossi, musico alla corte dei Gonzaga: studio biografico', 100–1; and Colorni, 'Una correzione necessaria a proposito di Anselmo Rossi, musico mantovano del Seicento'.

[128] See Parisi, 'Ducal Patronage of Music in Mantua, 1587–1627', 490, 651–2.

[129] See respective entry by Pierre Tagmann in Sadie (ed.), *The New Grove Dictionary of Music and Musicians*, xvi. 215.

[130] ASAG 3141, 1589: 'Lista della spesa della Ducale Camera di Mantova', under 'Straordinario', that is, special expenses, esp. fo. 578ᵛ ('a Sebastiano di Rossi osti per haver allogiato li sonatori da Viola ch'erano venuti a servir Sua Altezza').

[131] The records are not clear here: both persons are referred to as count of San Secondo (for Carlo, see F. Amadei, *Cronaca universale della città di Mantova*, ed. G. Amadei et al., iii. 236; for Federico, Rossi's dedication).

[132] From Modena's foreword to the collection.

Contemporary Appraisal

Two kinds of evaluative evidence may be assembled: from the dedications to his publications and from their number and diffusion. We may leave aside the laudatory remarks in the prefatory matter to the Hebrew songs, where Rossi is described as the first and greatest Jewish composer of music since the time of the Ancient Temple. Rossi's popularity within the Jewish community, or at least that part of it open to change and innovation, is not to be doubted. His name probably became a household word in Jewish circles over Northern Italy, where he was seen to bring honour to his people.

Rossi paints a different picture of himself in the eyes of his Christian colleagues. As a Jew, competing for favours ordinarily conferred on Christians, Rossi was subject to slander. Thus he appeals to Duke Vincenzo and other dedicatees for their protection against his critics. How? By accepting and approving his collections. He asks Vincenzo, then, to keep him 'safe from the hands of detractors' by lending his 'felicitous name' to his madrigals in Book 1 *a* 5, which 'without such great support would either soon fall into oblivion or, among the hands of such persons, be torn and wasted as if by raging dogs'. Felicita Gonzaga is entreated to 'protect and defend' the madrigals in Book 2, for 'no slanderer or detractor would ever dare to censure something that is protected and favoured by a Lady of such great distinction'. Dedicating his fourth book of madrigals to Federico Rossi, the composer hoped that his name would be 'an impenetrable shield for resisting the fierce darts of malevolent detractors', thus preventing the book's being 'lacerated by a furious tooth'. The tide of criticism did not wane, for in Book 3 of the instrumental works he petitions Don Ferrante Gonzaga 'to defend' him from 'slanderous and deprecating tongues'. It was imperative to demonstrate fidelity to his patrons, and Rossi craved signs of approval from them in order 'to give proof to the world' of their favour; or 'to become illustrious' by having their illustrious name apposed to his collections; or 'to acquire greater fame and greater renown' by flaunting their support.[133]

Perhaps more telling is the record of Rossi's publications. Publishing houses then, as now, were unwilling to take on works that seemed unprofitable. Not only did Rossi have thirteen collections issued in his lifetime, which by any standard speaks for a certain popularity, but of these, some seem to have been in special demand, thus were reprinted. Book 1 of the five-voice madrigals, for example, had four later editions; Book 2 had two; Book 3 of the *sinfonie*, three; and so on, for a total of twelve reprints, two of them posthumous.[134] Thus Rossi has a total of twenty-five publications to

---

[133] Quotations from the dedications to, respectively, Bks 1–2 and 4 of madrigals *a* 5. For a complete transcription of the dedications (along with their translation), see respective volumes in *CW*. On the dedications as a source of biographical information, see Harrán, 'Salamone Rossi, Jewish Musician in Renaissance Italy', esp. 48–53 (for the Italian ones), and Ch. 2 below.

[134] See listing in App., i. 'Collections', and, in detail, the portion 'Sources' in the introductory material to the various volumes of *CW*.

his name, one of them printed in Antwerp.[135] That he was known and 'marketable' outside Italy is clear from the inclusion of his works in an anthology of madrigals printed in Copenhagen and in two others printed, again, in Antwerp.[136] Even more interesting is his appearance in the large anthology of madrigals copied by the recusant Francis Tregian, while incarcerated in the London Fleet Prison, between the years 1613 and 1619: there Rossi is represented by nineteen works.[137] In their pastoral tone, and unaffected simplicity, these works must have struck a resonance with English audiences, used to similar ones by their own madrigalists. It is no wonder that the composer Weelkes reworked six of Rossi's *canzonette* in his own versions.[138]

[135] The last edition of his Bk 1 *a* 5 (P. Phalèse, 1618).

[136] Copenhagen: *Giardino novo bellissimo* (Waltkirck, 1605), two madrigals *a* 5. Antwerp: *Il Parnasso* (Phalèse, 1613), two *a* 6; *Il Helicone* (Phalèse, 1616), one *a* 5.

[137] London, BL MS Egerton 3665 ('The Tregian Manuscript'), nos. 452–70 (eleven from Bk 1 *a* 5, five from Bk 2, and three from Bk 3); the manuscript is available in a fac. edn. (with intro. by F. A. D'Accone).

[138] Cf. J. Cohen, 'Thomas Weelkes's Borrowings from Salamone Rossi'. On the Italian madrigal in England, see Hamessley, 'The Reception of the Italian Madrigal in England'.

2

The Publications

ALL of Rossi's surviving works are known from early printed editions. There may have been others originally in manuscript and no longer extant, among them those for the theatre. Four of his madrigals for an *intermedio* by Chiabrera illustrate the problem: the texts remain, but not the music.[1] Since Rossi was active in the theatre, it stands to reason that more was composed than the lone musical example, for a Christian play, to be found in the sources.[2] As for the Hebrew songs, Rossi, we learn, worked, over a number of years, to assemble a collection of them, from which he selected various ones for publication:[3] here, too, it may be assumed that manuscript copies of others were once available.

To what we do not have in manuscript may be added what we do, but probably not the composer's: a vocal arrangement of a *sinfonia* from the second book of his instrumental works;[4] and an anonymous collection of Hebrew polychoral works, of which only one part remains, in a style quite different from Rossi's.[5]

General Features

Of the thirteen collections, six appeared in one or more reprints, for a total of twenty-five publications, which, as noted at the end of the previous chapter, might signal Rossi's popularity. Except for two of the reprints, all publications were issued during his lifetime. They fall into three categories, depending on language, medium, or function: secular works in Italian, instrumental works, and sacred works in Hebrew.

By far the largest category is the first, with eight collections covering the full span of the composer's career. Rossi began in 1589 with a set of *canzonette* for three voices and ended in 1628 with a set of *madrigaletti* for mainly

---

[1] *Il ratto di Proserpina*; for texts, cf. CW viii. app. 2.

[2] 'Spazziam pronte' (Andreini). On Rossi and the theatre, see Ch. 6 below.

[3] Rossi, in his dedication, speaks of 'constantly multiplying the psalms of David', eventually to terminate '*many of them* ... I realized it would be good to favour the public by bringing out *a choice of my songs*'. Leon Modena, in his foreword, says of the composer that 'daily he would enter into his notebook a psalm of David or a certain text used for praying or offering praise ... until he succeeded in gathering *some of them* into a collection'.

[4] 'Partirò da te': for details, see App.

[5] Cincinnati, Hebrew Union College, MS Birnbaum, Mus. 101 (dating from the 1630s?). For details, see Ch. 7.

two voices plus *continuo*. Between them lay five books of madrigals for five voices (1600, 1602, 1603, 1610, 1622) and one for four (1614).

The second category is represented by four collections for three to five voices (1607, 1608, 1613, 1622), having *sinfonie, canzoni*, sonatas, and various dances between their covers. For the third category there is the one collection of Hebrew songs for three to eight voices (1622/3).

In their contents, the Italian collections number 144 works,[6] the instrumental ones 130, and the single Hebrew collection thirty-three. Since Rossi's instrumental works, with the exception of sonatas, tend to be shorter than his vocal ones, the repertory is heavily weighted on the vocal side. Counted by bars, the Italian works total over 8,000 bars, to which more than 3,500 for the Hebrew works should be added; the instrumental ones, by contrast, total somewhat less than 5,000. Still, with his four instrumental collections, Rossi is one of the few vocal music composers of his time, and the only one at the court of Mantua, to publish instrumental works, and a sizeable number at that. One reads in a recent study that 'the main preoccupation of the Mantuan court under both Vincenzo I and Ferdinando was clearly with vocal music and theatrical entertainments rather than with abstract instrumental compositions'.[7] Lasso, Palestrina, Marenzio, Monte, Gesualdo and, in Mantua, Wert, Pallavicino, Gastoldi, Monteverdi, Baccusi, Orlandi, Dognazzi, Franzoni, Nascimbeni, Rasi, Striggio, Taroni, Viadana, and so on, were almost exclusively composers of vocal music. Or at least officially: were one, for example, to extract the instrumental portions from Monteverdi's vocal collections and operas, Monteverdi, too, would appear as a major composer of instrumental music.[8] Still, compared with him and the rest, Rossi is special for having published 'independent' instrumental works, and with the addition of his Hebrew collection, he is obviously unique.

Seen as a whole, the collections reveal certain tendencies. One is to proceed from less to more challenging kinds of composition. Rossi started with a modest set of *canzonette*, then continued with madrigals, which, for Morley, exemplified the most 'grave', i.e. eloquent, species of secular composition.[9] In his instrumental music, he began with diminutive and often relatively simple *sinfonie* and dances and only later tackled sonatas, by comparison more extended and exigent.

Another tendency, concomitant with the first, is, in the vocal works, to start with fewer voices and gradually increase their number. Where the *canzonette*, for example, are for three voices, the next five books are for

---

[6] Plus another six, already mentioned, from other sources (four from Chiabrera's *Ratto di Proserpina*; 'Partirò da te' from a collection of *canzonette*; and 'Spazziam pronte' from *Musiche...composte per La Maddalena*, 1617).

[7] Allsop, *The Italian 'Trio' Sonata*, 9.

[8] On Monteverdi's contribution to the sonata (via his vocal works), see e.g. Selfridge-Field, *Venetian Instrumental Music from Gabrieli to Vivaldi*, 3rd rev. edn., 119–24 (concerning the years 1615–30).

[9] Morley, *A Plain and Easy Introduction to Practical Music*, ed. Harman, 294–5.

five. Though published in 1614, the madrigals for four voices were composed around the time of, or perhaps even before, the first three books for
five, that is, anywhere from the later 1590s to 1603;[10] in which case, again,
the tendency would be to proceed from fewer to more voices, perhaps from
three to four and only then to five. If the sequence of works in the Hebrew
collection, from three to eight voices, reflects the order of composition, then
here, too, the composer proceeded *a minimis ad maxima*. Stylistically, there is
a difference between the Hebrew works for fewer voices, which, melodically, are fairly ornamental, and those for more voices, especially eight,
which, by contrast, seem plain. But any assumption that the former preceded the latter cannot be unconditionally sustained. The three-voice 'Barekhu', no. 3 in the collection, would, for liturgical reasons, have called for an
embellished style no matter when it was composed; and, moreover, for the
same reasons, would not have been written for any more than three voices.

The tendency to expand the ensemble, at least in the Italian collections, is
significantly reversed, however, in the instrumental ones. There the composer started, equivocally, with works for three or four voices, providing, for
many of the three-voice ones, optional versions for four or five, only to
delimit the ensemble, in the later collections, to three voices. The explanation for the change has to do, as will be explained, with the growing
predilection, among early Baroque chamber music composers, for trio-
sonata texture.

Still another tendency is to work on different kinds of pieces at different
times. Thus the *Canzonette* stand as an only work, separated, by ten years,
from the next publication, which inaugurated four books of five-voice
madrigals, from 1600 to 1610. In the interim, the composer published two
collections of instrumental music (1607–8). The four-voice madrigals, from
1614, are, as said, probably to be grouped before or with the first books of
five-voice ones.

A further tendency is to proceed, over the years, from greater to lesser
predictability in the contents of the collections. Rossi's works may roughly
be divided into two periods, the first until 1610, the second from 1613 on to
1628. In the first, Rossi composed his various books of stylistically related
madrigals and his first two books of stylistically related instrumental works.
In the second, he seems to be searching for another mode of composition, as
is clear from his novel sonatas. But the search extended to the rest of his
publications: thus his fifth book of madrigals (1622), to judge from its *basso
continuo*, quite unlike any other in his earlier publications, suggests a set of
upper parts in what must have been *stile concertato*; his Hebrew collection
(1622/3), expanding from three to eight voices, shows the composer grap-
pling with the textural demands of different ensembles and, at the same
time, forging a style in accordance with the requirements of Hebrew

---

[10] On the hypothesis of an earlier date for the madrigals *a 4*, see Ch. 3.

prosody; and the *Madrigaletti*, his last collection (1628), are removed, as chamber duets, from anything he wrote before. Signs of change are vaguely apparent in certain traits of the fourth book of five-voice madrigals (1610), if its sometimes more independent *basso continuo* and vocal parts can be taken as an indicator.

The publications fall, then, into two groups: the earlier, more conservative books; and the later ones, more varied in their styles and structures. Rossi made his 'declaration of independence' in 1613, describing the first work in Book 3 of his instrumental works as 'in the modern manner'. In the following years he attempted, it would seem, to realize its implications. Not content with a single genre, he moved in different directions, seeking new means of expression: the virtuoso sonata, the vocal duet, *concertato* madrigals, sacred Hebrew songs. Rossi's change of manner, though initiated and often conspicuous in his instrumental works, penetrated his vocal ones, where it is more subtly reflected.

It follows that there were two critical years in Rossi's production: 1589 and 1613. In 1589, the composer made an initial statement. Ten years intervened until his second publication. In the interim he mastered the craft of composition, as we learn from the dedication to Book 1 *a 5* (1600). The results are evident in the several publications, six in all, plus four reprints, from 1600 to 1610. Around then, Rossi seems to have changed course, leading him, in 1613, to make a second statement. The course he chose was more strenuous, the search for *novità*. Thereafter the number of his publications decreased, yet the variety of their contents increased. The years must have been taken up, in large part, with the preparation of the Hebrew collection, for which Rossi had no precedent beyond sporadic attempts at choral singing, in the synagogue, starting from the early years of the seventeenth century.[11] Though there is nothing stylistically earth-shaking in Rossi's Hebrew songs, they are none the less quite different from any of his previous works in their directness and unabashed emphasis on choral recitation. Learning to cope with the demands of Hebrew, the constrictions of liturgical propriety, and, possibly, the limited vocal skills of his Jewish singers might have been beneficial in releasing Rossi from the conventions of his madrigals. Be that as it may, the second decade marked a turning-point in his composition.

Strangely though, it was Rossi's earlier, more conservative vocal collections that struck a responsive chord in his listeners. The first book of five-voice madrigals was popular enough to go through four reprints; the reason may have been its poetry, mainly by Guarini. But the music, too, in its lack of pretence, must also have been appealing. Book 1 was the principal source, moreover, of the various madrigals that made their way into the transalpine anthologies, including Tregian's ample selection for his own. Rossi's

---

[11] Cf. Adler, 'The Rise of Art Music in the Italian Ghetto', esp. 334–60.

popularity declined in the following books of madrigals, from two reprints for Book 2 and one for Books 3–4 to none thereafter.

Quite another situation prevails with regard to his instrumental works: not the functionally useful Books 1–2, with their *si placet* versions of certain *gagliarde* and *sinfonie*, were chosen for reprints, but the more stylistically advanced Books 3–4: Book 3 reappeared another three times, the last towards the end of the 1630s; and Book 4 in a single reprint, now from the early 1640s. The public thus seized, first, on Rossi's early vocal works, conventional as they were, from 1600, before they became outmoded by works of other composers cultivating a more fashionable idiom; and, only later, on his instrumental works, at their moment of greatest novelty. When Rossi wrote his *madrigaletti*, as innovative as they were, he had been pre-empted by composers who wrote duets (among them Monteverdi and Sigismondo d'India)[12] or who published sets of *madrigaletti* (Biagio Marini and Stefano Bernardi).[13]

The Publications as a Source of Biographical Information

That a Jewish musician of the later sixteenth and early seventeenth centuries was a composer is unusual; that he wrote over three hundred works, or to be exact, 313, of which we know, plus presumably many more, of which we do not, is remarkable; that 307 of them were published in thirteen separate collections of his own authorship is no less than astounding. It should be remembered that Rossi's status on the payrolls was that of one of the lesser and sometimes least paid musicians at the court. Still, there must have been interest in his works, otherwise it is hard to explain his tenacity. Since there were a number of other, better paid composers in Mantua whose works were in greater demand, including those naturally of the various court chapel masters, one can only wonder how Rossi's were prepared and financed.

Some information about the mechanics of composing and publishing can be gleaned from the dedications to the collections. That they are addressed to specific individuals as patrons suggests one of two contrary possibilities: the collections were either commissioned or not, in which case they were offered as gifts. Who paid for them? One might think: the patron; or the publisher, in anticipation of expected sales' revenues; or a third party, perhaps Rossi's banker friend Moses Sullam.[14] All this is speculation, on which the dedications put a damper by implying, first, that the collections

---

[12] On the beginnings of the chamber duet, see Liebscher, *Das italienische Kammerduett (ca. 1670–1750)*, esp. 31–79 (with emphasis on Monteverdi); and Whenham, *Duet and Dialogue in the Age of Monteverdi*, esp. i. 49–68, tracing the 17th-c. duet to 16th-c. prototypes.

[13] Marini, *Madrigaletti...lib. 5°* 1–4 v. (1625); Bernardi, *Madrigaletti* 2–3 v. (1626).

[14] See e.g. Bernstein, 'Financial Arrangements and the Role of Printer and Composer in Sixteenth-Century Italian Music Printing', esp. 49 (on the different ways patrons supported publications).

were mainly prepared on the composer's own initiative and, second, that the patron was being solicited for help in defraying the costs of publication.

There is still another possibility: the composer himself paid in part or in full for one or another collection. The usual picture one paints of Rossi is as a destitute *ebreo* who depends, for financial help, on his patrons. Yet the information on Rossi's business dealings, to which we referred in Chapter 1, may modify the palette. Take the Hebrew songs, for one. It has been assumed that Rossi's patron Moses Sullam, to whom they were dedicated, underwrote their publication. Yet discrepant evidence may be adduced from the reference, in the copyright, to the composer's 'having gone to a tremendous expense', for which he should be duly protected ('it is not right for someone to come along and harm him by reprinting the songs or buying them from someone else').

Of the dedicatees, addressed in most of his Italian publications as 'patron mio colendissimo', or in his Hebrew one as 'ketsini verozni hanisgav' ('my exalted lord and leader'), only two seem to have been full-fledged patrons: Duke Vincenzo and Moses Sullam, the first as Rossi's employer, until 1612, at the court, the second as his Jewish protector, at one time or another, within the community.[15] The rest were patrons in the sense that they might have asked Rossi, on different occasions, to lend them his services as composer or performer. To Vincenzo the composer expressed his 'infinite obligation': the first and second publications are dedicated to him as a token of gratitude for his kindness ('you listened to, let alone indulged my many imperfections').[16] Vincenzo took Eleonora, daughter of the grand duke of Tuscany, Francesco de' Medici, for his second wife in 1584, and Rossi celebrated the two of them, in his first publication, in the opening number:

> You two earthly divinities
> Rise in flight above the heavenly beams,
> Vincenzo and Leonora;
> No wonder the earth and bending heavens adore you.[17]
>
> (*three stanzas follow*)

The publication was one in a series of twenty-three collections, from 1577 to 1606, dedicated to Vincenzo, known for his love of music and the arts. They included books of madrigals by no lesser figures than Wert, Gastoldi, Pallavicino, Orazio Vecchi, Monteverdi, Alessandro Striggio the elder, Marenzio, and Sigismondo d'India.[18]

---

[15] The 'patron' of Bk 5 is unknown, for the dedication is absent from the one part that survives.

[16] For the dedications in the original and translation, see variously in the *CW* edition; and for their yield of biographical information, Harrán, 'Salamone Rossi, Jewish Musician in Renaissance Italy'.

[17] 'Voi due terrestri numi' (Cte: 1); for later stanzas, see Ch. 6.

[18] All of them *a* 5, as follows: Wert, Bks 6 (1577) and 9 (1588); Gastoldi, Bk 1 (1588), as well as his *Balletti* (1591) and an earlier book of *canzoni* (1581); Pallavicino, Bk 4 (1588); Vecchi, Bk 1

Moses Sullam[19] and, before him, his parents encouraged the composer by word and deed. Rossi speaks of him as 'courageous and energetic, combining wisdom and greatness'.[20] He had the 'courage' and 'energy' to defend Rossi from his critics, real and potential, within the community ('you placed your glory upon me and upon the work of my hands'); he had the 'wisdom' and 'greatness' to recognize his talents and provide him, so it would seem, with financial support ('I am bound by the ties of the kindness and the favours with which you and your illustrious parents—may their souls know Paradise!—rewarded me; were I to count them, they would outnumber the sands'). Yet the question whether Sullam underwrote the Hebrew publication—it was already raised—cannot be unequivocally answered.

The Sullam family was one of eight Jewish families authorized to run loan banks in Mantua from the end of the sixteenth century.[21] Moses' father Angelo (Mordecai) amassed a considerable fortune, which allowed his son to extend his largesse to cultural endeavours. The family was so solidly ensconced in the financial dealings of the duchy that it received a permit, during the preparations for the ghetto, to reside outside the walls and, moreover, to run its own synagogue.[22] On coming to power, Francesco, it is true, rescinded the permit, though only that part relating to outside dwellings.[23]

Private synagogues were known in Mantua from earlier times. The first one appears to have been in the home of the banker Abraham, son of Bonaventura (Meshulam), originally from Forlì, at the end of the fourteenth century.[24] In 1489, Pope Innocent VIII authorized Leone (Judah) Norsa to lend money and maintain a synagogue in his home.[25] Duke Francesco II, in

(1589); Monteverdi, Bks 3 (1592) and 5 (1605); Striggio, Bk 3 (1596); Marenzio, Bk 9 (1599); and d'India, Bk 1 (1606). From 1589 there is, in addition to Rossi's *canzonette*, another set by Trofeo, now *a 6*. At least ten collections by lesser composers (Arnoni, Biffi, Faà, Leoni, Massaino, Mazzone, Perabovi, Preti, Riccio, Tresti) remain, mostly of madrigals *a 5*.

[19] Sullam, or in Italian *scala*, 'ladder', denotes the original derivation of the family, before settling in Italy, from L'Escalette, in Provence: see Colorni, 'Cognomi ebraici italiani', 78. On Moses Sullam, see Simonsohn, *History of the Jews in the Duchy of Mantua*, 41, 120–1, 127, 231–2, 275, 278, etc.

[20] This and next quotations from the composer's dedication to Sgs.

[21] On Angelo Sullam, see Simonsohn, *History of the Jews in the Duchy of Mantua*, 65–6, 221–2, 230, 569.

[22] ASAG, Decreti 53, fos. 261ᵛ–262, with the following marginal comment: 'Per Moisè e Fratelli, e Figliuoli di Angelo Bonaventura Ebrei. Concessione di poter avere abitazione in città fuori del Recinto del Ghetto, ivi esercitando il Banco Feneratizio—tenendo la loro Sinagoga,—esercitando ogn'altro traffico, e alloggiando per sei giorni continui Ebrei forestieri' (18 Aug. 1611).

[23] Cf. Simonsohn, *History of the Jews in the Duchy of Mantua*, 122 n. 67 (reporting a meeting of the community council, on 4 Mar. 1612, to deal with the problem of lodgings for the few families once allowed to live *extra muros*). The authorities received a request to provide the bankers and their families with suitable premises within the ghetto (JCA, file 11, doc. 18; cf. Simonsohn, *History of the Jews in the Duchy of Mantua*, 230).

[24] See ibid. 567.

[25] ASAG, Decreti (3 July 1489); cf. Simonsohn, *History of the Jews in the Duchy of Mantua*, 759–61 (also 204). On the Norsa synagogue, founded by another member of the family in 1513, see Ch. 7.

1540, decreed that the Jews 'be allowed to run their synagogues that are presently open and used both privately and publicly and to celebrate their offices, ceremonies, and rites as they have done in the past'.[26] Angelo Sullam, Moses' father, received permission, in 1588, to have a private synagogue.[27] When the Sullam family became installed in the ghetto, after 1612, it no doubt retained its synagogue, and it is there, perhaps, that Rossi first tried out his Hebrew compositions. Comments were made about them, suggestions advanced for their improvement. One might infer as much from Rossi's words: 'oh, how many times did I, at your command, toil until I found the way to order the material of the songs with joyful lips'.[28]

Additional 'patrons'—five more Gonzagas and five members of other families[29]—bestowed more limited favours. They listened to Rossi's compositions, which the composer deemed an act of goodwill. Prince Vincenzo, later Duke Vincenzo II, 'did not disdain', in moments of leisure, 'to hear some of my musical *concerti*'; and Paolo Guglielmo Andreasi, count of Rodi, displayed his 'affection' by 'not scorning' them.[30] The favours themselves might have been no more than a kind glance or a word of encouragement. Don Ferrante Gonzaga, prince of Guastalla, honoured the composer, so the latter wrote, by 'listening to some of my compositions' and showing approval, for Rossi continued: 'it appeared to me, as far as I could perceive, that they left you somewhat satisfied'.[31] Cesare, duke of Modena, is thanked for 'having shown that you were pleased, in days gone by, with my compositions'; and Alessandro Pico was 'kind enough to take pleasure in listening, these last few months, to some of my rough madrigals'.[32]

---

[26] ASAG, Decreti (28 Oct. 1540): 'che possano tener loro sinagoghe che al presente sono aperte et usate così particolari come universali et celebrar gli loro ufficii cerimonie et riti come hanno potuto far per il passato'.

[27] Cf. Simonsohn, *History of the Jews in the Duchy of Mantua*, 569.

[28] From composer's dedication to Sgs.

[29] Felicita Gonzaga was the wife and, after 1590, widow of Luigi Gonzaga, marquis of Pallazuolo, and at one time the mistress of Vincenzo I. Great-grandson of the marquis Francesco Gonzaga (d. 1519), Ferrante Gonzaga, prince of Guastalla, was born in 1563 and died in 1630 (cf. F. Amadei, *Cronaca universale della città di Mantova*, ed. G. Amadei et al., ii. 712–13). I have not been able to identify Francesco Lodovico Gonzaga. Paolo Emilio Gonzaga, brother of Fabrizio Gonzaga, belongs to the Novellara branch (cf. ibid. iii. 30–1, 357). Prince Vincenzo, son of Duke Vincenzo I, reigned as Duke Vincenzo II from Feb. to Dec. 1627. Paolo Guglielmo Andreasi was count of Rodi (Rodigo), a territory once belonging to the Gonzagas of Bozzolo, yet ceded by them to Vincenzo I (cf. ibid. iii. 39); there is a reference to an Ascanio Andreasi, count of Rodi ('Pro D. Ascanio Andreaseo Comite Roddi...'): ASAG, Decreti 52 (Aug. 1597). Count of San Secondo, Federico Rossi was possibly the son of Carlo Rossi, Mantuan court official. [Cesare] d'Este was duke of Modena and cousin of Alfonso II, last of the Este dukes in Ferrara; with Alfonso's death in 1598, and the absorption of Ferrara into the papal territories, the family settled in Modena, where Cesare reigned until his death in 1628. Alfonso d'Este, Cesare's son: shortly after becoming duke in 1628, he abdicated in order to enter a Capuchin order. Alessandro Pico, prince of Mirandola, married Laura d'Este, Cesare's daughter, in 1604 (see Ch. 1).

[30] From dedications to, respectively, S4 and S1.

[31] From dedication to S3. Ferrante patronized other composers, among them Marenzio (Bk 8 *a* 5, 1598).

[32] From dedications to, respectively, S2 and Bk 3.

Other times the favours might have been more remunerative, resulting in a gift or a paid commission for one or more individual works. Federico Rossi is said to have clearly shown the composer his 'remarkable kindness and infinite affection' in times past, namely the years when Rossi undertook his 'studies of harmonic composition', thus the later 1580s and the 1590s.[33] Don Alfonso d'Este, prince of Modena, seems formerly to have been particularly cordial, for Rossi speaks of his 'infinite kindness and greatness'.[34]

But in none of these dedications does the composer say that the goodwill of his dedicatees extended to their having commissioned the collection that was being offered to them or to their having subsidized its publication. What one reads is that the composer, remembering their erstwhile kindness, found the courage to dedicate his works to one or another of them, from whom he hoped to gain protection, i.e. fame, and, by implication, some sort of reward.

Rossi plays at the game of bonding: the act of bestowing favour creates an obligation—Rossi becomes indebted to the patron; he therefore repays his debt by dedicating a collection to him; the patron, in turn, is supposed to be obliged to Rossi for his kindness, whereby leading him to request and reward Rossi's services; Rossi is then further obliged to the patron; and so there emerges a mutual pattern of favours and obligations in a game played for enhancing the reputation of its participants. Thus where Rossi had his fourth book of madrigals 'honoured by the name of Your Most Illustrious Lordship' Federico Rossi as its dedicatee, he was at the same time honouring Federico, and Federico, accordingly, was expected to feel honoured. The only problem is that in the chain of events there were missing or broken links, with the anticipated gratuities not forthcoming.

What is touching, even saddening, is that Rossi seems to be grasping in every direction to achieve protection and security. The majority of the dedicatees were secondary figures in court and political life. If they paid him a mere compliment or appeared amicably disposed to him it may, for the composer, have been reason enough to curry their favour. Ten dedicatees in thirteen collections: their very number and the overly obsequious tone in which they were addressed would suggest that Rossi's attentions were inadequately rewarded. Only once did the composer come out openly and say what he really wanted: keep in mind my being your 'devoted servant', he adjures Paolo Guglielmo Andreasi, 'should you have an opportunity to employ me in your service'.[35] Andreasi, though, was at best a small fish in the pond of Mantuan affairs, and catching it could not have been lucrative for the composer: Andreasi is not known to have had a musical establishment, nor did any other composer, as far as can be determined, honour him with a publication.

---

[33] From dedication to Bk 4.

[34] From dedication to M4. Alfonso's benevolence extended to other composers, who dedicated their own collections to him (D'India, 1618; Saracini and Turini, 1624).

[35] From dedication to S1.

It is difficult to know how much of the dedications is sincere and how much engineered. In the Hebrew collection Rossi tells us how he chose Moses Sullam as the dedicatee. 'I searched in my heart for the one ruler to whom I would turn, to place on his altar the offering of this thanksgiving. Then I lifted my eyes and saw that it would be better for me to show my affection to you, honoured and important in Israel, than to anyone else',[36] a decision that the composer justifies by citing the many favours he received, and continues to receive, from him. Despite the rhetorical veneer, the tone is genuine. Yet when Rossi dedicates his four-voice madrigals to Prince Alfonso d'Este, he speaks in another language, long-winded, cloying, syco-phantic:

My mind, particularly disposed to serving Your Highness forever, and your infinite kindness and sublimity have given me the courage not only to dedicate to you these few efforts of mine but also to make me hope, at the same time, to be able to see them, by means of your most felicitous name, consecrated to the immortality of your fame, resting assured that you will not disapprove of my receiving this favour of your kindness, which is to reveal to the world, with my meagre demonstrations, the most ardent signs of my reverent devotion to Your Highness, whom I, in all humility, beseech, with deepest affection, to accept these trifling notes of mine, assuring you that every wearisome undertaking is bound to become the lightest load for me, inasmuch as I am stirred by an immense desire to serve Your Highness to whom I pay my humblest respects by entreating the Lord God that, in His benignity, He rain all favours upon you and Your Most Serene Household.

Where in the previous dedication the composer thanks for what he received, now he begs for what he did not, but would like to receive. He couches the dedication in the language required in appeals of subordinates to superiors. This is not Rossi talking as he normally would—the contents are too cunningly fabricated.[37] Rather it is Rossi framing his thoughts after the conventions of panegyric rhetoric. Only infrequently does he break its cocoon to say something clever, as in comparing the dedicatee of his *Madrigaletti* to the attributes of music ('these musical works of mine could not meet with an object more proportioned than Your Most Illustrious Lordship, for they have as their goal Harmony, and you possess it in the affections of your spirit, which, in its kindness, has, for its rhythm, the delight of whoever encounters it [harmony] and, for its measure, the gratitude of whoever observes it') or in begging forgiveness for being so bold, in presenting his fourth book of instrumental works, as 'to join the warbling of singing swans', though he be no more than a 'marsh bird'.

We are grateful for the dedications, yet can only be irked by them: the true story of Rossi's relations with his 'patrons' lies hidden behind their veil. The

---

[36] From Rossi's dedication.

[37] Whether he wrote them, then had them styled, is another question. He could have used an epistolarian handbook. Cf. Quondam, *Le 'carte messaggiere': retorica e modelli di comunicazione epistolare*; also Polak, *Medieval and Renaissance Letter Treatises and Form Letters*.

dedication is a literary genre unto its own, albeit directed by the mechanics of epideictic oratory. It depended, for its efficacy, on three kinds of proof, as outlined by the ancients (Aristotle, Cicero, Quintilian): emotional (awakening the sympathy of the dedicatee), ethical (stressing his moral eminence), and logical (framing the appeal in a language that, structurally and stylistically, hangs together). The aim was to win protection, for oneself and one's work, by linking with a meritorious dedicatee.

Composers, musicians, music theorists: all sought benevolent patrons. We learn of their motives from Franchino Gaffurio, who wrote that 'among the ancients there was a custom handed down by tradition which posterity has preserved up to the present. According to this custom learned men offered their lucubrations to some illustrious person so that the authority of such a man would deliver their works from malicious and scurrilous attacks. Thus they dedicated the results of their labours to notable men.'[38] Rossi's complaints, and apprehensions, of slander, as expressed in at least four dedications,[39] were shared by most persons who relinquished their works for publication. In a poetic anthology from 1622, for example, we read that the printer decided to dedicate it to his patron because, 'with the glorious name of Your Most Illustrious Lordship on the cover of the printed works, I will not have to fear their being a victim, at any time, of untoward fortune, not to mention that the name will put a brake on the tongues of those who bite and will preserve the works from whoever be so brazen as to tear them to shreds'.[40]

Rossi's fears of libel were aggravated by widespread hostility to Jews. Whatever they did, wherever they went, the Jews were subject to censure and abuse. The composer's quest for protection, lest his name and works be denigrated, is not a rhetorical ploy. It is real, following from the general tendency, in the fifteenth to seventeenth centuries, to make false accusations against Jews. The Jews were not allowed to hold positions of power over Christians or compete with them for social or economic advantage. Yet the Christians depended on them for money, for services. In everyday life, the Jewish bankers, by exacting interest on their loans, antagonized their debtors;[41] and the Jewish musicians, by seeking benefits, riled their colleagues. The papacy published severe decrees from the mid-sixteenth century, restricting the activities and privileges of the Jews; anti-Jewish sentiments were incited by calumnious sermons in the churches; Jews were molested on the streets; they were arrested on trumped-up charges; they invited ridicule by wearing the requisite signs of identification; they were squeezed

---

[38] Gaffurio, *De harmonia musicorum instrumentorum opus* (1518), tr. Miller, 33.

[39] See Ch. 1, under last section ('Critical Appraisal').

[40] Angelo Salvadori, in the dedication to Romano (comp.), *Prima raccolta di bellissime canzonette musicali e moderne di auttori gravissimi*, fos. 2ᵛ–3.

[41] On the vicissitudes of Jewish bankers within the larger frame of Church policy, see the classic study by Poliakov, *Jewish Bankers and the Holy See from the Thirteenth to the Seventeenth Century.*

dry by exorbitant taxes; they were expected to underwrite the productions of the Jewish theatrical troupe; Jews were kidnapped, then returned for ransom; their books were censored; their movements were confined. God forbid if any Jew were seen on the streets during an ecclesiastic procession or on a solemn holiday. Unless restrained, Christians went on the rampage against them at Easter.

The situation worsened in Mantua towards the end of the sixteenth century with the hardening of Church policy. The Jews appealed to the rulers for protection. Decrees were published to discourage malevolence and strife. Duke Francesco, in 1612, proclaimed the 'displeasure' of the authorities at seeing that 'the Jews, tolerated in this city, are so often injured and maltreated through sheer spite of those who dislike them.... Therefore we order that nobody, whatever his rank, station, sex, or condition, harass by word or deed the said Jews, wherever they be, in neither their person nor their property.'[42] Such decrees had been published before and continued to be published until, with the French Revolution, the Jews were emancipated. They temporarily thwarted anti-Semitic outbursts, yet were too laxly enforced to eradicate them.

Francesco himself fanned the flames of animosity. Before entering office, he was known as a Jew hater—even the pope said so—and as likely to drive the Jews out of Mantua.[43] The prediction was partly accurate, for his first actions, on becoming duke, were directed to imposing a more restrictive legislation on his Jewish subjects.[44] He was responsible for accelerating and completing the arrangements, begun by Vincenzo under order of the pope, though Vincenzo dilly-dallied in their execution, for confining the Jews to a ghetto. Francesco is said to have been grave and reserved whereas Vincenzo was open and affable.[45] That Rossi got along with Vincenzo, who, as a contemporary Jewish annalist wrote of him, 'favoured the Jews and spoke kindly to them',[46] may be assumed from the content of his two dedications to him. It is uncertain what his relations were with Francesco or his successor Ferdinando: all we have to go on is that while they were dukes the circumstances of the Jews deteriorated and, as for Rossi's collections, none of them was dedicated to either.[47]

---

[42] ASAG, Gridario A-75, fos. 761–2 (12 June 1612); after Coniglio, *I Gonzaga*, 410–11.

[43] From two letters (1612) of the Mantuan ambassador to Rome (Aurelio Recordati); after Parisi, 'Ducal Patronage of Music in Mantua, 1587–1627', 227, 257–8.

[44] According to the Venetian ambassador to Mantua (Pietro Gritti): see Segarizzi (ed.), *Relazioni degli ambasciatori veneti al Senato*, i. 120.

[45] On Vincenzo's temperament, see again the report (now by Francesco Morosini) in ibid. i. 88 ('principe di spirito grande, di generosi pensieri e così largo nel spendere che sempre si trova in bisogni e necessità; affabile, benigno e clemente con suoi sudditi...').

[46] Joseph Hakohen (d. 1578), '*Emek habakha* ('Vale of Tears'), according to a later version with annotations, until 1605, by an unknown editor (after Simonsohn, *History of the Jews in the Duchy of Mantua*, 31).

[47] Rossi may, though, have dedicated to Francesco the *gagliarda* entitled 'il Marchesino' in S1 (1607), if 'marchesino' be construed as a surrogate form of endearment for 'principe' (on the

Beyond the dedications to the collections, there are, as another source of biographical information, inscriptions affixed to certain instrumental works. Most occur in the *gagliarde*, twenty-three to be exact, while the rest occur in *sinfonie* and sonatas (two for each). A long list of names may be drafted, indicating the breadth of Rossi's associations within courtly and Jewish circles. The dedicatees are referred to by their first or last name, generally feminized (thus 'Gagliarda detta la Norsina'), or by a pseudonym (thus 'Gagliarda detta la Sconsolata').

The following identifications, in alphabetical order, are inferable, though not infallible (except when noted, all apply to *gagliarde*). 'L'Andreasina'[48] specifies the dedicatee of its collection: Paolo Guglielmo Andreasi. 'La Cavagliera'[49] might refer to the string player Cavalier Luchesino, on the court payroll from 1622.[50] But the connection is tenuous, for others bore the same title. The virtuoso tenor Francesco Campagnolo, for one: he served at the Mantuan court from 1594 to 1626, receiving, in time, the honorific Cavaliere (and is thus addressed in at least three documents).[51] Francesco Rasi, for another: it was the new doge of Venice, Antonio Priuli, who, in 1618, named him Cavaliere of San Marco.[52] True, Giovanni Battista Buonamente also achieved knighthood: Buonamente was at the Mantuan court in the first decade of the seventeenth century and, while in Vienna, in the 1620s, he maintained connections with the Gonzaga family, and possibly with Rossi, to judge from the structural and stylistic resemblances between their instrumental works. Yet he is ruled out, for the designation Don or Cavaliere occurs in various documents from 1627 on, long after Rossi composed his *gagliarda* 'detta la Cavagliera'.[53] The chivalrous title was even conferred on certain distinguished Jews, especially physicians, among them members of the Norsa family.[54] Other Jews bore the family name Cavaglieri, Cavaglione, or Cavalieri.[55]

'La Cecchina', in a *sinfonia* so called,[56] probably refers to Settimia Caccini, the younger daughter of the singer and composer Giulio Caccini. His other daughter Francesca did in fact receive the nickname 'la Cecchina', but there is no record of her having been in Mantua. By contrast, Settimia did take up residence at the court, together with her husband Alessandro Ghivizzani,

---

term, see below). To redress the balance, it might be mentioned that Ferdinando was the recipient, by dedication, of the Jewish composer David Civita's *Premitie armoniche* 3 v., 1616.

[48] S1: 23.

[49] S4: 23.

[50] ASAG 395, fo. 67 (with earnings more than three times those of Rossi, who immediately precedes him on the same payroll).

[51] Cf. Parisi, 'Ducal Patronage of Music in Mantua, 1587–1627', 567 n. 178 (the documents are a letter from 1617 and the court payrolls from 1621–2).

[52] Cf. Kirkendale, 'Zur Biographie des ersten Orfeo, Francesco Rasi', 316.

[53] See Nettl, 'Giovanni Battista Buonamente', for the relevant documents.

[54] Cf. Simonsohn, *History of the Jews in the Duchy of Mantua*, 32 n. 115.

[55] Cf. Schaerf, *I cognomi degli ebrei d'Italia*, 18.

[56] S3: 9.

from 1612 to 1619: the first edition of Book 3, where the *sinfonia* appears, came out in 1613; in 1617, Rossi collaborated with four other composers, among them Ghivizzani, in writing music for the sacred drama *La Maddalena* (see Plate 6).[57] But there are other possibilities: Cecchina as a character in a play, as, for example, the servant so named in Bernardino Pino da Cagli's comedy *I falsi sospetti* (1597); or Pier Maria Cecchini ('Frittellino'), head of the professional acting troupe called the 'Accesi'; or even his wife, the actress Orsola Cecchini ('Flaminia').

'La Corombona', in a *gagliarda*,[58] is perplexing: if not a person, it might signal an instrument (*corombona* as a garbled spelling for *trombone*? or for *cromorno*, Italian for crumhorn?). Or is it a combination of Corona and Bona, both of them Jewish female names?[59] 'La Emiglia', in a *sinfonia*,[60] might refer to Paolo Emilio Gonzaga, dedicatee, fifteen years hence, of the *Madrigaletti*. Yet one cannot be sure, for the name, in either feminine or masculine form, is ubiquitous. For a feminine example, one might mention that, in 1605, the Mantuan poet Muzio Manfredi dedicated five lyrics to Emilia Finetti Rasponi, who apparently gave him a rose, for which he reciprocated in verse.[61] Emilio is also the Italian equivalent for the Hebrew Meir.[62]

To return to the *gagliarde*, 'la Giustiniana'[63] could relate to the Giustiniani, who ran a publishing house, in Venice, for Jewish books.[64] 'L'Herba'[65] is a mystery. There were Christians so named, among them the Dominican friar Benedetto Erba, who was sent to Mantua in 1568 to serve as Inquisitor.[66] Erba awakens a vague association with the Piazza Erbe, or the 'fruit and vegetable market', otherwise known as the Piazza dei Mercanti: it bordered the ghetto on one side, where it formed the continuation of the Jewish market in the Piazza dell'Aglio (see Plate 14*b*). Yet the designation *Erbe* appears to be later, moreover the idea that Rossi dedicated a *gagliarda* to a market is clearly far-fetched.

---

[57] All five *intermedi* may be found in Rossi's CW viii. app. 3.

[58] S4: 24.

[59] For Corona, daughter of Consilio Porto Sacerdote, see Simonsohn, *The Jews in the Duchy of Milan*, iii. 1475–6 (for the year 1567), iv. 2631 (for the year 1577). For compound names with Cara, see e.g. Stow, *The Jews in Rome*, i, the document for 1537: Cara Bona, which, not inconceivably, could become Corombona.

[60] S3: 8.

[61] Manfredi, *Madrigali* (1605), 142–4 ('Rosa donata. Per la Sign. Emilia Finetti Rasponi, la quale un dì mi donò una Rosa'); for Manfredi's connections with the Mantuan court, see Bertolotti, *Muzio Manfredi e Passi Giuseppe*. There is a notation, in 1591, for the actress and singer Emilia Pilastri: cf. id. *Musici alla corte dei Gonzaga in Mantova dal secolo XV al XVIII*, 71.

[62] Colorni, 'La corrispondenza fra nomi ebraici e nomi locali', 811.

[63] S4: 22.

[64] One of two such houses in Venice: the other was run by the Bragadini brothers, and it was there that Rossi's 'Songs' were published. On the Hebrew press, see Amram, *The Makers of Hebrew Books in Italy*, and with particular attention to Venice, Benayahu, *Haskama urshut bidfusei venetsya*.

[65] S3: 22.

[66] See Coniglio, *I Gonzaga*, 351.

Was 'Marchesino'[67] in reference to Paolo Guglielmo Andreasi? It seems unlikely, for Andreasi, in the same collection, was the recipient of another *gagliarda*. Furthermore, why marquis, or literally 'little marquis', when Paolo was a count?[68] Marchesa and Marchigiana occur as Jewish female names.[69]

'La Norsina'[70] points to a member of the Norsa family, of considerable repute—for its rabbis, scholars, loan bankers—in the Jewish community.[71] 'La Massara'[72] is probably in allusion to the Jewish dancer and musician Isacchino Massarano.[73] 'La Silvia'[74] might refer to or, if added to a later edition, might commemorate Don Silvio Gonzaga, son of Vincenzo by his mistress Agnes de Argotta, marchioness of Grana: Silvio, much acclaimed at the court, died in 1612, at the age of 20.[75] Yet the name could indicate a theatrical personage, for example, Silvia in Dionisio Rondinelli's 'favola boscareccia' *Il pastor vedovo* (1599); or, again if added to a later edition, Silvio in Giovanni Battista Andreini's *Amor nello specchio* (1622). It could also indicate a Jewess.[76]

For 'la Soriana'[77] there is the possibility of at least one singer: the bass Don Ottavio Soragna, on the court registers from 1621–2; and, less likely, one of two persons at Santa Barbara, Marco Soragna, singer, and also bell-ringer, during the years 1609–14, and Don Pietro Antonio Soragna, singer during the years 1609–11, then officiant until his death in 1629. Or perhaps it points to someone from Soragna, where there was a line of marquis. Closer in spelling is the name of the composer Francesco Soriano, who, in 1592, dedicated his second book of madrigals to Cardinal Scipione Gonzaga and might have been in Mantua around 1613. Still another possibility is Soriana as a nickname for Sara Copio Sullam, Moses Sullam's daughter-in-law, whom Rossi must have known from his visits to Venice.[78]

'La Turanina'[79] is obscure: the composer and contralto Don Antonio Taroni, in the service of Vincenzo, Francesco, and Ferdinando? Carlo de Torri, mentioned in a letter by Monteverdi?[80] The composer Francesco Turini, whose madrigals and sonatas were published in the early 1620s?

---

[67] S1: 19.

[68] On the possibility of 'Marchesino' for Francesco Gonzaga, see n. 47. Another possibility is an allusion to Silvio Gonzaga, the marchioness Agnes de Argotto's son: see below.

[69] See index to Stow, *The Jews in Rome*, i.

[70] S1: 25.

[71] See above, and for a general study by a later descendent, cf. Norsa, *Una famiglia di banchieri, la famiglia Norsa (1350–1950)*.

[72] S1: 26. Note the adjacency of nos. 25–6, to Jewish dedicatees.

[73] Variously discussed in Ch. 1.

[74] S3: 18.

[75] Cf. Parisi, 'Ducal Patronage of Music in Mantua, 1587–1627', 222–3.

[76] Simonsohn, *The Jews in the Duchy of Milan*, iii. 2155 (for the year 1685).

[77] S4: 27.

[78] See Ch. 1. For a Jewish Soriana in Rome, cf. Stow, *The Jews in Rome*, i. 40 (for the year 1536).

[79] S3: 21.

[80] 9 Dec. 1616: see *The Letters of Claudio Monteverdi*, tr. Stevens, 115 (Torri is described, in the notes, as possibly a Mantuan gentleman visiting in Venice).

The city Turin? The answer may lie elsewhere: Turra (or possibly Tura) is a Jewish cognomen.[81]

'Venturino'[82] might denote the composer Stefano Venturi del Nibbio: Ferdinando Gonzaga tried to secure his music.[83] Yet it could also denote a younger member, hence *ino*, of the Ventura family in the Jewish community. Ventura was, further, a first name given to Jews, male and female.[84] The Italian equivalent for the Hebrew (female) Mazal Tov is Venturina, or elsewhere Bona Ventura or Bonaventura.[85] Yet one should not exclude the possibility of a theatrical character: there is, for example, a later play by Andreini, with the servant Venturino.[86]

'Il Verdugale'[87] is problematic. Less so 'la Zambalina':[88] it might refer to Vincenzo Zampoli, singer at Santa Barbara from 1605–9;[89] or, with a stretch of the imagination, to Angela Zanibelli, a Ferrarese singer engaged, in 1608, to perform in Gagliano's *Dafne* and Chiabrera's *intermedi* (for Guarini's *L'Idropica*).[90]

Other dedicatees are mentioned by pseudonym, in allusion perhaps to theatrical figures: thus 'la Disperata', 'la Gratiosa', 'l'Incognita', 'l'Ingrata', 'Narciso' (i.e. Narcissus), or 'la Sconsolata'.[91] Grazia and Graziosa are common as Jewish female names.[92] 'L'Incognita' might betoken the presence of a certain noble, who turns up incognito at a social gathering in the ghetto, whether Don Ferrante, the dedicatee of the collection in which the piece appears, or any other Christian under official order not to fraternize with Jews (recall the masked participants at a reception in the house of Isacchino Massarano).[93]

The epithet 'Amor perfetto'[94] is more difficult: as already suggested in Chapter 1, it might designate the part of Amore, in an *intermedio*, danced by Giovanni Battista Perfetti, with whom Rossi entered into a business arrangement in the 1620s.[95]

[81] Cf. Schaerf, *I cognomi degli ebrei d'Italia*, 28.

[82] S1: 18.

[83] As emerges from three dispatches (1608): cf. Bertolotti, *Musici alla corte dei Gonzaga in Mantova dal secolo XV al XVIII*, 89.

[84] See, e.g. Simonsohn, *History of the Jews in the Duchy of Mantua*, 208; and for extensive listings, the index to id., *The Jews in the Duchy of Milan*, esp. iv. 3080–1.

[85] Colorni, 'La corrispondenza fra nomi ebraici e nomi locali', 814. Bonaventura is also a male given name (ibid. 811). The Hebrew Aaron is rendered as Ventura (ibid. 808), as are other Hebrew prenomens: Gad, Josef, Shmuel (ibid. 810–11, 813).

[86] *Lelio bandito* (1624).

[87] S3: 23.

[88] S2: 24.

[89] Cf. Tagmann, 'La cappella dei maestri cantori della basilica palatina di Santa Barbara a Mantova (1565–1630)', 387.

[90] Reiner, 'La vag'Angioletta (and others)', *passim*.

[91] 'La Disperata': S3: 19; 'la Gratiosa': S4: 20; 'l'Incognita': S3: 17; 'l'Ingrata': S4: 25; 'Narciso': S2: 32; 'la Sconsolata': S4: 19.

[92] See index to Stow, *The Jews in Rome*, i.

[93] See Ch. 1 (under section 'Outside Earnings').

[94] S3: 20.

[95] See Ch. 1 (under section 'Outside Earnings').

'La Turca'[96] would seem, likewise, to refer to a theatrical part. With Vincenzo's military campaigns against the Turks at the turn of the century, the Turkish question came to the forefront of Mantuan politics.[97] It sharpened when, in 1607–8, negotiations were undertaken with the duke of Savoy to spearhead a war against the Turks in the Balkan countries.[98] From politics it entered the theatre, as evident in Andreini's La turca, produced in Casale in 1608 on the occasion of the nuptials of Francesco Gonzaga and Margherita of Savoy; nor did the same author tire of the vein, to judge from La sultana (1622), with a cast that called for a 'Turk, father of the sultana', and 'six noble Turks'. The plays must have included Turkish-styled intermedi, along the lines of the Ballo di donne turche that Gagliano composed, to a text by Alessandro Ginori, for a court entertainment in Florence, 1615.[99]

Yet one should not exclude the possibility of the Florentine composer Giovanni del Turco, who seems to have had connections with the Mantuan court: in his Book 2 of madrigals a 5 (1614), for example, he included 'Ecco cinto di gloria', in honour of Ferdinando Gonzaga; there are letters of his to the court from 1607 on (he was instrumental in procuring singers for the duke).[100]

In two cases, the dedicatees seem to be places, namely, Vienna ('Sonata detta la Viena')[101] or the Villa La Favorita ('Gagliarda detta la Favorita').[102] Why Vienna? Perhaps because of a visit, to Mantua, of someone from the imperial family; or, conversely, because of a visit, to Vienna, of someone from the duke's establishment (say, the Rubini brothers, with whom Rossi appeared in instrumental concerti; they, along with others, were variously connected with the Habsburg court);[103] or even because of a Viennese commission or an offering to someone at the Viennese court. Vincenzo's military campaigns against the Turks took him to Hungary, with side visits to Prague, Vienna, and Innsbruck; his son Vincenzo junior visited Vienna in 1612, on his way to Germany. There is no evidence that Salamone was part of their retinue, though he could well have been.

In a sense, Mantua was a fief of the Empire, for the title 'duke of Mantua' was originally bestowed on the Gonzagas by Emperor Charles V in 1530.

[96] S3: 16.
[97] For its ramifications on music of the later 16th c., after the Battle of Lepanto (1572), see Fenlon, 'In destructione turcharum'.
[98] Vincenzo eagerly responded to Emperor Rudolf II's appeal to wage war on the Turks: cf. Coniglio, 'Le spedizioni di Vincenzo contro i Turchi', in his I Gonzaga, 363–78, namely, the campaigns undertaken in 1595, 1597, and 1601; Errante, ' "Forse che sì, forse che no" '; and, on the preparations for war during 1608–12, Tamborra, Gli stati italiani, l'Europa e il problema turco dopo Lepanto, esp. 23–68.
[99] See Ghisi, 'Le musiche per "Il ballo di donne turche" di Marco da Gagliano'.
[100] On Giovanni del Turco, who seems to have been the duke's secretary in Florence, there are various annotations in ASFD, esp. xvi. 594, 762, 801.
[101] S3: 6.
[102] S4: 21.
[103] Cf. Harrán, 'From Mantua to Vienna' (for both the Rubinis and relevant literature).

Mantua and the imperial court were welded through family ties: in 1561, Vincenzo's father, Duke Guglielmo, married Eleonora, daughter of Emperor Ferdinand I; in 1582, Vincenzo's sister Anna Caterina was wed to Archduke Ferdinand, brother of Emperor Rudolf II; and in 1622, his daughter Eleonora was wed to Emperor Ferdinand II. It could even be that the 'Sonata detta la Viena' was annexed to Rossi's Book 3 of instrumental works in its third edition—the first and second ones are no longer extant—to mark the festivities surrounding this last set of nuptials.[104]

One final, and rather surprising, point: the name Viena or Vienna, it turns out, was also held by females: I found it, on three occasions, in a catalogue of sixteenth-century Venetian courtesans.[105]

'La Favorita' probably alludes to the so-named villa in which Rossi may, on various occasions, have been invited to appear (construction on the villa, on the outskirts of Mantua, began in 1616).

In one case, the name of a city indicates the provenance of the dedicatee: the 'Sonata detta la Casalasca'[106] was addressed to one or both of the Rubini brothers, originally from Casale.

Until now, Rossi has been described as needing protection from his Christian detractors. Yet in the Hebrew collection the tables are turned: fearing a reactionary outcry, perhaps, from whoever might have been averse to polyphony in the prayer services, he counted on Moses Sullam, as a leading figure in the Mantuan Jewish community, to lend him support. More official support came from Leon Modena, who, by throwing his weight behind the 'Songs', assured the composer of rabbinical sanction. Further sanction came from the signatories to the copyright. They were, in the order of their rank in the Venetian rabbinate, Isaac Gershon, Moses Cohen Port, Leon Modena, and Simha Luzzatto. Of these, Luzzatto, in 1638, came to the defence of the Jewish community at large (in his *Discorso circa il stato degli ebrei*).[107]

Ordering of Contents

In Rossi's vocal collections, there are usually nineteen works, inclusive of their *partes*; or up to twenty-one, if the *partes* are reckoned separately, as they originally were.[108] In his instrumental collections, the works vary from

---

[104] For a contemporary account, see Bertazzolo, *Breve relatione dello sposalitio fatto dalla Serenissima Principessa Eleonora Gonzaga con la Sacra Cesarea Maestà di Ferdinando II* (1622).

[105] *Il catalogo delle più onorate cortigiane di Venezia nel Cinquecento*, 72–3.

[106] S3: 2.

[107] On Luzzatto (c.1585–1663) and the background and context of his 'discorso', see Ravid, *Economics and Toleration in Seventeenth-Century Venice*, and id., '*Contra Judaeos* in Seventeenth-Century Italy'.

[108] Thus five of the eight vocal collections have 19 works (Cte and Bks 1–2, 4–5), with fewer works (18, 17, 14) in the others. Four collections number 21 separate items (Bks 1, 3–5) while the rest have one or two less (the Mti, with 18 works, are an exception in having 24 separate items).

twenty-seven to thirty-five (none of them in *partes*).[109] It should be remembered that their number is in inverse proportion to their length: except for sonatas, instrumental works are noticeably shorter than vocal ones, often by as much as 50 per cent.

The principles of ordering in the various collections were mainly five: by number of voices, by modes, by poets or their verses (in vocal works), by genres (in the instrumental ones), and by the differentiation between regular and special compositions. Not always do the principles work together, nor are they always fully applied in one or another collection. But the evidence is strong enough to suggest that they were immanent in their planning.

1. *By number of voices.*   Except for the *Canzonette* and Book 3 of the instrumental works, all collections have one or more items for additional voices, in which case the bulk of the works, for the regular ensemble, appears first. Thus, among the secular vocal collections, Book 1 *a* 5 has seventeen works for five voices, then two for six; or the *Madrigaletti* has fifteen duets, then three trios. The rest of them conclude with one work for either six or eight voices. In the first two instrumental collections, the number of works for larger ensembles increases, as does the number of those for optional ones (by contrast, the last two collections consist entirely of three-voice works).[110] The ordering, again, is by size of ensemble: in Book 1, the fifteen works *a* 3 are set first, then followed by the five *a* 4 and the seven *a* 5. Book 2 varies the plan by having its works for optional ensembles in the middle, thus twenty-one *a* 3, five *a* 4/3, six *a* 5/3, and three *a* 4. The most systematic arrangement of works by size of ensemble occurs in the Hebrew 'Songs': there they line up in ascending order from three to eight voices, with six works *a* 3, five *a* 4, eight *a* 5, and so on, until the final eight *a* 8.

In one collection, the *Madrigaletti*, the works are disposed not only by their number of voices, but also partly by their clefs. Thus, in the first twelve numbers, duos for higher voices precede those for lower ones, in order: six with the top voices in soprano clef, two with them in treble clef, two with them in tenor clef, and two with one voice in the alto and the other in the tenor clef.

2. *By modes.*   Works in the same mode tend to be placed together in pairs or in larger groupings. Of the nineteen in the *Canzonette*, nos. 3–5, 15–16, and 18–19 are in Dorian transposed to G; 6–11 in Mixolydian; and 12–14 in Ionian. Still larger groupings may be detected: in the same collection, by combining nos. 3–5 and 6–11, one obtains a series of nine works all having G as their *finalis*. The same kind of planning is clear from the other collections.

---

[109] Different statistics emerge if one considers that of the 35 works in S2, nine appear in an optional version, thus reducing the total number to 26; and that of the 35 in S4, five (of the six) *correnti* are paired with *gagliarde*, thus reducing the total number to 30. Said otherwise, Rossi's instrumental collections run from 26 to 33 works.

[110] With one exception: the last work in S4, for 6 v.

Book 1 *a* 5, for example, has nos. 3–4, 16–17 in Mixolydian; 5–7, 12–15 in Dorian transposed to G; and 10–11 in Lydian with B flat. Again larger groupings emerge for works having G as their *finalis* (nos. 3–7, 12–18). Yet the modal planning goes even further in the same collection: works in Aeolian are placed at the beginning and in the middle (nos. 1, 9) and those in Lydian with B flat in the middle and at the end (8, 10–11, 19). One final example will suffice: Book 4 *a* 5 alternates works in G (Dorian on G, Mixolydian) with others in A (Aeolian) to form the symmetrical succession A (no. 1), G (2–9), A (10–11), G (12–14), A (15–16), followed by two works in Lydian with B flat and one in G. What is interesting is how the composer or editor juggles modal with other considerations in the set-up of the collections, as when the arrangement by numbers of voices or by poets, etc., cuts across or forces changes in the modal sequence.

3. *By poets.* There is a tendency to group works, in the secular vocal collections, by their poets. Thus, in Book 1 *a* 5, Guarini has his poems arranged in twos or larger sequences of four or five (nos. 1–2, 5–8, 12–13, 15–19), with the two selections from *Il pastor fido* in apposition (15–16), as, moreover, the two poems by Rinaldi (3–4). Anonymous poems tend, similarly, to be set together, as in Book 4 *a* 5 (nos. 14–15, 17–19). Naturally, the greater the number of anonymous poems, the more widely dispersed they become: in the madrigals *a* 4, they are everywhere, though typically in clusters (nos. 1–2, 7–9, 11–12, 16–17), with Guarini's verses filling the interstices (4–6, 10, 14–15); in the *Madrigaletti*, they form their own nuclei spread over the collection (nos. 5–8, 10–11, 13–17), with four works by Marino (1–4) preceding them. In Book 3 *a* 5 Marino's poems are placed at the focal points of beginning, middle, and end (nos. 1–2, 5–8, 12–14, no. 14 being the last work in the collection).

Other considerations in grouping works relate to the verses, particularly their form. All multistrophic poems in the *Canzonette* precede the two monostrophic ones; and in the same collection there are clusters of works according to their number of lines per stanza: nos. 1–4, 13–16, 18–19 have four-line stanzas and 5–6 five-line ones. Most madrigals are prosodically *madrigali*, so they clearly dominate, hence appear in groups; when other types are intermixed, they are sometimes set together, as in Book 2 *a* 5 where nos. 10–11 are *ballata*-madrigals, or in Book 5 *a* 5 where nos. 12–17 are sonnet octaves, or in the *Madrigaletti* where nos. 13–15 are strophic *canzonette* (or more precisely, *scherzi*).

The acrostic that forms from the initial letters of the first seven pieces in the *Canzonette* may have been one reason for setting them in that order. So, too, the fact that two pieces in Book 5 *a* 5 and three in the *Madrigaletti* were later settings of texts already composed in earlier books may have influenced their placement: at the end in the first (nos. 18–19), at the beginning in the second (1–2, 4). In Book 2 *a* 5 the two narrative poems (by Rinuccini) were set at the beginning and an atypically optimistic poem at the end; in the *Canzonette* the one poem in honour of the patron and his spouse opens the collection; and in the madrigals *a 4* the two poems in which the speaker is rather uncustomarily a woman form a pair (nos. 5–6).

The planning of the Hebrew 'Songs' likewise proceeded according to textual considerations (beyond those concerning their arrangement by number of voices). Thus the same text appears in two different settings at the beginning and in the middle (the prayer Kaddish, nos. 1, 16); or in three different settings, with the second and third of them marking a new voice group (Psalm 128, as no. 2; then as no. 12, the first of the pieces for five voices; and as no. 20, the first of those for six). Most texts are drawn from the Book of Psalms, hence inevitably fall into clusters (nos. 4–5, 8–14, 17–18, 20–4, 30–2). Yet other text types, when they occur, are ordered with a structural purpose in mind: all but one of the *piyyutim*, i.e. post-biblical verses, appear together (nos. 25–9); and the two selections from Scriptures each close a certain voice group (no. 6 from Leviticus the group for three voices, no. 19 from Isaiah the group for five).

4. *By genres.*   In the instrumental collections, works of one type precede those of another. Thus in Book 1 the fifteen *sinfonie a 3* are set at the opening, and within the next two groups for four and 5/3 voices the *sinfonie* precede the *gagliarde*,[111] only to be followed at the end of the first group by a single sonata (more correctly, *ricercare*) and at the end of the second by a portion of a *balletto*. A similar situation prevails in Book 2,[112] yet now the collection ends with *canzoni*. Books 3–4 are even more explicit in their differentiation between abstract and dance types: they begin with a group of sonatas and another of *sinfonie*, then continue with groups of dances, in the order *gagliarde*, *correnti*, and *brandi* (with five of the six *correnti*, in Book 4, paired there with as many *gagliarde*).

The sonatas seem to have been ordered in accordance with their structural design or their length and complexity. In Book 3, for example, the *canzona*-sonatas come first (nos. 1–2), with the shorter one (55 bars), having three metres in succession, preceding the longer one (71), having five; there follow the variation sonatas (nos. 3–5), arranged by their length (64, 128, 160 bars) and degree of complexity (ground basses respectively of 8, 16, and again 16 bars, with the last having three metres in succession); and, as the final sonata, a 'special' one, 'in dialogo' (no. 6). Book 4 illustrates further how structural considerations determined the ordering of the sonatas, which now number thirteen: first come the *canzona* sonatas (nos. 1–4), then the variation ones (5–12) and, as the last number of the collection, a special sonata that, in its construction and content, is quite unlike the earlier ones.

[111] With one exception: in the 5/3-v. group the first *gagliarda* (no. 23) is wedged between the second and third *sinfonie* (nos. 22, 24); two *gagliarde* follow (nos. 25–6).

[112] Twenty-one *sinfonie* 3 v., four *sinfonie* 4/3 v. (with one *gagliarda* separating the first two from the second two), five *sinfonie* plus one *gagliarda* 5/3 v., and three *canzoni* 4 v.

Within the variation sonatas, moreover, the shorter examples (nos. 5–8) precede the longer ones (9–11).

5. *By differentiation between regular and special works.* Such a differentiation seems to have been crucial in ordering the contents of the collections. Beyond the practice of relegating all works for larger ensembles to the end, one might mention that these same works were usually endowed with other distinctive traits: thus in Book 2 *a* 5 the last work was a 'dialogo' *a* 8, as was the last in Book 5 *a* 5 and in the madrigals *a* 4. Book 3 *a* 5 has as its next to last work—no. 13—a piece that tops the scales in Rossi's vocal œuvre: it is a *canzone* in seven stanzas plus envoi, totalling 102 lines, and the composer emphasizes its singularity by adding a *basso continuo*, the only piece in the collection to have one. The problem of an appropriately 'conclusive' last work—no. 14—remained: Rossi solved it both poetically (the verses are completely different, in their content, from the *canzone* that precedes) and musically (an extra voice was added to form six, though without a *continuo*).

In the *Madrigaletti*, of the three trios at the end, the last is special in being written for either two or three voices, as the performers choose. Other special works were, in Book 1 *a* 5, the six optional versions, for voice and chitarrone, of madrigals nos. 12–17, again forming a group; and, already mentioned, two monostrophic *canzonette* at the end of the same-named collection and three multistrophic ones in the *Madrigaletti* (nos. 13–15), of which two have an instrumental *ritornello*; not to forget the eight *madrigali concertati* that close Book 5 *a* 5.

In the instrumental collections, the composer goes out of his way, in Book 4, to emphasize the end: he wrote a sonata for an ensemble of four violins and two chitarroni, with music that resembles that of no other sonata in the collection—a fitting conclusion, perhaps, to the four books of instrumental works. In the Hebrew 'Songs', the last eight works are not only written for the largest ensemble in the collection, eight voices, but differ from the rest in their use of antiphonal choruses. As the last number, Rossi wrote a piece set to a wedding hymn and having echo effects. Its text is laced with mystical overtones that lift the collection, at the end, to a higher semantic level.

Opus Numbers

Three of the later collections bear opus numbers: the madrigals *a* 4 (1614), Opus 9; the third book of instrumental works, in its third edition (1623), Opus 12; and the *Madrigaletti* (1628), Opus 13. The numbering is uncertain. True, there are thirteen known printed collections, so that the *Madrigaletti* would count as Opus 13. But between Opuses 9 and 12, not two, but three collections were published, which would change the numbering of Opuses 12–13 to 13–14.

The opus numbers of the collections preceding Opus 9 may easily be reconstructed:

[Opus 1]	1589	*Canzonette*		[Opus 5]	1607	Inst. wks, Bk 1
[Opus 2]	1600	Bk 1 *a* 5		[Opus 6]	1608	Inst. wks, Bk 2
[Opus 3]	1602	Bk 2 *a* 5		[Opus 7]	1610	Bk 4 *a* 5
[Opus 4]	1603	Bk 3 *a* 5		[Opus 8]	[1613]	Inst. wks, Bk 3

Problems begin thereafter. Were one to continue the numbering until opus 13, the results would be as follows:

Opus 9	1614	Madrigals *a* 4		[Opus 12]	1622/3	Hebrew songs
[Opus 10]	1622	Bk 5 *a* 5		Opus 13	1628	*Madrigaletti*
[Opus 11]	1622	Inst. wks, Bk 4				

But that is not the way the publications were numbered, for there, as said, Book 3 of the instrumental works, in its third edition, counted as Opus 12. It would appear, then, that both the first and the third editions of Book 3 of the instrumental works received separate opus numbers ([8], 12) and that the Hebrew songs did not figure in the tabulation. One explanation might be simple confusion, which happens in the best of composers' repertories. Another might be that the third book of the instrumental works was sufficiently revised to warrant a separate number, yet that is unlikely: in its 1623 edition, it was labelled not 'revised and reprinted', as customary when the contents of a book are reworked, but only 'third printing'.[113] Why omit the Hebrew 'Songs' though, unless, again, the omission was inadvertent, or the publisher, catering, in the secular vocal and instrumental works, to an Italian audience, considered a non-Italian collection to lie outside his jurisdiction or be thoroughly irrelevant? Or, contrarily, unless the composer, knowing that the collection was directed to a small, select Jewish audience, thought it pointless to count it among his otherwise widely circulated non-Jewish publications, the more so since no Christians, because of the Hebrew, would ever be performing its works?

So far the numbering of the collections, and it is safe to assume that beyond those that were printed the composer prepared no others. There is some question, however, as to the possibility of a Book 2 of *canzonette* or a Book 2 of madrigals *a* 4, since both collections were labelled 'libro primo'. But that seems to have been standard procedure, even if there were no follow-up to the first book. The locution both left an opening for a continuation and referred to the book as the first of its kind among the composers' works. There were thirteen printed collections and, presumably, no more. But, in point of fact, only twelve of the thirteen are complete: Book 5 *a* 5, as already indicated, is extant in the *basso continuo* only; the loss of the vocal parts is all the more lamentable since the collection seems, from the texts

---

[113] 'Terza impressione', whereas the 1638 edition was labelled 'terza impressione nuovamente ristampata'.

and the writing for *continuo*, to have marked a major change in the composer's style.

Though it is hardly likely that manuscripts of additional vocal and instrumental works will ever surface, the idea that it may some day be possible to
retrieve the vocal parts of Book 5 *a* 5 in at least one of its original printed
copies fires the imagination.

3

Italian Vocal Music

WITH but few exceptions, Rossi's Italian vocal works were published in eight collections, forming, in their bar count, nearly 50 per cent of his repertory.[1] There are three different ways to gauge size: number of collections, number of works, and number of bars. In all three areas, the secular collections stand in the forefront. Of the three, the peculiarities of the last have yet to be considered.

In length, the collections vary from 379 bars, in the *Canzonette*, to 1,277 in Book 1 *a* 5.[2] Between the two, in ascending order, range the *Madrigaletti* (725 bars),[3] the madrigals *a* 4 (928), and, of those for five voices, Books 2 (1,059), 4–5 (both 1,080), and 3 (1,090). Correlated with the number of items per collection and their individual length, the figures indicate that, on the average, three-voice *canzonette* are Rossi's shortest works, around twenty bars; that two- or three-voice *madrigaletti* are nearly double their size, or thirty-six bars; that four-voice madrigals run even longer, or forty-six; and that five-voice madrigals are the composer's longest secular works: they range from fifty-one bars in Books 3–5 to fifty-five in Book 2 and sixty-one in Book 1. The number of voices thus determines the length of the separate works while in the five-voice collections the longer madrigals occur in the first two books.

Put on a graph, the development would show a sharp leap from the short works in the first collection to those sometimes three times as long in the second one, with a modest tapering off of dimensions in the succeeding collections, only to end midway between the extremes in the last collection. The development is the reverse of that in the instrumental collections, where each book becomes progressively longer (in the total number of its bars), as the result of certain extended works, particularly sonatas.

Said otherwise, the *canzonetta*, with which Rossi started, and which he abandoned for the madrigal in the following collections, never really disappeared: it asserted itself, in their contents, in the gradual paring down of dimensions and increasing simplicity of expression. The *canzonetta* and madrigal, as lighter and more serious types, may be posited as two different, competitive models on which Rossi based his Italian vocal works. Yet the *canzonetta* infiltrated into the madrigal, changing its complexion. By ending

---

[1] The exceptions occur in anthologies (see the end of Ch. 1 and the beginning of Ch. 2).

[2] Excluded are the optional monodic versions of six madrigals in the same book, or another 394 bars.

[3] Or, adding the written-out strophic repeats in two works, 862 bars.

with a collection of *madrigaletti*, Rossi seems to be proclaiming the victory of the *canzonetta*.

The *canzonetta* was also influential in shaping other composers' works, among them Monteverdi's.[4] It reflects a new interest in the shorter, simpler madrigal, as a counter-tendency to the more emotionally charged dramatic type, available, in Mantua, in the works of Wert, yet eschewed there by Rossi, along with Gastoldi, Pallavicino, and, in his early books, Monteverdi.

Problems of Chronology

Fairly firm dates can be established for all collections but two: Book 4 *a* 5 and the madrigals *a* 4. The question is not when the two were published, but rather when they were composed.

Possible evidence for the earlier composition of Book 4 (1610) might be its inclusion of poetry by Guarini and Rinaldi, two authors present in the first two madrigal books, yet, with few exceptions, eliminated thereafter. Occasional settings of Guarini cannot, however, be taken as an indicator of early composition, no more than occasional settings of that favourite poet of the early madrigal composers, Petrarch, who appears, in a single example, in Rossi's last collection. More substantial, perhaps, would be Rossi's reference, in the dedication to his patron, Federico Rossi, to the many favours he received from him during his years as a student of composition, that is, presumably, the mid-1580s until the end of the century. Since these favours, or as Rossi put it, the patron's 'special kindness and infinite solicitude', were the reason why the composer thought it appropriate to dedicate the collection to him,[5] Rossi was ostensibly in his patron's debt for some twenty years before showing him his gratitude. Waiting such a long time to discharge his obligation would seem to evidence patent ingratitude, unless the collection was composed earlier, yet, for technical reasons, perhaps financial, deferred in its publication.

There are musical reasons for suspecting an earlier date. Book 4 reveals certain similarities to Book 3 (1603): both have madrigals of about the same length; both favour major over minor modes. Book 4 has various works with extensive musical repeats of their final verse or verses,[6] thus returning to a procedure exemplified by Books 1–2. It leans not to homophony for its basic texture (as was the case in Book 3) but rather to a mixed chordal and imitative style, reminiscent of Book 1 and, in certain works, of Book 2;[7] it

---

[4] See Ossi, 'Claudio Monteverdi's *Ordine novo, bello et gustevole'*.

[5] 'Thus finding myself obliged to you for some time now, I considered it my duty, as your devoted servant, to show you my indebtedness with this small offering.'

[6] 'Perla che 'l mar produce' (with a repeat of the last six lines), 'Lidia, ti lasso' and 'Clori mia' (with a repeat of the last four), and 'Movetevi a pietà' (with a repeat of the last two).

[7] Bk 2: 'Amarillide mia', 'E così pur languendo', 'Occhi, quella pietà', 'Per non mi dir', 'Dove, misero, mai'.

sometimes has the top voice separated from the others,[8] as if harking back to the examples, in Book 1, of pseudo-monody.

One must be realistic: since Rossi's five-voice madrigals were published in the first decade of the seventeenth century—with the exception, of course, of Book 5—and since they tend towards overall consistency in their style and structure, the various arguments recited in support of earlier composition for Book 4 could easily be construed as referring to small nuances in a fairly solid general palette.

The most compelling reason for redating Book 4 would seem to be the indication, in the title, that its 'publication'—to be distinguished from its 'composition'—was recent. Rossi's collections have two kinds of wording in their titles: one in which both the composition and the publication are said to be recent ('novamente composti e dati in luce'), as in the first three and last books a 5 and in the *Madrigaletti*; another in which only the publication is said to be so ('novamente posti in luce'), as in the *Canzonette*, the madrigals a 4, and, in the present case, Book 4 a 5. Of the last three, the *Canzonette* are not likely to have carried the designation 'recently composed': as Rossi's first publication, its content would in any case have been 'recent'; and the book of madrigals a 4 does seem to have been composed earlier than its publication (see below), which would explain why 'recently composed' was out of place. That leaves Book 4 a 5 with an interrogation mark around its origins.

The time span may be narrowed to that between 1603 and 1610, for Book 4 includes nine poems by Marino, whose works appeared, for the first time in Rossi's publications, in Book 3 a 5 (1603). Book 4, then, could, theoretically, have been composed either between Books 2 and 3—Book 2 came out in 1602, as did the earliest printed collection of Marino's poetry—or sometime after Book 3, in which case the question is: how long after? The evidence is inconclusive.

More conclusive is the evidence for the earlier composition of the madrigals a 4. It is of three kinds: general, poetic, and musical. To the first category belongs the wording of the title, which, as just mentioned, omits the formula 'recently composed'. Other details of a general order regard the authorship of the verses. Book 1 a 4 includes six madrigals to lyrics by Guarini, a poet whom Rossi favoured in his Book 1 a 5 (1600), to the extent of thirteen selections; two are drawn from the *Pastor fido*, presented in the 1590s. Guarini increasingly loses ground thereafter.[9] Starting with Book 3 a 5, Marino became Rossi's privileged poet. Yet Marino is conspicuously absent from the madrigals a 4. Were Guarini represented there by, say, a single work, that would hardly be enough to raise eyebrows. But six works, among them four from the *Pastor fido*, does seem a rather large number, unless, of course, and this is the main point, the four-voice madrigals were composed during Rossi's earlier 'Guarini period'.

[8] As in 'Io parto'.   [9] Bk 2 has three poems by Guarini, Bks 4–5 each have one.

True, as a counter-argument one might note that any such division into poetic periods is tenuous. Monteverdi, for example, at earlier and later stages, composed a large number of madrigals by Guarini, including ten (out of thirteen) in Book 5 *a* 5 (1605) and, fourteen years later, six (out of thirty-four) in his *Settimo libro*. Nor on this account has anyone suggested that Monteverdi's seventh book be redated to the time of his fifth.

Beyond Guarini, the lion's share of poems in Rossi's book *a* 4 is of uncertain authorship, which, too, might be significant. Except for the *Madrigaletti*, the book has the largest number of anonymous works, nine in all, in any of his madrigal collections, and in this sense the madrigals *a* 4 seem to revert, in concept, to the unidentified *poesia per musica* of the early *Canzonette*.[10]

As for the structure or content of the verses, i.e. the more specifically 'poetic' evidence, most poems are, in their prosody, madrigals, as in Book 1 *a* 5, whereas succeeding collections had several other verse types (*ballata, canzone,* sonnet, and hybrid varieties of the madrigal).[11] Two poems are delivered by a female, who, after Book 2 *a* 5, disappears as the speaker of the madrigals.[12] The *partenza* is the main theme of five works, which sets the collection in the ambience of Books 1–2 *a* 5, after which it waned in importance. Two other themes in the madrigals *a* 4 had appeared in Book 1, but are omitted from the later ones: the first, in 'Mia vita', is 'You do not believe I love you', comparable to two examples in Book 1;[13] the second, in 'Com'è dolc'il gioire', is about the happiness of the lover whose affection is—*mirabile dictu*—reciprocated, comparable to one example in Book 1.[14] As to the 'kiss theme', whose vogue started in Rossi's Book 3 *a* 5, but not before, it does in fact appear in one poem of the madrigals *a* 4 ('Dolcemente dormiva'). It concerns a kiss the lover steals from his sleeping beauty as an innocent pleasure, without the erotic overtones of Marino's *Canzon de' baci*. One last point: three other poems in the madrigals *a* 4 contain invocations to Amor, who is rarely addressed in Rossi's five-voice madrigal collections; such invocations seem rather to typify his *Canzonette*.[15]

The musical evidence for redating the collection has to do with the length of its madrigals, their forms, their texture, and their *continuo*. Averaging forty-six bars, the madrigals *a* 4 are shorter than the five-voice ones—varying

---

[10] Bks 1 and 3 each have two unidentified poems, 2 and 5 each have three, and 4 has five (while Mti, returning to the *canzonetta* type in various examples, as will be shown below, has eleven).

[11] Madrigals constitute 82% of the poetry in M4, comparable to the 89% in Bk 1; they amount to considerably less thereafter (Bk 2, with 52%; 3, with 35%; 4, with 63%; and 5, with 57%).

[12] The two are 'O Mirtillo' and 'Tu parti', comparable to two examples in Bk 1 ('Anima del cor mio', 'Tirsi mio') and one in Bk 2 ('Filli, mirando il cielo').

[13] 'O com'è gran martire', 'Dirmi che più non ardo?'.

[14] 'Felice chi vi mira'.

[15] The three poems are 'O Mirtillo', 'O dolcezz'amarissime', 'Amor, se pur degg'io'; cf. Cte: 4, 6–7, 11–12, 15.

from about fifty to sixty bars in the five books—and seem in several works to occupy the middle ground between them and the even shorter *canzonette*.[16] There is a correspondence between the length of the single madrigals and that of the collection as a whole, which, in its total number of bars, stands, similarly, between the collections of madrigals and the *Canzonette*.[17] Structurally, the works resemble those of Book 3 *a* 5 (1603) in having no literal repeats of their last section; texturally, they resemble them in their emphasis on homophony. Where in Book 4 *a* 5 (1610) the *basso continuo* showed a modicum of independence from the vocal bass, a tendency that led in time to the highly independent *continuo* of the *Madrigaletti*, in the madrigals *a* 4 it is a servile *basso seguente*, as in the composer's early publications.

Putting the three kinds of evidence together, one might conclude that the madrigals *a* 4 are likely to have been composed well in advance of their publication. One possibility is towards the end of the 1590s, i.e. 'Opus 2' between the *canzonette* for three voices and Book 1 for five, as if Rossi learned his craft by a gradual increase from three to four, then five voices. Another possibility is during the period of Books 1–3 *a* 5 (1600–3), though probably preceding Book 3 from which Guarini, as already said, is absent.

Poets and Poetic Forms

Of the 150 Italian lyrics, the majority (95) are assignable to a poet on the basis of one or more literary sources while the remainder (55) are still of uncertain authorship. From the following list of the twelve poets that can be identified, it is clear where Rossi's preferences lie: Giovanni Battista Marino (37 settings), Battista Guarini (24), Gabriello Chiabrera (11), Ottavio Rinuccini (8), Cesare Rinaldi (7), Livio Celiano (2), and, with one setting each, Giovanni Battista Andreini, Alessandro Gatti, Alessandro Guarini (son of Battista), Petrarch, Tomaso Stigliani, and Torquato Tasso. Marino and Guarini, as said, belonged to different periods in Rossi's production: works of the former were first included in Book 3 *a* 5, dominating those of all other poets there and in later collections; works of Guarini appeared from Book 1 *a* 5 on, though, in Book 2, were already outnumbered by those of Chiabrera and Rinuccini. Thus where Guarini was replaced by Marino, Marino held his own, at least in Books 4–5 *a* 5, only to be replaced in the last collection (*Madrigaletti*) by that most popular of madrigal poets: anonymous.[18]

---

[16] Cf. M4: 2, 4 (in its separate *partes*), 6–8, the third *pars* of 10, and 11–12, 14, and 16, all about double the size of a *canzonetta* (averaging 20 bars.).

[17] M4, 928 bars; Bks 1–5, each over 1,000 bars; Cte, 379 bars. J. Cohen emphasizes stylistic connections between M4 and Cte (e.g. the first madrigal *a* 4 and the last two *canzonette*): see 'Salamone Rossi's Madrigal Style', esp. 151–2.

[18] Guarini: Bks 1 (13/19, i.e. 13 out of 19 poems in the collection), 2 (3/19), 4 (1/19), 5 (1/19) (cf. M4, of possibly earlier composition, with 6 poems by Guarini out of a total of 17). Marino: Bks 3 (10/14), 4 (9/19), 5 (13/19), Mti (4/18, compared with 11 anon. poems in the collection).

In his choice of works by Guarini, Marino, Chiabrera, and Rinuccini, Rossi reflected the most modern lyric trends.[19] Rossi continued and intensified the Guarini cult that followed the *Pastor fido*.[20] Guarini was sometimes heavy and overbearing, especially in the selections from his play. Rinuccini, Rinaldi, and, particularly, Chiabrera represented a more congenial vein: lightness, directness, playfulness. Only with Marino, however, does Rossi seem to have found his true self. He latched onto this most fashionable of poets before most other composers had discovered him.[21] With the publication of Marino's *Rime* in 1602, he set his verses almost with a vengeance: Book 3 *a* 5 is 70 per cent Marino as is Book 5. Few other composers dared to tackle the prime example of poetic derring-do, Marino's *Canzon de' baci*, and when they did, usually settled for one or two stanzas.[22] Rossi set all seven plus the envoi:[23] together they occupy nearly half of his Book 3 *a* 5 (436 bars; see Plate 7).

Marino seemed to correspond to the composer's poetic tastes: brevity, cleverness *à tout prix*, charm, sensuality.[24] Rossi matched his verses with terse madrigals, pared down to their essentials, stylistically, to let the poet's voice be heard. It became clearer in time that Rossi's preference lay with the *canzonetta* of his first collection; or the smaller madrigal of Books 3–4; or the *madrigaletto* of his last collection. Even the extensive *Canzone de' baci* is an aggregate of eight short works, after the eight strophes of its verses. In his choice of poetry, Rossi tended increasingly to favour short, concentrated examples: thus the noticeably epigrammatic twist in the selections from Book 2 on, due not only to their emphasis on concise (heptasyllabic) verses, but also to their pointed expression.[25] It is paralleled, structurally, by the gradual reduction in the size of madrigals by at least ten bars, on an average, from Book 1 to Books 3–5.

How did Rossi select his poetry? Most of the poets whose works he set were affiliated at one time or another with Mantua, through stays at the

---

[19] The chief study on contemporary poetry is Elwert, *La poesia lirica italiana del Seicento*. For Monteverdi's poetic choices, differing from Rossi's, see Pirrotta, 'Scelte poetiche di Monteverdi' (and, on their mannerist component, Fabbri, 'Tasso, Guarini e il "Divino Claudio"'); also Tomlinson, 'Music and the Claims of Text'.

[20] It led, in some cases, to whole collections of madrigals so entitled, for example: Ph. de Monte, *Musica sopra il Pastor Fido...lib. 2° 7 v.* (1600); Piccioni, *Il pastor fido musicale...il 6° lib. di madrigali 5 v.* (1602); and Mezzogorri, *Il pastor fido armonico...2° lib. de madrigali 5 v.* (1617). On the musical repercussions of the *Pastor fido*, see Hartmann, 'Battista Guarini and *Il pastor fido*'.

[21] On Marino's poetry in musical settings, see Simon and Gidrol, 'Appunti sulle relazioni tra l'opera poetica di G. B. Marino e la musica del suo tempo' (and for monodies in particular, Laki, 'The Madrigals of Giambattista Marino and their Settings for Solo Voice').

[22] 1603, Il Verso (stanzas 1–2); 1607, Salzilli (stanza 1); 1610, Scialla (stanza 1); 1628, Locatello (stanza 1); 1630, Delipari (stanzas 1–3).

[23] As did Priuli (1607) and Magni (1613).

[24] On the peculiarities of Marino's poetry (as distinct from Guarini's and Rinuccini's), especially in relation to Monteverdi, see Tomlinson, *Monteverdi and the End of the Renaissance*, 151–214.

[25] Cf. Bk 2: 5, 7–8, 10; Bk 3: 1, 3, 7–8, 11; Bk 4: 3, 11, 15, 18–19; M4: 2, 7–8, 14–15; Bk 5: 1–4, 6–7, 9, 11.

court or commissions for it (Guarini, Tasso, Chiabrera, Rinuccini, Andreini, Marino). But presence in Mantua was not essential to being chosen: the Gonzaga family entertained a vast network of connections with different courts and cities through its resident ambassadors in Milan, Turin, Genoa, Venice, and Rome; or through its agents who travelled over Italy on specific missions; or through journeys of court officials to places outside the Mantovano; or through family ties, with the Medici in Florence, the Este in Ferrara and later Modena, and the dukes of Savoy in Turin. Thus the poetry of all Italy was, potentially, available, and could have been exploited.

Sometimes poets, away from Mantua, offered their services, as did Chiabrera, who wrote to the court from Florence, telling where he could be found. 'Now that I am in Florence, to which I have been summoned by their Royal Highnesses, I thought it my duty to write and let you know where you can order works from me, should you, perchance, so wish to honour me.'[26] Or they sent their works to the court, as did, again, Chiabrera, who, in the years 1608–12, expedited various poems and *favole* for musical setting.[27] Other times poets were recommended to the authorities, as when Francesco Gonzaga, visiting Turin in 1608, wrote to his brother Ferdinando that 'here I met Marino, who is the most charming man in the world both in writing beautiful verses and in his life style'.[28]

More practically, though, Rossi probably chose his lyrics by perusing single authors' collections, or poetic anthologies, or manuscript copies of individual poems. Thus for 'Parlo, misero, o taccio?' and 'Al partir del mio sole' in Book 1 and 'E così pur languendo' in Book 2, he might have consulted Guarini's *Rime* (1598); for 'Dirmi che più non ardo?' in Book 1 or 'Spasmo s'io non ti veggio' and 'O tu che vinci' in Book 2, Rinaldi's *Delle rime...parte sesta* (1598); and for the ten poems by Marino in Book 3, Marino's *Rime* (1602). For 'Soave libertate', by Chiabrera, in Book 2, he might have consulted *Le maniere de' versi toscani* (1599); and for certain poems of Rinuccini, e.g., 'Amarillide mia' in Book 2, manuscript copies in circulation, not to speak of such copies for anonymous verses.[29]

All poems were set to music by Rossi as either their only composer or the first in a series of two, three, or often many others. Here it should be remarked that Rossi is known as the only composer to have set thirty

---

[26] 'Hora ritrovandomi in Firenze chiamato da queste Alt. SS.^me mi è paruto mio debito scriverne, acciò ella sappia ove commandarmi se a forte volesse degnarmi di tanto' (25 Aug. 1608); after ASFD xv. 790.

[27] After same source. On Chiabrera's connections with Mantua, see Neri, 'Gabriele Chiabrera e la corte di Mantova'.

[28] ASFD xvi. 585. On the relations between Mantua (under Ferdinando) and Turin, see Quazza, 'Ferdinando Gonzaga e Carlo Emanuele I', also Rivoire, 'Contributo alla storia delle relazioni tra Carlo Emanuele I e Ferdinando Gonzaga'.

[29] For example, the anon. lyrics that constitute the Cte; or nos. 8, 12, and 16 in M4. Rossi might also have consulted manuscript copies of works by Chiabrera and Marino. That Marino's poetry circulated well before its first printed edition is clear from Montella's setting of 'Vivo mio sol' in his Bk 2 *a* 5 (1596).

poems in the literature, among them five by Marino and four by Chia-brera,[30] and the first composer to have set forty-one others, among them thirteen by Marino and four by Guarini.[31] In all, seventy-one works, or close to half of Rossi's Italian ones, are involved: they mark the composer's unique contribution to the late sixteenth- and early seventeenth-century Italian secular repertory.

Were one to rank composers of the time by the originality of their poetic choices, Rossi would definitely score high. Not only that, but by launching a particular work, Rossi seems to have triggered a chain reaction, to the extent of anywhere from one to thirty-one additional settings after his example. Among those of particular appeal to others, one finds three poems by Guarini, first set by Rossi in Book 1, and five by Marino, first set by him in Book 3.[32]

Just as other composers may, on occasion, have looked to Rossi's works for their texts, so Rossi may have looked to theirs for his own. Three of the texts in his Book 1 *a 5* had already been set by Monteverdi in 1592; three of those in his madrigals *a 4*, by Marenzio in 1595; nine of those in Books 2–4, by Caccini in his *Nuove musiche* (1601); and so on. A fascinating pattern of mutual dependencies can be drawn for his and other composers' choices of poetry.[33]

Since, in Rossi's madrigals, the poetry is 'the thing', determining in its structures and thematics the form and content of the music, in this and the next section an attempt will be made to present the verses in an overview. A different review of the poetry, from a theatrical standpoint, will be under-taken in Chapter 6.

Structurally, most of the poems (82) in Rossi's collections are madrigals proper, in the specific sense of a madrigal as a free admixture of usually 7–13 lines each having seven or eleven syllables in iambic metre. The rest exhibit one or another of the following forms, in descending order:

> *canzonetta* in one or more stanzas (27)
> sonnet complete (7) or first octave only (6)
> *ballata* (10)
> *ballata*-madrigal (6)[34]
> *canzone* in a single stanza (5) or in seven stanzas plus envoi (1)
> *canzone*-madrigal (5)
> *balletto* (1)

---

[30] Plus one each by Stigliani, Andreini, and Rinaldi, and eighteen anon. ones.

[31] Plus five by Rinaldi, four by Chiabrera, two by Rinuccini, and thirteen anon. ones.

[32] Guarini, in Bk 1: 'Deh com'invan chiedete' (17 additional settings); 'Parlo, misero, o taccio?' (30); 'Al partir del mio sole' (15). Marino, in Bk 3: 'Io moro' (19); 'Taci bocca' (12); 'Ch'io mora?' (25); 'Se la doglia e 'l martire' (31); 'Riede la primavera' (22).

[33] For details, see the commentary to the separate madrigals in *CW*, vols. i–viii, as well as the compilative index to 'other composers' settings of the same texts', i. pp. xliv–xlix.

[34] On the *ballata*-madrigal and, below, *canzone*-madrigal, see Harrán, 'Verse Types in the Early Madrigal', esp. 33–6, 44–6.

Madrigals occur in all but one collection, the *Canzonette*, while *canzonette* do largely in the one so named, though also in Books 2 and 4 of the five-voice madrigals and in the *Madrigaletti*. Full sonnets turn up in various collections (Books 1 and 4–5 *a 5*, the *Madrigaletti*), but sonnet octaves are confined to Book 5 *a 5*; the *ballata* appears mainly in Books 3–4 *a 5* and the *ballata*-madrigal in Book 2 *a 5*.

These distinctions, interesting as they are for showing the varying degrees of prosodic rigidity in Rossi's poetic choices, tend to blur when the madrigals are judged as a whole. All the poems are, in effect, madrigals, now in the generic sense of a madrigal as a secular lyric, in Italian, set to music for two or more voices (and, towards the end of the sixteenth century and beyond, even for one). Some of them are longer, others shorter; some have set rhyme schemes or verse lengths, others are more flexible in their construction.

Even the notion of a *madrigaletto* as a small and slight madrigal does not hold up: two of the *madrigaletti* are set to complete sonnets, one is a ten-line *ballata*. With few exceptions, the rest have 7–10 lines, as do regular madrigals, and treat typically madrigalesque themes with no lesser sobriety. It is not in its poetry that the *madrigaletto* is scaled down from the madrigal, but in its musical proportions and two-voice texture. The term, in its literal sense of a 'little madrigal', with implications of *piacevolezza*, has an earlier history: it may be traced to the mid-sixteenth century.[35]

Despite their uniformity, the madrigals in Rossi's collections exhibit at least one basic distinction, namely between poems in a single stanza and those in several. It corresponds to the distinction between non-iterative and iterative types, whereby Rossi's verse choices divide into about 85 per cent of the former and fifteen per cent of the latter. Musically, it obtains only to the extent that the stanzas of multistrophic works are separated from each other and repeated to the music of the first. That eliminates one poem in Book 2 *a 5*, and another in Book 4 *a 5*, where the stanzas are run together and set as if they were a single larger one;[36] and, in the *Canzonette*, two poems, which, though nominally *canzonette*, have a single stanza.[37] It also eliminates the large multistrophic *Canzon de' baci* in Book 3 *a 5*, where each of the stanzas is set to its own music.

The exceptions illustrate how fragile the typology is. On the one hand, a multistrophic poem, such as a *canzonetta*, may be condensed to a single stanza, in which case it becomes a madrigal; or it may be treated, on the other, as two or more stanzas without musical repetition, in which case it becomes a chain of madrigals or 'madrigal cycle'. Said otherwise, a thin line divides the *canzonetta* from the madrigal. Yes, a *canzonetta* is ordinarily an

---

[35] In the dedication to the *Primo libro delle muse* 4 v. (1555), Antonio Barré, referring to its 'madrigaletti', qualifies them as 'ariosi e piacevoli'. See Haar, 'The "Madrigale arioso"', 207.

[36] Bk 2: 'Soave libertate'; Bk 4: 'Io parto'.

[37] Cte: 'Mirate che mi fa', 'Se 'l Leoncorno corre'.

iterative type, yet it may purposely be written in a single stanza, thus simulating a madrigal.

The strophic poems (23), confined, with few exceptions, to the first and last collections, usually comprise four stanzas, of four or, less often, five lines. Some are distinctive in having all stanzas end with the same or nearly the same final verse or couplet as a refrain (nos. 1–3 below); others are in having a returning end rhyme or rhyme word in successive stanzas (no. 4).[38] Thus to the iterative larger structure the poet adds lower level repetition, either literal or varied, as in the following examples:

(1) Chè donna bella senz'amor non vale (x 4)

(2) Anzichè 'l Dio d'Amore
Vuol che fuggendo mi nodrisch'il core (x 4)

(3) Sì grave è 'l mio dolore *varied in successive stanzas to*:
Sì grave è 'l mio martire
Sì grave è la mia pena

(4) -ore *in stanza 1* (amore, core, dolore)
in stanza 2 (splendore, core)
in stanza 4 (core, amore)

In one *canzonetta*, the last line of each stanza, a declaration, is incorporated into the first line of the next as a question: thus 'Non è vero!' becomes 'Non è vero? ah, simplicetta', etc., the result being a chain form.[39]

The strophic poems should be distinguished from the more usual non-strophic ones, which, in Rossi's repertory, average between seven to nine or less often ten lines. Those exceeding twelve lines tend to be sonnets or works divided into two or more *partes*: the sonnet into a *prima pars* for its octave and a *secunda* for its sestet, and the others into *partes* more irregularly ordered, such as 'O dolcezz'amarissime', with three parts respectively of twelve, ten, and six lines, for a total of twenty-eight.[40] To complicate matters, some of the iterative poems with identical music for the separate stanzas are divided into *partes*, but here the *partes* designate stanzas: thus 'Vo' fuggir lontan da te', in four *partes*, is, in reality, a *canzonetta* in four stanzas.[41] The longest poem in Rossi's repertory is, obviously, the *Canzon de' baci* in eight *partes*, or 102 lines. *Pars*, in this case, stands for both a stanza and, since the seven stanzas plus envoi are set to their own music, an autonomous *pars*.

Metrically, the poems, be they madrigals, *ballate*, or other types, adhere to a combination of seven- and eleven-syllable verses in iambic metre, though

[38] Same final verse: Cte: 7, 10, 17. Same final couplet: Cte: 3, 6, 13, and Mti: 13. Returning end rhyme or rhyme word: Cte: 5, 7–8, 11, 15, 17. The examples quoted are, in order, Cte: 10, 3, 7, 5.

[39] Cf. Mti: 14 (the *pastourelle* referred to below).

[40] From M4: 10. Compare with 'Com'è dolc'il gioire' (M4: 4), having 7 lines for the first part and 10 for the second. Both poems are drawn from speeches in Guarini's *Pastor fido*, which might explain the irregularities in their division.

[41] Mti: 15.

sonnets, of course, are restricted to hendecasyllables. Other verse lengths are exceptional, among them a poem in *versi sdruccioli*, i.e. twelve syllables with the terminal accent not on the penultimate, but the antepenultimate;[42] two poems with one or two pentasyllables added to their regular seven- and eleven-syllable lines;[43] two in trochaic octosyllables;[44] and three with mixed verse lengths, from four to eleven syllables, of which one reads as shown in the table below.[45]

No. of syllables	Verses 1–10
6	Gradita libertà
7	Pur ricovrato ho l'alma!
7	Ecco la verde palma,
6	Trofeo d'empia beltà.
5	Più non s'apprezza
5	Finta bellezza,
11	Nè più cieco è 'l desio, piagato il core,
7	E non vedrete, amanti,
5	Stillarmi in pianti
7	A sospirar d'amore.
	(two stanzas follow)

All but one of these irregularly constructed poems were multistrophic and confined, for the most part, to two collections: the *Canzonette* and the *Madrigaletti*. It is not by chance that they appeared in Rossi's first and last collections, which are stylistically kindred in their emphasis on lighter musical forms. The single theatre piece of the lot ('Spazziam pronte') was, symptomatically, written as a *balletto*; and the one monostrophic example, 'Partirò da te', belonged to a collection whose contents are described as 'canzonette'. Another work ('Ne le guancie di rose') appeared in Book 5 *a 5*, of which several others have the dimensions of *madrigaletti*, in the present case thirty-nine bars; though the voice parts are lacking for this collection, one may assume, from the bass, a stylistic propinquity with the *Madrigaletti*.

Lighter forms, then, are the locus for prosodic irregularities. In contrast to regular *canzonette*, those that have them are probably to be designated 'scherzi', such as are found in Monteverdi's collection *Scherzi musicali* (1607), based largely on Chiabrera's *scherzi*. Their tone, too, becomes lighter.

---

[42] 'Voi che seguite il cieco ardore di Venere, | Udite, amanti: la mia cara Fillide', etc.: Cte: 8.

[43] 'Correte, Amanti [*5 syllables*], | A' miei sospiri e pianti', etc.: Cte: 15. 'Ne le guancie di rose e 'n sen di latte', etc., with, as lines 5–6, the 5-syllable 'Occhi amati, | Occhi bramati': Bk 5: 4.

[44] 'Spazziam pronte, o vecchiarelle': from the play *La Maddalena*; 'Pargoletta che non sai', with the last line of its five stanzas a tetrasyllable: Mti: 14.

[45] 'Gradita libertà': Mti: 13; 'Vo' fuggir lontan da te': Mti: 15; 'Partirò da te': Brescia, Bibl. Quer., MS L. IV. 99, no. 20.

Indeed, in 'Pargoletta che non sai', a coarse country lass rebuffs the advances of an unctuous wooer (in the tradition of the *pastourelle*), and in 'Spazziam pronte', three hags vigorously sweep the floors to clear them of bird droppings.

On a microstructural level, the poetry is sometimes built around a single word, followed through by its reiteration, exact or varied: thus, when 'exact', 'ohimè' five times in a poem of eight lines and 'cor' six times in a poem of ten; or, when 'varied', 'vedrò (×2)/vedroll'/vista/veder'; 'parto (×2)/parte/partita/partire'; 'baci (×6, twice as verb, four times as noun)/baciata/bacio (×2)/baciarla (×2)/baciatrice'; and so on.[46] Other times the word is more an idea, presented in a string of synonyms: the lady's *eyes*, referred to as stars, beams, sun; her *obduracy*, as marble, hard, rocks; the *air* that carries the lover's words to the lady, as a breeze (varied to read fresh breeze, gentle breeze, graceful breeze, lovely breeze, charming breeze), blowing, stiff North Wind, searing South Wind; the *blindness* of love, as a menagerie of myopic (and obnoxious) animals, viz. a basilisk, a mole, a viper; *music*, as hearing, siren, song, accents, voice, harmony, sound; and, in another example, even more impressively, as beautiful sounds, songful caverns that increase harmony, the blend of dear and joyful notes of love, singing, the murmur of bushes, dancing flowers.[47] In the last example, the poet (Rinuccini), in a display of verbal pyrotechnics, combines the set of musical images with another set of vernal ones, namely, sun, fields, green bushes, grasses, flowers, sweet fragrances, the waft of the Zephyr.

Sometimes the poet takes a single idea and varies it through a process of augmentation (happy/happier/happiest) or of diminution (a full glance becomes a ray, then a part of the pupil, then the semblance of a glance).[48] Other times he creates an extended simile, as when Cynthia is said to resemble the moon in being fickle, frigid, inconstant, uncertain; or when the lady is conceived as a tigress (who has no pity) or the lover as a unicorn (with the difference that where the unicorn does not know it will be trapped, the lover does); or when the loss of the lady is compared to that of a bird's mate; or when life is acted out in a playhouse (veil [= curtain], stage, spectacle, spectator, theatre).[49] Or if not one simile, he creates a chain of them, as when Milady's teeth are likened to the pearls of the sea, her eyes to the stars, and her cheeks to April's flowers.[50]

---

[46] 'Ohimè': Bk 1: 12 (Guarini); 'mio core': Bk 4: 16 (Marino); 'vedrò', etc.: M4: 10 (Guarini); 'parto', etc.: Bk 5: 3 (anon.); 'baci', etc.: Bk 4: 1, later Bk 5: 19 (Marino). See also M4: 2 (Guarini): 'dolcemente (×2) /dolce (×3)'.

[47] Eyes: Bk 1: 9 (Celiano); obduracy: Bk 5: 1 (Marino); air: Bk 5: 10 (Marino); blindness: Bk 5: 2 (Gatti); music: Bk 1: 5 (Guarini), then Mti: 18 (Rinuccini).

[48] Enlargement: Bk 1: 2 (Guarini); diminution: Bk 2: 8 (Chiabrera).

[49] Cynthia: Bk 5: 17 (Marino); tigress: Cte: 16; unicorn: Cte: 19; loss of lady: Mti: 12 (Petrarch); life as a play: Bk 5: 14 (Marino).

[50] Bk 4: 5 (Chiabrera).

Elsewhere the poet piles up variations of single words as well as of their synonyms in a triple set of images, for example, death ('mori/il morir/ morir/morte') followed by the negation of life ('non ha vita/non vive/ove vita non è'), plus killing ('uccidesti'); or escaping ('fuggitivo/fugga/fugge') followed by wandering ('vagar', though also 'vago' [×2, once as a noun, then as an adjective]), plus leaving ('parti/partir').[51] In the latter example the poet (Guarini) plays on the added connotations of 'vagar', wandering, as wishing and wooing, and all this within seven lines, held together with the glue of their rhymes (aBBcCdD) and of heavy alliteration (*parte, pena, partir, ponga; ferma, fede, fugga, fugge*)![52] Of the various poets, Marino took the palm for verbal wizardry.

More often, the verses are typified not by a unifying idea, but by contrast motifs, or oxymora, of which the most widespread is, naturally, life versus death. The poet plays the life/death conflict 'to death': it is the very essence, or 'life', of the madrigal.[53] Other contrast motifs combine with it, or work alone, in single examples, to illustrate the theses and antitheses of which love is about, though particularly (in the madrigal) its antitheses: weeping/ rejoicing, cruelty/pity, departure/staying, departure/return, bitterness/ sweetness, silence/speech, fire/ice, winter/spring, and so on.[54]

Contrast is endemic to the madrigal, yes, but in reading over the poetry of Rossi's madrigals, one has the impression less of the verbal dichotomies within single poems than of the continuities within the repertory as a whole. As amorous poetry, the content revolves about the trials of lovers to gain bodily and psychic control over one another. The 'head' and the 'heart' appear to play a major role in determining the language. Not only are they detailed in the separate poems (face, countenance, eyes, looks, mien, brow, cheek, mouth, lips, tongue, etc., for the *head*; soul, spirit, bosom, breast, etc., for the *heart*), but they give rise there to more specific vocabulary.

Thus the eyes, designated otherwise as pupils or by epithets for vision (seeing, beholding, looking, glances), become, by extension, the source of

[51] Death: Mti: 4 (Marino); escaping: M4: 6 (Guarini).
[52] For another example pivoting about the double meaning of 'partir' as parting and parti-tion, see Bk 4: 4 (Marino).
[53] Cf. Bk 1: 8, 11–13, 15, 19; Bk 2: 14–15, 18; Bk 3: 1, 5, 10–13; Bk 4: 3, 7, 10, 12, 17; etc.
[54] Weeping/rejoicing: Bk 1: 19 (or varied to suffering/rejoicing: M4: 16; sorrows/joys: Bk 5: 17; pains/joys: M4: 7; sighing/rejoicing: Mti: 6; weeping/laughing: Bk 3: 8, Mti: 10). Cruelty/ pity: Bk 4: 19; M4: 5, 9; Mti: 2, 7 (or varied to feigned pity/real pity: Bk 2: 14). Departure/ staying: Bk 4: 11; M4: 8; Bk 5: 3 (or varied to escaping/not escaping: Bk 4: 8; escaping/being caught: Bk 5: 7). Departure/return: Bk 1: 19; M4: 6. Bitterness/sweetness: Bk 2: 10; Bk 4: 1, 13; M4: 4, 10; Bk 5: 19 (or varied to poison/ambrosia: Bk 4: 13; poison/milk: Bk 5: 4). Silence/ speech: Bk 1: 5, 17; Bk 3: 2; Bk 4: 4, 6; Mti: 7. Ice/fire: Bk 1: 7; Bk 4: 2, 13; Mti: 3, 11 (or varied to ice/sun: Bk 3: 13). Winter/spring: Mti: 2, 12. See, also, darkness/sun (Bk 2: 3; or varied to moon/sun: Bk 5: 14); not loving/loving (Bk 2: 15); not kissing/kissing (Bk 4: 1, Bk 5: 19); pallor/ colour (Bk 5: 9, Mti: 11); infidelity/fidelity (Bk 5: 5); severing/binding (M4: 5); night/day (Mti: 12–13; or varied to blindness/sight: Mti: 2; hiding/disclosing: Bk 5: 11–12, Mti: 1); dreaming/ seeing (Bk 1: 1); war/peace (Bk 3: 1, 13); to die/to be born (M4: 14); to harden/to soften (M4: 1).

light imagery: Rossi's madrigals are replete with references to the sun (or the Great Planet), the moon, stars, beams, rays, lights, mirrors, lightning, flashing, shining, sparkling, glittering. But the light that shines becomes, in turn, the source for fire motifs, of a dazzling variety: flint, tinder, fires, flames, beams, blazes, sparks, that ignite, kindle, burn, scorch, sting, melt, consume, incinerate; all of them are metaphors for love as ardour. To return to the eyes proper: they not only shine and burn, but they cry: thus a new set of motifs concerned with weeping, tears, liquid; which themselves, by extension, generate still another set of motifs concerned with lamentation: misery, lament, suffering, sorrow, mourning, torture, pain, worry.

The mouth, to follow through another bodily idea, becomes the source of vocabulary for speech and song (words, voices, sounds, harmony, the lure of female sirens) and, of course, of an endless set of images for osculation: kisses and kissing, lips, rubies, pearls, i.e. drops of moisture, dewy spirits, the food of nectar, ambrosia, tongues that sometimes turn to biting vipers, etc.

What of the heart? It has the power to give life or cause death; it is thus either kind (courteous, gentle, gracious, compassionate, merciful, benevolent) or malevolent (cruel, wicked, fierce, merciless, pitiless, thankless, haughty, arrogant). In its kindness, it sends arrows and darts of love or thunderbolts; in its malevolence it brandishes weapons that wound, hurt, kill, destroy. Thus we return, full circle, to the 'heart' of the madrigal, as signalled in its most blatant contrast motif: life versus death.

The separate words are grouped into lyric outpourings of the speaker, who is usually *he*, though in a few cases, in the earlier books, also *she*.[55] The word *usually* should be emphasized: there are a large number of madrigals that, in their gender, are uncertain.[56] Grammatically, they could have been spoken by *he* or *she*; the context, more often than not, indicates that it is *he*. The pronoun *we* is unusual: it stands for *I*, the *pluralis majestatis*, in the dedicatory piece that opens the *Canzonette*, and for *lovers* in 'Come il ferir sia poco': there a female archer, stationed on a high rock, hurls at them a thousand bolts of ice. Sometimes *he* and *she* hold a dialogue, as in the one between Thyrsis and Phyllis in a sonnet by Celiano:

> 'Stay in peace', said Thyrsis, sighing,
> To sorrowing and beautiful Phyllis.
> 'Stay in peace, I must go, thus I've been ordered
> By law, by wicked destiny, by harsh and stubborn fate'.
> And she, distilling a bitter liquid now from the one,
> Now from the other star, fixed her beams
> On the beams of her Thyrsis and pierced
> His heart with most merciful darts.
> At that point he, with death stamped on his face,

---

[55] Bk 1: 14, 16; Bk 2: 1; M4: 5–6.
[56] Cf. Bk 1: 1, 6–7, 10, 12–13, 19; Bk 2: 4, 7, 9, 14, 17–18; Bk 3: 2, 4, 9, 11; etc.

Said: 'alas! without my sun, how will I survive,
Going from pain to pain, from sorrow to sorrow?'
And she, oppressed with sighs and tears,
Feverishly formed these words:
'Oh my dear soul, who takes you away from me?'[57]

Or the words of the one or other are quoted in the course of a narrative, as at the opening of Book 2 in two poems by Rinuccini, of which the first reads thus:

Phyllis, beholding the heavens,
Spoke sorrowfully and, all the while,
Filled a white veil with hot pearls:
'I burst into tears,
I languish and die from love,
Nor can I find pity, oh heavens, oh stars!
I still am young and have a head of gold;
Coloured and fair,
My cheeks look like fresh roses.
Oh how painful it will be
When I have a face of gold and a head of silver!'[58]

Other times *he* vents his frustrations in a soliloquy, as when, in the following anonymous *canzonetta*, *he* admits that try as he may he cannot escape from the pains of love:

1 I tried to flee from Love
To avoid feeling sorrow;
Now my fate is so cruel
That I constantly crave for death.

2 I tried to go away
To avoid being further consumed,
Yet a fresh arrow
Now renews all my troubles.

3 I tried, by leaving,
To make my suffering end,
But Love, everywhere,
Increases the flames of my fire.

4 Thus the more I flee,
The more I'm consumed and dissolved,
For Love wants
My pain to be eternal.[59]

Thematics

The poems revolve around the usual topics of madrigal verse, namely, the pains of love and, less often, its delights. A more exact typology reveals

[57] Bk 1: 9: ' "Rimanti in pace", alla dolente e bella | Fillida Tirsi, sospirando, disse', etc. See also Bk 1: 11, Mti: 14.

[58] 'Filli, mirando il cielo, | Dicea doglios'e 'ntanto', etc. See also Bk 2: 2; Bk 3: 7, 13; M4: 13; Mti: 3. Bk 2: 1–2 (by Rinuccini) are similar in their themes (in the first a young woman vents her sorrow, in the second a young man does his), their location of the speakers (under the heavens, to which they appeal), and their order of presentation (narration, quotation).

[59] 'Cercai fuggir Amore | Per non sentir dolore', etc.: Cte: 9. Cf. Cte: 13, 18–19; Bk 1: 7, 16; Bk 2: 16; Bk 3: 11 (in which the lover frames his thoughts in three conditional 'if' clauses); M4: 3, 7, 10; Bk 5: 15.

certain emphases and, in the course of time, changes in the thematics of Rossi's repertory, as determined, obviously, by his poetic choices. The 150 Italian lyrics group into various subject categories, which, because of their persistence, qualify as topoi. One might perceive anywhere from ten to twenty or more such topoi, depending on how finely one slices the repertory for its main and subsidiary themes. For present purposes, a more circumscribed differentiation seems preferable, in keeping with the overall uniformity of the repertory.

The most persistent theme—it appears in close to half of the poetry, spread over the composer's collections—is 'to love is to suffer'. It runs the gauntlet from charges that Milady makes the lover suffer to his wish that he be relieved of his suffering. The variants are as many as the kinds of suffering, which, in poetry as in life, are countless. Pursuing the basic theme, one finds it developed in such arguments, from simple to more complex, as:

> I suffer from love[60]
> The more one loves, the more one suffers[61]
> You purposely make me suffer[62]
> If you love me, why do you make me suffer?[63]
> I suffer, but you hardly care[64]
> If I suffer, why shouldn't she too?[65]
> I suffer, weeping day and night[66]
> I suffer in silence[67]
> I will keep silent, telling nobody of my love for you[68]
> Though you make me suffer, my suffering is sweet[69]

Various adjunct notions slip in, such as cruelty:

> Her cruelty makes me suffer[70]
> Your cruelty removes my speech[71]
> Why are you cruel to me even in springtime?[72]
> Though you are cruel, you appear to be merciful[73]
> You are cruel, yet I remain faithful[74]

or burning:

> You make me burn, though you do not share my ardour[75]
> Lady burns Love, then freezes him[76]

---

[60] Cte: 18; Bk 2: 1.   [61] Bk 2: 16.   [62] Cte: 11; Bk 1: 4; Bk 3: 12; M4: 9.
[63] Bk 1: 12; Bk 3: 3.   [64] Bk 2: 3, 13, 15.   [65] M4: 17.   [66] Bk 3: 9.
[67] M4: 3; Bk 5: 15.   [68] Bk 5: 11.   [69] M4: 2.   [70] Bk 1: 15.   [71] Bk 1: 5.
[72] Bk 3: 14; Mti: 2.   [73] Bk 4: 9.   [74] Bk 5: 1, 15.   [75] Mti: 8.   [76] Mti: 3.

or the contrast between joy and sorrow:

> Milady is the source of my joy and sorrow[77]
>
> If she is my happiness, why am I so miserable?[78]
>
> You are beautiful, but your cruelty makes me miserable[79]

and so forth through such others as weeping,[80] the pain of looking,[81] the urge to escape,[82] and, in endless variations, loving as destruction or dying.[83] The topos reflects in a number of complementary themes, among them: I am happy in my misery; I want to renew my love for you, though you make me suffer; and I wish I could stop suffering.[84]

Second in frequency is the topos 'parting is painful', or the *partenza*. It accounts for about 15 per cent of the repertory, though is confined mainly to the earlier books. The expression of grief over the departure of the beloved may be his or hers,[85] or even both of theirs, as when, in one example, the departure of Thyrsis makes both him and Phyllis sorrow or, in another, reversing the sexes, the departure of Sylvia makes both her and Amyntas sorrow.[86] Annexed to the basic theme are such variations as the lover's plea for his lady not to abandon him for another man; or his worry over how he will survive once he has left her; or the lady's declaration that though her lover departs, she will not cease loving him; or the question of what good it does either of them to love each other if they must be separated.[87] As complementary themes, one finds escape and hiding; or a plea for return; or the contrast between departure and return.[88]

[77] Bk 5: 17.

[78] Mti: 6.

[79] Cte: 17.

[80] Outwardly I smile, inwardly I weep (Bk 3: 8); we weep while our flames turn to ice (Bk 4: 2); looking at her makes me weep (Bk 4: 15).

[81] To see you is to die (M4: 14); whether I look at you or not, I suffer (M4: 11); by looking at me, you make me suffer (Mti: 9).

[82] There is no way I could escape sorrow (Cte: 9); if my love is as intangible as a shadow, why not escape instead of clinging to it? (Bk 4: 6); I will escape her who makes me die (Cte: 12); you lovers had better escape, for loving causes sorrow (Cte: 15).

[83] Destruction: my beautiful lady can destroy anything (Bk 5: 6); my love has been destroyed by her contempt (Bk 1: 7); once I loved her, but she ruined my love (Bk 5: 18). Dying: Lady makes me die (Cte: 2, 16); your beauty makes me die (Cte: 7); your cruelty makes me die (M4: 14); I am dying, for you killed me (Bk 4: 10; Mti: 4). Or adding the notion of speech: must I die before telling you so? (Bk 4: 3); I am dying and cannot say it (Cte: 13). Or playing on the contrast between living and dying: you want me to die, yet keep me alive (Bk 4: 7, 17; Mti: 17); you both kill and entice me (Bk 5: 2).

[84] The first in Bk 2: 11, Bk 5: 9, M4: 7; the second in Bk 5: 8; the third in Bk 1: 13, Mti: 15.

[85] Cf. M4: 8, 16.

[86] Bk 1: 9 (Thyrsis, Phyllis; quoted above), 11 (Sylvia, Amyntas): note their proximity in the collection.

[87] In order: Bk 1: 18; Bk 2: 4; Bk 4: 16; Bk 1: 14; M4: 5.

[88] For example: no sooner did you arrive than you fled (Bk 1: 1; M4: 6); why run away from me if you want me to die? (Bk 2: 5); to no avail do you hide from me (Bk 5: 12); return to me (Bk 3: 4); when you left I wept, but now that you are returning I rejoice (Bk 1: 19).

In another set of examples the notion of leaving is tied to dying,[89] though the departure-death equation admits such variations as: yes, I die, but since you remain in my heart, I live; or do not demur from kissing me before my death, with death described as 'my last harsh departure'.[90] The model for the equation is the poetry that Petrarch wrote *after* Laura's death, and Rossi does, in fact, set one such Petrarchan sonnet: there the suitor compares his state to that of two separated lovebirds, with the one difference that where the lamented bird may still be alive, Laura is 'stingily retained by death and the heavens'.[91]

A third topos, in about a tenth of the repertory, and distributed over various collections, is the invocation 'help me'. Sometimes it appears as such, though more often is presented as an appeal, to the lady, to show her love, to emit a sigh, to behold her suitor, to sense his agitation, to notice his tears, or to hear his sighs.[92] The gist of one poem is: if she made me fall in love, she should rightly love and comfort me; the gist of another is: oh, if she only knew how much I love her![93]

About 5 per cent of the repertory is concerned with kissing, or the *bacio*. It appears with the introduction of Marino's poetry in Book 3, and may be found in Books 4–5, but not in the *Madrigaletti*. The act of kissing is sometimes innocent, as when the lover says that he wants to kiss his lady; or that she asks for his kisses, but fails to return them; or that she should not escape, but stay and kiss him.[94] Other times the *bacio* is fraught with dangers: it not only causes joy and pain, but it kills, indeed, kissing now becomes an act of war—the lovers battle for gains, yet suffer losses.[95] The *Canzon de' baci* has, for its vocabulary, denial, refusal, robbing, binding, conquest, murder, warring, defying, hostility, insults, quarrels, battles, struggles, wounds, imprisonment, stabbing. Marino raised the *bacio* to the heights of lethal eroticism. Composers responded in single works or in whole collections entitled *baci*.[96]

The rest of the topoi, of more limited occurrence, add different nuances to the amorous theme. On the darker side of the palette one finds poems that work the ideas: you do not believe that I love you; you pretend to

---

[89] Bk 1: 16, Bk 2: 18 (the piece is entitled an 'aria di partenza'), Bk 4: 11, M4: 15 ('Ah dolente partita'). On musical settings of this last lyric, perhaps the most famous of madrigalesque *partenze* (altogether, 32 composers tried their hand at it from 1593 to 1621), see, for those of Marenzio, Wert, and Monteverdi, Petrobelli, '"Ah dolente partita"'.

[90] The first in Bk 5: 3, the second in Bk 3: 1.

[91] Mti: 12 ('Vago Augelletto').

[92] In order: Bk 1: 8; Bk 5: 4; Cte: 10; Bk 2: 10, 19; Mti: 11, 14; M4: 1; Bk 5: 10; Bk 4: 19.

[93] Cte: 6; Bk 2: 2.

[94] In order: Bk 3: 6; Bk 4: 1; Bk 5: 13, 19.

[95] Cf. Bk 3: 13 (the *Canzon de' baci*) and Bk 4: 12–13.

[96] Cf. Puliti, *Baci ardenti: 2° lib. de' madrigali* 5 v. (1609; of the 17 items, four are by Marino, including 'Io moro', set by Rossi in Bk 3: 1); Delipari, *I baci: madrigali ... lib. 1°* 2–4 v. (1630, opening with first three stanzas from the *Canzon de' baci* [see above]; of the two other items by Marino, one is 'Taci, bocca', set by Rossi in Bk 3: 2).

love me; should I speak or be silent?; it does no good to escape from love.[97] On the brighter side, rather infrequently seen in Rossi's repertory, one finds others that work the ideas: I am free of love (thus disproving the notion that it is useless to escape); he is happy who enjoys his lady's love; the remembrance of past love is reason to rejoice; I love you and you alone; lady is beautiful; and love rules the universe.[98] A poem in a category of its own is the dedication piece, at the beginning of the *Canzonette*, to Duke Vincenzo and his spouse Leonora: it hails them as 'worthy of sacred and glorious dominion'. Though anonymous, it may have been written after the example 'A voi, Coppia felice', published two years earlier and 'celebrating, in lofty and sonorous rhymes, Mantua, Vincenzo, and Leonora'.[99]

All of these topoi can be signalled as such if one selects what seems to be the basic idea of single poems. Yet, in reality, the poems move, here and there, on compound thematic planes, thereby impeding, if not impairing the process of selection. Thus in one example there is an appeal for help (as one topos) to prevent dying (which happens when one suffers from love, as another topos)[100] by having his lady return (which shows that, at one point, she departed, as a third topos). In another, where it is clear that, despite the pain the lady causes, the suitor loves her dearly, the poetry oscillates between the topoi 'to love is to suffer' and 'I love you'. In a third, to the effect that it is only right to love a beautiful woman, there is a combination of the topoi 'I love you' and 'lady is beautiful'.

One poem is unique among Rossi's works: it develops the idea that though Milady is cruel, she appears to be beautiful. Why 'appears'? Because the painter so depicted her:

> Kind artificer, chosen for such a worthy labour,
> You adorned (I see it!) the face at least
> Of this haughty and wicked fair beast,
> Hostile to love and to me, with a meek affection.
> Not only did you provide her simulated appearance
> With beauty, grace, loveliness, and comeliness,
> But you represented her, so cruel, as cordial and charitable,
> Whence my heart may have peace and delight.

---

[97] Disbelief: Bk 1: 6, 10; M4: 12. Pretence: Bk 2: 7, 14. Speech or silence: Bk 1: 17; Bk 3: 2; Mti: 7. To escape is to no avail: Bk 4: 8; Bk 5: 7.

[98] Freedom from love: Bk 2: 17 and Mti: 10, 13 (to be compared with the counter-theme of having lost one's freedom: Bk 2: 6). Love requited: Bk 1: 2; M4: 4. Remembering past love: Bk 5: 16. I love you: Cte: 3–4, 19; Bk 4: 18; Mti: 1, 5, 16. Beautiful lady: Bk 4: 5; Bk 5: 15. Love as ruler: Bk 2: 12.

[99] 'Per celebrar con rima alta e sonora | E Mantova e Vincentio e Leonora': from Toscano, *L'edificazione di Mantova e l'origine dell'antichissima famiglia de' principi Gonzaghi e d'altre nobilissime familie di detta città* (1587), p. 1, octave 2. Tasso composed his own celebratory rhymes: see his *Canzone della coronatione del Serenissimo Sig. Don Vincenzo Gonzaga duca di Mantova et Monferrato, etc.* (1587).

[100] For this and examples in next two sentences, see Cte: 5; Cte: 3; Mti: 16.

On her face, in itself harsh and savage,
I already perceive, midst your shadings, a kindly ray
Flashing in the one and the other star;
Afterwards, indeed, someone might say: 'if nature
Made her defiant of mercy, behold! this man, wiser still,
Made her both merciful and beautiful'.[101]

The poem illustrates its own topos, namely, painting as imitation. Marino, the author, addressed it to Ambrosio Figino, well known for his portraits, among them one of Carlo Emanuele, duke of Savoy. He paid tribute to the portrait and its painter in an extended poem—238 stanzas—entitled 'Il ritratto del Serenissimo Don Carlo Emanuello, duca di Savoia, panegirico del Marino, al Figino', in which he alludes, via Figino's name (from *fingere*, to simulate), to the dichotomy, in art, of real and make-believe:

Wise Figino, 'twas you who, through a fateful mystery,
Received your name from 'feigning', and while you feign
You make the appearance of the object you feigned true to life...[102]

The topos may be traced in earlier literature, as, for example, in a poem by Rinaldi, with the same contrast between real and simulated, sweet and cruel:

From life did you depict,
Doctor Painter, the image,
In order to make my heart be satisfied with a sweet object.
But, carelessly, you did not notice
That instead of pleasing
The effect turned out to be contrary to your desire.
Oh, marvellous success:
Cruel became the very act that was produced through piety.[103]

Muzio Manfredi was fascinated with the topos, addressing three poems to the painter Andrea Lunghi, who apparently failed, after three attempts, to capture the beauty of Manfredi's wife. He wrote another three about a portrait of Barbara Sanseverina, countess of Sala, in which he chided the painter (Scipione da Gaeta) for distorting the countess's mouth.[104]

Except for Rossi, no composer is known to have set Marino's 'Figinian' sonnet, and one can only wonder what moved him to do so. Therein lies a story still to be told.

---

[101] 'Ornasti, il veggio, a sì degn'opr'eletto, | Fabro gentil, di quest'altera e ria', etc.: Bk 4: 9.

[102] Published in 1609, the poem, of which the first three lines are quoted ('Saggio Figin, che per fatal mistero', etc.), was written at least a year earlier: Marino refers to it in a letter, dated 1608, to another famed portrait painter, Bernardo Castello; cf. his *Lettere*, ed. Guglielminetti, 69. The theme of 'real and make-believe' might further be explored in relation to Figino's treatise on art theory: *Il Figino, overo del fine della pittura* (1591).

[103] Rinaldi, *De' madrigali...prima...parte* (1588), 124.

[104] Manfredi, *Madrigali* (1605), 109–12, 204–5.

Music

The larger number of works—eighty-four out of the 146 that remain[105]—are written for five voices. In this Rossi stands in good company: the five-voice madrigal tradition encompasses the major composers of the late sixteenth and earlier seventeenth centuries, most notably, for Mantua, Wert (11 books), Pallavicino (8), and Monteverdi (6).[106] Yet where the tendency, in the seventeenth century, was toward a *concertato* idiom for fewer voices, Rossi maintained the five-voice ensemble until 1622.

Works for larger ensembles occur at the ends of collections, to provide a more impressive close (four madrigals *a 6*, three *a 8*).[107] Those for smaller ensembles range from three voices (22 examples), mainly in the *Canzonette*, to four (16) in the book of madrigals *a 4*, and two plus *continuo* (15) in the *Madrigaletti*.

With the three-voice *canzonette*, Rossi, again, stands in good company: such works were the rage, in Mantua, in the 1580s–90s, including those by Monteverdi, Wert, and Gastoldi.[108] The four-voice madrigals, on the other hand, mark a retrenchment: there are few such collections after 1600.[109] In writing for two voices and *continuo* (1628) Rossi joined the modernists, though in retard: Monteverdi turned to the genre in 1619, preceded by Sigismondo d'India.[110] The *Madrigaletti* close with two works for three voices and *continuo* and one for two voices and *continuo* plus a third 'si placet', the only work of its kind in Rossi's Italian repertory. Its real locus is in his instrumental music (18 examples).[111] But where the *si placet*

[105] Four others are known from their texts only (for Chiabrera's *Il ratto di Proserpina*); cf. *CW* viii. app. 2.

[106] On the 5-v. madrigal collections of Wert, see the detailed treatment under his 'works' in MacClintock, *Giaches de Wert (1535–1596)*, and on those of Pallavicino, Monteath, 'The Five-Part Madrigals of Benedetto Pallavicino'. The literature on Monteverdi's madrigals is extensive, though the 5-v. ones are probably most thoroughly covered in Fabbri, *Monteverdi*.

[107] 6 v.: Bk 1: 18–19; Bk 3: 14; Bk 4: 19. 8 v.: Bk 2: 19; M4: 17; Bk 5: 19.

[108] In chronological order: 1581, Moro (dedicated to Giulio Cesare Gonzaga); 1584, Monteverdi; 1589, the year of Rossi's publication, Bonfilio (dedicated to the Mantuan friar Don Anselmo Compagnoni), Trofeo (dedicated to Duke Vincenzo), and Wert (dedicated to the duchess Leonora); 1591, Bozi; 1592, Gastoldi (Bk 1, dedicated to Alessandro Magno, canon at Sant'Andrea, Mantua); 1595, Gastoldi, Bk 2 (dedicated to Guidobuono Guidobuoni, adviser to Duke Vincenzo; not to forget, in 1591, Gastoldi's *Balletti* 5 v., dedicated to the duke, and, in 1594, his *Balletti* 3 v., dedicated to Alessandro Angosciola, the duke's chamberlain); 1599, O. Bargnani.

[109] 1601: Soriano, Bk 1. 1603: Alberti, Bk 1. 1604: Alberti, Bk 2; Montella, Bk 1. 1607: Alberti, Bk 3; Marsolo, *Madrigali boscarecci*; Montella, Bk 2. 1608: Oddi, *Madrigali spirituali*; Quagliati, Bk 1; Roccia, Bk 1. 1610: G. de Macque, Bk 3. 1613: Nenna, Bk 1. 1614: Pace, Bk 4. 1623: G. Merulo, *Madrigali . . . in stile moderno*.

[110] Monteverdi, in Bk 7 (*Concerto*) 1–6 v.; d'India, in five books of 'musiche' 1–2 v. (1609–23); cf. Joyce, *The Monodies of Sigismondo d'India*. See also G. F. Anerio, *Ricreatione armonica* 1–2 v. (1611), *Diporti musicali* 1–4 v. (1617), *Selva armonica* 1–4 v. (1617), *La bella Clori armonica* 1–3 v. (1619), *I lieti scherzi* 1–4 v. (1621); Barbarino, *Canzonette* 1–2 v. (1616); and others.

[111] See Ch. 4 (and, on performance, Ch. 6). One more *si placet* work can be found among Rossi's Hebrew songs (no. 9, for 4/3 v.).

instrumental works were originally written for three voices, then enlarged to four or five, with the added voices creating dissonances and awkward voice leading, the last piece in the *Madrigaletti* works equally well for two or three voices.[112]

All the collections but one (the *Canzonette*) were supplied with a *basso continuo*. Book 1 *a* 5 had it in its fifth and last edition (1618) and Book 3 *a* 5 for its capacious *Canzon de' baci* only.[113] Except for the *Madrigaletti* and Book 5 *a* 5 (to judge from the *continuo*, its one remaining part), the *continuo* serves rather as a *basso seguente*, following, with few changes, the bass voice or, when the bass drops out, the voice—whichever it be—that sounds the lowest notes. On the instrumentation of the *continuo*, see Chapter 5.

Rossi's Italian works belong, basically, to three categories of composition: the *canzonetta* for three voices; the madrigal for four and five; and the *madrigaletto* for two plus *continuo*. Each comprises one or more collections, from different periods. Thus the *Canzonette* (1589) are a first period collection, separated from the next by eleven years, during which Rossi, in his own words, learned his craft. From Opus 2 on, we are dealing with a middle period, to which the first to fourth books of five-voice madrigals and the one of four-voice madrigals may be assigned: in all, five books, from the first decade of the seventeenth century (assuming, as we have, that the four-voice madrigals, published in 1614, were composed much earlier). The last period, from 1622 on, comprises Book 5 *a* 5 and the *Madrigaletti*. That leaves two gaping holes in Rossi's secular vocal production, notably 1589–1600 and 1610–22, the first, as said, corresponding to the years of his apprenticeship, the second filled by other forms of composition (instrumental music and preparations, probably from 1612 on, for the Hebrew collection, which, stylistically, forms a category *sui generis*).

Sensible as it would seem to treat the collections of the three periods individually, the lines between them are not that well drawn to warrant their separation. Rather, they are blurred by continuities in the overall development. The early *canzonetta* has well-defined characteristics as a short form for three equal voices, treated lightly, and unaffectedly, as befits its concise and facile poetry. But it links in size, shape, and content with the *madrigaletto* of the last period, as if Rossi reverted, in his later years, to his original mode of composition. True, the *madrigaletto* is written for two voices plus *continuo*, after the texture, perhaps, of the instrumental works. But the texture was already foreshadowed in the *Canzonette* (Ex. 3.1).

Not only does the *canzonetta* adumbrate the *madrigaletto*, but it links with the madrigal: in effect, a *canzonetta* in a single stanza is, to all intents and

---

[112] Unlike the two pieces *a* 3 and *continuo* (Mti: 16–17), where the three voices are rhythmically and melodically equivalent, the last piece (Mti: 18) is basically written for 2 v. and *continuo* plus optional bass; indeed, the bass here acts as support.

[113] Bk 2 omits the *continuo* from its last piece *a* 8, as does M4.

Ex. 3.1 'Torna dolce, il mio amore' (*Canzonette*, no. 5, bars 14–20)

purposes, a madrigal.[114] The nexus is provided, in the first collection, in its last two works, which are monostrophic and, were it not for their three voices, have the formal and stylistic characteristics of the four- and five-voice madrigals. Like the *canzonette*, the madrigals tend often to divide into three parts, conventionally a beginning, middle, and end; to display a clear rhythmic and melodic profile; to move texturally between homophony and light imitation; and, especially from Book 3 *a 5* on, to be diminutive in size, in accord with their increasingly epigrammatic poetry. In Rossi's hands, the madrigal, in time, became more and more like a *canzonetta*, and it seems only natural, in retrospect, that his last collection was a set of *madrigaletti*.

The development from one to another category is 'dramatic' only in the sense that it is from one kind of ensemble to another: a trio; four or five voices; a duet plus *continuo*. Otherwise, it seems continuous, with small changes of form and content in the transfer from *canzonetta* to madrigal and then to *madrigaletto*, marked, one and all, by a fairly uniform compositional approach. The repertory will be treated, accordingly, as a whole, with reference, where suitable, to the differences between its parts. To be considered are metres and modes, counterpoint, textures, macro- and microstructures, and the relation between music and poetry. Needless to say, they work together to form what, synthetically, is Rossi's, and no other composer's, Italian vocal œuvre.

---

[114] On the gradual infiltration of lighter elements into the madrigal, see DeFord, 'Musical Relationships between the Italian Madrigal and Light Genres in the Sixteenth Century'.

1. *Metres.* Almost all the vocal works—137 out of 146—are written under C, or duple mensuration. With C the norm, interest immediately focuses on the exceptions: each of them has a textual or functional explanation. The only work in triple metre from beginning to end is the theatrical *balletto* 'Spazziam pronte',[115] performed as a rollicking dance song; like the text in trochaic metre (– ᵕ), so the music in 3/2, on which more will be said in Chapter 6. Other works, in alternating duple and triple metres, include a madrigal and various *canzonette* and *canzonetta*-like *madrigaletti* ('*canzonetta*-like' by virtue of their strophic construction). The madrigal occurs at the end of Book 2: Rossi put it there, no doubt, because in its five sections under different metres,[116] as well as in its composition as a 'dialogo a 8', it was special, hence worthy to close the collection. Being 'lighter' than madrigals, *canzonette* and *madrigaletti* seem, by nature, to invite playful metrical changes. Yet, with regard to the present examples,[117] there are semantic or prosodic reasons for them.

In the *canzonette*, the portions in triple metre serve the text—they are written in black notes, meant to suggest love's blindness and frenzy.[118] 'Crazy is he', the poet exclaims, 'who falls in love with a woman' (Ex. 3.2).

In the three *madrigaletti*, the irregularities of metre or verse lengths or both encourage temporal shifts, to the extent, in one of them, of six metres in succession, more than in any other Italian work by the composer.[119] These irregularly measured *canzonetta*-like *madrigaletti* were already reviewed under 'Poets and Poetic Forms', where they were called *scherzi*.

Ex. 3.2 'Non voglio più servire' (*Canzonette*, no. 12, bars 11–16)

---

[115] The Hebrew songs likewise have a single work in triple metre (no. 16). Works under 3, as will be seen, abound in the instrumental collections.

[116] C (40 bars.), Ø 3/2 (6), ¢ (17), Ø 3/2 (6), ¢ (15). On the relationship of C and ¢ to one another and to 3/2, see Ch. 5.

[117] Cte: 8, 12, 17. Mti: 2, 13, 18.

[118] 'Voi che seguit'il cieco ardor di Venere' (Cte: 8; first line, first stanza): triple metre, bars 1–12, duple, 13–19. 'Pazz'è colui ch'in donna s'innamora' (Cte: 12, with *capoverso* 'Non voglio più servire'; first line, first stanza, paralleled by 'Di non girmene più per Donna matto', last line, last [= fourth] stanza): duple metre, bars 1–12, triple (starting from 'Pazz'è', 13–21 (see Ex. 2). 'Scherzan intorno i pargoletti amori' (Cte: 17; first line, first stanza): triple metre, bars 1–7, duple, 8–18.

[119] Mti: 13 (six metres), 14 (with one change implied in the short final line of each stanza), 15 (three metres).

It might be mentioned that where the ratio of mixed metres is obviously low in Rossi's Italian works, it is relatively high in his Hebrew songs and instrumental works, amounting, in both, to about 25 per cent.[120] Yet the link between the three parts of the repertory is in the *canzonette*: there they meet, if not in practice, at least in concept. Indeed, the metrical changes of the instrumental and Hebrew works were presaged in the first collection. That the madrigals went their own way thereafter, adhering to a single metre, shows that however close they were to the *canzonette* in their origins, as can be demonstrated in their melodies, rhythms, and textures, they developed according to their own metrical logic.

The question, of relevance to performance, how sections in duple metre relate to those in triple will be discussed, at length, in Chapter 5.

2. *Modes.* In his modal choices, Rossi noticeably favours Dorian on G (48 works) and Mixolydian (39). The two modes represent different inflections—minor, major—of a single scale having G as its *finalis*. Next in order are Aeolian (27) and Lydian with B flat, i.e. Ionian on F (20). Thus the F–A area of the tonal compass, with its corresponding modes, is the one explored if the majority of Rossi's secular vocal works. Of the twelve works that remain, six are in Dorian and another six in Ionian: they might be subsumed, as variants, under those in Dorian on G and Lydian with B flat.

All in all, the repertory is based on minor and major as its prime modal orientations, as if signalling the breakdown, in the later Renaissance, of the modal system and its replacement with an inchoate tonal one: out of the eight or twelve modes there seem to crystallize two larger ones, minor and major, defined mainly by the inflection of their thirds and sixths. The modes are still not equalized in Rossi's secular repertory, for minor (Dorian, Dorian on G, Aeolian) outnumbers major (Mixolydian, Lydian, Ionian) by 81 to 65. Nor would one expect them to be, for we are still in the early Baroque.

Changes in Rossi's modal choices can be plotted over the collections. Ionian appears in the first two, yet falls into disuse by Book 5 *a* 5; its function seems to be fulfilled by Lydian with B flat, appearing in all collections, though most notably in the first three books *a* 5 and in the *Madrigaletti*. Where Dorian on G is the leading mode in Books 1–4 *a* 5, it shares equal rank with Mixolydian in the *Canzonette* and in Book 5 *a* 5. In the *Madrigaletti*, however, the composer's preference clearly lies with the Mixolydian.[121]

But these data are not accurate: one major change in Book 5 and the *Madrigaletti* is the introduction of Dorian (untransposed) in, altogether, six examples (curiously, their introduction in Book 5 corresponds to that in the Hebrew songs, published around the same time).[122] Were one to group the examples of Dorian with those of Dorian on G in the last two collections,

---

[120] Eight of the 33 Hebrew songs, thirty of the 130 instrumental works.
[121] In seven works, compared with two in Dorian on G.
[122] Sgs: four works in Dorian (9, 11, 16, 19).

then compare them with the number of examples there in Mixolydian, the result is basically that signalled in the *Canzonette*: Mixolydian and Dorian are more or less equal in importance.

The data are still not accurate: to appraise the composer's modal preferences from one to another collection, all minor modes (Dorian, Aeolian) must be tallied against all major ones (Mixolydian, Ionian, Lydian). The results have been summarized in this table of percentages (representing, for each collection, the number of works in either minor or major modes).

	Cte	Bk 1	Bk 2	Bk 3	Bk 4	Bk 5	M4	Mti
Minor	41	52	51	56	68	57	76	44
Major	56	47	47	42	31	42	22	55

There is, thus, an edge of minor over major in all the madrigal collections, though it becomes increasingly clearer in Books 3–5 *a 5* and is most startlingly profiled in the madrigals *a 4*. The percentages are reversed in the *Canzonette* and the *Madrigaletti*. All this means that, as said before, the first and last collections are inherently related and stand apart from the madrigals; and that the madrigals *a 4* form a category of their own within the larger repertory of the madrigal, or at least that their collection has a distinct modal physiognomy (enhanced, moreover, by its having the largest number of madrigals in Aeolian, indeed, Aeolian is its leading mode, used in particular for the poetry of Guarini).[123]

3. *Counterpoint.* In his secular works, Rossi was a careful composer, observing the proprieties of sixteenth-century counterpoint. He learned his craft in a gradual progression from three-voice writing to (perhaps) writing *a 4*, then *a 5*, assuming again that, in their composition, the four-voice madrigals preceded those *a 5*. As a contrapuntist, Rossi made few 'grammatical' errors: in the 6,675 bars of his seven (complete) Italian collections, only twenty-seven parallel consecutives could be detected. The *Canzonette* are free of them and, except for one or two instances, so are the madrigals *a 4* and the *Madrigaletti*.[124] Some may have been typographical errors; others might indicate a certain haste in composition, as, for example, the concentration of parallels in the *Canzon de' baci*[125] and, in general, in Book 4. Still another explanation, in one example, is word painting, as when the composer exacerbates us with consecutives not just for 'cruelty', but for '*double* cruelty' (Ex. 3.3).

---

[123] In M4, 41% of the works—seven in all—are in Aeolian, compared to 5% in Cte and, in Bks 1–4, 10%, 15%, 21%, and 26%: the upward curve is indicative (it is reversed in Mti, where only 11% of the works are in Aeolian).

[124] Three in Bk 1, six each in Bks 2–3, and nine in Bk 4.

[125] Of the six in Bk 3, the *Canzon* contains four.

Ex. 3.3 'Occhi, quella pièta' (Book 2 *a* 5, no. 14, bars 13–23)

The picture would not be complete without considering other categories of consecutives, though less objectionable. One category is interrupted parallels, i.e. standing between two phrases or separated by a rest within a single phrase: they are spread over the repertory, with the largest concentration in Book 1 (nine examples). But these are petty infractions of contrapuntal propriety, which none of the madrigalists, moreover, ever observed to the letter. Another category occurs in works for larger ensembles, particularly those *a* 8 for two choruses, between their basses, as for example in the antiphonal works that close Book 2 and the madrigals *a* 4, with certain passages in parallel unisons and octaves. It is not as if Rossi had a 'harder

Ex. 3.4*a* 'Pur venisti, cor mio' (Book 1 *a* 5, no. 1, bars 7–9, esp. 8[1])

time' with eight-voice writing; rather he took the liberties that other composers did with the basses of *cori spezzati*, particularly in those sections where the
separate choirs joined to form an aggregate.[126]

Signs of inexperience may be detected in the early madrigal collections, in
the presence, here and there, of thirdless chords on prominent beats (Ex.
3.4*a*), with a consequent thin texture. Or so one might think: thirdless
chords, it turns out, are typical of the three-voice *canzonetta*, sacred and
secular (and not only at the beginning or in the middle of a phrase, but
frequently at the cadence; cf. Ex. 3.4*c*)—examples may be gleaned from
works by no lesser lights than Palestrina and Monteverdi.[127] Seeming
moments of awkwardness, again in the early collections, are passages that
move stodgily towards the cadence (Ex. 3.4*b*) or that sound rather feeble in
their intervallic progression (Ex. 3.4*c*). It is not always clear, though, where
to draw the line between awkward and bold or between careless and
intended. One would expect the composer to exercise a certain initiative in
modifying the contrapuntal profile by occasional licences: after all, he does
not compose by the book; and, historically, he stands at the junction

---

[126] See e.g. Wert, 'Cara Germania' 8 v. (*Opera omnia*, iv. 76–80), and 'Ch'io scriva' 8 v. (ibid. i.
103–9). Similar infractions are to be found, even more pronouncedly, in the last work (no. 19) of
Rossi's Bk 5; but they occur between the lines not of the basses, but of the two *continuo* parts
(thus the extended parallels in bars 25–9, 38–40, 48–51, 59–66, etc.), as they do, moreover,
between the two parts for chitarrone in the sonata *a* 6 that closes S4 (no. 30). On compositional
practices in writing for split choruses, see Carver, *Cori spezzati*.

[127] Palestrina, 'Jesu, rex admirabilis', *Werke*, ed. Haberl *et al.*, xxx. 3 (bar 6); 'Ahi che
quest'occhi miei', ibid. xxviii. 135 (bar 4). Monteverdi, 'Qual si può dir maggiore', *Tutte le
opere*, ed. Malipiero, x. 2 (bars 6–7, 11). Ex. 4*a* by Rossi does, in fact, thin out to three voices in its
thirdless formation in bar 8. For similar spots in the composer's *canzonette*, see 4: 3, 5: 3, 17: 15,
18: 7, 19: 19 (all of them non-cadential); only one of his six three-voice Hebrew 'Songs', though,
has them (1: 23, 74, 126, again non-cadential).

Ex. 3.4*b*   'Hor che lunge da voi' (Book 2 *a 5*, no. 4, bars 13–15)

Ex. 3.4*c*   'Torna dolce, il mio amore' (*Canzonette*, no. 5, bars 5–7)

Ex. 3.4*d*   'S'io paleso il mio foco' (*Madrigaletti*, no. 7, bars 18–19)

between two practices, the *prima* and the *seconda*, though signs of the latter are still modest in his madrigals. The farthest he went in this direction is in the *Madrigaletti*, with two examples of parallel seconds at the cadence, an early instance of what has been referred to, in the literature, as the 'Corelli clash'. But as much, if not more, might be anticipated in a last collection and one, moreover, in *stile concertato* (Ex. 3.4*d*).

Ex. 3.4*e* 'Cor mio, deh non languire' (Book 1 *a* 5, no 13, bars 6–8)

A number of what otherwise would seem unusual passages are engendered by word painting, hence receive musical legitimacy on textual grounds. In Book 1, for example, an F cadence, in 'Cor mio', is approached not by the dominant, as might be expected, but by a flaccid supertonic in first inversion: the word reads *languir* (Ex. 3.4*e*). (If I use terminology, here and elsewhere, with tonal harmonic associations, it is for its convenience and not because I am implying chordal functionality.[128]) In Book 4, Rossi practises dissonant voice leading, in various spots, in reaction to 'how he burns and stings'; or 'poison'; or 'bitter'; or 'dying, alas!' (Ex. 3.4*f*).[129] None of the infractions is that overbold, though, as to disrupt the flow; nor can they be compared to anything but the mildest of dissonances that pepper the works of the more pictorial madrigalists, from Marenzio to Gesualdo.

4. *Textures.* Three main textures may be discerned, as implicit in the three categories of composition: that of the *canzonette*, with three equally melodic voices, having light imitations, though a basically homophonic complexion; that of the *madrigaletti*, with the two upper voices forming a duet while the bass accompanies them as a true *continuo*—the writing is flecked with touches of monody; and that of the madrigals, for four, five, and, occasionally, six or eight independent voices, varying from chordal simultaneity to quasi-chordality and different degrees of syntactic imitation. More often

---

[128] One could make a case for emerging tonality in European music of the 16th–17th centuries, as did, among others, Dahlhaus in his *Studies on the Origin of Harmonic Tonality* (see e.g. the section 'Between Modality and Tonality', 234–47, taking off from the thesis that 'scale degrees in 16th-century chordal technique were understood primarily as degrees in a diatonic system and only secondarily as degrees in a mode').

[129] Cf. Bk 4: 8, bars 24–5 ('com'ard'e punge'; Ex. 4*f*); 13, bars 24–5 ('tosco'); 14, bar 52 ('aspro'); 19, bars 32–5 ('morend'ohimè').

Ex. 3.4*f* 'Troppo ben può' (Book 4 *a* 5, no. 8, bars 22–6)

than not, the madrigals stand midway between the extremes of homophony and imitative counterpoint, in a compromise style with restrained rhythmic gestures, few decorative melismas, and a discreet use of word painting. The modal orientation, in all three styles, is preponderantly diatonic.

Such a description is too generalized, however, to do justice to the individuality of the separate collections. The foundations of Rossi's madrigals were laid, as said, in his *canzonette*. Yet the *canzonelle* have a story of their own. Though tending to homophony as their main texture, they exhibit other modes of writing: the duet, in which two voices are paired against a third; quasi-imitation; and imitation. In bipartite *canzonette* (AB), both parts are likely to begin with homophony and continue with imitation or quasi-imitation.[130] In tripartite ones (ABC), the first and last parts are usually in imitation while the middle one maintains a quasi-imitative or homophonic stance. Tripartite forms often are tucked away under bipartite ones, thus ||: A :||: BC :||.[131] Most *canzonette* have from two to four textural changes, as dictated mainly by verbal considerations.[132]

From the heterotextural *canzonetta* it was a small step to the madrigal, which appeared similarly flexible in its shifting styles from one verse to another. But perusing the collections one detects changes in emphasis. Book 1 *a* 5 gravitates towards intermediate or hybrid textures (animated homophony, or quasi-polyphony) as its main modes of discourse. Book 2 continues in the same vein,[133] yet seems to favour homophony. The tendency towards homophony is even more noticeable in Book 3: there it results, in

---

[130] See Cte: 1–2, 11, 13.

[131] All but one of the twelve bipartite *canzonette* have their second section divided textually and musically into a B transition, then a C closing part (the one exception is no. 10).

[132] Cte: 4 is unusual in maintaining a single stance from beginning to end: homophony.

[133] As in Bk 2: 3, 13–16.

many works, in passages with simultaneous declamation. Book 4 marks a
return, here and there, to the mixed chordal and imitative styles of Book 1
(and, in certain works, Book 2), as congruent with the argument, at the
beginning of this chapter, for its earlier date of composition.

As to the madrigals *a 4*, they show a stylistic propinquity to those in Book
3 *a 5* in their emphasis on homophony, be it chordal or slightly animated.
Yet, rather than couple them with Book 3, one might conceive of them, in
their frequent chordality,[134] as corresponding to the notion of the four-voice
madrigal, by the time of the early seventeenth century, as a simpler, less
artful mode of composition than the five-voice one.

A major change occurs in Book 5. In the absence of the voice parts, one
turns to the *continuo* for information. It carries 846 signs, more than Rossi
inscribed in any other collection. In content, the *continuo* acts as an
independent instrumental part, not dispensable, as was the *basso seguente*
of the earlier publications, but forming an integral part of the composition. It
is 'instrumental' in the sense that it often breaks into short phrases, extends
a single note over one or more bars, moves by leaps, and, in its rhythms,
seems overly labile, if not jerky.[135] One may assume that Book 5 took a new
compositional tack after the rather conservative traits of the previous books;
more in the direction of the seventeenth-century *concertato*, in which the
tendency was to divide the ensemble into smaller groups, to juxtapose them,
to impart clear rhythmic and melodic definition to their motifs, to charge the
writing with rhythmic energy, and, last but not least, to differentiate
between voices and *continuo*. Book 5 is more 'Baroque', no doubt, than the
composer's other collections, except for his last, the *Madrigaletti*, not to
speak of his last two instrumental books.

The change of course in Book 5 is validated by the *Madrigaletti*. There, too,
the *basso continuo* functions as a true *continuo*, in the sense that in its pace,
rhythms, and motifs it is largely different from the upper voices. What
results, in all but the last numbers (*a 3*), is the duet plus accompaniment,
or trio-sonata texture, to be found in the majority of Rossi's instrumental
works. More specifically, the *madrigaletti* tend to have their voices conceived
in homophony or light imitation, with either whole pieces or their larger
portions in the one or the other. The number of possibilities is extensive, as
corresponds to the variability of a *stile concertato*. Four pieces are written as
an imitative duet or trio more or less from beginning to end while three
adhere rather consistently to homophony.[136] Others are imitative at the
beginning; or at the beginning and in the middle; or at the beginning and
the end; or in the middle and at the end.[137] When so, their remaining

---

[134] Cf. M4: 2, 4–5, 8, 10, 12, 16–17.

[135] Cf. Bk 5: 4–5, 8–9, etc.

[136] Imitative duet or trio: Mti: 11, 13, 16, 17; homophony: 2, 6, 14.

[137] Imitative at beginning: Mti: 1, 4, 7; at beginning and in middle, 15; at beginning and end:
3, 9; in middle and at end: 5.

sections are, contrastingly, homophonic.[138] Sometimes imitation and homophony alternate with greater frequency, as in various *madrigaletti* with
protean shifts from one to another.[139] One work has a middle section in
recitative style; another harks back to the early *canzonetta* in having three
voices of equal importance.[140]

Two other textures form appendages to those already mentioned,
yet cannot be overlooked, for they confirm the modernist tendencies in
Rossi's secular repertory. The first is pseudo-monody, in the six monodic
arrangements—for voice and instrument—of madrigals 12–17 in Book 1 *a* 5:
Caccini tells us that it was 'common practice' for madrigals for several
voices to be sung by a single one.[141] Rossi's monodic versions are his only
works of the kind and, moreover, among the earliest printed ones at
large.[142] The composer may, from the start, have planned the five-voice
originals for their adaptability to a rendition by voice and instrument.
Thus, here and there, their canto tends to dominate the other parts, which,
in turn, are obliged to support it (Ex. 3.5).[143] For their full effect, one
must imagine these pseudo-monodies as garnished, in performance,
with appropriate ornaments, according to the instructions that, among
others, Bovicelli, Conforto, and Caccini provided in their vocal
manuals;[144] and as projected over the rippling accompaniment of the chitarrone (or archlute?) for which they were written (Rossi provided a full
tablature for all six works; on questions of tuning and instrumentation, see
Chapter 5).

Though Rossi did not continue in this vein, there are indications, in later
collections, of monodic influence. It may be plotted under two guises:
recitative; soloism.

Rossi's madrigals, from the first book on, contain passages in declamatory
style: they illustrate the penetration of the operatic (or monodic) recitative
into choral writing (Ex. 3.6*a*). The result has been dubbed, most aptly,
choral monody.[145] It is particularly evident in Book 3 and the madrigals *a*
4, not to speak of the Hebrew songs, in which it prevails over all other
textures.

Soloist traits may also be signalled, though to a lesser extent. Take Book 2,
for one, where, at the end of 'Sfogava con le stelle', the melismas in dotted

---

[138] Mti: 5 at the beginning; 9 in the middle; 1, 4, 7 in the middle and at the end; etc.

[139] Mti: 1, 8, and 18.

[140] Middle section in recitative: Mti: 3; three equal voices: 14.

[141] Caccini, foreword to *Nuove musiche* (1601), ed. Hitchcock, 43–56, esp. 45–6.

[142] They should be studied within the frame of monodic developments at large: cf. Fortune,
'Italian Secular Monody from 1600 to 1635'.

[143] The tendency is especially evident in Bk 1: 12–14 and part of 16.

[144] Bovicelli, *Regole, passaggi di musica, madrigali et motetti passeggiati* (1594); Conforto, *Breve et
facile maniera d'essercitarsi…a far passaggi* (1593); Caccini, as above. To these one should add
such practical collections as Brunelli's *Varii esercitii…per 1, e 2 voci, cioè soprani, contralti, tenori,
et bassi, per i quali si potrà con faciltà acquistare la dispositione per il cantare con passaggi* (1614).

[145] Newman, 'The Madrigals of Salamon de' Rossi', 126 and elsewhere.

Ex. 3.5 'Cor mio, deh non languire' (Book 1 *a* 5, no. 13, bars 17–26)

rhythms not only highlight the words 'make me amorous', but serve to strengthen the close (Ex. 3.6*b*); or Book 4, for another, where, in 'Io parto', to convey the notion of separation, the top voice is lifted above the others (Ex. 3.6*c*; after the example of the pseudo-monodies in Book 1). The real continuation of the soloist idiom is in various ornamental passages within the *madrigaletti*, some of them rather exuberant (Ex. 3.6*d*). There must have been others in (the missing vocal parts of) Book 5.

Both choral recitative and soloism, as conceived by Rossi, are examples of what has been called, more generally, 'cantar recitando': what it means, in

Ex. 3.6a 'Taci, bocca' (Book 3 *a* 5, no. 2, bars 7–11)

Ex. 3.6b 'Sfogava con le stelle' (Book 2 *a* 5, no. 2, bars 64–8)

five-voice madrigals or in pseudo-monodies, is that singing has an edge over reciting (as opposed to 'recitar cantando').[146]

The second modern-styled texture is represented by the *madrigali concertati* in Book 5, of which the last eight pieces (nos. 12–19) were so described in the *tavola*. To all appearances, the voices split into smaller ensembles, set antiphonally to similar or contrasting music. Then they came together to form a full ensemble at the end, indeed in six of the eight (nos. 13–18) the concluding section, amounting to the last third or fourth of their content, is marked 'insieme' (one can only wonder whether the word was intentionally or inadvertently omitted from nos. 12 and 19). As already

---

[146] The terms, after G. B. Doni, were explored by Pirrotta in various writings (among them *Music and Theatre from Poliziano to Monteverdi*).

Ex. 3.6c 'Io parto' (Book 4 *a* 5, no. 11, bars 13–21)

noted, the *Madrigaletti*, with their vocal dialogues, confirm the *concertato* tendency. It may be further confirmed by the instrumental works, particularly in Books 3–4, and by those Hebrew songs written for larger ensembles.

5. *Macro- and microstructures.* Of the 146 vocal works, twenty-three are strophic and another fourteen consist of two, three, four, or eight *partes*. Some of those in *partes* are, in fact, multistrophic, with their separate strophes marked *prima parte*, *seconda parte*, etc., yet performed to the same music. Others have changing music for their *partes* and, to all intents, are a composite of separate madrigals, though linked by their stylistic

Ex. 3.6d 'Vago Augelletto' (*Madrigaletti*, no. 12, bars 10–14, on 'joyous')

uniformity (thus, for example, the multistrophic *Canzon de' baci*, already discussed).

On a lower level, almost three-quarters of the secular works (107, to be exact) are through-composed, while the remainder demonstrate various repeat forms. The division corresponds more or less to that between madrigals and *madrigaletti*, on the one hand, and *canzonette*, on the other: that is, the *madrigaletti*, which, in their size and lighter texture, usually group with *canzonette*, are, with few exceptions, akin to madrigals in their formal design. Structurally, then, there seem to have been two models for Rossi's works: the *canzonetta* and the madrigal.

Repetition exists on different levels, from strophic repeats, just mentioned, to repeats of single verses. Strophic repeats occur in the multistrophic *canzonette*, of which there are seventeen examples in the *Canzonette* and three in the *Madrigaletti*. On a lower level, repeats are sometimes indicated by repeat signs surrounding whole sections, as in the same works, though now in respect to a single stanza. Thus, in the *Canzonette*, the composer uses one of two different forms: ||: A :||: B :|| or ||: A :|| B ||: C :||. He seems to prefer the first of them (occurring in twelve of the nineteen pieces), yet it is actually the second form, with B serving as a short transition between A and C, that prevailed: all but one of the ||: A :||: B :|| *canzonette* have their second section divided textually and musically into a B transition, then a C closing part, thus ||: A :||: BC :||. The endings of sections, as well as of the transitions between or within them, are marked by larger cadences (most *canzonette* have tonic cadences at the close of the first and last sections and cadences on other degrees at the close of the transitions, as accords with their 'transitional' function).[147] It might be noted that bipartite forms with repeat signs are particularly rampant among Rossi's instrumental works: the scheme ‖: A :‖: B :‖, for example, can be found in the larger part of his *sinfonie* and dances, as well as in about half the sonatas and all three *canzoni* (altogether ninety-three works out of 130).

Yet the *canzonette* do not have a monopoly on repetition, and it is on still lower levels of iteration that the distinction between *canzonetta* and madrigal as model types for structuration breaks down. True, repeat signs are rare in the madrigals.[148] Yet one finds, in fourteen of them, written-out repeats usually for the last phrase or phrases (followed, in three examples, by a codetta): some of the repeats tend to considerable length, covering four or even six lines of poetry.[149] Two other madrigals were composed as ABA' or ABC...B, in emulation of the poetry: in the first, the first two verses return, varied, at the end; in the second, the second verse returns, unchanged, as the last.[150] In other madrigals, textual-musical repeats again reinforce the close, yet their music is varied by melodic, rhythmic, and, most often, tonal (sequential) changes.

Were one to summarize the procedure in the madrigal books, the following changes seem pertinent: Books 1–2 have a small, but significant number of works with literal textual-musical repeats of one or more final verses, as does, moreover, Book 4, which thereby evidences a structural propinquity to the earlier books;[151] Book 3 and the madrigals *a 4* are, except for varied repeats of their closing material, almost completely through-composed; and Book 5, to judge from its *continuo*, is similarly through-composed, with one exception ('Sì ch'io t'amai', cast as ABB, with the repeat referring, it would seem, to the last five lines of the eleven-line poem). Thus the madrigals fluctuate between greater and lesser repeats, with Books 1–2 the standard for the one and Book 3 for the other.

The *madrigaletti* have a logic of their own. In their poetry and music, they usually fall into three sections, with breaks between them and often contrasting textures. So far they resemble *canzonette*. They differ from them, however, in the tendency to build a longer final section, for the concluding verse or verses, with multiple textual-musical repeats: in some examples the

---

[147] Yet four *canzonette* have a V cadence at the end of their first section. As for transitional cadences, six occur on V, five on IV, three each on III and VI, and one on VII.

[148] Except for Bk 1: 17, with a repeat sign for the last two lines (bars 33–46), followed by a 6-bar coda; and Bk 2: 5, with a repeat sign in the *continuo* (though not in the vocal parts) for the last two lines (bars 29–42, restated as 43–56).

[149] For examples, see Bk 1: 12, in which bars 26–44 (three lines) recur as 45–63; Bk 4: 16, in which bars 22–40 (four lines) recur as 41–59; and Bk 4: 5, in which bars 16–32 (six lines) recur as 32–48.

[150] Bk 2: 7 ('Spasmo s'io non ti veggio, | Moro se tu non m'ami...Spasmo s'io non ti sfido, | Moro s'io non t'uccido') and 12 (in the *prima pars* only: 'Con la sua forz'in mar, in terr', in cielo | Vince ogni cosa Amore...Vince ogni cosa Amore').

[151] Cf. Bk 4: 5 (bars 16–32/32–48); 16 (bars 22–40/41–59); 18 (bars 13–32/32–52); 19 (bars 27–44/45–62).

final section averages from 30 to 37 per cent of the total and in two it averages almost 50 per cent.[152] In addition to these extended, highly iterative final sections, there are many varied repeats of single verses as a whole or in part, far more in fact than in any of the composer's previous collections: the quicker rhythmic pace (in quavers) and the interlocking duet writing of the *madrigaletti* seem to invite greater repetition.

Other peculiarities may be recited for the *madrigaletti*. Certain works have a double exposition.[153] 'Messaggier di speranza', a *ballata*, carries a repeat sign for its last three lines (the *volta* and *ripresa*) and, moreover, the indication 'presto' for the third of them, the only tempo marking in Rossi's vocal repertory. The three strophic *canzonette* are written, after the example of the *canzonette* in Opus 1, as bipartite forms, with signed repeats of each part, yet with the addition, in two of the three, of an instrumental *ritornello* (which, motivically, grows out of the vocal material).[154] An innovation in Rossi's collections,[155] the *ritornello* serves, of course, as another means of organization, demarcating the various stanzas and imposing overall unity on the whole.

In the three *dialoghi* for eight voices, in various madrigal books, unique structural solutions are found to the alternation of different ensembles. These are musical, not textual dialogues, though the composer simulates a spoken dialogue through choral antiphony. In 'Riede la primavera', at the end of Book 3, the form is trisectional, corresponding to the division of the poetry into lines 1–3, 4–6, and 7–9, as follows (diagonals indicate divided choruses, capitals full-voice ones):

section 1	a/a	b/b	C		
section 2	d/d	e/e'			
section 3	‖: F	g/g	gh/i	j/j :‖	K (= codetta)

The plan of the *dialogo* 'Amor, se pur degg'io', at the end of the madrigals *a 4*, provides for the strategic placement of full ensembles near the opening, in the middle, and at the end (a/- A' b/b' c/d e/e' F g/h i/j K). To the phrase repeats the composer adds verbal ones, as in the word *ferrisci* in line 6: it is multiply reiterated in the separate voices to drive home the idea of 'striking'. As for the *dialogo* at the end of Book 5, it is even more impressive, for each of the two choruses has its own *continuo*. From the two continuo parts, the design may be reconstructed, more or less, as follows: *prima parte*, a/a' B c/d E; *seconda parte*, f/- G -/h I.

The only reservation one might have about these *dialoghi* is that there seems to be a certain disproportion between the slight size and triviality of

---

[152] 30–37%: Mti: 4, 7, 16, 11, pt. 2 of 18, and 1, in ascending order; almost 50%: 5–6.

[153] Mti: 1, 9, 13.

[154] Mti: 13–15. They differ from the *canzonette*, Op. 1, in having each of their stanzas written out in full (see below). In no. 13, the *ritornello* derives from the opening motive; in no. 15, it elaborates the closing one.

[155] There is one other example: his theatre piece 'Spazziam pronte' (see Ch. 6).

their poetry and the imposing ensemble used for its transmission: especially is this true in the dialogue at the end of the madrigals *a 4*, where *cori spezzati* are exploited to lend grandeur to an otherwise insignificant eight-line poem, which, in any case, the composer does not sustain beyond sixty-seven bars. The problem of disproportion will come up again in discussing the large-scale sonata that closes Book 4 of the instrumental works.

There is still another kind of structural articulation in the secular vocal works: the shaping of their music from one or two skeletal motifs. The usual conception of the madrigal is one of phrases gradually unfolded and so individuated as to conform to changes in the content of their verses. Rossi, however, never lets the specificity of words overrule the general theme: he follows the words without overemphasizing them, attempting, through a consistent elaboration of motivic material, to preserve the message of the poem in its integrity. Thus, from the first publication on, there is a tendency to develop certain ideas for their intervallic or rhythmic implications. Take the *canzonetta* 'Se gl'amorosi sguardi', where the initial repeated-note motif, in step-wise descent, infiltrates into the remaining phrases, sometimes in melodic inversion (Ex. 3.7*a*); or the madrigal 'Lumi miei', in Book 2, where the rising third (x) followed by a descending leap of a fourth (y) is transformed into a variety of subtly analogous shapes (Ex. 3.7*b*); or the *madrigaletto* 'Non è quest'il ben mio?', where the rhythmic and melodic figure of the opening bars, including its repeated note ending, occurs throughout, as a unifying device, in related forms (Ex. 3.7*c*).

Thus to the thematic logic of the verses the composer imparts a musical logic: it derives from the verses, yet has an existence of its own; it supports the verses, yet adheres to rules of compositional coherence. The separate madrigals have their separate stories, which can be reconstructed by considering their music from textual or inherently musical points of view. We are on the brink of a new period in music, where the composers carved out *Figuren*, both in response to the text and in compliance with demands of musical cogency. Joachim Burmeister's analysis of one of Lasso's motets for its specifically 'musical' content is relevant to developments within the literature at large.[156]

6. *Relation between poetry and music.* The relation may be considered on three levels: syntactic, accentual, and semantic. Though Rossi's vocal works, as emphasized, can be considered *qua* music, still it was for the sake of their texts that they were composed. Because his music is texturally transparent, it conveys the words in all their structural and thematic specificity, as detailed in the first part of this chapter.

Syntactically, the music follows the divisions of the poetry, marking them with musical caesurae of different weight: half cadences, cadences on a first

---

[156] The motet is 'In me transierunt' (discussed in *Musica poetica*, 1606); see Palisca, '*Ut oratoria musica*'.

Ex. 3.7a 'Se gl'amorosi sguardi' (*Canzonette*, no. 6, bars 1–4, 8–10, 20–3)

inversion triad, and full cadences, on different degrees of the mode, with the tonic reserved for ends of sections and other degrees for intermediate points of articulation. Accentually, the lines are shaped to reflect the verbal stresses, with accented syllables set to longer values or higher pitches or sometimes to two or more notes forming a short melisma. Semantically, the music underlines the words by presenting them straightforwardly in one or more textures with suitable rhythmic or tonic inflection of the melodies in response to the changing sentiments.

Since the text is so clearly projected on all three levels, it would seem superfluous to illustrate the compositional procedure by more specific examples: what Rossi did is what most other madrigalists, conscious of the primacy of the text, did in their own works, except that Rossi practised discretion as the better part of valour. The discussion will focus instead on two aspects of the word-tone symbiosis: the accommodation of music to

Ex. 3.7*b* 'Lumi miei' (Book 2 *a* 5, no. 9, canto, bars 1–4, 8–10, 12–28, 31–3, 36–9)

successive stanzas of the *canzonette*; and, as a more specific demonstration of the composer's 'discretion', his use of word painting.

In the *canzonette*, the music was adapted to the words of the first stanza only, and but for minor infractions was exemplary in observing their prosody. After the first stanza, the singers were left on their own to fit the additional ones, printed at the bottom of the page, to the same music. They no doubt encountered many difficulties, for the additional stanzas, when correlated with the music, are replete with wrongly accented words and poorly articulated phrases. 'Torna dolce', for example, has, in its second to fourth stanzas, twenty-seven misplaced accents (spread over the three voices): 'su*bi*ta' (2), 'spir*to*' (1), '*ai*ta' (1), 'vi*va*' (3), 'luce' (3), 'chia*ro*' (3), 'es*ser*' (3), 'trop*po*' (4), '*pun*genti' (1), 'tor*na*' (2), 'sospi*ri*' (1), 'ar*di*' (1), 'sor*da*' (2). Whole syntactical units have to be split to match them to their musical phrases, hence 'e non mi dar/dolore'; 'Hora ti chiegg'/aita'; 'Se vuoi ch'io mi/consoli'; 'De l'amor tuo, o mia/lucente Stella'; 'Chè come ad altri non/ho dato il core'; 'Torna, ti/priego'; 'Così non/vivo'. Elsewhere among the *canzonette* vowels have to be added to words (e.g. 'amor' → 'amore'), or dropped from them (e.g. 'struggevi' → 'struggev''), or words

Ex. 3.7c 'Non è quest'il ben mio?' (*Madrigaletti*, no. 6, bars 1–5, 8–10, 14–19)

have to have their syllables split between phrases (e.g. 'fie-/ ra'), or single notes have to be divided (when there are fewer notes than syllables): they are the only way to get the text to fit the music.

In the light of the difficulties in adjusting later stanzas to the music of the first, one wonders whether they were sung at all or whether it made any difference to the composer if they were. When Rossi really wanted later stanzas properly performed, he took steps to assure they would be, as in 'Gradita libertà' and 'Vo' fuggir':[157] there the same music is written out in full for the separate stanzas, with various small changes made for its suitable adaptation to the words. Are we dealing with two different approaches to the multistrophic song: one in which confusion must necessarily prevail, which goes against all humanistically-inspired doctrines of a seemly accentual and syntactic relationship between words and music; and another in which order rules their accommodation, as it ordinarily would in a monostrophic work? No easy answers are forthcoming, but the musical evidence is uncomfortable, for it forces us to rethink the matter of proper accommodation (what is proper?) and of how much of a stanzaic work was actually performed or intended to be heard.

As regards word painting, Rossi was, as said, more interested in preserving the general tone of the text than in highlighting its individual words. The poet Stigliani spoke of musicians imitating happy words in sad poetry or sad words in happy poetry, only to 'damage the affection that dominates the subject, for they introduce into it part of its contrary'.[158] That is precisely what Rossi tends not to do. Thus, as a rule, one finds few blatant pictorialisms. Rather, Rossi underlines evocative words by modest rhythmic, melodic, or harmonic changes, as for example on 'ahi che languire, ahi che perire', where he slows down the movement and introduces E flats;[159] on 'in quest'estrema mia dura partita', where, somewhat more extensively than he is wont, he uses suspensions and, towards the end, decelerates the movement, has the quinto expand in a melisma, and colours the harmony with alterations (B natural, E flat; Ex. 3.8).

Though Rossi uses little linear chromaticism, and if he does, it is of a conjunct variety, he does exploit the melisma, on occasion, as an expressive device. Summarizing his procedure here, one might note two or three stages in its application. The first stage is in Books 1–2, where the melisma emphasizes a select number of evocative words: laughter, song, turning,

---

[157] Mti: 13, 15.

[158] Stigliani, treatise on poetry in *Libro primo del Rimario nel qual si contiene il trattato del verso italiano*, esp. 211–16 ('Perciochè avvenendo spesso ch'in un componimento doloroso sieno molte parole allegre, e che in uno allegro ne sieno molte dolorose: i musici con immitar la particolare significanza di quelle, danneggiano l'affetto che domina il soggetto, perchè vi metton parte del suo contrario'). On Stigliani's contribution to 16th-c. literature, see Menghini, *Tommaso Stigliani*.

[159] Bk 2: 4, bars 16–19. See, also, Bk 3: 3, bars 1–7, where, on the words *Amarilli crudele*, the composer divides the ensemble (three upper voices in imitation, two lower ones in slower, fairly simultaneous motion) and introduces five G sharps.

Ex. 3.8   'Io moro' (Book 3 *a* 5, no. 1, bars 20–34)

dispatching, blessed, faith, cruelty, grief. Some of these melismas can be rather elaborate, as the one for 'laughter' in Ex. 3.9.

Stage 2 begins with Book 3 or the madrigals *a 4*, depending, again, on which came first, and continues into Book 4. Here the melisma seems to crystallize into three varieties: (1) running scalar figures in quavers, set to a single syllable (Ex. 3.10*a*); (2) lively quaver patterns, with each quaver having its own syllable (Ex. 3.10*b*); and (3) expansive melismas, as those in Books 1–2 (Ex. 3.10*c*).

The words that carry the melisma denote love, as conveyed through kissing, smiling/laughing, singing, breathing, burning; or movement, as conveyed through turning, playing, fleeing, trembling; or general states of

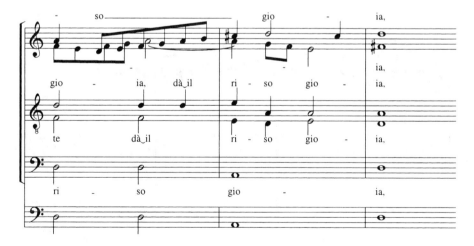

Ex. 3.9 'S'io miro in te' (Book 1 *a* 5, no. 3, bars 28–34)

mind (happiness, cruelty) or body (life, death). Yet they are usually enmeshed in the otherwise unruffled rhythmic and melodic content of the madrigals as a whole. Where Books 3–4 are fairly uniform in their procedure, the madrigals *a 4* differ from them in having the smallest number of melismas in any of the three categories, in conformity, perhaps, to Rossi's conception of four-part writing as more reserved or restrained than writing *a 5*.

Ex. 3.10*a* 'Io moro' (Book 3 *a 5*, no. 1, bars 35–7, canto, on 'kiss')

Ex. 3.10*b* 'O baci aventurosi' (Book 3 *a 5*, no. 13, bars 232–5, on 'escapes while murmuring')

Ex. 3.10*c* 'Io rido' (Book 3 *a 5*, no. 8, bars 26–30)

Stage 3 is marked by the *Madrigaletti*. Though, as in the earlier books, melismas are still few and far apart, they are now invested with new technical demands, in line with the more soloist orientation of the contents. Thus some of the melismas have rapid semiquaver figuration in one or usually both voices of the duet (see Ex. 3.6d above).

By contrast, the melismas in the four- and five-voice madrigals appear much tamer. No wonder, their context is not the modern style of the *Madrigaletti* but sixteenth-century counterpoint, typified, in its classic Zarlinian presentation, by vocal equanimity.

Despite his aversion to obtrusive word painting, Rossi connects with the humanist currents that, in large part, informed Italian music of both the Renaissance and the early Baroque.[160] He was as much concerned with verbal considerations as Zarlino believed Willaert to be in the mid-sixteenth century or Monteverdi believed himself to be in the early seventeenth.[161] Yet he treated texts not with the often intricate contrapuntal devices of the Renaissance polyphonists and not with the highly variegated melodic, rhythmic, harmonic, and textural gestures of the more dramatic sixteenth- and seventeenth-century madrigalists. It is not that he was less intent than they on underlining their accentual, syntactical, and affective qualities. Rather, his means were unassuming: he exploited diatonic scales, simple rhythms, conjunct melodies, and principally homophonic textures to serve his ends.

Rossi's secular works should be pondered from new perspectives, whereby their seeming conventionalities lend to reversed interpretations: the composer's solicitude for the audibility of the text concurs with the most forward-looking tendencies of his time. By assuming a more relaxed attitude towards vocal music, Rossi seems, after his fashion, to have advanced its composition by emphasizing the continuities between sixteenth- and seventeenth-century practices.

The new principle of the words as the 'mistress of music', according to which Monteverdi explained how the *seconda pratica* differed from the *prima*, was not new at all. Indeed, it formed the cornerstone of the *prima pratica*: it is enough to peruse the writings of the earlier theorists and the works of the earlier composers to discern its ubiquity.[162] Where, in applying the principle, the Renaissance composers resorted mainly to polyphony, the Baroque ones did mainly to monody or *stile concertato*, at least at the beginning. But not for long: counterpoint was hardly the exclusive property of the early

---

[160] On the pervasiveness of humanist conceptions in the writings of the Renaissance theorists and their relevance to the *seconda pratica*, see, at length, Harrán, *In Search of Harmony*, esp. ch. 9 on 'music and rhetoric' and ch. 10 on 'Galilei and the new humanism'.

[161] Zarlino, in *Le istitutioni harmoniche* (1558), and Monteverdi, in the forewords to Bk 5 (1605) and the *Scherzi musicali* (1607). On Willaert as a paradigm for the 'expressive composer', again as conceived by Zarlino, see Harrán, *In Search of Harmony*, esp. ch. 7 on 'music and expression'. On basic concepts in Monteverdi's musical thought, see Ehrmann, *Claudio Monteverdi*.

[162] Cf. Harrán, *Word-Tone Relations in Musical Thought*, 76–101, 161–304.

composers, rather it was preserved, and heightened, in the Baroque, to the extent of becoming one of its most salient characteristics. If Rossi abided by counterpoint, he did so not in adherence to an earlier tradition, but because the earlier tradition formed an integral part of contemporary practice.

The story of Italian Baroque music, as of Baroque music at large, turns about the different ways the *stile antico* was incorporated into the *moderno*. One need only point to Bach's magnificent contrapuntal inventions at the end of the period to show how deeply the old penetrated the new and how dependent the new was on the old for its modes of composition.

Vocal composers of the earlier and later periods were usually concerned with conveying the words as expressively and, counting on the performers, as effectively as possible. So much of their music, including Rossi's, is indebted to the *verbum* for its substance. With Rossi, moreover, the indebtedness carries over into his Hebrew songs, now based, in large part, on the *verbum sacrum*.

Thus the idea that Rossi's homophonic madrigals, with restrained rhythmic gestures and a chiefly diatonic shaping of melodies, denote *antico* might be overturned to demonstrate the contrary: namely, by refraining from complications, the composer strove for a clear and communicative transmission of his works so as to impress their poetic contents more forcefully on the listeners. In his Hebrew collection, he described the listeners he had in mind as those discriminating persons 'who test words'.[163]

[163] From the composer's dedication.

4

Instrumental Music

O F Rossi's four instrumental collections, the first two came out almost together (1607–8) while the third was separated by a break of nine years from the fourth (1613, 1622). All four were intended for string instruments, with the exception of the first, which offers the option of playing the upper parts on cornetts.[1]

Books 1–2 contain some of the earliest works to be published as instrumental chamber music, or according to Agazzari's designation, 'dolci conserti' (to be contrasted with his other category, the 'conserti strepitosi e grandi').[2] A tradition of instrumental music seems to have become established in Mantua by the time of Rossi's first books. Indeed, a ducal collection of instruments is known from the 1550s, if not earlier.[3] Yet there were no instrumental music publications of Mantuan composers until Rossi's, which, in their many *sinfonie*, might have been stimulated by the theatrical activities for the nuptials of the crown prince Francesco.[4] Ever since Hugo Riemann, who emphasized Books 1–2 as the earliest publications to contain compositions for the 'trio' medium, the composer has been characterized as an innovator.[5] It was Manfred Bukofzer's contention, for example, that with Book 1 Rossi 'established' the trio sonata, 'the classic medium of Baroque chamber music'.[6] True, Venice was crucial in the early development of the sonata, as Peter Allsop demonstrates in a recent study. Yet he concedes that 'the only comparable development—remarkable for its precocity if not for the quantity of its contribution—was that of the dukedom of Mantua, where from 1607 until 1622 Salamon Rossi produced four volumes of instrumental music mainly for the "trio" medium'.[7]

Though the four books share many similarities, they divide into Books 1–2 and 3–4, with the second pair illustrating novel formal and stylistic conceptions in part of its contents, chiefly the sonatas. Books 1–2 are close to each

---

[1] On all matters of performance, see Ch. 5.

[2] Represented by works of the Venetians, particularly Andrea and Giovanni Gabrieli. For Agazzari's two categories, see his *Del sonare sopra 'l basso* (1607).

[3] For information on the collection's curators, including, for the years 1553–9, Giovanni Maria de Rossi (a Christian), see variously Fenlon, *Music and Patronage in Sixteenth-Century Mantua*, 67, and Parisi, 'Ducal Patronage of Music in Mantua, 1587–1627', 538.

[4] On this point, see Hansell, 'The Origins of the Italian Trio Sonata', 116–19.

[5] Riemann, *Handbuch der Musikgeschichte* (2 vols.; Leipzig, 1904–13), ii. 86.

[6] Bukofzer, *Music in the Baroque Era* (New York, 1947), 53.

[7] Allsop, *The Italian 'Trio' Sonata*, 8.

other in their overall length and the number of their works;[8] so are Books 3–4, but now there is a substantial expansion, indeed they more than double the length of the previous books.[9]

All in all, Rossi published 130 instrumental works, or actually fewer, for nine appeared twice (in Book 2) and five *gagliarde* were paired with five *correnti* (in Book 4), which leaves a net repertory of 116. The majority, or 103 works, were composed for three voices: two melody instruments and a chitarrone or other foundation instrument. Books 1–2, however, admit a small number of works for four voices (8) and for alternative ensembles of three or five (13) or (in Book 2 only) three or four (5). Book 4 ends with a sonata for six voices: four violins and two chitarroni. The composer seems then, in his first two books, to have been experimenting with diverse group-ings until deciding on three voices as his preferred ensemble. All works are complete, but for one: a *balletto*, transmitted in its first section only[10] and, in all likelihood, originally composed for voices. It made its way into the instrumental collections for one reason: to fill in the empty space on the last page of Book 1.

Of the various instrumental types, two run through the four collections, viz. the *sinfonia* and the *gagliarda*. The *canzona* is confined to Book 2, while the sonata, *corrente*, and *brando* are to Books 3–4. True, there was a single sonata in Book 1, yet formally it might be designated a *ricercare*. Rossi's instrumental works divide then into six types, his favourite being the *sinfonia* (65 examples), followed by the *gagliarda* (23), the sonata (20), the *corrente* (13), the *brando* (5), and the *canzona* (3).

In reality, Rossi wrote more music for sonatas (1,703 bars) than he did for *sinfonie* (1,577 bars). The *sinfonie* formed the larger part of the earlier collec-tions (fifty out of their sixty-two works), yet were displaced by sonatas in the later ones: the *sinfonia* fell from (only) nine examples in Book 3 to six in Book 4 while the sonata rose in the same books from six to thirteen. Or in actual bulk: the *sinfonia* constituted 14 per cent of Books 3–4 while the sonata did 51 per cent, showing clearly where the composer's preference lay.

Another way of considering Rossi's instrumental works is through their basic division into abstract instrumental types (*sinfonia, canzona,* sonata) versus dances (*gagliarda, corrente, brando, balletto*). The abstract types are represented by more than double the number of dances (88/42) and, except for the *canzona*, would seem to reflect the 'modern' style in the composer's repertory (the dances, by contrast, may be traced to Renaissance models). Where the dances were probably used as such in court or domestic festiv-ities, the abstract types fulfilled other functions. *Sinfonie*, relatively short,

[8] Length: S1, 614 bars; S2, 860. Number of works: S1, 27; S2, 35 (of the latter, 9 appear first *a 3*, then again for the same ensemble plus an optional two voices, thus a net total of 26 works).

[9] S3 runs to 1,470 bars (and has 33 works) and S4 to 1,762 bars (and has 35).

[10] It complements his one vocal *balletto* ('Spazziam pronte'), written for the sacred play *La Maddalena* (see Ch. 6).

may have introduced vocal or instrumental works in similar festivities or in theatrical productions.[11] *Canzoni* and sonatas, sometimes of considerable dimensions, are likely to have been played for various audiences, including those in the *accademie*, as music *per se*, or if you wish, 'concert music', independent of any function beyond being heard and judged on their own merits. The dances evidence their contextual associations in their titles, which carry various references to persons and events ('la Massara', 'Amor perfetto', 'l'Incognita', 'la Favorita', etc.). Of the twenty-seven inscriptions in the instrumental collections, all but four occur in *gagliarde*.[12]

General Aspects of Composition

Rossi's instrumental works can be approached in two ways: summarily, as a repertory; specifically, as generic types. The one presupposes the other, so that any discussion must inevitably deal with both. Here an attempt will be made to state the characteristics of the repertory as a whole, though clearly the repertory, as a composite, is defined by its different genres. The discussion thus oscillates, dialectically, between higher (repertorial) and lower (generic) levels of analysis.

1. *Size of works*. Classified by length, the repertory divides into three categories: the shortest works, consisting of *sinfonie* and the various dances; medium-sized ones, or the *canzoni*; and still longer ones, or the sonatas. Since the *canzoni* are represented by only three examples, they may fairly be ignored, which leaves the two basic categories of short and long. How short is 'short', how long is 'long'?

Each genre sets its own length, yet allows room for variation. The *sinfonia*, for example, ranges from about twenty to thirty bars, depending on the particular piece and more significantly on the collection in which it figures: there is an increase in its size from Books 1–2, where it averages twenty-two bars, to Books 3–4, where it averages thirty-one. Thus 'early' and 'later' varieties of *sinfonia* may tentatively be delineated among Rossi's works. Its expansion, modest as it is, may be due to the influence of the sonata.

Still within the 'short' category, the *gagliarda* ranges from about twenty-three to thirty-three bars, though slightly longer examples (up to thirty-eight bars) occur in Book 3. Its average length for the four volumes is twenty-six. Choreographically, the number of bars is actually half, for two bars of three minims are combined to form a larger one of six; but for purposes of comparison with other genres, the *gagliarda* has been defined here by its music *as written*, and not *as performed*. *Correnti* and *brandi* are, by this account, slightly longer, averaging for Books 3–4—the only books in which they appear—thirty-four bars.

---

[11] Cf. Troilo, *Sinfonie, scherzi*, etc. (1608); Bernardi, *Concerti accademici* (1615).
[12] As against two each in *sinfonie* (S3: 38–9) and sonatas (S3: 2, 6).

From the *sinfonia* and dances there is a leap to the intermediate and, as said, rather negligible category of the *canzona*, averaging about forty-nine bars, then on to the third category, or the sonata. Sonatas vary in length, in Books 3–4, from fifty-one to 160 bars,[13] or an average of eighty-six bars. Yet no such average can be sustained, for, in reality, the sonatas, in their length, demonstrate two varieties: shorter ones, averaging about seventy bars, and longer ones, averaging about 131. Morphologically, the (trio) sonata, of all the forms mentioned so far, is the most open, subject to changes of proportion in the works of Rossi and, as known from its development in the early seventeenth century, of others, among them Buonamente, Castello, Fontana, and Marini.

2. *Modes.*   Rossi's preferred mode, in all four collections, is Dorian on G (45 works), followed by Mixolydian (33), Lydian with B flat (20), (untransposed) Dorian (13), Aeolian (7), and Phrygian (3). There remain a number of 'special' modes, some of them transposed, others constituting major or minor scales, used each in two examples (D major, D minor, E minor) or in one (Ionian, C minor, G minor). Noteworthy is the predominance of works on the *finalis* G (altogether 79, or about 60 per cent of the repertory). While Dorian on G and Mixolydian maintain similar percentages throughout the four books, Lydian suffers a sizeable drop in Books 3–4, where it is replaced by works in Phrygian and the various 'special' modes just mentioned, none of which appeared in the earlier books. The composer seems, in the later ones, to be searching for a new tonal orientation, according to which major and minor scales inchoately substitute for the traditional modes. These 'new' modes enter the repertory mainly through the dances. Thus it is in the *gagliarde* and *correnti* that one finds C minor, D major, E minor, and G minor.[14]

The disparity between the earlier and later collections is confirmed, moreover, by the tendency towards major modes in the former and minor in the latter. What this means is hard to say, beyond the conclusion: changing times, changing modal preferences. In Books 1–2, for example, Rossi favours Mixolydian, Lydian, and Ionian over Dorian on G, Dorian, and Aeolian, by thirty-four to twenty-eight examples; in Books 3–4, he reverses his preferences, rather conspicuously, by forty-three minor works to twenty major ones.

3. *Metres.*   Rossi employs three kinds of metres: duple (44 works), triple (52), and mixed (34). Here his instrumental works differ noticeably from his Italian ones, where duple metre prevails.

Duple metre is designated by C, except for its replacement by ₵ in three *brandi*[15] and, often, after sections in triple metre in *sinfonie* and sonatas. But

---

[13] Were the longer sonatas in 3/2 to be counted in duple metre, they would extend to 225 bars.

[14] C min.: S3: Gagl. 3. D maj.: S4: Gagl. 2 and its *corrente*. E min.: S4: Gagl. 5 and its *corrente*. G min.: S4: Gagl. 1.

[15] S3: 24–6.

the original signature is not always an indicator of the actual metre, indeed, C, in several *sinfonie* and sonatas, stands for 3/2 (a typical early seventeenth-century convention).[16]

Except for the *brando*, the dances (*gagliarda*, *corrente*) are all in triple metre, as are ten of the fifty *sinfonie* in Books 1–2. With the inclusion of many more dances in Books 3–4, it follows that the same two books show a sizeable increase of works in triple metre, indeed, they more than double those in the earlier books.

Sinfonie may have anywhere from one to three metres, sonatas anywhere from one to five. Sonata 2 in Book 3, for example, has the succession C/3/ ₵/3/₵.

The question of how the various metres are to be read in performance will be treated in Chapter 5.

4. *Counterpoint.*   Building on his experience in writing vocal works for 3–5 voices,[17] Rossi approached the relatively easier task of writing for two voices plus chitarrone with a deft hand. All in all, some twenty examples of consecutive parallels can be tabulated in the four collections (compared to twenty-seven among his secular vocal works), excluding several more, less reprehensible, between the two *continuo* basses of his six-voice sonata (similar bass parallels appear in his eight-voice Italian and Hebrew works).

A comparison with the vocal works is revealing. In the madrigals, the parts move for the most part in minims and crotchets, and they seem to disport themselves with intervallic variety, while remaining within the bounds of contrapuntal propriety. The *canzonette* and *madrigaletti* are another matter: there the rhythmic activity often moves down a level, to reside in crotchets and quavers. Intervallically, the difference can be perceived in the tendency towards indirect, i.e. mediated fifths or octaves on succeeding minims (Ex. 4.1).

Ex. 4.1   'Donna, il vostro bel viso' (*Canzonette*, no. 11, bars 6–8)

---

[16] *Sinfonie*: S2: 8–9, 17–18, 25 (= 8, i.e. another version of no. 8), 28 (= 9), 29 (= 18); S3: 3; S4: 6. Sonatas: S3: 3, 5; S4: 6, 10.

[17] Assuming, as we have, that his madrigals *a* 4 (1614) were composed around the time of his first books *a* 5 (see Ch. 3).

The instrumental works resemble *canzonette* and *madrigaletti*, though now the contrapuntal infractions are not confined to crotchets, but occur on quavers and semiquavers as well. Thus indirect consecutives lurk in the voices of rhythmically slower and faster pieces, as characteristic of a particularly instrumental approach to voice leading (Ex. 4.2*a–b*).

The eighteen works for alternative voice combinations *si placet* (i.e. should the performers so choose)—thirteen for 5/3 voices, the rest for 4/3—are another matter: they were originally written for three voices, and as such they work very well. Then the composer decided to graft onto them another

Ex. 4.2*a*   Sinfonia 14 (Book 1, no. 14, bars 9–13)

Ex. 4.2*b* Sonata 3 'sopra l'Aria della Romanesca' (Book 3, no. 3, bars 6–11, 50–2)

Ex. 4.3 Sinfonia 3 'a 4 et a 3 si placet' (Book 2, no. 25, bars 1–4)

one or two voices, the result being various gaucheries of voice leading, among them inadmissible parallels[18] (Ex. 4.3).[19]

These *si placet* works form a separate category, subject, contrapuntally, to its own laws. They differ, moreover, from Rossi's two *si placet* vocal works, one a *madrigaletto*, the other a Hebrew song, in which the extra voice was carefully co-ordinated with the others. Two degrees of optionality may thus be detected in Rossi's repertory: one in which contrasting ensembles for one and the same work are contrapuntally viable, another in which the choice of a larger one is at the expense of intervallic rectitude.

5. *Forms.* Two formal levels may be distinguished: the overall form, as determined by its number of sections; the internal parcellation, as determined by repetitions of *ostinato* patterns or basic themes. Here the discussion will be confined to overall forms, with their internal parcellation considered under the section 'From *sinfonia* to sonata'.

Most instrumental works—ninety-two, to be exact—are in two sections (AB), with a repeat of each. Among them are all the *correnti*, the three *canzoni*,the majority of *sinfonie*, six sonatas, all but three of the *gagliarde*, and four of the five *brandi*. One *sinfonia* modifies the form by adding a coda. Seven sonatas modify it further by having a long first section A, unrepeated, then a short closing section B, repeated, thus A ||: B :||.[20]

---

[18] Seven in S1, seventeen in S2.

[19] See, for parallel fifths, canto 1 and alto, bars 1–2, and alto and bass, bar 2; and for awkward voice leading, all voices in relation to alto.

[20] *Sinfonia* with coda: S3: Sinf. 9. Sonatas in AB, with B repeated: S3: Son. 3–6; S4: Son. 6, 11, and the sonata *a 4* plus two chitarroni.

Trisectional works (ABC) are few. Either they have A and C repeated, with B acting as a transition, thus ‖: A :‖ B ‖: C :‖ (three *sinfonie*); or they have all three sections repeated, thus ‖: A :‖: B :‖: C :‖ (one *brando*, three *gagliarde*).[21]

There remain twenty-two works in one section, restricted to *sinfonie* and sonatas.[22] The *sinfonie* are so short that they could have been repeated one or more times, depending on the function they were meant to fulfil (marking a change of scene in an *intermedio*, accompanying a procession, introducing a vocal or an instrumental work, etc.) or on the inclination of the performers. Thus the hypothetical form AAAA, etc., may be surmised; and, in fact, in one monopartite *sinfonia*, a repeat sign was indicated.[23] In the six mono-partite sonatas there is no possibility of large-scale repetition, for they unfold in a sequence of short-term variations.

That leaves one more sonata so labelled at the end of Book 1; or perhaps mislabelled.[24] Unlike any of the sonatas in Books 3–4, it seems closer, in its four-voice imitative writing, to the imitative portions of the three four-voice *canzoni* in Book 2. Yet where the *canzoni* are in two parts, with repeats of each, and have changing textures (imitative, homophonic), changing themes, and (in two of them) changing metres, the sonata in Book 1 comprises a single (unrepeated) section and is otherwise uniform in its components. Perhaps it is best designated a (monothematic) *ricercare*, after similar examples in Claudio Merulo's *Primo libro de ricercari* 4 v. (1574).[25] As such, it constitutes the only work of its kind in Rossi's repertory (Ex. 4.4).

The confusion between sonata, *canzona*, and *ricercare* is not peculiar to Rossi. One finds it everywhere in the contemporary literature: thus Cesario Gussago wrote *Sonate* 4, 6, 8 v. (1608) that are in one section with no contrasts and so rhythmically staid as to suggest the vocal motet as a model; Antonio Mortaro wrote *Canzoni da sonare* 4 v. (1600) that are, but for three examples, in one section and, again, with no contrasts; Floriano Canale published a collection of *Canzoni* (1600), of which a number are actually *ricercari*;[26] and so on.[27]

6. *Textures.* Various textures are employed, from imitative, in the *canzoni*, to chordal, in dances and certain *sinfonie*, with intermediate gradations: animated homophony, pseudo-imitation. The preferred texture is a duet

---

[21] For ‖: A :‖ B ‖: C :‖, see S1: Sinf. 14 *a* 3, Sinf. 1–2 *a* 5/3. For ‖: A :‖: B :‖: C :‖, see S1: Gagl. 2 *a* 4; S3: Br. 3, Gagl. 1, 3.

[22] *Sinfonie*: S1: Sinf. 2–4, 6–8, 11, 13 *a* 3; S2: Sinf. 5, 7, 11, 18 *a* 3, Sinf. 2 *a* 4/3, Sinf. 3 *a* 5/3; S4: Sinf. 4. Sonatas: S4: 5, 7–10, 12.

[23] S2: 11.

[24] As evidence of a certain confusion over its identity, it is designated a sonata in all parts but the tenor, which has it as a *sinfonia*.

[25] Two other books followed (1607, 1608); see Bibliography.

[26] See Bibliography for various eds. of Gussago, Mortaro, and Canale.

[27] On the uncertainty of generic designations in the early Baroque, see Allsop, *The Italian 'Trio' Sonata*, ch. 3 ('Genre and Function'), esp. 47–50.

Ex. 4.4   Sonata (properly *ricercare*; Book 1, no. 20, bars 1–10)

Ex. 4.5   Sonata 4 'sopra l'Aria di Ruggiero' (Book 3, no. 4, bars 82–8)

with *continuo* accompaniment. It was already evident in the three-voice *sinfonie* of Books 1–2. Yet by Book 3 the duet assumed virtuoso traits in the sonatas and parts of the *sinfonie*, with running semiquaver passages reeled off between the voices (Ex. 4.5).

Book 3 marks a stylistic divide in Rossi's instrumental works: the sonata, particularly the variation sonata, engendered a new mode of writing, based on a clearer differentiation between duet and *continuo* in content and function. By comparison with the more conservatively written Books 1–2, Rossi's last two books strike one as being in *stile moderno*. The composer seems to have been aware of the change: he labelled the first work in Book 3 'in modern style', which applies not to the specific work, but to the genre it represents: the sonata. In this he anticipates Dario Castello, who, in the 1620s, published two collections of 'sonate concertate in stile moderno'.[28] But Rossi seems here to be formally announcing a style change that he had already inaugurated in certain *sinfonie a 3* of Books 1–2 (see Ex. 4.6). The sonata thus underwent an early gestation.

Ex. 4.6 Sinfonia 11 (Book 1, no. 11, bars 1–9)

By contrast, the two *sinfonie a 4* in Book 1 evidence an entirely different texture, one in which the voices are conceived as a homogeneous chordal ensemble. It is as if the composer oscillated between two different conceptions of the *sinfonia*, one *moderno*, the other, plain and processional, *antico* perhaps (Ex. 4.7a).

Like the *sinfonia*, the *gagliarda* appears in all four books. But, stylistically, it lacks the dialectic tension sensed in the *sinfonia*, indeed, except for its modes the *gagliarda* hardly changes from one book to another. Whether in three, four, or five voices it displays a fairly uniform homophonic texture, with the minims, as units of beat, divided into crotchets in one part or, simultaneously, in two or more (Ex. 4.7b).

---

[28] Cf. Castello, *Selected Ensemble Sonatas*, ed. Selfridge-Field. On the *stile moderno* sonata, see Allsop, *The Italian 'Trio' Sonata*, 85–105.

Ex. 4.7*a*   Sinfonia 1 *a* 4 (Book 1, no. 16, bars 1–13)

Ex. 4.7*b*   Gagliarda 4 'detta la Disperata' (Book 3, no. 19, bars 1–8)

From Sinfonia *to Sonata*

Rossi seems to have inaugurated the *sinfonia*, though in its brevity and
its function sometimes as an introduction to other works it follows in
the earlier tradition of the organ prelude and *intonazione* or the lute *ricercare*
(the term *sinfonia*, traceable to the ancients, was kept alive, moreover,

in humanistic writings).[29] But a closer antecedent to the *sinfonia* would seem to be the *canzonetta*, as we know it from Rossi's Opus 1. The connection between Rossi's *canzonette* and his *sinfonie* inheres in their common forms, their ensemble *a 3*, their varying textures, and their lightness and often popular character. What Thomas Morley said of the *canzonetta* might also apply to the *sinfonia*, namely, that it is neither heavy nor frivolous; that it is short; that its sections, or 'strains', are repeated, with the exception of the middle one; and that they often begin with a light point of imitation.[30]

Morley's prescription that the middle section of a *canzonetta* not be repeated must be modified to meet the realities of Rossi's Opus 1. There only seven of the nineteen pieces have the form ‖: A :‖ B ‖: C :‖. The remainder are in bipartite form, yet still divide into three sections, now with B serving as a transition within the second part, thus: ‖: A :‖: BC :‖. Most *sinfonie*, as already said, are in two parts, each repeated.[31] The *sinfonia* in three sections, with the middle one unrepeated, is, in fact, almost a rarity.[32] Yet the bipartite *sinfonie* do, like the *canzonette*, have their second part divide into a transitional B and a C. That explains why bipartite *sinfonie* have a longer second part, exceeding the first by anywhere from one to thirty bars.

As in the *canzonette*, sectional divisions in the *sinfonie* are reinforced by the cadence structure. In bipartite works, the tendency is to have both parts end on the modal *finalis*. In tripartite works or in those bipartite ones that divide into three sections, the tendency is to have a different cadence at the end of the middle part or section (usually on the fifth or fourth degree of the mode).

Textural changes provide further reinforcement of the overall form, again after the model of the *canzonetta*. Most three-voice *sinfonie* have the two upper voices begin imitatively, continuing in the first or second part sometimes as a homorhythmic duet (in minims or crotchets or running quavers) or as a series of playful echo imitations. The bass may either stand apart from the upper voices, serving as a rhythmic and (with its realization) harmonic prop for their activity; or occasionally join their imitative or homophonic writing as a third equal voice. Sinfonia 15 in Book 1, for example, begins with an imitative duet, then for the first (transitional) section of the second part has homophony in all three voices,

---

[29] Referring to Cicero, Dolet, for example, speaks of *symphonia* in the sense of *concentus*, or harmony: 'Symphonia est musicus concentus. Cicero familiar. lib. xvi', etc. He then defines *concentus* as 'quasi consensus, vel concordia', again after Cicero (the portion 'De somnio Scipione', in *De re publica*, VI. xviii. 18). See Dolet, *Commentariorum linguae latinae tomus secundus* (1538), cols. 1294–8.

[30] Cf. Morley, *A Plain and Easy Introduction to Practical Music*, ed. Harman, 295.

[31] By 'most' is meant 47 out of 65 *sinfonie*.

[32] It occurs in three works only (see above).

only to end with echo imitations in the upper ones (supported by a slow bass).

The *canzonetta* may be traced to the earlier *canzone villanesca*; and the *sinfonia*, to the earlier *canzona da sonar*. But the line of descent is not so direct. Rather, there is a mixing, along the way, of vocal and instrumental types, all of them emerging from a prototypical *chanson* or *canzone*. What they share is their division into two or three parts or sections, usually repeated and marked by textural and sometimes metrical changes; their use of the ubiquitous *canzona* motif (in dactylic rhythm) at the opening (Rossi has it in six of his *canzonette* and in several *sinfonie*, and, as might be expected, in his *canzoni*, though only one);[33] their light and lively treatment of motifs; and their small dimensions. Each of the types went its separate way, yet the generic links remain, which makes a meticulous structural and stylistic differentiation of instrumental types difficult, if not perhaps irrelevant, in the late sixteenth- and early seventeenth-century repertory. The genius of the types is their variability.

The links are such as to reinforce the connection, in Rossi's instrumental works, between the *sinfonia* and the sonata and to raise the question, pertinent or not, where the line may be drawn between them. There are three kinds of sonatas in Books 3–4: *canzona* sonatas, variation sonatas, and special sonatas. It is in the *canzona* sonatas, usually referred to in the literature as 'free sonatas',[34] that the *sinfonia* and sonata meet and reveal their mutual affinity to the *canzonetta* and the *canzona* as model types.[35] The first two sonatas of Book 3 and the first four of Book 4 are *canzona* sonatas in the sense that they comprise two parts, each repeated, and of the two, the second is longer and has metrical changes, as shown in the table below.

Such forms can be found in *sinfonie*, the only difference being that the *canzona* sonatas tend to greater length, as is clear from various similarly built *sinfonie*, shown in the second table (next page).

			No. of bars
Book 3	Sonata 1	‖: C :‖: 3, C :‖	24 ‖ 31 = 55
	Sonata 2	‖: C :‖: 3, ¢, 3, ¢ :‖	22 ‖ 49 = 71
Book 4	Sonata 1	‖: C :‖: C, 3, ¢ :‖	26 ‖ 47 = 73
	Sonata 2	‖: C :‖: 3, ¢ :‖	25 ‖ 36 = 61
	Sonata 3	‖: C :‖: C, 3, ¢ :‖	13 ‖ 38 = 51
	Sonata 4	‖: C :‖: 3, ¢ :‖	21 ‖ 48 = 69

[33] For example, Cte: 1, 3, 6–7, 11, 14; S1: Sinf. 13, 16–17; S2: 6, 14, 30–1; and for the middle section of the first *canzon per sonar*, S2: 33 (bars 33–40).

[34] See e.g. Allsop, *The Italian 'Trio' Sonata, passim*, and with respect to Rossi, 106.

[35] For the impact of the *canzona* on the sonata, see Crocker, 'An Introductory Study of the Italian Canzona for Instrumental Ensembles and its Influence upon the Baroque Sonata'.

Book 1	Sinfonia 12	‖: C :‖: 3, ¢ :‖	8 ‖ 30 = 38
	Sinfonia 15	‖: C :‖: 3, ¢ :‖	7 ‖ 17 = 24
Book 2	Sinfonia 2	‖: C :‖: C, 3, ¢ :‖	7 ‖ 19 = 26
	Sinfonia 12	‖: C :‖: C, 3 :‖	8 ‖ 18 = 26
	Sinfonia 15	‖: C :‖: 3, ¢ :‖	6 ‖ 22 = 28
	Sinfonia 21	‖: C :‖: 3, ¢ :‖	6 ‖ 16 = 22
Book 3	Sinfonia 4	‖: C :‖: 3, ¢ :‖	11 ‖ 19 = 30
	Sinfonia 6	‖: C :‖: 3, ¢ :‖	10 ‖ 17 = 27
	Sinfonia 9	‖: C :‖: 3, ¢ :‖ ext.	22 ‖ 20 ‖ + 10 = 52
Book 4	Sinfonia 1	‖: C :‖: 3 :‖	21 ‖ 18 = 39
	Sinfonia 2	‖: C :‖: C, 3, ¢ :‖	22 ‖ 29 = 51
	Sinfonia 3	‖: C :‖: C, 3 :‖	13 ‖ 22 = 35

By way of comparison, two of Rossi's *canzoni per sonar* divide as follows:

Book 2	Canzona 1	‖: 3 :‖: ¢, 3 :‖	22 ‖ 35 = 57
	Canzona 3	‖: C :‖: C, 3 :‖	20 ‖ 26 = 46

The *sinfonia* may thus be designated a smaller sonata. It would seem that, potentially, the *sinfonia* could, when expanded, become a *canzona* sonata. If so, one might conclude that the *canzona* was the matrix for the particular species of *sinfonia* having two or three sections with metrical changes; that the *canzona* sonata evolved from the *sinfonia*; and that the difference between the two of them is mainly one of length.

But the differentiation is not so firm: the works listed above show smaller sonatas, which, ordinarily, might be *sinfonie*, or larger *sinfonie*, which, ordinarily, might be sonatas. Sinfonia 9 in Book 3 and Sinfonia 2 in Book 4 are cases in point. Not only are they the longest *sinfonie* in their books (52, 51 bars), but, in their structure and character, they resemble the *canzona* sonatas in them. If length is a determining factor, then they should rightly have been labelled sonatas. Contrarily, Sonata 1 in Book 3 and Sonata 3 in Book 4 are the shortest ones of their kind (55, 51 bars), and since we already know that *sinfonie* topped the fifty-bar point, or so at least the two just mentioned, then the two sonatas could well have been designated *sinfonie*.

The basic problem remains: at what point does a *sinfonia*, in its length, qualify as a sonata: at fifty bars? Sixty bars? Perhaps the only answer is when it is 'noticeably' longer than most *sinfonie*, yet how does one define 'noticeably'? With no fixed yardstick for measuring generic differences, any comparison of one work with others of its kind must necessarily be relative. The adverb 'noticeably', as unsatisfactory as it is in descriptive analysis, does make pragmatic sense: indeed, in its uncertainty it is congruent with the morphological uncertainty of seventeenth-century instrumental chamber music.

Variation Sonatas, Special Sonatas

The source of the variation sonatas, which form the majority of the sonatas that Rossi composed for Books 3–4, is, clearly, the variation, particularly that on ground bass patterns. Rossi's variation sonatas are among the earliest works of their kind.[36] They are much, if not considerably longer than his *canzona* sonatas and are 'modern' in their being composed in an advanced idiom. The influence of monody, *stile concertato*, and vocal and instrumental ornamentation may be perceived in their complex and often dotted rhythms, their runs, echo effects, contrast motifs, and, in general, virtuosity.[37]

Vocal ornaments were, from the early sixteenth century, available for imitation by instrumentalists. Silvestro Ganassi, in his *Fontegara* (1535), advised recorder players to look to the singers for their examples. 'The aim of the recorder player is to imitate as closely as possible all the capabilities of the human voice'.[38] Similar remarks can be found in the later vocal manuals, as when Giovanni Luca Conforto wrote that his ornaments, or *passaggi*, 'might serve as well for those who wish to practise the viola or wind instruments'.[39]

The three variation sonatas in Book 3 are related to one another by being constructed on a ground. They seem to have been arranged in the order of their length and degree of complexity. Sonata 3 on the 'Aria della Romanesca' has sixty-four bars and a ground of eight; Sonata 4 on the 'Aria di Ruggiero' has 128 bars and a ground of sixteen; and the expansive Sonata 5 on a melody entitled 'Porto celato il mio nobil pensiero'[40] has 160 bars and, again, a ground of sixteen, with a metrical change in the middle section. Each of the three sonatas has eight variations on its ground, with the eighth one repeated at a faster tempo.

Book 4, with its thirteen sonatas, more than doubles those in Book 3 while retaining their separation into *canzona*, variation, and special sonatas. Its variation sonatas tend, by comparison with those in the earlier book, towards greater diversity of content and complexity of structure, not to speak of the heightened technical demands they make on the performer. To the variations, in Book 3, on a ground bass or a melody plus ground bass, Book 4 adds variations on a melody in the top voice (nos. 5, 7) and on a

---

[36] Piperno, in fact, described them as the first examples of sonatas composed to *basso ostinato* patterns ('I quattro libri di musica strumentale di Salamon Rossi', esp. 354).

[37] Allsop tends to view Rossi as falling behind Fontana or Castello in degree of virtuosity. Yet he bases his conclusion on the composer's 'free', i.e. *canzona* sonatas only, as he himself admits ('Nor was he particularly concerned with technical display, for these free sonatas never match the virtuosity of his own sets of variations'; *The Italian 'Trio' Sonata*, 109).

[38] *Fontegara*, tr. Peter, 9 (and similar remarks elsewhere, e.g. 18, 87, 89).

[39] Conforto, *Breve e facile maniera d'essercitarsi a far passaggi* (1593), fo. [4]ᵛ.

[40] It appears in Bargnani's *Canzonette, arie, et madrigali 3–4 v.* (1599), 11, as well as in d'India's *Musiche 2 v.* (1615), 38.

chordal scheme (no. 12). Two works effect a combination of the variation and *canzona* sonata types (nos. 11, 13).

Other changes in Book 4 are the increase in the number of variations, ranging from three to twenty-one (Book 3 had a single scheme of eight variations); a wider assortment of 'thematic' lengths, ranging from four to forty-four bars (via eight, sixteen, and twenty-one; Book 3 had 'themes' of eight and sixteen bars only); and an inverse relationship between the number of variations and the length of the 'theme' (in Book 3, no matter how long the theme, the number of variations remained eight).

The discussion here focuses on the particularities of the variation sonatas in Book 4. Each sonata creates its own frame of reference, thus represents an 'opus perfectum et absolutum' (Lampadius).

Sonata 5 comprises five variations on an (unidentified) 'Aria francese' placed in the top voice. The length of the tune is sixteen bars, originally written, it would seem, as two four-bar phrases each repeated, thus AABB (though in Rossi's setting the connection between statement and repeat rests not on their melodic but on their harmonic similarity). Beginning in F major (for the A section), the tune moves (for the B section) to D minor, so that the effect, in the separate variations, is one of modal oscillation (Ex. 4.8).

Sonata 6 has twenty-one numbered variations on a four-bar theme called the 'Aria di Tordiglione' (the last variation is repeated). Consisting of both a melody and a ground bass, the theme, as handled by Rossi, resembles the 'romanesca'. It appears in Fabritio Caroso's *Il ballarino* (1581) and his *Nobiltà di dame* (1600), though in major and in twelve semibreve bars (Rossi's theme, in minor, covers twelve minims, or four bars under 3/2).

Sonata 7 recalls Sonata 5 in having five variations on a sixteen-bar theme built on two repeated four-bar phrases, hence AABB. The theme, drawn from an (unidentified) *balletto*, occurs, ornamented, in the top voice.

Sonata 8 has four variations on the theme 'È tanto tempo hormai', placed in the upper voice and bass and, as used by Rossi, stretching over twenty-one bars, thus: A (4), A (3), B (7), B (7) (Ex. 4.9; see also Plate 8).

By comparison, Francesco Turini treated the same theme as a three-voice sonata plus *continuo*.[41] Now the theme is presented in five variations of diverse length, from twenty-two to twenty-four bars. The overall structure lies halfway between a variation set and a *canzona*, with its typical changes of metre and character from one section to the next (variations 1–2 are under C and 3–4 under 3/2, while variation 5, a kind of gigue, is under 6/8).

Sonata 9 has three variations on the 'Tenor di Napoli', which, as employed by Rossi, is a forty-four-bar 'theme' in the bass line, so divided: A (8) twice, B (8) once, and C (10) twice. Each segment forms a chordal scheme of (more or less) I–IV–V–I (in G). The first bass strain is given in Ex. 4.10.

---

[41] Turini, *Madrigali . . . con alcune sonate a 2–3 lib. 1°* (1621, also 1624²), differently paginated in the four partbooks.

Ex. 4.8 Sonata 5 'sopra un'Aria francese' (Book 4, no. 5, bars 1–17)

The 'Tenor di Napoli' appears elsewhere in the literature: Antonio Valente wrote a keyboard work entitled 'Tenore grande alla Napolitana con sei mutanze';[42] and Carlo Milanuzzi used the 'Tenor di Napoli' as the basis of a sonata for Spanish guitar.[43] Milanuzzi provides a key to his

[42] Valente, *Intavolatura de cimbalo....con alcuni tenori...lib. 1°* (1576), 71–4.
[43] Milanuzzi, *Secondo scherzo...opera ottava* (1625), under 'Sonate facili intavolate per la chitarra alla spagnola', 49–50.

Ex. 4.9   Sonata 8 'sopra l'Aria "È tanto tempo hormai"' (Book 4, no. 8, bars 1–21)

Ex. 4.10   Sonata 9 'sopra l'Aria del Tenor di Napoli' (Book 4, no. 9, bars 1–8)

intabulation in an 'Alfabetto per la chitarra alla spagnola' (at the opening of his collection). It allows one to reconstruct the 'Tenor di Napoli' as consisting of three strains that, in their length and harmonies, are identical with those in Rossi's sonata. The only difference is that Milanuzzi repeats not just the first and third strains, but the second as well.

Sonata 10 is constructed on the 'romanesca' ground (and its implied upper voice melody). The 'theme', in Dorian mode, occupies eight bars (under 3/2, though the work is printed under C) and is treated in twelve variations. Book 3 has its own sonata on the 'romanesca' (likewise in eight ternary bars and prefixed by a duple sign), yet with its eight variations it is one third shorter; its mode, moreover, is Dorian on G.

Sonata 11 is designated 'la Scatola', a title of infrequent occurrence in the literature (Marco Uccellini composed an instrumental work on 'la scatola degli agghi').[44] The 'theme', as used by Rossi, covers sixteen duple bars, and to all appearances is identical with the 'romanesca' bass and melody (yet Rossi's 'romanesche' are eight ternary bars long). It is presented in nine variations, with four different tempo markings and three different metres, as shown in the table (next page). The performers are instructed to repeat Variation 9, but at a faster tempo (as in the three variation sonatas in Book 3).

The division of 'la Scatola' into contrasting sections accounts for its box-like structure. At the same time it turns the work into a combination of *canzona* and variations, thus creating a hybrid *canzona*- and variation-type sonata, as in the work by Turini mentioned above.

---

[44] Uccellini, *Sonate, correnti, et arie 1–3 v.* (Op. 4, 1663), 67.

	Metre	Tempo
Variation 1	C	Adagio
Variations 2–6	C	Presto
Variation 7	3/2	Presto
Variation 8	¢	Adagio
Variation 9	¢	[Presto]

Sonata 12 on the 'bergamasca' consists of eight variations on an eight-bar chordal scheme in G, as I–IV–V–I / I–IV–V–I. Instrumental examples of the 'bergamasca' date from the 1560s: Giacomo Gorzanis, for example, wrote a 'Saltarello dito il bergamasco' for lute.[45] Chordal guitar, lute, and keyboard accompaniments are known from the beginning of the seventeenth century. Rossi thus connects with an established tradition.

There are two sonatas that stand apart, hence our designation 'special sonatas'. That the composer related to them as 'special' is evident from their placement: in Book 3, as the last of the six sonatas; in Book 4, as the concluding work. In their form, they recall the *canzona* sonata; but not in their content and its elaboration, where they are singular.

Sonata 6, in Book 3, is marked 'in dialogo'. It has the semblance more of a solo than of a duo sonata. Structurally, it divides into two sections, with a repeat sign about three-quarters of the way through (bar 55) and at the end (bar 73). For most of the piece, or the first section, the two violins plus bass accompaniment are heard alternately in long stretches of solo playing. It is only in the shorter second section that they come together as a duet, marked 'tutti insieme'. The sonata forces the question: what is the difference between duo and dialogue?[46] A duo, or duet, might be defined, quite simply, as two parts performing together; in a trio sonata of the kind that Rossi and most other composers wrote, it refers to the upper voices. A dialogue differs from the duo in that both participants make a separate statement before they join in a conclusion. It remains to be seen how this differentiation works itself out in the literature at large.

Sonata 6 forces a second question: in bipartite repeat forms, how much is to be repeated, both sections or only the second? Book 3, in its notation, is not clear on this account, for the repeat sign—a double bar with two dots on both sides—occurs in the middle and at the end of bipartite works, and thus could mean a repeat of the first and second parts or a repeat of the second one starting from the first repeat sign. In the *sinfonie, gagliarde, correnti*, and *brandi*, the repeat sign, similarly placed, refers to both parts.

---

[45] Gorzanis, *Il 3° lib. de intabolatura di liuto* (1564), fo. E 1.

[46] For the relation of solo, duo, and trio, see Jensen, 'Solo Sonata, Duo Sonata, and Trio Sonata: Some Problems of Terminology and Genre in Seventeenth-Century Italian Instrumental Music'.

Problems arise mainly in longer works having an extended first section and a brief second one. Sonatas 3–5 (in Book 3) have a second section ranging from one-seventh to one-tenth of the whole, and reason dictates a repetition of the second section only. In Sonata 5, for example, the first section totals 144 bars and the second one sixteen, and it is inconceivable that the composer intended a repeat of the first. The only uncertain case is no. 6, the 'special sonata', and this because of its slightly different proportions: fifty-four bars for the first section and nineteen for the second, now about one-fourth of the whole. Yet the same principle would seem to obtain, namely that in works having a considerably shorter second section only the second is to be repeated.[47] Were one to repeat the first section of Sonata 6, a form of unwieldy dimensions would result, not to mention that, musically, the repeat of the long solo portions in section 1 (before the 'tutti insieme' of section 2) leads to monotony.

Sonata 13, at the end of Book 4, is unique among Rossi's sonatas, as among his instrumental works at large, in being designed for six voices arranged as two trios, with the bass (*continuo*) of each played on its own chitarrone; in having its instruments—four violins and two chitarroni—specified in the title (it has been described as the earliest known composition for four violins);[48] in being written in a *stile concertato*, with the two trios played off against each other or contrasting with full-voice ensembles; in having conflicting signatures—one set of them in bar 1, a second in bar 23, while from bar 40 to the end all voices share the same signature—and, as a result, modal uncertainty (the piece wavers between untransposed Dorian and Dorian on G, with an admixture of Mixolydian and Aeolian as well); in toying with echo effects, marked *forte* and *piano*, though, to be sure, dynamic indications had already occurred in Book 3;[49] in having metrical changes that suggest the imposition of a *canzona*, in its contrasts of metre and material, on the overall form; and, in general, in displaying a rather complex design, in six sections, of which the last three are repeated (see table).[50]

It would seem that Rossi was pulling out all stops to provide an unusual final piece not only for his Book 4 but for all four collections of his instrumental music. The only question one might ask is why confine such complexity to seventy-eight bars? Set between contrary forces, Sonata 13 has a certain imbalance about it: one would have expected greater amplitude.

---

[47] The principle does not apply to S3: Son. 1–2, where, as in other *canzona* sonatas and in most *sinfonie* and dances, the second part is somewhat longer than the first.

[48] Apel, *Die italienische Violinmusik im 17. Jahrhundert*, 15.

[49] S3: Son. 4, Corr. 7 (see Ch. 5).

[50] In the table, under 'Ensemble', the voices are numbered 1–3 for the first trio and 4–6 for the second, with diagonals indicating the division between them.

Part	Section/bars	Metre	Ensemble
A	1: 1–23	C	Two trios (1, 3/4 and 2/5–6) in alternation
	2: 23–39	—	Same two trios
	3: 40–54	—	Same two trios in quicker alternation (with *forte, piano* markings), then all six voices
‖: B :‖	4: 55–61	—	All six voices
	5: 62–6	3	Two trios (1, 3/4 and 2/5–6) in alternation
	6: 67–78	₵	All six voices

The Sinfonia *as a Composite of Abstract and Dance Types*

The connections between *sinfonia* and *canzonetta* have already been emphasized. Structurally and stylistically, the vocal form, with its various links to
madrigals and instrumental *canzoni*, adumbrated the instrumental one. Yet
no sooner did Rossi launch the *sinfonia* than it replaced the *canzonetta* as a
model for other types in his instrumental repertory. The *sinfonia* can be seen
as a composite of and precedent for abstract and dance types. Rossi, in a
sense, was writing all his instrumental music within his *sinfonie*, and if this
primordial function of the *sinfonia* in his repertory has been overlooked it
may be due to the very designation 'sinfonia', implying a genre unto its own.

The abstract types include the *ricercare, canzona*, and sonata, as well as the
ritornello. Among Rossi's *sinfonie* there are examples that could, under other
circumstances, be described as any one of these. Thus Sinfonia 2 in Book 3 is
a *ricercare* in the sense of a *ricercare* as mainly a fugal type based on one or
more points of imitation. Sinfonia 2 consists of two such points, one developed in bars 1–13, the second in the remainder (13–29)[51] (Ex. 4.11).

Yet the resemblance ends there: the texture is more heterogeneous than in
a *ricercare* (it varies between a duet in the upper voices, accompanied by the
bass, and three-part imitation); the motifs are livelier than those in imitative
ricercari; and the structure is bipartite. But since the only other *ricercare* in
Rossi's repertory is one which, by default, was labelled a sonata, there is
little to compare this one *sinfonia* to: the relation to the *ricercare* cannot be
easily substantiated.

More significant are the links between the *sinfonia* and the remaining
abstract types, among them the *canzona*. As has already been demonstrated,
the *canzona* is implied in a number of *sinfonie* in one or more ways: their
structure (two or three parts, often with changing metres and textures);[52]
their use of the typical *canzona* motif in dactylic rhythm, often with repeated
notes;[53] and their general liveliness. These *sinfonie* relate further to the three
canzoni per sonar in Book 2, though the latter are slightly longer.

[51] With first point incorporated into bass, bars 17–18, and, in inversion, into canto 1, bars
15–16.

[52] S1: Sinf. 12, 15; S2: Sinf. 2, 4, 6, 8–9, 12, 15, 19, 21; S3: Sinf. 4, 6, 9; S4: Sinf. 1–3.

[53] S1: Sinf. 13 *a* 3, 1–2 *a* 4; S2: Sinf. 1–3, 6, 9, 14, 18, 20, Sinf. 1 and 4 *a* 4/3, 2–5 *a* 5/3; S3: Sinf. 5;
S4: Sinf. 2–3.

Ex. 4.11   Sinfonia 2 'detta la Emiglia' (Book 3, no. 8, bars 1–7, 13–19)

The sonata is, of course, implicit in the *sinfonia* via the relationship between the *sinfonia* and the *canzona* and *canzona* sonata. *Sinfonie* often resemble the *canzona*, as do *canzona* sonatas, which have all its lineaments, yet tend to greater length. Identity problems of when a *sinfonia* having the structure of a *canzona* becomes a bona fide sonata have already been discussed. The upshot is that much confusion prevails in their differentiation, to the extent that, as shown, one *sinfonia*, because of its larger size, should probably have been designated a sonata and two sonatas, for just the opposite reason, should probably have been designated *sinfonie*. It was the road of the *sinfonia*, then, that the composer travelled on his way to the *stile moderno*. He did this not only in matters of structure, but also in those of style: the *sinfonie*, from the early books on, contain rapid passages in the virtuoso manner of the variation sonatas; like the variation and 'special sonatas', they show the influence of monody in the use of dotted figures or precipitous runs (Ex. 4.12*a–c*).[54]

The influence of monody may further be felt in various *sinfonie* that evidence an 'affective manner', as characterized by one or more traits: diminished fifths, minor modes, suspensions, syncopations, and the

Ex. 4.12*a*   Sinfonia 7 (Book 1, no. 7, bars 5–7, 19–22)

Ex. 4.12*b*   Sinfonia 15 (Book 2, no. 15, bars 1–4)

[54] Virtuoso writing (in semiquavers): S1: Sinf. 7, 11; S4: Sinf. 4. The influence of monody (dotted notes): S2: Sinf. 10, 15, 21. Quick runs: S3: Sinf. 1, 4, 9.

Ex. 4.12c Sinfonia 1 (Book 3, no. 7, bars 1–3)

intermittent outbursts of rhythmic energy just mentioned. It is the more palpable when the basic movement is in minims, thus providing a clear metric frame for grasping rhythmic or melodic peculiarities. Typical is Sinfonia 8 in Book 3 (Ex. 4.13a): it displays 'durezze e ligature' (discords and suspensions) in Phrygian, a mode of writing that, once introduced by Giovanni de Macque, entered the seventeenth-century composer's lexicon (compare Frescobaldi's three 'Toccate per l'Elevazione' in his *Fiori musicali*). Examples occur in Rossi's earlier books as well (Ex. 4.13b–c).

Ex. 4.13a Sinfonia 8 (Book 3, no. 14, bars 1–11)

Ex. 4.13b Sinfonia 9 (Book 1, no. 9, bars 1–5)

Ex. 4.13*c* Sinfonia 16 (Book 2, no. 16, bars 1–10)

The 'affective manner' might be perceived as a transfer from the madrigals (and *canzonette*) to an instrumental medium. It marked the big change announced by Rossi in the sonata 'detta la Moderna': instrumental music invested with the expressive power and stylistic variety of vocal music (Ex. 4.14).[55] Affective dissonances and suspensions became standard fare, later, in the first, slow movement of the *sonata da chiesa*.

Ex. 4.14 Sonata 1 'detta la Moderna' (Book 3, no. 1, bars 1–10)

[55] See, also, various portions of the 'romanesca' sonatas in S3–4; S3: Son. 5 ('Porto celato'), bars 80–96; S4: Son. 2, first part.

Certain *sinfonie* might also be characterized as *ritornelli*. Praetorius tried to eliminate the terminological confusion, remarking: 'Although some authors, I find, do not properly distinguish the words *sinfonia* and *ritornello*, let me clarify that a *sinfonia* is not unlike a lovely pavan and a grave sonata, while a *ritornello*, written for 3–5 voices to be played on violins, cornetts, trombones, lutes, or other instruments, is not unlike a *gagliarda*, a *saltarello*, a *courante*, a *volta*, or even a *canzona* larded with quavers and imitations.'[56] By *sinfonia* Praetorius seems to be referring to various solemn four- or more-voiced (homophonic) *sinfonie* of the type one finds in Acts III–V of Monteverdi's *Orfeo*; such *sinfonie* also occur among Rossi's works.[57] By *ritornello*, he has in mind a livelier sort, to be found in most of Rossi's *sinfonie* and in Monteverdi's *ritornelli* in his *Scherzi musicali* (1607).

Praetorius was right in conceiving the *ritornello* as a catch-all for different types; so can the *sinfonia* be conceived, which makes it difficult, then, to distinguish them. Yet Praetorius overlooked one important point: Rossi's *sinfonie* approximate the *ritornello* when they are written not in two parts (‖: A :‖: B :‖), as is usually the case, but in one (with a caesura of some sort in the middle). Some eleven monopartite *sinfonie* may thus be described as *ritornelli*: they are mostly in 3/2 metre and have the rhythmic traits, now and then, of various dances (*gagliarda*, *corrente*, *brando*, *balletto*).[58] What is interesting is that the *ritornello*-styled *sinfonia* and, further, its manifestly solemn type are confined, mainly, to Rossi's earlier books. The later ones favour the bipartite, livelier *sinfonia*, which, for all that, is no less suggestive, at times, of various dances.

Before pinpointing the dances in Rossi's *sinfonie*, one ought to describe their metrical and stylistic characteristics, as conditioned by their step patterns. There is a difference between the outwardly similar *gagliarda* and *corrente*. The *gagliarda* was so danced as for a complete step pattern to cover six beats (with the leap falling on 5–6), thus single bars under 3/2 are expanded to pairs of bars under 6/2 (or 3/1); the *corrente*, by contrast, was so danced as for a complete set of steps to cover four bars under 3/2, thus 12/2 (two *sottopiedi* to the left side and two to the right or, if not sideways, then forward and backward, as described by Cesare Negri in his *Gratie d'amore*, 1602).[59]

These macrorhythmic groupings—marked, in the examples that follow, with thicker bars—are reinforced by harmonic or cadential emphases. The

---

[56] Praetorius, *Syntagma musicum*, iii. 129 [*recte* 109].

[57] S1: Sinf. 16–17 *a* 4.

[58] S1: Sinf. 2 (*corrente*), 3 (*brando*), 4 (*gagliarda*), 6 (*gagliarda*), 8, 13; S2: Sinf. 5, 7 (*corrente*), 11 (*corrente*), 18 (*balletto*); S4: Sinf. 4.

[59] I am grateful to Professor Yvonne Kendall for clarifying the step sequence. For Negri's account, with music example, see *Le gratie d'amore*, 265–6, entitled 'Balletto a due detto la Corrente, messo in uso dall'auttore'; according to Kendall, it represents one of five extant choreographies, from the period, for the *corrente*, though of the five only one other includes music (Thoinot Arbeau's *Orchésographie*, 1589; in fac. repr. of 1596 edn., 65–6).

gagliarda begins on the upbeat portion of its dance pattern (beats 4–6), which suggests that it follows immediately upon a *sinfonia* or a dance ending on a downbeat. By contrast, the *corrente* begins at the end of the second bar of its four-bar group, which suggests that it, too, follows upon a previous piece, probably a *gagliarda* that typically ends with a single chord on a downbeat. The *gagliarda* places fairly equal weight on all beats, though particularly on the fifth minim, or leap, of its step pattern; it abounds in hemiola figures, thus oscillating between 6/2 and 3/1 (Ex. 4.15*a*). Less subtle is the *corrente*, which emphasizes the first beat of its bars by doubling or dotting it, with

Ex. 4.15*a*   Gagliarda 3 'detta la Silvia' (Book 3, no. 18, bars 1–8)

Ex. 4.15*b*   Corrente 3 (Book 3, no. 29, bars 1–10)

some syncopation on second beats (Ex. 4.15*b*). In all, the *gagliarda* tends to be slower and more stately than the *corrente*.

There are at least thirteen *sinfonie* that in one or more sections might qualify as *gagliarde*. Usually it is the middle section that is so paced; other times, a whole second part and, in two cases, a complete piece.[60] When the middle section proceeds as a *gagliarda*, the final one may continue as a *brando* (Ex. 4.16).[61]

Some eight *sinfonie* could be described as *correnti*: two of them in one part, hence analogous to a *ritornello*; and the rest constituting a second part or, less often, its middle or last section.[62] Not always do they group as regularly in four bars as do *correnti* proper. An extra bar may be interpolated towards the end, to extend the final phrase. Otherwise the rhythmic pulse is that of a *corrente*.

The *brando*, as conceived by Rossi, differs from the *corrente* and *gagliarda* in its duple metre and its character: the upper voices, paired in thirds or sixths, move along in sometimes breakneck quaver figuration towards a cadence, at the end of a phrase or section, on two repeated chords. One has the impression of an uninterrupted stream of activity, coming to a sudden halt (Ex. 4.17).

Of the five *brandi* in the later books, Brando 2, in the fourth, may have been a *corrente*: it is the only one to have a triple metre signature. In form and style it resembles the *correnti*, with one exception: where 3 in *correnti*

Ex. 4.16   Sinfonia 15 (Book 1, no. 15, bars 6–11, 16–21)

[60] Middle section: S1: Sinf. 12, 15; S2: Sinf. 2, 21; S3: Sinf. 4, 6, 9; S4: Sinf. 2. Whole 2nd pt.: S1: Sinf. 1; S2: Sinf. 4; S4: Sinf. 1. Complete piece: S1: Sinf. 4; S2: Sinf. 5.

[61] S1: Sinf. 15; S2: Sinf. 2; S4: Sinf. 2.

[62] One pt.: S1: Sinf. 2; S2: Sinf. 11. 2nd pt.: S1: Sinf. 5; S2: Sinf. 6, 19; S4: Sinf. 3. Middle section: S2: Sinf. 15. Last section: S2: Sinf. 12.

Ex. 4.17 Brando 2 (Book 3, no. 25, bars 15–20)

means 3/2, in Brando 2 it means 3/4.[63] The question is obvious: if the work is a *corrente*, why was it labelled a *brando*? Rossi may originally have composed it as a *corrente*, then realizing he had only one *brando* for Book 4, and wishing to add another, took one of his *correnti*, rewrote it in 3/4, and renamed it a *brando*. But why rewrite it? Perhaps to make it have the generally black appearance of other *brandi*, with their many quavers. As an aside, it might be mentioned that none of these generic problems occur in the four *brandi* published by Buonamente in his *Quarto libro*.[64]

Another approach to Brando 2 in Book 4 is that it is neither a mislabelled *corrente* nor a *corrente* rewritten as a *brando*. Rather it exemplifies a *branle gai*, or *branle de Poitou*, typically in triple metre. Thomas Morley pointed to the resemblance between the latter and the *corrente*: 'Like unto this [the *branle* in triple time], but more light, be the Voltes and Courantes which being both of a measure are, notwithstanding, danced after sundry fashions'.[65]

The *brando*, in its duple variety, is present in at least nine *sinfonie*, in one or more sections: either the first or second parts of a bipartite work; or its last section only.[66] To these one might add still others, whole pieces, in fact,

---

[63] The only other instrumental piece that reads under 3/4 is S1: Gagl. 2 *a* 5/3. Yet it is special because of its black notation, vaguely alluding, perhaps, to the dedicatee (Norsa).

[64] Buonamente, *Il 4° lib. de varie sonate, sinfonie, gagliarde, corrente, e brandi per sonar con due violini et un basso di viola* (1626), 36–9. Other composers of *brandi* were Rognoni, *Pavane, e balli con 2 canzoni, e diverse sorti di brandi per suonare* 4–5 v. (1603; no longer extant); and Farina, *Il 3° lib. delle pavane, gagliarde, brandi*, etc. (1627). Buonamente and Farina had early connections with the Mantuan court. For formal and stylistic affinities between the works of Buonamente and Rossi, see Romanstein, 'Giovanni Battista Buonamente and Instrumental Music of the Early Baroque'; and, as they impinge on the dance suite, Harrán, 'From Mantua to Vienna' (and, below, Ch. 5).

[65] Morley, *A Plain and Easy Introduction to Practical Music*, ed. Harman, 297.

[66] 1st pt.: S2: Sinf. 12, 20. 2nd pt.: S3: Sinf. 7. Last section: S1: Sinf. 15; S2: Sinf. 2, 8, 10; S3: Sinf. 6; S4: Sinf. 2.

which, in the pacing and pairing of their upper voices, might be identified as *brandi*.[67] The question may be asked why they were not called *brandi* in the first place.

The same question applies to the last of the six *sinfonie* in Book 4: in almost all respects, the same *sinfonia* answers the description of a typical *brando* (except for being written in C, though scanning rhythmically under 3/2). Comparing it with Brando 1 in the collection, as well as with the *brandi* in Book 3, one finds similarities in size, structure, and, more significantly, content: a duet in quavers, moving hurriedly and almost seamlessly toward the section cadences. Since Sinfonia 6 is the last of its kind in Book 4, one wonders whether it might not have originated in the composer's decision to add yet another *sinfonia* to the five already assembled, in which case Rossi might have drawn on a conveniently available *brando* and relabelled it a *sinfonia*.

The *sinfonia* can also be a *balletto*. Thus Sinfonia 17 in Book 2 and Sinfonia 3 in Book 3 evidence the typical rhythmic stance of a triple metre *balletto*, as we find it in Rossi's theatrical *balletto* 'Spazziam pronte'.[68] Their music bounces along in a lively alternation of 3/2 and 6/4 patterns, with hefty accents on repeated-note cadences (Ex. 4.18).

Ex. 4.18   Sinfonia 3 'detta la Cecchina' (Book 3, no. 9, bars 1–4)

Again the question might be asked why the composer did not refer to his *balletto*-like *sinfonie* as *balletti*. The answer is obvious: *sinfonie* were many different things, as were, say, first movements of eighteenth-century symphonies. Rossi was not negligent in his use of terminology. Rather, the tendency to blur types by designating them in one way or another inheres in the multiple connotations of the music itself, which, in the early seventeenth century, resisted pat schemes of classification.

It is but one step from the notion of a *sinfonia* as a repository of different instrumental types to that of the *sinfonia* as itself a generic composite. Thus one finds in many examples a concatenation of a *sinfonia* proper with a middle section in *gagliarda* rhythm, then a final section reminiscent of a

[67] Whole piece written in one part: S1: Sinf. 3. Or written in two parts: S1: Sinf. 10; S2: Sinf. 13. Or written in two parts with a transitional section (‖: A :‖ B ‖: C :‖): S1: Sinf. 14.

[68] See Ch. 6, Ex. 6.1.

brando; or of a sober *sinfonia* in the first part with a *gagliarda* or a *corrente* in the second. Just as certain *sinfonie*, in their similarity to *canzoni*, acted as prototypes for the sonata, so others, in their succession of dance types, acted similarly for the seventeenth-century dance suite, which, itself, had an earlier history (dance pairs are known from the fourteenth century on). On potential dance suites in Rossi's collections, more will be said in Chapter 5.

Comparison with the Italian Vocal Works

Two kinds of differences between instrumental and vocal works may be signalled: general and musical. The general differences have to do mainly with the size of the collections and their constitution. Where the vocal works were published in eight collections, the instrumental ones were published in four, yet amount, in their bar count, to about three-fifths the size of the vocal repertory. In their number of works, the two repertories are actually very close, 146 extant vocal works as against 130 instrumental ones, thus can be said to represent two fairly parallel sides of Rossi's œuvre. The instrumental collections gradually increased in their length, unlike the vocal ones, where differences in length were determined by the various genres: the short book of *canzonette*, the longer book of *madrigaletti*, and the six still longer books of madrigals. Where most madrigals are for five voices, most instrumental works are for three. They are analogous not to the three-voice *canzonette*, but rather to the duet-plus-*continuo* texture of the composer's later *madrigaletti*. Eighteen instrumental works were written for alternative ensembles, compared to one Italian work of the kind.

The musical differences are no less notable. To start with, the instrumental works have their own generic types: *sinfonia*, sonata, *canzona*, various dances. They depart in construction and content from the various kinds of madrigal, though *sinfonie* sometimes resemble *canzonette* and certain *madrigaletti* in their brevity, their liveliness, and their bipartite forms. Instrumental works are, in general, shorter than vocal ones, but in their longer examples, namely, some of the sonatas, they far exceed them. Where madrigals became somewhat shorter in time, *sinfonie* and *gagliarde* became somewhat longer.

Modally, the two repertories emphasize Dorian on G, followed, in second place, by Mixolydian. Yet the instrumental one demotes Aeolian to a lower rank than among the vocal works and, moreover, introduces, in the later books, several 'special' modes, best described as scales: C minor, D major, D minor, E minor, G minor.

Where the overwhelming majority of vocal works is under a duple sign, the instrumental repertory shows a different constitution: about two-fifths of its works are in triple metre and one fourth in mixed metres.

Most madrigals are through-composed, whereas repeat forms are preferred for instrumental music. These repeat forms occur in both the abstract types and the dances, which usually consist of two parts. In the sonatas, though, the repeat is often reduced to a short final section.

Where the *continuo* serves largely as a *basso seguente* in the vocal collections, with the exception of the *Madrigaletti* and, as far as may be determined, Book 5 *a 5*, it functions as a foil for the parts, hence a more genuine *continuo*, in the instrumental ones. In two vocal collections there is mention of 'stromenti' for the *continuo*. The instrumental ones, by contrast, refer to a single chitarrone or similar instrument. Trio-sonata texture was the preferred mode of writing for the instrumental works, in marked contrast to the varying degrees of chordal or imitative counterpoint that typify the madrigal. The only vocal works to approach the duet-plus-*continuo* texture of the instrumental ones are the *madrigaletti*.

The innovations of the instrumental works, again by comparison with the vocal ones, are several: idiomatic generic types (*sinfonia*, sonata, dances); various dedications, mainly in *gagliarde*, to persons or families; dynamic and tempo markings in a selected number of works; references to borrowings, from other composers or from a repertory of tunes or ground basses; indications that certain works were meant to be transposed; trio-sonata texture; and finally, in Books 3–4, the new, technically demanding style of writing that comes to the fore particularly in the variation sonata. Attention turns, in Chapter 5, to the problems of translating these innovations into performance.

5

From Composition to Performance

I N the following chapter a line will be drawn from the composition of Rossi's works to their performance. The treatment is far from inclusive, for it neither touches on the special problems, mainly liturgical, that relate to the Hebrew 'Songs', nor does it deal with any more than a select number of musical parameters from within the secular vocal and instrumental collections. This is not an essay, then, on early seventeenth-century performance practice in the full panoply of its interpretative associations. Rather, the discussion narrows to questions raised with particular urgency by Rossi's collections in certain well-defined areas: accidentals, metres, the *continuo*, melody instruments, alternative ensembles, tuning, transposition, tempo, dynamics, and the ordering of dances into suites. Most of the questions are familiar from other late sixteenth- and early seventeenth-century composers' works, yet Rossi's force us to re-examine them in a renewed search for their elucidation.

Accidentals

There are several uses of accidentals in Rossi's collections, all of them known from the literature,[1] with one exception: naturals that act as sharps. These naturals are not occasional, nor are they adventitious: they number twenty-three examples in the vocal works, including two in the Hebrew songs, and thirty in the instrumental ones; and they demonstrate a clear enough profile to suggest an intentional deviation from standard practice. Where it was customary to designate a sharp by a sharp, the composer, in the following *sinfonia*, also designates it by a natural (Ex. 5.1).

The origins of this clearly unorthodox use of a natural for a sharp would seem to lie in the older meaning of the natural, in hexachordal theory, as the higher of two semitones, or *b durum*, versus *b molle* for the lower one. In earlier music, *b durum* (or *quadratum*) was used for perfect fifths and major thirds, while *b molle* (or *rotundum*) was used for minor thirds.[2] But, more

---

[1] The known uses are sharps or flats for raising or lowering pitches by a semitone; implied accidentals, to be added as *musica ficta*; cautionary signs, such as E sharp or B sharp, warning against altering pitches by *musica ficta*; redundant accidentals, i.e. a sharp or a flat on notes of the same pitch in a single bar (where, by modern convention, one accidental suffices).

[2] See Marchetto da Padua, *Lucidarium*, 8. 1. 17–20 (ed. Herlinger, 279–81); and id., *Pomerium*, 17. 15–17 (ed. Vecchi, 73–8).

Ex. 5.1   Sinfonia 5 (Book 4, no. 17, bars 11–16, 30–4, with two F sharps and three F naturals as sharps)

practically, they can be traced to the operational equivalence of sharps and such naturals as cancel flats: both raise the pitch to which they are adjoined.

Except for Rossi's examples, there seem to be no others in the literature. Nor can one find an adequate explanation for the usage beyond the one just mentioned, namely, the similarity between sharps and certain naturals. The theorists refrained from saying so, perhaps because it was obvious. But, with changes in time and custom, what was once obvious eventually became obscure. We can only be grateful to Lorenzo Penna, for one, who, in a treatise on the rudiments of music, wrote that 'the natural has two further effects, the first being to raise or increase the pitch and the second to assign the syllable *mi* to the note before which the same square natural is placed.... The sharp likewise raises or lifts the pitch'.[3]

Still, whatever the explanation, Rossi must have realized that he was not adhering to conventional notation. In most instances, he placed the naturals before an F that functioned as part of a 'dominant' chord (B–D sharp–F natural, i.e. sharp) resolving to E minor. To clarify their reading, he connected them, in vocal music, with a rueful or evocative conceit, as in 'pianto' or 'piangeretemi', 'tormento', 'anima', and 'conforto'.[4] Elsewhere he set the

---

[3] Penna, *Li primi albori musicali per li principianti della musica figurata*, 4th edn. (1684), 34–5 (from Bk 1, ch. 13 'Delli accidenti della musica').

[4] Bk 3: 8, bars 26–7 ('pianto'); 10, bars 9–10 ('piangeretemi'). M4: 7, bars 26–7 ('tormento'); 5, bar 4 ('anima'). Bk 2: 11, bars 36–8 ('conforto').

Ex. 5.2 'Occhi, quella pietà' (Book 2 *a 5*, no. 14, bars 39–45)

naturals on the key words 'finta' or 'fingesti',[5] which, adverting to *musica ficta*, dispel any uncertainties about his intentions: the naturals connote 'fictitious' sharps (Ex. 5.2).

Problems begin when the music is bereft of textual hints, as in the instrumental works. There the context and, more substantially, the impossibility of proceeding otherwise without lapsing into intolerable dissonance confirm the reading of naturals as sharps. Sometimes the music helps by proffering its own hints, as when an F natural in one part occurs together with an F sharp in the *basso continuo*.[6]

---

[5] Cf. Bk 2: 14, bars 41–5 ('con finta pietà'), and Bk 4: 9, bars 34–6 ('fingesti').

[6] As in S4: Sinf. 5, Corr. 5. Such musical hints are also to be found in the vocal works, as in Bk 2: 14, where, in the passage 'con finta pietà', the alto has a D sharp against a D

Natural signs function, elsewhere, as bona fide naturals, which itself is rather unusual, for naturals were customarily designated via sharps or flats. In the passage shown in Ex. 5.3 the natural signs indicate a regular natural and cautionary accidentals.

Ex. 5.3 'Soave libertate' (Book 2 *a* 5, no. 6, bars 29–32)

The natural on B cancels the flat in the signature while those on E and G caution against their alteration (lest E approached from D be lowered to E flat and G proceeding to A be raised to G sharp). It might be noted that the naturals fall on the word *stretto*, in 'stretto in belle catene': by singing 'confined to beautiful chains', the performer would seem to be advised to 'confine' himself to the 'chains' of the written pitches (*stretto* meaning 'exact', or 'literal', as in the locution 'lo stretto significato delle parole').

True, accidentals are nothing new to the Italian literature. Giuseppe Caimo, for example, in his madrigals for four and five voices, from the 1560s and 1580s, uses them liberally, sometimes even wildly. Yet when he writes them, they function, in all instances, as they are supposed to: sharps raise pitches, flats lower them, and naturals cancel alterations. Thus, in one passage, there are D sharps in the quinto, F sharps in the alto and bass, A sharps in the canto and bass, and C sharps in the canto and quinto: all sharps are signed, and act, as sharps. In another, with four naturals—real naturals—alongside B in the tenor, the naturals cancel the B flat of the signature.[7] This is standard procedure, against which the aforementioned examples in Rossi's works stand out, all the more, for their singularity.

natural in the quinto (bar 41^3) or the tenor a D natural against a D sharp in the *continuo* (bar 45^4).

[7] For the sharps, see Caimo, *Madrigali and Canzoni for Four and Five Voices*, ed. Miller, 106 (bars 19–22); for the naturals, see there, 55 (bars 34–7).

Metres

What is the relationship between the mensuration signs C and ₵? Or between either of them and 3? These are questions that, in Rossi's time, must have tested, if not tried, the performers' knowledge and skills: they are still being argued today.[8]

Most of Rossi's vocal music is written under C, with the semibreve as the basic unit of measure (or *tactus*) for drawing barlines. Triple metre, under the sign 3, occurs principally in his instrumental works, where it designates 3/2, i.e. *sesquialtera minore*, with the *tactus* comprising three minims. Mixed metres, with two or more signs in succession, are to be found in certain vocal works and, more substantially, in the instrumental ones.[9]

In the *sinfonie* and sonatas, C is often replaced by ₵ after sections of triple metre, i.e. C/3/₵, in which, to all appearances, ₵ (*tempo maggiore imperfetto*) is synonymous with regular C (*tempo minore imperfetto*). The theorists recognized their equivalence, though also admitted the validity of ₵, in its older denotation, for cutting the time of C in half (*tempo imperfetto diminuto*).[10] But is the equation C = ₵ binding?

True, Michael Praetorius distinguished madrigals under C from motets under ₵, with the madrigals having shorter values, hence quicker movement (though a slower *tactus*) than the motets.[11] Yet he was referring to individual works under the one or other sign and not to changes within them. Thus in determining how C compares with ₵ one must take into account the proportional relationships both *between* and *within* works under different signs.

As for those *between* works, C and ₵ were, by and large, employed fairly indiscriminately in music of the later sixteenth and early seventeenth centuries, so much so that certain theorists called for their separation and individuation after the example of earlier music.[12] Their different applications, if there were such, depend for their determination, in vocal music, on

---

[8] See e.g. Bowers, 'Some Reflection upon Notation and Proportion in Monteverdi's Mass and Vespers of 1610'; it awakened a response from Jeffrey Kurtzman and a counter-response from Bowers (see under Bibliography).

[9] Of Rossi's (146) Italian vocal works, 137 were printed under C, one under 3, and the remainder (8) in changing metres (C/3, 3/C, C/3/₵ /3, etc.); of his (33) Hebrew works, twenty-four were printed under C, one under 3, and the remainder (8) in changing metres; and of his (130) instrumental works, fifty-three were printed under C (though twelve were meant to be read, partly or wholly, under 3), three under ₵, forty-four under 3, and thirty in changing metres.

[10] Brunelli writes e.g. that '*tempo minore imperfetto* can be ordered in two ways: the first is by singing it like *maggiore imperfetto*; the second, by singing all its notes in half their value, as well as calculating its pauses by half their value': *Regole utilissime per il scolaro* (1606), 17. Recent research by Margaret Bent has shown that the sign ₵ as a diminution is more often a theoretical fabrication than a practical reality (see e.g. 'Aspects of Mensural Usage in Ockeghem', forthcoming in the volume of proceedings of a quincentennial conference on Ockeghem, Tours 1997).

[11] Cf. Praetorius, *Syntagma musicum*, iii (1618), 50.

[12] Among them, again, Brunelli, *Regole utilissime per il scolaro* (1606), 17.

the content of the text or the pacing of its syllables; or in both vocal and instrumental music, on the density of the writing or on rhythm in conjunction with the *tactus*.

The relationship between C and ¢ *within* works can be construed in various ways. Here and there, especially in Rossi's instrumental works, the change to ¢, after 3, might, by comparison with an earlier section under C, indicate a slightly faster tempo. In Book 1, for example, Sinfonia 12 has a final section under ¢ that is rhythmically less active than the opening one under C, thus suggesting that, in performance, the final section might have been accelerated (Ex. 5.4a). It bears comparison with Sinfonia 15, having a final section under ¢ that, in its rhythms, resembles the opening one under C, thus suggesting that C and ¢ are equivalent (Ex. 5.4b).

Ex. 5.4a   Sinfonia 12 (Book 1, no. 12, bars 1–4, 17–21)

Yet reverse arguments could just as well be advanced for the two examples. One is that if the last section under ¢ was rhythmically less (or more) active than an earlier one under C, so the composer wanted it to be. Another is that if it was rhythmically equivalent to an earlier section, then for variety's sake it could well suffer an alteration in tempo when performed.

Evidence for the equivalence of C and ¢ is provided by 'O tu che vinci l'alba', the last piece in Book 2 *a 5*. Bars 56–78 are a (written-out) repeat of 33–55, with the portion in ¢ originally in C, which suggests that the signs C and ¢ are identical in their tempo implications. Thus the madrigal furnishes what appears to be an important nugget of information for gauging the relationship of C and ¢ in Rossi's works having mixed metres.[13] But again,

[13] Bowers supports such a conclusion with reference to the 'Ave maris stella' and the Magnificat *a 7* in Monteverdi's Vespers ('Some Reflection upon Notation and Proportion',

Ex. 5.4*b*   Sinfonia 15 (Book 1, no. 15, bars 1–4, 16–20)

to play the devil's advocate, the sign ₵ could, in theory, indicate an acceleration.

What of the relation of C or ₵ to 3? From the previous remarks one might infer that it varies in accordance with how quickly or slowly the *tactus* is paced in duple sections. The usual reading of 3 as *sesquialtera* leads, of course, to three minims in the place of two. But it must be squared with the pragmatics of performance: the kind of flexibility described in renditions of vocal music,[14] where the tempo resulted from contextual decisions, would seem equally to apply to instrumental music, the more so since vocal music was regarded as its model.[15]

Rossi's works not only force questions about duple/triple relationships, but confront us with other realities: namely, that 3 means one thing in a *gagliarda* and another in a *corrente*; and, further, that C should sometimes be read as 3.

In the dances triple metre is usually signed by 3, which, in the main, reads as 3/2, or *sesquialtera minore*, with three minims to a 'bar'. Needless to say,

363–7); as in the statement that 'in view of the lack of a practical distinction between C and ₵ they are effectively all consistent throughout' (365).

[14] See e.g. Vicentino's recommendations for affectively performing madrigals (*L'antica musica ridotta alla moderna prattica* [1555], fo. 88ᵛ [*recte* 94ᵛ]) or Giustiniani's report on the licences taken by the 'concerto delle donne' (*Discorso sopra la musica de' suoi tempi*, 1628, tr. MacClintock, 69).

[15] Ever since Ganassi, for one, instrumentalists were directed to vocal music as a paradigm for phrasing, articulation, tempo, and ornamentation. See his *Opera intitulata Fontegara* (1535), tr. Peter, 9: 'Be it known that all musical instruments, in comparison to the human voice, are inferior to it. For this reason we shall endeavour to learn from it and to imitate it....The aim of the recorder player is to imitate as closely as possible all the capabilities of the human voice'.

choreographic considerations influence the way the minims group. The 3 in a *gagliarda* is not 3/2, but a double bar under 6/2, indeed, a complete series of steps in the *gagliarda* occupies six minims. Rhythmically, though, the *gagliarda* oscillates between six minims and three semibreves, in typical hemiola, while at the same time retaining its initial subdivision into 3/2 plus 3/2 (Ex. 5.5*a*).

Ex. 5.5*a*   Gagliarda 1 'detta la Sconsolata' (Book 4, no. 19, bars 1–8)

Time was required for articulating these rhythmic subtleties, and the *gagliarda*, whether performed straightforwardly in six beats or with the beats divided by virtuosic footwork, was moderately paced. Not so the livelier, more earthy *corrente*, where the rhythms group into four bars of 3/2, thus 12/2 (or as transcribed here, 12/4) for a complete dance sequence, with strong accents on first beats and, at every fifth bar, a significant harmonic change (Ex. 5.5*b*; note naturals for sharps).

The difference between the two varieties of 3/2 comes to the fore when the two dances are performed in tandem, as in the *gagliarda-corrente* pairs in Rossi's Book 4, on which more below: there the tempo has obviously to be adjusted to the peculiarities of the one or other dance. But the difference also reflects upon the pacing of sections under triple metre in non-dance types, both vocal and instrumental. As it so happens, many of these sections, in Rossi's *canzonette, madrigaletti,* and Hebrew songs, or, among his instrumental works, in his *sinfonie*, sonatas, and *canzoni*, do, in fact, display the rhythmic traits of either a *gagliarda* or a *corrente*.[16] In such cases it might

---

[16] For examples from the instrumental works, see Ch. 4, under the section 'The *Sinfonia* as a Composite of Abstract and Dance Types'.

Ex. 5.5*b*   Corrente 5 (Book 4, no. 26, bars 1–12)

be assumed that the decisions that pertain to the tempo of a *gagliarda* and *corrente* as dances pertain to the tempo of sections resembling them in other genres.

Rossi's œuvre illustrates still another variety of triple metre, though now disguised by a duple sign. The use of C for 3/2 is particularly rampant among the instrumental works: of the fifty-three prefixed by C, four sonatas and nine *sinfonie* are either wholly or partly to be measured in 3/2 on the basis of their rhythmic and harmonic accents.[17] Belonging to those that are 'partly to be measured in 3/2' are certain *sinfonie* that have triple metre in the first section only, which turns them into works in mixed metres (Ex. 5.6).[18]

But 3/2 departs here from that in pieces prefixed by 3 and having minims as their chief units: in such pieces the minim is probably to be measured in sesquialteral relationship to one under duple metre, hence to be taken about one third faster. In C used for 3/2 the rhythmic circumstances are different, as may be illustrated by the sonata on the 'theme' of the *romanesca* in Book 3. It has passages in which the minim divides into semiquavers, which would suggest that the minim should probably be taken not at a faster pace, but more or less at the same pace as one in a piece under duple metre (Ex. 5.7).

It is now clear why the pieces were marked with C to start with: their measurement is on the level of the minim, itself equivalent to the minim in duple compositions.

[17] Sonatas: S3: 3, 5; S4: 6, 10. *Sinfonie*: S2: 8–9, 17–18, 25 (optional version of no. 8, now *a* 4), 28–9 (optional versions of, respectively, nos. 9 and 18, now *a* 5); S3: 3; S4: 6.
[18] See, specifically, S2: 8–9, 25, 28.

Ex. 5.6   Sinfonia 9 (Book 2, no. 9, bars 1–3, 8–12)

Ex. 5.7   Sonata 3 'sopra l'Aria della Romanesca' (Book 3, no. 3, bars 52–7)

The use of C for 3, to summarize, is of two kinds: a faster 3/2, as in various *sinfonie* prefixed by C, where the movement is basically in crotchets and quavers; a slower 3/2, as in various sonatas also prefixed by C, yet where the movement is extended to embrace semiquavers. Both qualify as triple metres, though, practically, the second is too heavily weighted with shorter notes to be performed as quickly as the first.[19]

Sonata 5 in Book 3 is more complicated: it has two varieties of triple metre, 3/2 and, it would seem, 3/4, and of the two, 3/2 is disguised by duple signs (C, ₵). The succession is C for the first section, in which C equals 3/2; 3 for the second section, in which each bar reads as 3/4; and ₵ for the third section, in which ₵ equals regular C, though again as 3/2 (Ex. 5.8).

The conclusion is twofold: the metres have to be determined as a function of their rhythmic content; and the tempo of 3 is not unitary, but variable,

Ex. 5.8 Sonata 5 'sopra Porto celato il mio nobil pensiero' (Book 3, no. 5, bars 1–4, 95–100, 126–30)

---

[19] For slower and faster triple metres under C, see Aldrich, *Rhythm in Seventeenth-Century Italian Monody*, 42–3, 57 (and for examples, 45).

both in single works under 3 (or sometimes under duple metre), among them *gagliarde, correnti,* and the aforementioned sonata on the 'theme' of the *romanesca,* and in works having mixed metres. In the latter, the relationship between two and three minims depends largely on their context.

Bass Part, Basso continuo

An instrumental bass was provided for most of the vocal collections, the exceptions being the *Canzonette,* all but one work in Book 3 *a 5,* and the book of Hebrew songs. In the first four madrigal books *a 5* and the book of madrigals *a 4* it acts as a *basso seguente,* doubling the notes of the vocal bass. Not so in the *Madrigaletti* and, one might assume, the incomplete Book 5 *a 5,* where it is considerably more independent.[20] Unlike the vocal collections, the instrumental ones contain no separately printed bass, for the lowest part was its own bass, hence could if necessary have functioned as *continuo.*

The only collections to be figured are Book 1 *a 5,* for which a *continuo* was supplied in the last edition (1618, eighteen years after the first; it contains 261 figures); Book 5 *a 5* (846 figures); the *Madrigaletti* (775); and, of the instrumental books, the fourth (646). In the remaining collections either no figures or very few occur. Since Books 1–3 of the instrumental works are relatively bare of them, it is possible that their lowest part was played melodically, with some harmonic filling, on a single instrument (about which more below).[21] It is also possible that the *continuo* in the last edition of Book 1 *a 5* should be taken as an indicator that, in practice, it was realized from the first edition on (1600). Yet the opposite conclusion might also be drawn, namely, that the deferral of the *continuo* to the last edition implies its purposeful omission from the four earlier ones. As to Book 3 *a 5,* where the only work to carry a *continuo* is the extra special *Canzon de' baci,* it would appear that the others were definitely to be performed with voices alone. But here, too, one might argue differently: it could be that the omission of the *continuo* in the others was meant to highlight the *Canzon,* by contrast, as a unicum within its collection, which both poetically and musically it indeed is, without necessarily implying that the remaining numbers were to be kept free of a *continuo* in actual performance.

Three questions should be asked. Was the *continuo* compulsory in the vocal and instrumental works? How many instruments did it comprise? Which instruments were they?

[20] All in all, thirty-seven works out of 110 with a *continuo.* These represent the more 'modern' side of Rossi's vocal repertory.

[21] Such a conclusion is supported by Borgir, *The Performance of the Basso Continuo,* 51–2. In opposition to the 'generally held view that all Baroque ensemble music includes the *basso continuo',* he claims that 'secular instrumental music throughout the period allowed for performance by single-line instruments'. He considers Rossi's three-part compositions 'harmonically complete', hence self-sufficient in their ensemble.

The questions are answered in part from within the titles to Rossi's collections. Those to the instrumental ones specify, for the bass, a 'chitarrone' (Book 2), 'a chitarrone or another similar instrument' (Books 3–4), or 'a chitarrone or another foundation instrument (*istromento da corpo*)' (Book 1). From the titles one may conclude, first, that the *continuo* was compulsory in the instrumental works and, second, that it was to be played on the chitarrone, i.e. theorbo, which could, however, be replaced by another 'foundation instrument' (the term is Agazzari's).[22] Since the chitarrone was described (in Book 1) as a 'foundation instrument', it follows that the 'similar' instrument for substitution (according to Books 3–4) also belonged to the 'strumenti da corpo'.[23] Rossi speaks of a single bass instrument for his instrumental works: there is no need, then, to reinforce it. Neither does one find evidence for multiple instruments in the titles to his and other contemporary composers' instrumental collections, nor does one find it in early seventeenth-century theorists' manuals.[24]

By contrast, the titles to the vocal collections are more general, referring to a *basso continuo* 'to be played' (*Madrigaletti*), or 'to be played *in concerto*', i.e. together with the voices (Book 2 *a* 5), or 'to be played on foundation instruments' (Book 3 *a* 5), or merely 'for instruments' (Book 4 *a* 5). It would appear that the *continuo* was compulsory, though the music, as constructed, might indicate otherwise. With the exception of the *Madrigaletti* and Book 5 *a* 5, the vocal works were either written for voices alone (the three-voice *canzonette*) or principally conceived for voices (the madrigals for four and five voices).[25] The *continuo* part, by functioning as a *basso seguente*, and that is the way Rossi wrote it, adds nothing of its own, thus is easily dispensable in most madrigals. It might have been furnished as a commercial ploy: to make the music more fashionable, hence more attractive to potential buyers.

The composers recognized the possibility of omitting the *continuo*, and this in the first flower of the Baroque, thought, by those who preach the conventional wisdom, to be premised on the inevitability of a *continuo* accompaniment. Girolamo Diruta and Maurizio Cazzati, for example, said of certain collections that the bass may be played 'se piace'.[26] The Baroque is

---

[22] Agazzari, *Del sonare sopra il basso* (1607).

[23] The only one of the four books not to mention the possibility of alternative instruments is S2 ('con un chitarrone').

[24] On this point, see Borgir, *The Performance of the Basso Continuo*, 19. He concludes that 'in Italy…titles of instrumental sonatas are reliable guides to the number of instruments the composer considered necessary', 21. For a general study on bass practices, see Hodgkinson, 'Terminology, Performance, and Structure of the "Bass" in Few-Voiced Seventeenth-Century Italian Instrumental Music'.

[25] Where the Mti tended to a trio-sonata texture, Bk 5 seems, to judge from the *continuo*, to have been conceived differently from the other madrigal books, namely with a more independent and active *continuo* in a blatant *stile concertato*.

[26] Diruta, *Salmi intieri 4 v.…con il basso per l'organo, se piace* (1630); Cazzati, *Salmi per tutto l'anno 8 v. brevi, e commodi per cantare con 1, o 2 organi, e senza ancora se piace* (1660).

obviously many things, including the perpetuation, within its practice, of the *continuo*-free Renaissance.

There is no mention of the chitarrone in the vocal collections, yet it may be assumed from their indication of 'foundation instruments' (Book 3 *a* 5) or by reference to what we know of the latter from the instrumental collections. Like Monteverdi's Book 5 *a* 5 (1605), allowing the realization of the *basso continuo* on a 'clavicembalo, chittarone od altro simile istromento', so Rossi's vocal collections could have had their *continuo* played on one or more supporting instruments: remember, the composer spoke, in their titles, of 'instruments'. Given the option of substituting 'similar' instruments for the chitarrone,[27] the choice of the instrument seems to have been left to the performers' better judgement. The only obligation was to stay within the perimeters of 'foundation instruments'.

In both the instrumental and the vocal collections the chitarrone could, then, be replaced by another stringed instrument (archlute, viola da gamba, violoncello) or by a wind or keyboard instrument (bassoon, harpsichord, spinet) in the older tradition of playing instrumental music 'con ogni sorte de strumenti musicali' (as in Biagio Marini's *Affetti musicali*, 1617). The formula 'chitarrone or other similar instrument' might intimate a certain predilection for the chitarrone over the rest. But what did Rossi mean by chitarrone?

One would be inclined to take the word chitarrone at face value were it not for the evidence of the six pseudo-monodies, for voice and chitarrone, in Book 1 *a* 5.[28] Could the meaning be stretched to refer to an archlute?[29]

On the tuning of the chitarrone, the theorists, among them Alessandro Piccinini, Praetorius, and Marin Mersenne, seem to have been in agreement on transposing the first and second courses down an octave.[30] In this respect, the chitarrone differs from the archlute, which retains them at their original pitches. But tuning the two upper courses of the chitarrone to the lower octave does not work well for Rossi's pseudo-monodies: various lines in the vocal original now cross below the bass, producing 6/4 chords (Ex. 5.9a).[31] Nor does the other option offered by the theorists, namely, to lower the first course only, prove helpful, for it leads to jagged leaps in melodies clearly intended to be conjunct (Ex. 5.9b).[32]

---

[27] The option extended into the 18th c. as well, as when e.g. B. Marcello specified that the *continuo* of his flute sonatas could be played on either a violoncello or a harpsichord (*Suonate a flauto solo con il suo basso continuo per violoncello o cembalo* [1712]).

[28] Specifically, Bk 1: 12–17.

[29] The possibility was discussed in the introduction to *CW* i, and, independently, by David Nutter in recent research, still unpublished.

[30] On the tuning of the chitarrone, see e.g. Mason, *The Chitarrone and its Repertoire in Early Seventeenth-Century Italy*, and Spencer, 'Chitarrone, Theorbo, and Archlute'.

[31] Bars 28–9, 38, 45, 47–8, 57.

[32] Bars 21, 24–25, 32, 39–40, 52, 58–9.

Ex. 5.9*a*   'Ohimè, se tanto amate' (Book 1 *a* 5, no. 12), bars 20–1, 26–7, etc.

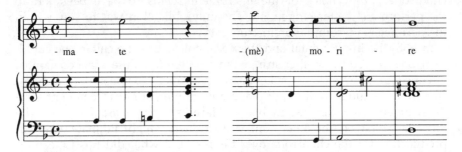

Ex. 5.9*b*   bars 4–5, 15–17, etc.

True, the octave transposition is convenient, in many places, for keeping the top voice of the accompaniment from duplicating the sung melody or from exceeding it by a third or more. Yet the advantages of maintaining the bass line in its integrity and of having 'normal' chordal progressions would seem to outweigh those of separating the voice from its accompaniment. The chitarrone tablature reads best without octave lowering, either as d–g–c'–e'–a'–d" (in two examples) or as A–d–g–b–e'–a' (in the rest),[33] plus their added (unstopped) bass strings.

As it so happens, the theorists were not unanimous in advocating octave transposition. Adriano Banchieri suggested a tuning in which course 2 was left intact while course 1 might or might not be transposed 'come piace'.[34] Though Rossi specifically mentions the chitarrone in his various publications, he allows its substitution, as is evident from the instrumental ones, by 'similar instruments'. Since, as said, one basic difference between the chitarrone and archlute was in the octave transposition of the one and the fixed notation of the other, it could be that Rossi either left the tuning of the chitarrone to the discretion of the musician or actually intended an archlute.[35]

---

[33] Bk 1: 12–13 (d–g, etc.), 14–17 (A–d, etc.).

[34] Banchieri, *Conclusioni nel suono dell'organo* (1609), 53.

[35] Nutter (see above) goes so far as to suggest that a single archlute, tuned to A, was used, which means that the voice part of two of the pseudo-madrigals (nos. 12–13) would have to be tuned down a fourth.

The problem is not easily resolved: the theoretical statements need to be re-evaluated and other examples of chitarrone tablatures from the period—by, say, Johann Kapsberger and Flamminio Corradi[36]—studied for their spacing of voice and accompaniment.[37]

One thing is certain, though: the chitarrone, or archlute, or surrogate instruments for playing the accompaniment in the pseudo-monodies or in the madrigals or *madrigaletti*, were 'foundation instruments', providing the infrastructure for the voices or, in the instrumental collections, for the 'melody instruments'.

Melody Instruments

Books 1–3 of the instrumental works are, as far as is known, the earliest chamber music publications to indicate melody and bass instruments; they precede, by a decade or more, collections of Biagio Marini and Stefano Bernardi, themselves followed by Rossi's Book 4.[38] Focusing on the melody instruments in Rossi's collections, one finds varying specifications from one to another: Book 1 calls for *viole* or *cornetti*, Book 2 for *viole*, Book 3 for *viole da braccio*, and Book 4 for *violini*. Can the differences be reconciled?

That *cornetti* could be substituted for *viole* conforms to the practice in other composers' collections, including those, already mentioned, of Marini and Bernardi.[39] The question is whether Rossi limited the exchange to his first book or regarded it as feasible in the subsequent ones too. On the assumption that the titles are exact in their requirements and that Rossi, because of his own skills on the violin, favoured string instruments over others, it seems likely that *cornetti* were meant for Book 1 and possibly Book 2, though not for the rest. String and wind instruments are so remote in their sonorities that one wonders whether the *cornetti* were not confined to those works in Books 1–2 calling for one or two extra instruments ('se piace').

Yet the question of instrumental exchange is not so easily dismissed. Books 3–4 have *sinfonie* and *gagliarde* basically in the same style as those in Books 1–2, from which one might infer their similar instrumentation (*viole* or *cornetti*), and this in contravention of their specifications. Further evidence may be adduced in support of substitution: the perpetuation of the alternative violin or *cornetto* practice into the 1640s, as, for example, in the

---

[36] Kapsberger, 1610, 1612, 1619; Corradi, 1616.

[37] See e.g. Buetens, 'Theorbo Accompaniments of Early Seventeenth-Century Italian Monody'; and for a broader study, North, *Continuo Playing on the Lute, Archlute, and Theorbo.*

[38] Marini's *Affetti musicali*, including *sinfonie, canzoni*, sonatas, a *balletto, arie, brandi, gagliarde*, and *correnti* 1–4 v. 'con violini cornetti et con ogni sorte de strumenti musicali' (1617) and, next in order, Bernardi's *Madrigaletti* 2–3 v., with various sonatas to be played on 'due violini over, cornetti, et un chitarrone, trombone, overo fagotto' (1621).

[39] On the practice in general, see Allsop, *The Italian 'Trio' Sonata*, 29–30; and in detail, Lewis, 'The Use of Wind Instruments in Seventeenth-Century Instrumental Music'.

'violinist' Giovanni Battista Fontana's well-known instrumental collection from 1641, with sonatas for 1–3 voices to be played, in their melody parts, on a *'violino* or *cornetto'.*[40]

Another problem is whether the differentiation between *viole, viole da braccio,* and *violini* was casual or intended: do they represent separate instruments or are they synonyms, one and all, for the violin? Either possibility may be envisioned, but the evidence for the second of them, to the effect that violins were meant, seems stronger.

For one thing, except for the addition of sonatas to Books 3–4, Rossi's four collections are closely related in their contents: *sinfonie* and *gagliarde,* the mainstay of the four, demonstrate structural and stylistic connections throughout the four; some of the more technically demanding *sinfonie* in the earlier books adumbrate the sonatas of the later ones.

For another, the term *viola,* though used to refer to viols, was also sometimes used as a generic term for the 'violin family'. Francesco Todeschini published a collection of *gagliarde, correnti,* etc., to be played on 'four *viole,* i.e. two violins, a viola, and a cello'. Although the collection dates from 1650, it is by a Mantuan musician working for the later duke Carlo II, from which one might assume the existence of a Mantuan tradition.[41]

For a third, the term *viola da braccio* does not necessarily refer to an arm viol, but rather to a string instrument (viol, violin) played 'on the arm', as opposed to 'between the legs' (viola da gamba, cello). Since Book 4 does indeed call for *violini* and, in content, continues in the same vein as Book 3, it is likely that *viole da braccio* and *violini* are equivalent. Pursuing this same line of reasoning back to the earlier books, it is equally likely that the *viole* to which they refer are no different from the *viole da braccio,* i.e. *violini,* in the later ones.

Yet another possibility should be considered. Since we know, from Chapter 1, that there were two instrumental ensembles at the court in Rossi's time, one with violins for his 'concerto', another with viols, if they were indeed viols, to be used for accompanying dances, and that both ensembles may have been under his direction, we might envisage a situation where the 'abstract' types, i.e. *sinfonie, canzoni,* and sonatas, were played by violins and the dances, i.e. *gagliarde, correnti,* and *brandi,* by viols. The only problem is that, in the title to Book 4, which, again, has the same kinds of pieces as the previous books, plus an increased number of dances, a single instrument is mentioned for the upper parts, *violini,* thus eradicating any distinction between abstract and dance types as a criterion for their instrumentation, or at least in Book 4.

---

[40] Fontana, *Sonate 1–3 v. per il violino, o cornetto, fagotto, chitarrone, violoncino, o simile altro instromento* (1641). See also Buonamente, who, in Sonatas 4–5 from Bk 6 (1636), allows the second violin to be replaced by a *cornetto.*

[41] Todeschini, *Correnti, gagliarde, balletto, et arie, 4 v. da sonare con quattro viole cioè due violini, viola, e basso...lib. 1°* (1650).

Perhaps the terminology should be understood more loosely, in the sense of 'ogni sorte de strumenti musicali', whereby one kind of melody instrument could be substituted for another, after the example of similar exchanges, already discussed, between bass instruments.

Optional Ensembles, Tuning, Transposition, Tempo, Dynamics

The instrumental works are special in containing a number of specific performing indications, though, as was the case with instruments, their explanation or implementation is often fraught with difficulties.

1. *Optional ensembles.* In Books 1–2 Rossi scored various *sinfonie* and *gagliarde* (plus one fragment of a *balletto*) for different-sized ensembles. He allowed the performers to choose *si placet* between settings for three or five voices (in thirteen works) or, in Book 2 only, for three or four voices (in five works).[42] Basically, the works were composed for the smaller ensemble, and as such are faultless in their voice leading. In this sense, they recall Gastoldi's five-voice *balletti*, described by one critic as 'puffed out versions of a trio texture'.[43] With the addition of two middle voices, however, a number of parallels and dissonances emerge.[44]

The enlargement to four or five voices may have been at the behest of the publisher, seeking to amplify the rather limited amount of music in Books 1–2 or to increase its chances of performance by offering the choice of larger or smaller ensembles. Rossi complied, but does not seem, in Book 2, to have had enough material at hand. So, if the assumption of a 'collusion' between publisher and composer can be sustained, he resorted to a compromise: he took nine of the three-voice *sinfonie* from the earlier part of the book and placed them, in alternative versions for three or four voices or for three or five, in the later part. The net result, as far as the number of original works in Book 2 is concerned, is nine less than the total.

Which version did the composer prefer? If he were a stickler for contrapuntal propriety, the three-voice version would clearly have been his choice. But since he and other composers seem to have been working within the bounds of a tradition that allowed for a modicum of freedom in the constitution of ensembles,[45] he is likely, as pointed out in Chapter 4, to have

---

[42] *Sinfonie* 5/3 v.: S1: 21–2, 24; S2: 27–31. *Sinfonie* 4/3 v.: S2: 22–3, 25–6. *Gagliarde* 5/3 v.: S1: 23, 25–6; S2: 32. *Gagliarda* 4/3 v.: S2: 24. *Balletto* 5/3 v.: S1: 27.

[43] Denis Arnold, in a review in the *Journal of the American Musicological Society*, 21 (1968), 107.

[44] The only exception is S1: 22, which seems to have originally been conceived *a 5*.

[45] The practice extends into the 1650s, as in the same collection by Todeschini already mentioned with reference to *viole* meaning *violini*. There he allows the omission of the middle parts ('e si possono sonare a tre, a due, lasciando fuori le parti di mezzo'). Alternative ensembles are specified, here and there, in later collections, among them Marco Uccellini's *Sinfonie boscarecie a violino e basso* (1669), for two to four instruments at the performers' discretion. For further examples, see Mangsen, '*Ad libitum* Procedures in Instrumental Duos and Trios'.

recognized the viability of different approaches to voice leading: one according to the conventions of *prima pratica* counterpoint, the other according to a more casual treatment whereby the rules were bent for the sake of a larger performing group.

The question of 'preference' was raised, in the chapter on 'Italian Vocal Music', in considering strophic repeats in the *canzonette*, where the accommodation of words to notes resulted in barbarisms of accentuation and syntax. There, too, one had to acknowledge that while textual propriety was expected in non-strophic works, a different approach may have been tolerated in strophic ones. Otherwise, one would have to conclude that such repeats were probably never executed, in which case the addition, in the prints and manuscripts, of multiple stanzas was merely *pro forma*, with no relevance *pro pratica*.

2. *Tuning.* In Book 4, two *gagliarde*, and their corresponding *correnti*, carry the instruction that 'the octave of the chitarrone be tuned to the four-string *contralto*'.[46] They are the only works in this and the other instrumental books to have a key signature with two sharps (on F and C), which would have posed a problem for the bass courses, i.e. the added bass strings, on the chitarrone. Rossi, as already mentioned, seems to have employed two different chitarrone tunings for his pseudo-monodies in Book 1 *a* 5, one beginning on A, the other on d: the bass courses for the A tuning would have been C–D–E–F–G and for the d tuning F–G–A–B flat–c. In the two *gagliarde* (and their *correnti*) in Book 4 the lowest pitches are E–F sharp–G–A. Yet F sharp is clearly absent from the bass courses of the two tunings (as is E from the one on d). To provide the F sharp (and C sharp), the chitarrone might have been tuned down one whole tone (from A) to G, thus G–c–f–a–d'–g', with the bass courses BB–C sharp–D–E–F sharp.

How does such a tuning relate to the instruction for tuning the octave of the chitarrone to the four-string *contralto*? By four-string *contralto* one might assume a (modern-styled) viola tuned to c–g–d'–a'. Since Book 4 calls for two *violini* (and chitarrone), the instrument could just as well have been a violin. Moreover, the upper parts of the two *gagliarde* and their *correnti* lie as high as those of other works in the collection and are more easily negotiated on a violin than on a viola. To all appearances, the violin was meant, and the usual tuning of the violin to g–d'–a'–e" coincides with a G tuning on the chitarrone. In short, the performer seems to have been advised to tune his chitarrone to G, whereby the lowest string concurs with the lowest one, an octave higher, on the violin. What we have here, in essence, is one of the earliest known indications of *scordatura*.

3. *Transpositions.* Six instrumental works seem to call for transposition either upwards by a fourth or a second or downwards by a fourth or a

---

[46] S4: Gagl. 2, 5, and their *correnti* ('si accorda l'ottava del chitarrone con il contr'alto a quattro tasti').

third.[47] One reason for doing so would be their adaptation to another vocal or instrumental work in a different mode. If, for example, they were used in theatrical performances, they might have been paired with *canzonette* or madrigals written higher or lower, in which case some sort of accommodation of the *balli* to the register and mode of the vocal works would have been necessitated.

Since transpositions were probably undertaken, in performance, as a matter of course, it is strange to find their indication in a printed source, all the more so since the work to which the transposed one was to be adjoined is not specified. If Rossi wanted his pieces to be transposed, why did he not write them at their intended pitches to start with?

In the literature it has been asked whether works marked 'va sonata alla quarta alta' or similarly were not intended to be kept at their written pitches, thought already to represent a transposition.[48] But why go to the trouble of warning not to transpose? In the end, performers probably did as they chose, moving works up or down at their own convenience; and, barring further information, any direction not to do so makes little sense, or so on the face of it it would seem. The progressive verb form 'va sonata' is quite explicit: it means 'is played' or 'is to be played' at whatever transposed pitch is indicated.

The solution to the problem might seem to reside in the range of the pieces as notated: are they already written unusually high or low, thereby precluding further alteration upward or downward? Checking them from this angle leads to inconclusive results. Two of those to be transposed up a fourth do, in fact, lie rather high: they reach b″ flat, hence, to all intents, rule out further transposition.[49] On the other hand, one example to be transposed down a fourth is written in an overly high register (its top voice reaches d‴), and its downward transposition does seem justified.[50] Even so, the higher notes could have been negotiated by *viole da braccio* or *cornetti*, as required for the upper parts in Rossi's instrumental works.

To sum up, whether the works were transposed or not would seem to be the lesser of two problems. There remains the greater one of providing an explanation: if they were to be transposed, then why at the specified pitch? And if the reason was their conjunction with a particular vocal or instrumental work, which work was it and why did the composer not refer to it by name? But if, on the other hand, they were not to be transposed, what

[47] S1: Sinf. 1 and 10 *a* 3 ('va sonata alla quarta alta'), Sinf. 2 *a* 4 ('alla quarta alta'); S3, Corr. 5 ('va sonata una voce più alta de l'ordinario'), Gagl. 1 ('va sonata a la quarta bassa'), Gagl. 2 ('va sonata una terza più bassa di quello si sona all'alta').

[48] Cf. Parrott, 'Transposition in Monteverdi's Vespers of 1610', with reference to Rossi's works on p. 506.

[49] Cf. S1: Sinf. 1, 10.

[50] S3: Gagl. 1. The same may be said of the one example to be transposed down a third (S3: Gagl. 2): it reaches b″ flat.

possible reason could the composer have had for forewarning the performers against transposition?

The information concerning the transposition of works to the upper
fourth or other intervals is too spotty to allow one to draw firm conclusions
about causes or motivations. As noted, the practice of transposition seems to
have been fairly widespread; and if it went beyond what is indicated in the
works themselves, then one might conjecture any number of transpositions
applicable to Rossi's and others' works for whatever reasons may have
stirred the composers or performers to undertake them.

So far the question of transposition has been confined to instrumental
music. When applied to vocal music it becomes even knottier. Practices of
transposition should obviously, for their fuller elaboration, be considered in
relation to *chiavette* as they occur in the secular and sacred vocal repertory.
The topic, bearing on Rossi's designation of clefs in his madrigals and
Hebrew works, has, because of its complexity, if not impenetrability, been
consciously avoided in this and other chapters (it demands, and will be
given, a separate investigation elsewhere). For the time being it might be
mentioned that in a recent study on *chiavette* a rather firm line was drawn
between vocal and instrumental practices.[51] When 'transposition clefs', i.e.
chiavette, are used in instrumental music, so the author contended, they
require 'to be performed at pitch, without any transposition'.[52] The words
are emphatic, lending support, albeit indirectly, to the notion, already argued,
that the instruction 'va sonata' at the upper fourth, or at other intervals, could
well call for transposition.[53] But, to repeat, the evidence for transposition,
from within the music, let alone the theoretical sources, is indecisive.

4. *Tempo.*   Sonata 11 in Book 4 has the markings 'Adagio', 'Presto', 'Adagio',
'[Presto]' for its principal sections and, for the repeat of the last section, 'più
presto'. It constitutes one of a small number of Rossi's works to carry tempo
indications. Book 1 had a 'sinfonia grave', though it is not clear whether the
term *grave* refers to its tempo or its 'serious' character: the writing is
rhythmically restrained.[54] Book 3 had three sonatas whose last section, like
that in the sonata above, is marked to be repeated faster (the instruction reads
'si replica l'ultima parte ma più presto').[55] Such tempo increases may

---

[51] Barbieri, ' "Chiavette" and Modal Transposition in Italian Practice (*c*.1500–1837)'.

[52] Ibid. 69. In Rossi's instrumental works, ten works have transposition clefs, or more
specifically an F clef on the third line for the lowest voice. Of the ten, five call for upper or
lower transposition (S1: 1, 10, 17; S3: 16–17) while the rest carry no such instruction (S1: 5; S2: 5,
13, 23; S4: 7). Another work that does call for transposition has the lowest voice in a regular F
clef on the second line (S3: 31). The clef usage, in short, is inconsistent.

[53] Even Parrott admitted that 'with the development of instrumental music, free of
vocal models, the concept of fixed pitches began to predominate' ('Transposition in Monteverdi's Vespers of 1610', 494).

[54] S1: 22. It is the only one of the eighteen *si placet* works in S1–2 to have had its two extra
voices—alto, tenor—conceived along with the rest as forming a whole, inasmuch as voice
leading and textural consistency are concerned.

[55] S3: 3–5.

have been standard practice in repeating final sections of works at large. Whether it applies, further, to repeats of whole sections of bipartite or tripartite works, be they *sinfonie, canzoni*, or dances, cannot be determined, though for variety's sake, in one or another example, it probably does. The question connects with that other thorny one, already addressed under metres, whether, in the succession C/3/₵, the section under ₵, coming at the end, was meant to be taken faster than the initial one under C. In matters of tempo, the performers were doubtless flexible, and again, by analogy with final sections to be repeated at a faster tempo, they are likely, here and there, to have accelerated final sections under ₵.

5. *Dynamics.* Dynamic markings occur in the later books. Sonata 4 in Book 3 combines them with echo imitations, signed 'Ecco Piano', 'Ecco Forte', the word *ecco* meaning, apparently, both 'echo' and 'behold!'. Corrente 7 from the same book has two instances of *piano* and *forte* placed rather arbitrarily: perhaps the only reason for adding them was to emphasize the work as the terminal one in the collection, hence something 'special'. More consistently placed are the *forte* and *piano* markings in the last work in Book 4, a sonata whose 'special' qualities—in instrumentation, style, modes, metres, echoes—were delineated in Chapter 4. Dynamics are 'special', though only in the sense of their being notated. In everyday practice, they were quite natural. The course of events in the seventeenth century was such as to increase the notational specification of dynamics, thus gradually changing their graphic status from special to ordinary.

The Ordering of Dances into Suites

In the chapter on 'instrumental music' the *sinfonia* was described as a composite, in various works, of abstract and dance types. Though Rossi did not compose full-fledged suites, he tentatively pointed in that direction in Book 4. There he formed five dance pairs of a *gagliarda* and 'its *corrente*' in the same mode.[56] True, *gagliarde* and *correnti* had already appeared in Book 3. But, in Book 4, they are as it were officially combined into two-movement 'suites'. From their example one might assume, in retrospect, that players were free to fabricate their own 'suites' in Book 3. Of the eight *gagliarde* and seven *correnti* in Book 3, three pairs are possible.[57]

In Book 4, three *gagliarde* and one *corrente* remain unpaired,[58] and were it desired, they could have been substituted for members of the fixed pairs or coupled with dances from the previous books, as long as they shared the same mode.

---

[56] S4: Gagl. 2–5, 8 (and their *correnti*).
[57] S3: Gagl. 1 or 4 with Corr. 6 (in Aeolian); Gagl. 5 with Corr. 2 or 3 (in Dorian on G); and Gagl. 8 with Corr. 4 (in Mixolydian).
[58] S4: Gagl. 1, 6–7; Corr. 5 (misnumbered 6).

Yet the modal restrictions on pairings are removed as soon as works are transposed, after the example of the various ones so marked in Books 1 and 3 (see above). That opens a wide field for potential pairings with other dances or even with the *sinfonia*. Buonamente, for example, has two dance suites at the beginning of his Book 5 (1629): there he links a *sinfonia* to a *gagliarda*, which, in turn, has 'its own *corrente*'. In his Book 7 (1637), after nine sonatas, he writes eight suites, about which he says that 'every *sinfonia* has its *brando*, *gagliarda*, and *corrente*'.[59]

The *sinfonia* combined not only with dances, but with abstract types as well. In a collection by Antonio Triolo (1608), for example, it preceded or followed *ricercari, capricci,* or (instrumental/vocal) *scherzi*.[60] But the *sinfonia* also entered the vocal domain. Praetorius spoke of placing *sinfonie* before and after vocal works.[61] Gastoldi included them in his *Concenti musicali* (1604) and Pietro Pace in his *Madrigali* for 4–5 voices (1617).[62] Of the twenty madrigals in Pace's collection, ten have *sinfonie*, about which the composer says that should one wish to sing the madrigals to which they are attached it is indispensable to play their *sinfonie*.[63]

With the knowledge that the *sinfonia* could be used in vocal and instrumental compositions, and that pairings of dances were already effected in Rossi's Book 4, one could have a field day in conjecturing possible linkings, for one, of *sinfonie* and *gagliarde, correnti,* and *brandi* throughout Rossi's four instrumental collections and, for another, of *sinfonie* and madrigals, *canzonette,* and *madrigaletti* in his eight Italian ones. The combinations are practically endless if one admits the possibility of transposition for purposes of modal accommodation.

Yet perhaps the most telling piece of evidence for linking *sinfonie* and dances, to return to the instrumental works, is contained in the music itself, as scrutinized for its final cadences or its openings. It is with the ends and beginnings, mentioned in passing in Chapter 4, but now considered in their potential for intimating dance suites, that we shall now be concerned.

Sinfonie end on a strong beat. *Gagliarde* so begin as for their first step to be on the fourth beat of their six-beat pattern, i.e. the upbeat bar of their

---

[59] On Buonamente and Rossi and the origins of the dance suite (and for Rossi as Buonamente's model), see Harrán, 'From Mantua to Vienna'. Buonamente's connections with Mantua, for which there is documentation from the first and third decades of the 17th c., are signalled by Nettl in 'Giovanni Battista Buonamente', esp. 528–30, 541–2; see also Allsop, *The Italian 'Trio' Sonata*, 10, though he writes that 'the precise relationship between Rossi and Buonamente must remain a matter of conjecture in the absence of the latter's first three collections' (111).

[60] Troilo, *Sinfonie, scherzi, ricercari, capricci, et fantasie 2 v. per cantar, et sonar, con ogni sorte di stromenti* (1608): 2, 'Sinfonia et Ricercar', and 5, same in reversed order; 3, 6, 15: 'Sinfonia et Capriccio', and 14, same in reversed order; 12, 'Scherzo et Sinfonia', and 20, same in reversed order.

[61] *Syntagma musicum*, iii. 132 [recte 112].

[62] Gastoldi, *Concenti musicali con le sue sinfonie, commodi per concertare con ogni sorte di stromenti* 8 v. (1604); Pace, *Madrigali* 4–5 v. (1617).

[63] 'avertendo però che quelli delle *sinfonie* non si possano cantare senza sonarli' (from title).

Ex. 5.10 Sinfonia 2 (Book 4, no. 14, bars 1–5, 49–51); Gagliarda 3 'detta la Favorita' (no. 21, bars 1–4, 25–6); 'its *corrente*' (bars 1–4, 30–3); Brando 1 (no. 28, bars 1–4)

two-bar groupings. Such a beginning allows their pairing with a previous *sinfonia* as if the *gagliarda* started in the second part of the same bar in which the *sinfonia* ended. As for the final cadence of the *gagliarda*, it falls on a strong beat in the first bar of a two-bar grouping, thus permitting its connection with a *corrente*. The *corrente* starts at the end of the second bar of its four-bar grouping, whereby it completes the first (or downbeat) bar of the previous *gagliarda*. It ends on a repeated chord (bars 1–2 of a four-bar unit), which could easily link with a *brando*.

One might, as an example, construct a hypothetical dance suite from various items in Book 4, viz. a *sinfonia*, a *gagliarda* and *corrente* (already paired in the original), and a *brando* (Ex. 5.10).

Note how smoothly the pieces combine, as if the *sinfonia* leads naturally into the *gagliarda*, the *gagliarda* into the *corrente*, and so on. Note, also, how uncannily the hypothetical suite is augured in the *sinfonia*, with its division into a sober opening section in duple metre, a middle section *alla gagliarda* in triple metre, and a final duple section, which, bustling with quavers, suggests a *brando* (Ex. 5.11).

Ex. 5.11 Sinfonia 2 (Book 4, no. 14, opening (see Ex. 5.10); middle, bars 30–3, etc.; end, bars 37–40, etc.)

The suite thus exists, on a prefigurative level, in the initial *sinfonia* and, *post factum*, in the actual concatenation of *balli* and a *sinfonia* to form a modally and rhythmically sensible whole.

Rossi, then, in his own modest way, links with the tendencies, in the later part of the seventeenth century, towards a distillation of two multipartite structures: the sonata and the suite, usually referred to under the designations *sonata da chiesa* and *sonata da camera*.[64] The 'da chiesa' sonata was foreshadowed in his *sinfonie*, his *canzoni per sonar*, and his *canzona* sonatas; the 'da camera' sonata, in the dance pairs of Book 4 and, more substantially, in the combinations of dances and *sinfonie* that could have been, and probably were, undertaken by musicians in performing his instrumental works.

[64] See Allsop, The *Italian 'Trio' Sonata*, for the most recent treatment of the sonata from its origins to Corelli; and with respect to the chamber sonata, Daverio, 'In Search of the Sonata da camera before Corelli'.

6

Music for the Theatre

WHILE previous chapters dealt with as much as is known of Rossi, biographically, from scraps of evidence in various documents and his works, the present one will piece together, from even fewer scraps, one side of his activity that is largely 'unknown': his connections with the theatre. Beyond two concrete instances of theatrical composition, which did not escape the scholars,[1] practically nothing remains, musically, to speak for closer ties with the theatre. Yet it is only reasonable to assume that, as the leading musician in the Mantuan Jewish community, Rossi contributed interludes of various sorts to the one or more annual productions of its theatrical troupe. Since the musical evidence for Rossi's theatrical associations concerns the non-Jewish theatre, it is no less reasonable to assume that Rossi furnished music for productions of non-Jewish companies as well.

Moving from certainties to suppositions, the discussion will cover four topics: Rossi's *intermedio* for Battista Guarini's comedy *L'Idropica*; his *balletto* for Giovanni Battista Andreini's 'sacred representation' *La Maddalena*; the evidence for his relations with the Mantuan Jewish theatrical company; and the possibility of reconstructing his theatre music, in part, by reference to his surviving works. Rossi's theatre music should be distinguished from his music for court entertainments, which, though replete with song and dance, lack a dramatic action. The examples to be mentioned relate to theatrical productions only.

The Intermedio *for Guarini's Comedy* L'Idropica

Guarini's *L'Idropica* was performed in 1608 as part of the week-long celebrations that marked the nuptials of Francesco Gonzaga and Margherita of Savoy. To the play itself the poet Gabriello Chiabrera added a prologue, four *intermedi*, and a finale, each of them set to music by different composers: Monteverdi, Rossi, Giovanni Giacomo Gastoldi, Marco Monco, Monteverdi's brother Giulio Cesare, and Paolo Virchi. Rossi's was the first *intermedio*, presented between Acts I and II, and like the other composers' portions,

---

[1] Becherini, Bertolotti, Canal, Nagler, Prunières, Solerti; for a review of the bibliography, see Harrán, 'Salamone Rossi as a Composer of Theatre Music', 96 n., 103 n. (and various references below).

what remains of it is not its music, but its story and lyrics.[2] Though it is foolhardy to talk about music in its absence, part of Rossi's *intermedio* can, nevertheless, be reconstructed from adjunct evidence, namely, the information contained in eyewitness reports of the court chronicler Federico Follino and, visiting in Mantua, the painter and art critic Federico Zuccaro.[3] True, Follino and Zuccaro were particularly drawn to the dramatic and scenic aspects of the *intermedi*, and only marginally interested in the music, which they invariably described as 'dolce', 'dolcissima', or 'dilettevole'. Still, they said enough between the lines of their reports to allow one to fit Rossi's music, in its content and performance, into the story.

The story, in this case, is 'The Rape of Proserpine' (*Il ratto di Proserpina*), or as its heroine is otherwise known, Persephone. Since her rape precedes her marriage, the story pays tribute, after its own heterodox fashion, to the newly-weds Francesco and Margherita. It was followed, in Intermedio II, by another notorious rape, that of Europe.[4] Chiabrera seems to have made a name for himself in writing this kind of poetry. For the wedding of Maria de' Medici and Henri, king of France, in 1600, an occasion which, for the music historians, is indelibly linked with the beginnings of opera (Jacopo Peri's *Euridice*), Chiabrera prepared a *Rapimento di Cefalo*.[5]

Rossi's *intermedio* opens with a dance of sixteen nymphs, who sing in praise of love's joys and pains. Pluto emerges from the bowels of the earth, driving a chariot; he snatches Proserpine and they vanish. General consternation follows. Descending on a cloud, Venus justifies Pluto's action as motivated by love. Enter Proserpine's mother Ceres on a chariot drawn by two dragons: she mourns the loss of her daughter. No sooner does she finish her lament than, in mid-air, Fame appears, propelled by the locomotion of her feathers. She consoles Ceres, informing her that Proserpine has left earthly parts to become queen of the nether world. 'Don't let the dark region disturb your thoughts', she says. 'In any domain, Ceres, it's great luck to win a great empire.'[6]

---

[2] For a general description of the various *intermedi*, see Solerti, *Gli albori del melodramma*, i. 73–103; and Nagler, *Theatre Festivals of the Medici*, 177–85. For the plots and the verses, see, in particular, Follino, *Compendio delle sontuose feste*, included, moreover, in Chiabrera, *Opere*, iv. 107–41. Chiabrera's *Ratto di Proserpina* should be distinguished from his *poemetto* entitled *Il rapimento di Proserpina*, an entirely different work, though sharing the same subject (*Opere*, iii. 152–63).

[3] Follino, *Compendio delle sontuose feste*, 72–99; Zuccaro, *Il passaggio per l'Italia*, 16–30. Their reports are contained in Solerti, *Gli albori del melodramma*, iii. 205–34 (Follino), 235–40 (Zuccaro).

[4] The third *intermedio* celebrates the nuptials of Jupiter and Alcmene, the fourth those of Hercules and Hebe.

[5] Florence: Giorgio Marescotti, 1600. On Chiabrera's connections with Florence, see Nagler, *Theatre Festivals of the Medici*, 96 ff.; on his connections with Mantua, see Neri, 'Gabriello Chiabrera e la corte di Mantova', 318–19.

[6] For the original Italian (and a translation) of all texts (poetic, descriptive) relating to Rossi's *intermedio*, see CW viii, pp. xl–xlvi, also Harrán, 'Salamone Rossi as a Composer of Theatre Music', 96–102. Unless otherwise stated, quotations below are drawn from Follino's report.

From the bare bones of this narrative, an *intermedio* was constructed that, in its scenery, costumes, and machinery, was so impressive as 'to stupefy the most balanced minds'.[7] The chroniclers concentrated on the *meraviglie*, from gushing fountains and shooting flames to black horses and fiery dragons. Music was of lesser interest to them, yet from their few remarks on it one can determine how many pieces Rossi wrote, their general character, and the way they were performed.

Rossi wrote five pieces, and not four, as might be thought from Chiabrera's four poems, set as four solo madrigals. The *intermedio* starts with what one eyewitness described as 'a delightful blend (*concerto*) of voices and instruments that made the whole theatre reverberate with a most agreeable harmony'. It is hard to define the exact nature of this initial piece. Because it included voices, it was not an instrumental *sinfonia* of the kind with which the remaining *intermedi* of *L'Idropica* seem to have opened.[8] The only other vocal-instrumental works in Rossi's repertory are a *balletto* written for Andreini's *Maddalena*, on which more below, and two *madrigaletti* with instrumental *ritornelli*.[9] It could be that the piece was simply a madrigal first performed vocally, then instrumentally, or a madrigal with its voices reinforced by instruments. Such double or mixed performances are known from the literature.[10]

Two kinds of information relate to the other pieces. The first concerns the main lines of their performance, the second the particularities of who did what and how. Regarding the first, we are told, for example, that in the chorus of nymphs ('Pingono in varii canti'), the instrumentalists played 'with the loveliest charm', the dancers moved 'with gracious manners and graceful motions', and the singers 'sweetly swayed their voices to the melody'. The overall effect was, apparently, to make hearing the piece as delightful as watching it.[11] Venus' song was intoned 'in a most gentle voice', and Ceres' 'in a plaintive . . . voice', which befitted her tearful appearance. Since nothing is said of how Ceres' *lamento* was received, it seems not to have been as powerful as that other *lamento* sung by Europe in the second *intermedio* (composed by Gastoldi). Europe is reported to have sung the dolorous notes of her melody so movingly that she awakened tears in the

---

[7] The description reflects Follino's opinion on the dramatic impact of the *intermedi* as a whole. Fame's aerial peregrinations, in Intermedio I, seem to have left the onlookers speechless ('they all remained astounded at such a beautiful and marvellous sight').

[8] For the other *sinfonie*, cf. Solerti, *Gli albori del melodramma*, iii. 228 (Follino), 248 (Zuccaro).

[9] Mti: 13, 15 (to be considered in the sections on 'theatrical implications' in Rossi's poetry and music).

[10] For example, the sixth *intermedio* for *La Pellegrina*; cf. *Les Fêtes du mariage de Ferdinand de Médicis et de Christine de Lorraine* (Florence, 1589), ed. Walker, p. li. See also Piperno, 'La sinfonia strumentale del primo Seicento—I', 155–6.

[11] 'the hearing of the listeners could for the moment only envy [the sight of] their eyes'.

listeners.[12] To all appearances, the part of Europe was performed by Rossi's sister, Madama Europa.[13]

From the second kind of information about the performance, namely, who did what and how, we learn that the initial chorus was executed by sixteen young girls posing as nymphs, and of the sixteen, four sang, four played instruments, and eight danced:

Sixteen maidens appeared from within the garden.... All at once, with exquisite grace, four of the maidens began to play a most delightful tune on the instruments they held in their hands. At the sound of the tune, another eight of them, moving in an orderly fashion, came out, in single pairs, from under those porticos, passing, with steps measured to the time of the dance, through the middle of the garden. After reaching the lawn before the same porticos, they faced the audience and began a ballet with such pleasing manners and graceful gestures that just to see them was reason for inestimable delight. The other four maidens who had stayed in the inner part of the porticos together with those who were playing [instruments] began themselves to move their voices sweetly to the [tune of the] song. As they accompanied, with their strains, the playing of the latter maidens and the dancing of the former ones, they fashioned a delightful melody...

The text, a *canzonetta* in four strophes, is one that Rossi composed as a dance song (see below).

Elsewhere we are told that Venus, perched on a hanging cloud, sang her 'madrigale' to the accompaniment of instruments off-stage[14] and that Fame sang hers while interspersing toots on a trumpet. Fame's entrance was announced by fanfares on a single silver trumpet so resonant, it appears, as to suggest 'a whole band (*concerto*) of trumpets playing together'.

Turning to the music proper, we have some idea of its general character. The opening vocal-instrumental number is described as a 'dolcissimo concerto' producing 'gratissima armonia'; the choral ballet as a 'dolcissima aria da ballo', with a 'dilettosa melodia' and a 'bel canto'; and the final madrigal as a work having a 'melodia dolcissima'. Aside from these vague indications, it may be assumed that the songs of Venus, Ceres, and Fame were monodies with instrumental support; perhaps not true monodies, but rather

---

[12] 'To the great delight and greater marvel of the listeners, she sang, in the most delicate and sweet voice, the madrigal that follows...singing, with the sweetest harmony, these tearful notes that, through pity, awakened tears in the listeners': cf. Solerti, *Gli albori del melodramma*, iii. 218–19.

[13] See above, Ch. 1, and, for a broader study, Harrán, 'Madama Europa, Jewish Singer in Late Renaissance Mantua', with arguments for and against Europa's participation in the *intermedio* on pp. 207–10.

[14] On the practice of concealing instruments in a staged performance, see Alessandro Guidotti's preface to Emilio de' Cavalieri, *La rappresentazione di Anima et di Corpo*, repr. in Solerti, *Le origini del melodramma*, 1–12, esp. 6 ('Gli stromenti, perchè non siano veduti, si debbano suonare dietro le tele della scena'). Instruments were placed behind the scenes in the performance of Monteverdi's *Arianna* (see Follino's report in Canal, 'Della musica in Mantova', 762), as they were in any number of *intermedi non apparenti* from the 15th and 16th centuries; for examples, cf. Pirrotta and Povoledo, *Music and Theatre from Poliziano to Monteverdi*.

pseudo-monodies, i.e. madrigals which, for performing purposes, were scaled down to a single voice plus accompaniment, after the example of the soprano-chitarrone arrangements in Book 1 *a* 5. It may be assumed, further, that the choral dance, written to a strophic *canzonetta*, shared traits, stylistically, with the *canzonette* published in 1589.

Beyond these assumptions, the only way left to get at the music is through the poetry. Chiabrera's poems for the *intermedio* might be compared with his other poems, seven in all, in Rossi's madrigal books. Of the seven, five appeared in his Book 2 *a* 5, six years before the *intermedio* for *L'Idropica*, while the other two followed the *intermedio* by, respectively, two and twenty years.[15] Thus, from a stylistic standpoint, only six works are viable for comparison, those falling within the 1602–10 time frame. The six share with the poetry of the *intermedio* common themes: chains of love, the search for freedom, relief from sorrow.[16] They might also have shared common musical traits, if one presumes that the way the composer related to Chiabrera's themes in one work is similar to the way he did in another. If such an argument can be sustained, then any of the Chiabrera settings in Book 2 *a* 5 might suggest the character of the pieces in the *intermedio*. The only problem is that the various themes noted in his verses are prevalent in madrigal poetry at large.

Still another way to consider the poetry of the *intermedio* is through its forms. Fame's madrigal has fourteen lines, and a search for similar examples among Rossi's works, excluding his settings, in two *partes*, of sonnets having fourteen lines,[17] leads, curiously, to a poem by Chiabrera, 'Soave libertate'; the two might profitably be compared.[18] Venus' aria, on the other hand, is a *ballata*-madrigal, allowing comparison, in its structure, with Rossi's fourteen settings of *ballate* or *ballata*-madrigals.[19] Among them is one of Chiabrera's *ballata* beginning 'Messaggier di speranza',[20] which, since it was published in 1628, is, for present purposes, too late to be

---

[15] Bk 2: 4 ('Hor che lunge da voi'), 6 ('Soave libertate'), 8 ('Un sguardo, un sguardo no'), 16 ('Dove, misero, mai'), and 17 ('Occhi, voi sospirate'). For the other two, see Bk 4: 5 ('Perla che 'l mar produce') and Mti: 9 ('Messaggier di speranza').

[16] Chains of love: from poetry of *intermedio*, 'E tra ceppi e catene | Appellano lor pene | Dolce mercè di gratioso Amore'; from another poem, 'et io rimango | Stretto in belle catene | D'altr'amorose pene | E d'altro bel desio' (Bk 2: 6). The search for freedom: from poetry of *intermedio*, 'Che dell'amata libertà ne priva; | ...Se di chi muor la libertade è viva'; from other poems, 'Là dov'è libertà non è tormento' (Bk 2: 17), 'Soave libertate, | Già per sì lunga etate | Mia cara compagnia' (Bk 2: 6). Relief from sorrow: from poetry of *intermedio*, 'Prender conforto da l'ardor interno', 'hor ti ricerco... | O de l'afflitto cor solo conforto?' and 'Ma de l'alta rapina, | Cerere, ti consola'; from other poems, 'Dove, misero, mai | Sperar deggio conforto a' dolor miei' (Bk 2: 16), 'Chi dà conforto al core?' (Bk 2: 4).

[17] Seven full sonnets, in four separate collections. For a 14-line madrigal, also set in two *partes*, see M4: 10 ('O dolcezz'amarissime d'Amore', by Guarini).

[18] The only difference between them is that Fame's madrigal ('Asciuga i pianti') has varying couplets of 7- and 11-syllable lines (Ab/Ca/Cd/ed/EE/fg/gF) whereas 'Soave libertate' has heptasyllabic couplets only (aa/bb/cc/dd/ee/ff/gg).

[19] On the terms *ballata* and *ballata*-madrigal, see Harrán, 'Verse Types in the Early Madrigal', 28–36.

[20] Mti: 9.

structurally or stylistically relevant. Even with regard to the choral *canzon-etta* that, as said, might be compared with other examples of *canzonette* from Rossi's first publication, it should be pointed out that it differs from all known *canzonetta* settings by Rossi in that it has six lines for each strophe; Rossi's *canzonette* are based on poetry with four lines to a strophe, or less often, three or five.[21] Having six lines, the choral *canzonetta* exhibits its own rhyme scheme, therefore its own structure, with concomitant implications for the phrasing and content of the music.

Clearly, there is no way of reconstructing the music of 'The Rape of Proserpine', short of actually finding it. Yet it might be noted, before the subject is dismissed, that the *intermedio* is Janus-faced. It points, for one, to the fifteenth- and sixteenth-century tradition of the *intermedio*, with which it shares such features as a chorus of nymphs, the contrast between earthly and infernal regions, the appearance of Venus, the singing of a lament, and the general theme of *omnia vincit amor*.[22] It points, for another, to the future: Chiabrera's 'Rape of Proserpine', to music by Rossi, seems to have inaugurated a trend. It was followed by various other Proserpian rapes written as *intermedi* or as operas, among them Giulio Cesare Monteverdi's *Rapimento di Proserpina* (1611), Girolamo Giacobbi's *Proserpina rapita* (1613), Claudio Monteverdi's *Proserpina rapita* (1630, music lost), and Francesco Sacrati's *Proserpina* (1644).[23] By studying the Chiabrera-Rossi *intermedio* in relation to earlier and later works, a fuller picture of its lost music might perhaps be obtained.

A Balletto *for a Sacred Play*

A second piece of evidence for Rossi's connections with the Mantuan theatre resides in his *balletto* for Giovanni Battista Andreini's play *La Maddalena*, a 'sacred representation' staged in 1617 as part of the celebrations for Duke Ferdinando's marriage to Caterina de' Medici.[24] Where, for 'The Rape of Proserpine', one was forced to speculate on the music, no longer available, one can now, for the *balletto*, fall back on a printed source: published in 1617, it includes the works of the four composers—Rossi, Monteverdi, Alessandro Ghivizzani, Muzio Effrem—engaged for the *intermedi*.[25]

[21] Excluded are the three *canzonette* in Mti: 14–16 (on which more below). Prosodically, they are best described as *scherzi*.

[22] For examples, cf. Pirrotta and Povoledo, *Music and Theatre from Poliziano to Monteverdi*, and Osthoff, *Theatergesang und darstellende Musik in der italienischen Renaissance*.

[23] For details, see Solerti, *Gli albori del melodramma*, i. 122, 139, 145–6, 157–61.

[24] *La Maddalena, sacra rappresentazione* (1617). The play was reworked for a Milanese production as *Maddalena lasciva e penitente* (1652). Andreini primed himself for the early version by composing a sacred poem, in three *canti* (totalling 360 octaves), on *La Maddalena* (1610). On Andreini and his theatrical troupe, see Bevilacqua, 'Giambattista Andreini e la compagnia dei Fedeli'; on the wedding festivities for 1617, see Portioli, *Il matrimonio di Ferdinando Gonzaga con Catherina de' Medici*.

[25] *Musiche de alcuni eccellentissimi musici composte per la Maddalena* (1617). In the 1617 version of the play, Andreini pays tribute to the four 'outstanding musicians, who honoured and

Son of the famed poet and singer Isabella Andreini, Giovanni Battista well figures in the literature on the Italian theatre. Yet his play *La Maddalena* has received scant attention while its musical insertions, if mentioned at all, are done so in passing. My immediate concern is with the text and music of Rossi's *intermedio*, its relation to the other composers' insertions in the play, and its position within the repertory of Rossi's works at large.

Rossi's *balletto* was sung and danced, in the earlier version of the play, in Act I, at the opening of Scene 3.[26] It might seem incongruous for a composer to write a piece of dance music for a 'sacred representation', especially since the other composers prepared fittingly 'sacred' works, all based on texts concerned with penitence and redemption. Yet the practice of writing dance songs for sacred dramas seems to have been well established. Such songs were used for purposes of variety and entertainment, as acknowledged in the preface to Emilio de' Cavalieri's 'sacred representation' *di Anima et di Corpo*: they 'enliven' the performance, they add 'grace and novelty'.[27] They were not absent, moreover, from previous plays on the theme of Mary Magdalen. In an early sacred representation on the 'conversion of Saint Mary Magdalen', the heroine, still in her sinful state, invites 'young men' into her house 'to make "music"' ('dare ne' suoni'); to the sound of instruments they dance and sing 'various stanzas to melodies' in praise of youth and worldly delights.[28] The story of Mary Magdalen, with its conflicts between her immorality and her penitence, clearly lent itself to secular insertions. But why did Rossi get to write the *balletto*, and not someone else? Probably because he was the only Jewish composer to participate, hence could not be asked, nor would have agreed, to set a text professing Christian doctrine.

Rossi's *balletto* consists of three voices, set to four lines of text, then followed by an instrumental *ritornello*, for a total of twelve bars (Ex. 6.1).

In the title, it is designated 'to be sung and played with three *viole da braccio*'. The music is complete,[29] but not the text: in the musical source, it has a single stanza. For the remaining stanzas, one can turn to two literary sources, namely, the 1617 version of the play and its rewrite for a performance in 1652. They share the first stanza of the musical source, then add three others, which read differently in the two versions (cf. Plate 6).

enriched his work with their illustrious compositions; as if torrents of devotion, they delighted in proceeding with him as tributaries to the great sea of Mary Magdalen's tears' (238). For the four madrigals, see *CW* viii. app. 3; for their texts, in the original and in translation, see there, pp. xlvii–lix.

[26] In the 1652 production, it appeared in Act I, at the opening of Scene 5.

[27] After Solerti, *Le origini del melodramma*, 6–7.

[28] *Rappresentazione della conversione di S. Maria Maddalena*, in *Sacre rappresentazioni dei secoli XIV, XV e XVI*, ed. D'Ancona, i. 255 ff.

[29] Though prefixed by a binary mensuration sign, it scans, rhythmically, as 3/2.

Va cantato et sonato con 3 viole da braccio

Ritornello

Ex. 6.1 Rossi's *balletto* for *La Maddalena*, after *Musiche...composte per la Maddalena* (1617), first stanza

1617 version

Spazziam pronte, o vecchiarelle,   *Come on, old women, let's sweep*
Questo suolo,   *This floor;*
Vaghe solo   *Our only wish*
Far d'augei prede più belle.   *Is to make birds our fairest prey.*

Su affrettiamo a gara i bracci,   *Hurry, let's have a race to move our arms,*
Già che 'l tetto   *For the rooftop*
È 'l boschetto   *Is the grove*
Ove stan le panie, i lacci.   *Where snares and traps are laid.*

Ecco al suon di Maddalena   *Behold! at the sound of the Magdalen*
Che volante   *Her lover*
Vien l'Amante;   *Comes flying,*
Già la pania il piè gli affrena.   *Yet the snare restrains his foot.*

Da la preda d'augelletti   *Of the prey of birdies*
Nostra parte   *Our party*
Già si parte,   *Now takes leave,*
Chè pur noi tendiam laccetti.   *For we just set little traps.*

(76 lines of spoken dialogue follow)

1652 version
Spazziam pronte, o vecchiarelle,   *Come on, old women, let's sweep*
Questo suolo,   *This floor;*
Vaghe solo   *Our only wish*
Far d'augei prede più belle;   *Is to make birds our fairest prey;*
Spazziam pronte, o vecchiarelle.   *Come on, old women, let's sweep.*

Al bel suon di Maddalena   *At the fair sound of the Magdalen,*
Qui volante   *Her lover*
Vien l'Amante,   *Arrives here in flight;*
Già la pania il piè gli affrena;   *Yet the snare restrains his foot;*
Al bel suon di Maddalena.   *At the fair sound of the Magdalen.*

D'abbellir qui il suol ci piaccia,   *Here we like to polish the floor,*
Suolo eletto   *A floor chosen*
Per boschetto,   *For a grove,*
Ove incauto augel s'allaccia;   *Where a careless bird gets entangled;*
D'abbellir qui il suol ci piaccia.   *Here we like to polish the floor.*

Maddalena in guancial d'oro   *The Magdalen, on a cushion of gold,*
È civetta,   *Acts coquettish,*
Amorosetta,   *Flirtatious,*
Chè atteggiando fa dir 'Moro';   *And, by coaxing, makes one say: 'I'm dying';*
Maddalena in guancial d'oro.[30]   *The Magdalen, on a cushion of gold.*

(8 lines of spoken dialogue follow)

The two literary sources suggest different musical adaptations. Where the earlier one had four-line stanzas, of which the fourth line was repeated for the concluding phrase of the music (as clear from the musical source; see, again, Ex. 6.1), the later one has five-line stanzas, of which the fifth line in each is identical with the first:

	1617 (corroborated by musical source)					1652				
Lines of text:	1	2	3	4	4	1	2	3	4	1
Phrases of music:	A	B	C	D	E	A	B	C	D	E

---

[30] 1617, p. 17; 1652, pp. 25–6. As is clear from what follows, the later version advances stanza 3 of the earlier one to stanza 2 (with the opening changed from 'Ecco al suon' to 'Al bel suon') and replaces stanzas 2 and 4 of the earlier one with two new ones (its stanzas 3–4).

1. Duke Vincenzo I Gonzaga (at the age of about 38–40, with the collar of the Order of the Golden Fleece and on the breast plate the motto 'Sic'), to whom Salamone Rossi dedicated his first two collections (1589, 1600). Oil painting by Frans Pourbus the Younger (1569–1622), c.1600–2. Fondazione D'Arco, Mantua.

2–3. Duke Francesco IV Gonzaga (at the age of about 26) and Duke Ferdinando (at the age of about 30). Engravings by an unknown hand (the first from c.1612, the second from c.1616), with inscriptions that translate respectively 'Francesco Gonzaga, fifth duke of Mantua and marquis [*recte* third duke] of Monferrato', 'Ferdinando Gonzaga, sixth duke of Mantua and marquis [*recte* fourth duke] of Monferrato'. Included in Antonio Possevino the Younger, *Gonzaga* (Mantua, 1617). Biblioteca Comunale, Mantua.

4. Letter that Salamone Rossi wrote on behalf of his brother Emanuele (21 February 1606); fair copy, with the close and signature in Salamone's own hand. Archivio Storico, Archivio Gonzaga, Mantua.

5. Salamone Rossi on a list of participants in a production of the Mantuan Jewish theatrical company (Acessi [sic] de Amor, 17 February 1605); detail, with name fifth from top. Jewish Community Archive, Mantua.

SCENA TERZA.

Stella, Rosa, Aurora, Aron, Leone.

PAZZIAM pronte ò vecchiarelle
Questo suolo,
Vaghe solo
Far d'augei prede più belle.
Sù affrettiamo à gara i bracci
Già, che'l terro
E'l boschetto
Oue sien le panie, i lacci.
Ecco al suon di Maddalena,
Che volante
Vien l'Amante,
Già la pania il piè gli affrena.
De la preda d'augelletti
Nostra parte
Già si parte,
Che pur noi tendiam laccetti.
Stel. Ecco il suol si polito,
Ch'à porui il piede il riguardante inuita.
Ecco il prato di fiori,
Che nel bel seno accoglie
L'amorosa cerasia,
Che con dente d'amore

B   Morde

6. Page from Giovanni Battista Andreini's sacred play La Maddalena (Mantua, 1617), from which the full text of Rossi's intermedio 'Spazziam pronte' may be reconstructed.

Ranquilla guerr'e ca ra Oue l'ira è dolcez-

za Amor lo sdegno e ne le risse e ne le ris-

sc'è pa ce Ou'il morir s'impara L'esser prigion s'apprezza L'esser pri-

gion s'apprez za Quel corallo mordace Che m'offende mi gio-

ua Quel dente che mi fere ad' hora ad hora Quel mi risana ancora Quel

bacio che mi priua Di vita mi rauuiua Di vita mi rauuiua On-

d'io ch'hò nel morir vita ogn'hor noua Per ferito esser più ferisco a proua.

7. Page from Salamone Rossi's setting of the notorious *Canzon de' baci* by Giovan Battista Marino (Book 3 of his five-voice madrigals, Venice, 1603; third stanza, alto). Bibliothèque Nationale de France, Paris.

8. Page from Sonata 8 'sopra l'Aria "È tanto tempo hormai"' in Salamone Rossi's later virtuoso manner (Book 4 of his instrumental works, 2nd edn., Venice, 1642; canto 1). Gesamthochschulbibliothek, Kassel.

9a–b. Leon Modena as portrayed on the title page (bottom) of his *Historia de riti hebraici* (Venice, 1638): full page, detail.

באסו

השירים
אשר לשלמה

מזמורים ושירות ותשבחות אשר
הביא בהכמת הנגון והמוסיקה
לשלשה ד'ה' ו'ח'קולות
כמ'ר שלמה מהארומים יצו
מדרי קק מאנטובה
להודו לה'ולזכר לשמו עליון בכל
דבר שבקדושה · חדשה
בארץ :

פה ויניציאה שפג

כמצות השירים
פייטרו ולורינצו בראגאדיני ··
בבית יואני קאליאוני

Appreſſo gli Illuſt. Sig.
Pietro e Lorenzo Brag.

10. Title page of Salamone Rossi's 'Songs of Solomon' (Venice, 1622/3; bass). Bologna, Civico Museo Bibliografico Musicale.

11. Page from Rossi's setting of Psalm 100 in his 'Songs of Solomon' (Venice, 1622/3; no. 14), with an exuberant vocalise on the word 'singing' (canto, end of second and beginning of third staves). Bibliothèque Nationale de France, Paris.

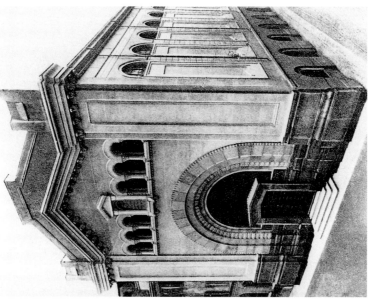

12. Street scene (Via Governolo) from the Mantuan ghetto in the 1920s (houses have since been renovated); beyond the entrance gate (to what is now the garden of the Archivio di Stato) is, three streets away, the twelfth-century Tower of Zuccaro (see Plate 14*b*, bottom, to the right of no. 97; see there, moreover, for Via Governolo: it runs to the left of the church of San Salvatore, no. 136, terminating at Via Dottrina Cristiana). Giovetti Photo Archive, Mantua.

13. The Mantuan Scuola Grande, or 'Great Synagogue' (founded in 1529 and, in 1633, installed in the palace of the marquise Felicita Gonzaga; the edifice was razed in 1938). Giovetti Photo Archive, Mantua.

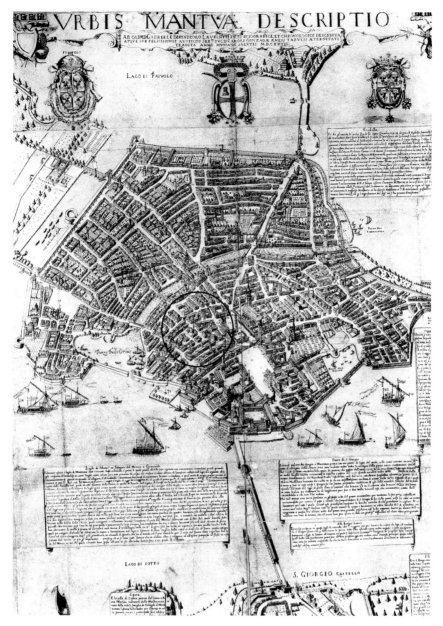

14a. Map: 'Urbis Mantuae Descriptio, a panoramic view of Mantua, with exhaustive descriptive marginalia; designed by Gabriele Bertazzolo and printed in two different versions, the first from 1596 (Francesco Osanna), the second as represented here, from 1628 (Ludovico Delfichi). Centre portion: a close-up of the city (the area of the ghetto has been circled; on the lower tip of the plan are the Ducal Palace and its adjoining edifices). Biblioteca Comunale, Mantua.

14b. 'Urbis Mantuae Descriptio' (1628, as in Plate 14a); detail, the ghetto

Numbers (as identified in marginalia) running from outer left to right side: 99 (twice, at entrance gates), Jews' Ghetto; 80, Office of Wool Trades; 98, Public Salt Vendor; 66, Clock Tower ('Torre dell'Horologio'); 57, Merchants' Market (later known as Fruit and Vegetable Market, 'Piazza Erbe'); 65, Time Tower ('Torre delle Horre'); 76, Mint, and next to it, 58, Grain Market ('Piazza del Formento'); 75, Prisons; 121, Jesuit Fathers' Convent Santissima Trinità; 68, Reverend Jesuit Fathers' Tower; and within the ghetto, from left to right: 136, church of San Salvatore; 71, Jews' Big Tower ('Torrazzo delli Hebrei'); 60, Garlic Market ('Piazza dell' Aglio'); 100, Christian Loan Bank ('Monte di Pietà'); 99 (at entrance gate to Via Dottrina Cristiana, running straight through to the opposite end with its own entrance gate, also marked 99, though barely legible), Jews' Ghetto (the second street from the latter gate is Via Governolo: see Plate 12); and to the left of it, 175, Oratorio di Dottrina Cristiana. Sites outside the ghetto: on the far right side, 59, courtyard of Sant'Andrea, with the church itself only partly shown on this detail; further down (facing 121), 139, church of Santo Zeno; on the upper left side, 141, church of San Martino; below it, 113, convent of Santa Maria del Carmine; on the bottom left, 62, courtyard of Santo Stefano, and 140, church itself; bottom middle to right corner, 97, San Cosimo Salt Supplies; Tower of Zuccaro (unnumbered); 3, Armoury.

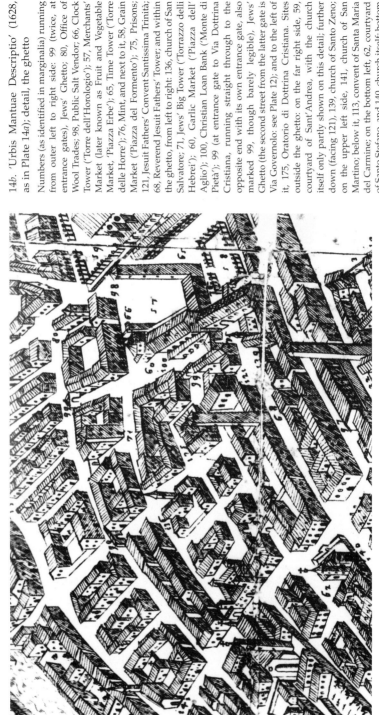

Not only do the two literary sources allow us to complete the text, but between the two of them they give fairly explicit instructions for performing the *balletto*. It was danced, we are told, by the Magdalen's two bonded dwarfs, Aron and Leon, and her three old, ignominious women servants, Stella, Rosa, and Aurora—all the names refer to Jews.[31] Holding watering-cans, the dwarfs sprinkle plants set in three flowerpots; holding brooms, the women, bent over, sweep the floor. While pacing their sprinklings and sweepings to the rhythms of the music, the five characters sing and artfully dance to the sound of hidden instruments.[32] Two violins and a viola were used for the *ritornello* that followed the separate strophes; they might have been used, moreover, for accompanying the singers in the strophes them-selves. It is less clear how the five characters negotiated the three vocal parts: two of the women might have sung the top voice, the third the second voice, and the two dwarfs the bass.

How does Rossi's piece compare with the other composers' insertions in the play? It resembles Monteverdi's prologue ('Su le penne de' venti') in having strophic poetry and a *ritornello*;[33] it deals, albeit facetiously, with one of the main themes of the play and its *intermedi*, Mary Magdalen's tears of repentance, leading to her baptism (let us not forget the cans of water the dwarfs used to spray the plants).[34] Yet it differs from the rest in its structure and content. Not only is it the shortest insertion of the five, but it is the only one to be written as a *balletto*; the only one in triple metre; the only one to be sung and danced; the only one to have a secular text; the only one to be composed for three voices and three instruments; and the only one for which definite performing instructions are given.[35] In its lively rhythms and its colourful staging, Rossi's *balletto* probably stole the show.

[31] For his comedy *Lo schiavetto* (1612), Andreini had, among the *interlocutori*, the four 'Hebrei' Semoel, Caino, Lion, and Sensale.

[32] The 1617 edition refers, in the *Ordine* (p. 235), to six participants (three women, three slave dwarfs), yet from the names of the characters at the beginning of the scene and the record of *interlocutori* elsewhere (fo. [⁺4]ᵛ), as well as from the instructions given in the 1652 edition (p. 25), it is clear that the three dwarfs are, actually, only two. In the list of *interlocutori* for 1617, the women are described as 'Vecchie di bassa stima serve di Maddalena'; to this the list for 1652 (fo. A 4) adds 'anderan curve, con bastoncelli'.

[33] The two pieces also share a common mode (Mixolydian, the others being in Aeolian and Dorian on G). Yet Monteverdi composed the seven strophes of his prologue as a monody, introduced and followed by a 5-v. *ritornello*; cf. Monteverdi, *Tutte le opere*, ed. Malipiero, xi. 170–1 (*ritornello* and 1st stanza only; for all stanzas, see *CW* viii. 48–55). Is it by coincidence that the first two items in the play were written by Monteverdi and Rossi, or does their order there follow the precedent established in the *intermedi* for 1608? (The music source has its own arrangement: of the four pieces, Rossi's is the last.)

[34] The poetry of the *intermedi* harps on the notion of water washing away sins, as in the following vocabulary (drawn from Monteverdi's prologue and the other composers' *intermedi*): *acqua, bebbe, Egeo, fonte, lagrime, lavar, lavò, (antico error) lavate, mar, piangete, pianto, piover, rugiade, stille*. As to plants (symbolizing the growth of life through baptism), the poetry is rife with botanical images (*d'Allor monili e fregi, boschetto, fiori, fronde, ghirlanda, giardinier, palma, palme divine, piante, seminando*).

[35] From the instructions in the 1617 version of the play, all we know about Monteverdi's prologue is that it was sung by Favor Divino ('un bellissimo fanciullo') to the accompaniment of

But its uniqueness does not end there. Compared with other works in Rossi's repertory, it is his only complete *balletto*;[36] his only work for which we have a set of performing instructions; his only secular vocal work in 3/2 metre;[37] and his only work with a specific instrumentation for the *ritornello*.[38] The antics of the two dwarfs and three old crones, cavorting about the stage with watering-cans and brooms, seem to have inspired Rossi to do something special.

The Jewish Theatre

So far the discussion has turned about the only known pieces that Rossi wrote for the theatre. More information may be obtained by pursuing another line of investigation: Rossi's association with the Jewish theatrical company active in Mantua before, during, and after his lifetime. Various references to the Jewish theatre may be assembled from the files of letters and the three folders labelled 'Ebrei' in the Gonzaga archive of the Archivio di Stato, Mantua, and more substantially from the extended files of the Mantuan Jewish community.[39] From these references, sparse as they are, there emerges a picture of uninterrupted theatrical activity extending from the second quarter of the sixteenth to the mid-seventeenth century.[40]

'hidden instruments'. Information on the other works is equally sparse (for details, see *CW*, pp. xlvii–lv). Further instructions are given in the 1652 version, but they seem to suggest that except for Monteverdi's and Rossi's insertions, the three others were replaced by new ones, probably in *stile recitativo*. Cf. Andreini's *La centaura* (1622), where in Act III, Scene 5, we are told that the various characters representing 'Dolore, Perdita, and Giustizia will come out one by one, and all three of their parts could be sung in recitative style' (p. 123).

[36] His only other *balletto* is a fragment printed, without text (and in duple metre), at the end of S1 (see below).

[37] Despite its binary mensuration sign (see above). In its 3/2 metre, it differs, moreover, from Gastoldi's 5-v. *balletti* (1591), of which only three pieces ('L'Innamorato', 'Il Piacere', 'Il Martellato') are in triple metre, though here not 3/2, but 3/4; see his *Balletti a cinque voci*, ed. Sanvoisin, nos. 1, 7, and 14. As to Gastoldi's 3-v. *balletti* (1594), one of them ('La Cortigiana') does, in fact, have a 3/2 metre (while four others are written in 3/4); see his *Balletti a 3*, ed. Benkö, no. 2 (3/2) and nos. 4, 11, 13, 16 (3/4).

[38] His only other pieces with an instrumental *ritornello* are Mti: 13, 15 (see below).

[39] On the Jewish theatre, with reference to the Mantuan Jewish files, see Simonsohn, *History of the Jews in the Duchy of Mantua*, 656–69, and, still earlier, though no less important, D'Ancona, *Origini del teatro italiano*, ii. 398–429 (limited, in its report, to the *Ebrei* files in ASAG). Schirmann's 'Hate'atron vehamusika bishkhunot hayehudim be'italya bein hame'a ha-16 veha-18' is concerned with Jewish theatrical performances for Jewish audiences only. See also G. Amadei, 'Note sul teatro a Mantova nel Rinascimento', and the various chronicles of musical events, from 1588 on, in Parisi, 'Ducal Patronage of Music in Mantua, 1587–1627', 152–69, 246–54, 300–21; also, more recently, ead. 'The Jewish Community and Carnival Entertainment'.

[40] D'Ancona carried his report up to 1605; Simonsohn provides documentation extending the activities of the Jewish theatrical troupe to 1650. See also Parisi ('Ducal Patronage of Music in Mantua, 1587–1627'), with listings of performances, by the troupe, for the years 1588, 1590, 1593, 1595–6, 1598 (revival of Leone de' Sommi's *Le tre sorelle*), 1601–4, 1605 (*Acessi de Amor*), 1606 (Tasso's *Intrichi d'Amore*), 1607–10, 1612–1613, 1615–18, 1620 (*Della palma*, author unknown), 1621, 1626.

The Jewish theatre became a major source of theatrical entertainment in Renaissance Mantua. Of the various reasons for its appeal, one might mention the practical one that the Jewish theatre was self-supporting, hence did not cost the dukes a farthing. Its repertory included new and old comedies by Italian authors (e.g. Ariosto, Tasso, Muzio Manfredi) and possibly by members of the Jewish troupe, though of such Jews only Leone de' Sommi is known.[41]

Music seems to have held the same importance in the performances of the Jewish theatrical troupe as in those of the Christian companies: it was included, at any rate, in the *intermedi* to Jewish productions of plays by, among others, Ariosto (*I suppositi*, 1563), Leone de' Sommi (*Gli sconosciuti*, 1575), and Bernardo Pino da Cagli (*Gli ingiusti sdegni*, 1584). But no record of their composers survives.[42] Salamone Rossi could have been involved in productions from the late 1580s on; indeed, it makes sense for a well-established theatrical troupe such as that of the Jewish community to have employed the services of its foremost composer to supply its musical needs. If Sommi, its foremost playwright, wrote a number of comedies for the troupe and directed it, and Isacchino Massarano, its leading dancer, planned and participated in its dances, then who wrote and supervised its music, if not Salamone Rossi?

It has been assumed, in the literature, that Rossi had professional ties with the Jewish theatrical troupe.[43] Can the assumption be sustained?

The records of the Mantuan Jewish community contain three explicit references to Rossi as a participant in performances of the Jewish theatrical troupe. He first appears in connection with the play *Acessi* [*Accessi? Eccessi?*] *de Amor*, presented on 17 February 1605 (see Plate 5); then, a second time, in connection with a play performed in February, 1606, at Carnival time; and yet a third in connection with a comedy performed in the autumn of 1615.[44] In all three instances, Rossi's name figures in listings of participants, which include up to sixty individuals belonging to families of the Jewish community. Nothing is said about the music or its performance, yet from documents

---

[41] Sommi composed a number of comedies, including the first known example of an original (i.e. untranslated) Hebrew play, *Tsaḥut bediḥuta dekidushin* ('A Comedy of Betrothal', from the 1550s). Few works remain: the manuscripts of Sommi's comedies were largely destroyed by fire, in 1904, in a wing of the Bibl. Naz., Turin (yet some have recently been retrieved: see Molin, 'Recovery of Some Unedited Manuscripts by Leone de' Sommi at the National Library of Turin'). For a comparative study of Rossi and Sommi, see Harrán, 'Jewish Dramatists and Musicians in the Renaissance'.

[42] Except for a lone reference to music by Wert for Manfredi's *Nozze di Semiramide con Memnone*, staged and directed by Sommi in 1591 (on Manfredi's connections with the Mantuan court, see Bertolotti, *Muzio Manfredi e Passi Giuseppe*).

[43] See e.g. Fenlon, *Music and Patronage in Sixteenth-Century Mantua*, ii, p. xiii; as well as his entry on Rossi in Sadie (ed.), *The New Grove Dictionary of Music and Musicians*, xvi. 223.

[44] The three references occur, respectively, in JCA, file 9, doc. 1: 10, headed 'Lista delle persone che intravengono nella comedia Acessi de Amor fatta 17 feb. 1605'; file 10, doc. 1: 19, signed by Fabio Gonzaga; and file 15, doc. 30, entering the expenses incurred in preparing the performance.

relating, for example, to the 1606 production, it is clear that both Mantuan and 'foreign' instrumentalists were employed.[45]

Other details are furnished in an expense account for comedy productions in 1611. There the community disbursed various sums to Rossi for his services, which included providing a box for storing shoes and seeing to the rental of various articles for performance (see Chapter 1). Small wages were paid to singers (1.7.6 lire) and an instrumentalist (6 lire). A major expense was 'for having the comedy and *intermedio* copied and renting a room for the singers', no doubt to rehearse in (96 lire).[46]

Though we can be sure that Rossi participated in these three productions, we still do not know in what capacity. As a composer? As a performer? With its limited resources, the Jewish community probably engaged Rossi as both, counting on him, that is, to provide the musical *intermedi* and to take part in them as a violinist or even singer. For all we know, he might have even acted a part in the comedy and one or more parts in the *intermedi*. Just as Sommi performed multiple tasks for the Jewish company, directing and staging its plays, and acting in them as well, so Rossi could have written whatever music was required, then rehearsed it with the musicians and joined variously in its performance.

The Jewish theatrical troupe was a company of actors, but Rossi may have had his own company, or 'concerto', within it. A 'concerto' may be understood as 'an ensemble of players and singers for performing pieces of music'.[47] It is in this sense of 'concerto' that Sommi refers, in his treatise on theatrical art, to the practice of concocting certain *bizzarie* for the transition from one act to another, such as having 'eight or ten tradesmen emerge from different streets while singing together *in concerto*, with each one announcing his trade and some of them playing separately on instruments hidden among their effects, as happens when a zither is contained in the kettle of a coppersmith, or a little violin in the boot of a cobbler, or a flute in the broomstick of a chimney sweep, or a spinet in the basket of a pastry cook, and other similarly contrived inventions'.[48] Rossi's 'concerto', of which much was said, or better surmised, in Chapter 1, may have been a small ensemble of voices or instruments, as many as needed to perform the standard-sized vocal and instrumental works that Rossi provided for the various performances of the Jewish theatrical group.

---

[45] The duke ordered Abraham Udine, in charge of finances for the production, to pay an honorarium of twelve pounds to the 'foreign' musicians and of fifteen to the five Mantuan players (letters dated 8 and 10 Feb. 1606).

[46] JCA, file 12: 'dati... per li cantori L 1.7.6'; 'per il sonaro L 6'; 'per far scriver la comedia e l'intramedo et fito di una camera per li cantori L 96'; after Parisi, 'The Jewish Community and Carnival Entertainment', 302 n. 40.

[47] After *Il nuovo Zingarelli*, 419 (the fifth of six definitions).

[48] *Quattro dialoghi in materia di rappresentazioni sceniche* (1565), ed. Marotti, 70 (from the fourth dialogue).

The theorist Praetorius equated a *concerto* with a *sinfonia*, writing that *concerto*, in Italian, derives from the Latin *concertatio*, meaning 'a disputation, in which the various voices or musical instruments are committed to producing harmony', and that it translates into German as 'ein Concert'.[49] Such an explanation would point to a vocal-instrumental work, of the kind that opened Rossi's *intermedio* for Guarini's comedy *L'Idropica*: it was described, to repeat, as a ' "dolcissimo concerto" of voices and instruments that made the whole theatre echo with a delightful harmony'.

Elsewhere Praetorius assigned the *sinfonia* alias *concerto* to the category of textless music ('cantilenae sine textu'), remarking that the Italians mean by *sinfonia* a work (*concentus*) 'composed for instruments alone, using no vocal parts'.[50] Such a description would cover the *sinfonie* composed by Rossi: they are textless pieces, written, in most cases, for an ensemble of three instruments, which, as the composer specified, were usually two *viole* or *violini* plus a chitarrone. This was, presumedly, the basic ensemble to which the composer entrusted the instrumental works in the *intermedi* for productions of the Jewish troupe.[51] When more players were required, the ensemble could have been expanded to four, five, or more parts, with other instrumentalists called in *ad hoc* from the Jewish community or, by special permission, from the court or elsewhere.[52]

What of the singers performing the madrigals and other vocal insertions in the Jewish productions? They might have been drawn from the same group of Jewish singers who performed Rossi's Hebrew works in the synagogue and private gatherings. Women singers were excluded from Jewish prayer services, though not from the theatre; Rossi's sister Europa is likely to have numbered among them.[53]

Three specific references to Rossi's participation in the Jewish theatre would lead one to suspect a more active part in its productions than hitherto reported. Rossi might have been involved in them through the full span of

---

[49] Praetorius, *Syntagma musicum*, iii. 4. The equation of *concerto* or *concentus* with *sinfonia* depends on their etymology: *syn* or *con*, for 'together'; *phon* or *cantus* (becoming *-centus* or *-certus*), for 'sound' or 'song'.

[50] Praetorius, *Syntagma musicum*, iii. 24.

[51] It has equivalents in the 3-v. *sinfonie* of other composers' theatrical works, for example, the 'Zinfonia su un triflauto' that Peri wrote for his *Euridice* (1600) or the *sinfonia a 3* that Gagliano wrote for his *Ballo di donne turche* (1615).

[52] Which might explain the mention of payments to Mantuan and 'foreign' instrumentalists participating in Jewish theatrical productions (see above). The reasons for expanding the ensemble were probably three: to enable the performance of instrumental works for four or more voices (as in various *sinfonie* and *gagliarde* by Rossi); to reinforce single parts in instrumental works *a 3*; and to double the parts of vocal works (madrigals) for five or more voices. Guidotti, in the preface to Cavalieri's *La rappresentazione di Anima et di Corpo* (1600), spoke of '*sinfonie* that could be played with a large number of instruments'; Gagliano, in the preface to his opera *Dafne* (1608), wrote of its opening *sinfonia* that it could be played by 'different instruments, which serve, moreover, to accompany the choruses and play the *ritornelli*'. For both prefaces, cf. Solerti, *Le origini del melodramma*.

[53] Likely, yes, but not certain: there is, unfortunately, no evidence of Madama Europa's activities for the Jewish theatre.

his career, from the late 1580s until the late 1620s. It was in the Jewish theatre that Rossi probably learned his craft.[54] It was there that he probably attained sufficient skills to earn commissions to compose *intermedi* for non-Jewish productions, among them Guarini's *L'Idropica*, Andreini's *Maddalena*, and, supposedly, others whose record has disappeared. The Jewish theatre may have provided him with an important outlet for his talents as performer and composer. Every time its actors performed in Carnival season, every time they appeared at court to mark wedding celebrations, anniversaries, birthdays, visits of foreign dignitaries, and so forth, Rossi's services may have been required as instrumentalist and composer of *intermedi*.

Large quantities of theatre music by Rossi may be hypothesized. Where is this music, then? Was it, like most other *intermedi* of the late fifteenth to early seventeenth centuries, prepared for one or more performances, then forgotten?[55] Were the original manuscripts destroyed during the sack of the ghetto in 1630? Is there any way Rossi's theatre music could be retrieved?

Theatrical Implications in the Secular Poetry

One might pursue another line of investigation, assuming that Rossi's theatre music may be preserved, in part, in his printed collections. Just as, in the early sixteenth century, *intermedi* for comedies by Machiavelli lay hidden within madrigal collections by Verdelot,[56] so it seems reasonable that other composers' *intermedi*, from the end of the sixteenth and beginning of the seventeenth centuries, might be included in their own collections.

At least seven kinds of textual evidence may be relevant for locating Rossi's still unknown theatre pieces. Of the various lyrics to be mentioned, some were already discussed from a prosodic or thematic standpoint in Chapter 3. Now, however, they will be reviewed, along with the rest, from a theatrical perspective:

1. *Settings having poetry that can be traced to plays.* Rossi composed music to six texts from Guarini's *Pastor fido.*[57] That, in itself, says nothing about their

---

[54] In the dedication to Bk 1, Rossi pays Duke Vincenzo the compliment that it was while he served him (in the 1590s) that he learned the rudiments of composition (see Ch. 1). There is no contradiction between Rossi's activities for the court and those for the Jewish theatre: both kinds were under the duke's sponsorship.

[55] Of the few *intermedi* whose music has been preserved, the most notable are those for Antonio Landi's comedy *Il Commodo* (see *A Renaissance Entertainment*, ed. Minor and Mitchell) and those for Girolamo Bargagli's comedy *La Pellegrina* (see *Les Fêtes du mariage de Ferdinand de Médicis et de Christine de Lorraine*, ed. Walker).

[56] In all, some five madrigals, as originally pointed out by this writer (*olim* Hersh), 'Verdelot and the Early Madrigal', i. 19–24, 105–6.

[57] Two of them in Bk 1: 15–16; the other four in M4: 4–5, 10, 15, composed, to all appearances, at an early date (see Ch. 3), thus falling within the time frame of the play's performances.

theatrical performance, for it was customary to set verses, detached from their dramatic surroundings, as separate madrigals. More than 550 madrigals, in fact, were written to lyrics from Guarini's play, and of these only a small number were heard in the theatre. We know very little about the performances of the *Pastor fido*, and even less about their musical insertions. Given the Mantuan venue of at least one of the performances (1598), it could be that one or more of Rossi's settings were written for it.[58]

2. *Poetry of a strongly scenic character.* In one text, Madonna, posing as an archeress, stations herself on a high rock, from which she hurls her weapons.[59] In another, the shepherdess Chloris sleeps; little Cupids scuttle about, surrounding her face; her lover bends down and steals a kiss.[60] In still another, night is described as silent, cloudless, and glistening with stars. The vocabulary, in the second part, turns theatrical: 'To such a sweet and joyous *spectacle* | May the spheres lend their harmony and the stars their light; | May the heavens be a *spectator* and the world a *theatre*'.[61] The only problem with this last text is that it is precisely the second part that Rossi did not set.

3. *Departure songs* (partenze). Rossi composed music to at least fourteen different poems describing the sadness of parting. A typical example is Rinuccini's 'Io parto', where the lover says: 'I'm leaving, beloved beams; | Behold once more the sorrow of my leaving | On this wan and bewildered forehead. | I'm leaving, oh sun, oh stars, | Eyes, heaven's deities whom I revere on earth; | I'm leaving, I'm leaving, alas, I'm no longer leaving, I'm dying'.[62] Situations of leave-taking are common enough in the theatre. Rossi's parting songs could have been used, to good advantage, in any number of plays; it seems likely, in fact, that some of them were.

---

[58] Other composers' theatrical works were scattered among various publications: for those of Gastoldi, see Fenlon, *Music and Patronage in Sixteenth-Century Mantua*, ii. pp. ix–x; for those of Giovanelli and Marenzio, see Chater, 'Castelletti's "Stravaganze d'Amore" (1585)'. On the performances of Guarini's *Pastor fido*, see D'Ancona, *Origini del teatro italiano*, ii. 535–75; Hartmann, 'Battista Guarini and *Il pastor fido*'; also Fenlon, *Music and Patronage in Sixteenth-Century Mantua*, 149 ff. The first Mantuan performance of the play, completed in the early 1580s, was due to take place in 1592, yet, for various reasons, had to be postponed to 1598. On the *intermedi* for this performance, as reported by Battista Grillo in a *Breve trattato* (1604), see Neri, 'Gli "intermezzi" del *Pastor fido*'; they were presented between the acts of the play, hence should not be confused with possible musical insertions (including Rossi's?) in the play itself. Only two musicians are mentioned in connection with the 1592 production, Wert and Rovigo; yet others might also have been involved in the preparations for it, among them Rossi (his co-religionist Isacchino Massarano was in charge of the choreography).

[59] 'Come il ferir sia poco' (Marino), Bk 4: 2.

[60] 'Dolcemente dormiva la mia Clori' (Tasso), M4: 13. In another text, Cupids play about Milady, braiding her hair with garlands ('Scherzan intorno i pargoletti amori', Cte: 17).

[61] 'Tace la notte' (Marino), Bk 5: 14 ('A sì dolce spettacolo e giocondo', etc.).

[62] 'Io parto, amati lumi; | Rimirate il dolor de la partita', etc. (Bk 4: 11). Other *partenze* are spread over the collections: Bk 1: 9, 11, 19; Bk 2: 18 (labelled an 'aria di partenza'); Bk 3: 7; Bk 4: 4, 16; Bk 5: 3; M4: 6, 8, 15 ('Ah dolente partita', from Guarini's *Pastor fido*), 16; Brescia, Bibl. Queriniana, MS L. IV. 99, p. 20 (see below, Ex. 6.2).

4. *Poems in dialogue.*[63]   Just because a poem is in dialogue does not mean that it was performed in the theatre: the madrigal literature abounds in examples of 'dialoghi fuor di scena'. Nevertheless, dialogues were increasingly put to use in *intermedi* of the sixteenth century, as, for example, in the first *intermedio* for Francesco d'Ambra's comedy *La Cofanaria* (Florence, 1569), a dialogue between Venus and Cupid.[64] Whether Rossi's dialogue settings were pressed into theatrical service cannot be determined.

5. *Poems naming a specific individual.*   Some of them were probably set to music for ceremonial occasions, such as birthdays and anniversaries. Others might have been employed in dramatic presentations, in which the persons named are those who participate in the action. Still others might have had no immediate usage beyond the merely hedonistic one of courtly or private entertainment.

The persons named, in Rossi's poetry, range from the ducal pair Vincenzo and Leonora[65] to the stock characters of pastoral poetry Amaryllis, Amyntas, Chloris, Clytia, Myrtilus, Phyllis, Thyrsis, and so on.[66] Amor appears in a number of examples, Venus in one.[67] Usually only one person is invoked. Yet there are poems where two, three, and even four persons come to the fore.[68] How many of these poems were integrated into a dramatic action remains an open question. Chances are that a certain number were.

6. *Poetry having irregular verse lengths.*   With few exceptions, all of the texts composed by Rossi show the usual admixture of seven- and eleven-syllable verses (in iambic metre). One wonders about the exceptions, particularly since the free alternation of different verse lengths was recognized as advisable for theatrical poetry. Alessandro Guidotti wrote, in connection with

---

[63] Two examples: 'Rimanti in pace' (Celiano), Bk 1: 9; 'Pargoletta che non sai', Mti: 14.

[64] On theatrical vs. non-theatrical musical dialogues, see Nutter, 'The Italian Polyphonic Dialogue of the Sixteenth Century', also his entry for 'Dialogue' in Sadie (ed.), *The New Grove Dictionary of Music and Musicians*, v. 415–21 (where the expression 'dialoghi fuor di scena' is traced to G. B. Doni).

[65] 'Voi due terrestri numi' (Cte: 1; see below). For other texts celebrating 'couples' and performed as part of *intermedi*, see e.g. 'Coppia gentil d'avventurosi amanti' (Rinuccini), composed by Malvezzi for the first *intermedio* of *La Pellegrina* (see *Les Fêtes du mariage de Ferdinand de Médicis et de Christine de Lorraine*, ed. Walker, 33–5), or the *canzonetta* 'Coppia real' sung by Hymen to music by Monteverdi in his prologue to *L'Idropica* (for text, see Solerti, *Gli albori del melodramma*, iii. 211–12).

[66] Amaryllis: Bk 2: 3; Bk 3: 3 (for more examples, see below). Amyntas: see below. Aurora: Bk 4: 17. Chloris: Bk 3: 14 (also Mti: 2); M4: 13 (for more examples, see below). Clytia: Bk 5: 5–6. Flora: see below. Lydia: Bk 3: 7; Bk 4: 16; Bk 5: 12. Myrtilus: see below. Phyllis: Bk 2: 1; Bk 3: 6; Bk 4: 1 (also Bk 5: 19), 6; Bk 5: 13; M4: 9; Mti: 16–17 (for more examples, see below). For Sylvia, Thyrsis, and Zephyr, see below.

[67] Amor: Cte: 4; Bk 1: 7 (also Bk 5: 18); Bk 3: 12; M4: 17 (for more examples, see below). Venus: see below.

[68] Two names: Cte: 6 (Amor, Phyllis), 8 (Phyllis, Venus); Bk 1: 9 (Thyrsis, Phyllis), 11 (Amyntas, Sylvia), 16 (Thyrsis, Phyllis); M4: 5 (Myrtilus, Amaryllis). Three names: Bk 5: 16 (Amor, Thyrsis, Chloris); Mti: 18 (Zephyr [if personified], Phyllis, Chloris). Four names: Bk 4: 18 (Chloris, Phyllis, Flora, Amaryllis).

Cavalieri's *La rappresentazione di Anima et di Corpo*, that 'it is fitting for it[s poetry] to be easygoing and full of shorter verses, not only of seven syllables, but also of five and eight, with an occasional *verso sdrucciolo* [i.e. a verse ending in a proparoxytone]; and when, for the charm of the music, it has adjacent rhymes, the effect is delightful'.[69]

Three of the exceptions were composed as strophic *madrigaletti*: one in trochaic *ottonario*, with a four-syllable closing verse;[70] the others in iambic or mixed metre, with anything from four to eleven syllables to a line.[71] Beyond their prosody, it might be noted that two of the three *madrigaletti* have a recurrent *ritornello*, perhaps, though not necessarily, an indicator of theatrical performance;[72] and that one is a dialogue, in the *pastourelle* tradition, between an ardent suitor and his recalcitrant shepherdess, who follows up his protracted expostulations, eight lines to a stanza, with curt one-line retorts ('It's not true!', 'I don't feel it!', 'I don't understand you!', etc.).[73]

Other exceptions are *canzonette*, the first a strophic poem in *versi sdruccioli*:

> Voi che seguite il cieco ardor di Venere,
> Udite, amanti: la mia cara Fillide
> Co'l suo bel viso m'ha ridott'in cenere.[74]

> *(two stanzas follow)*

The second is a *partenza*, in a single stanza, with alternating verses of four, five, and six syllables in mixed metre.[75] In its dotted semiquavers, and sharp rhythmic contrasts, it differs from Rossi's usual works. To all appearances, it represents, stylistically, his only example of a monody (to be distinguished from his pseudo-monodies in Book 1 *a* 5). Appearances, though, are deceptive: as it turns out, the vocal work is an adaptation of a *sinfonia a 3* in Rossi's second book of instrumental works (no. 21); thus it too, in its own way, is a pseudo-monody, though prepared, perhaps, by another composer.[76]

---

[69] From preface; after Solerti, *Le origini del melodramma*, 8.

[70] 'Pargoletta che non sai' (Mti: 14): five strophes, each nine lines long (rhyme scheme: abbacddee).

[71] 'Gradita libertà' (Mti: 13): three strophes, each having ten lines, of five, six, seven, or eleven syllables, in iambic metre (rhyme scheme: abbaccDeed, in the order of 6, 7, 7, 6, 5, 5, 11, 7, 5, 7 syllables; for verses, see Ch. 3). 'Vo' fuggir lontan da te' (Mti: 15): four strophes, each having eight lines of four, six, seven, or eight syllables, in mixed metre (rhyme scheme: abcacddb, in the order of 7, 4, 8, 7, 6, 4, 4, 4 syllables).

[72] See below, under possible musical evidence for theatrical connections.

[73] In one source of the poetry, the shepherdess's repartees are described as 'a cruel answer [to the words] of an invincible lover'; see Romano (comp.), *Prima raccolta di bellissime canzonette musicali e moderne di auttori gravissimi* (1622), 111–12.

[74] Cte: 8 ('You who follow the blind ardour of Venus, | Hear, lovers: my dear Phyllis | Has, with her fair face, reduced me to ashes').

[75] 'Partirò da te', Brescia, Bibl. Queriniana, MS L. IV. 99, dated 1610, p. 20; probably for 2 v., of which only the top one is extant. On this manuscript, see Kurzman, 'An Early Seventeenth-Century Manuscript of "Canzonette e Madrigaletti Spirituali" ' (and for 'Partirò', 171).

[76] On the problem of 'mehr Schein als Sein' in this and other works, see Harrán, 'The Fixed and the Changeable in the Problematic of Stylistic Definition'.

Still, with its free poetry and *stile rappresentativo*, it stands a good chance of having been used in the theatre: 'I will leave you, | Yes, I will take leave, | Oh traitor, | Causing this heart | To die; | I will no longer love you, | I will no longer follow | Your deceits, no! | No, no, no! | You traitor' (Ex. 6.2).

Ex. 6.2   Rossi, 'Partirò da te' (missing bass line supplied after corresponding *sinfonia*, Book 2, no. 21)

7. Poetry referring to music.   Many poems speak of 'songs' and 'singing', of 'voices', 'sounds', 'notes', 'harmonies', etc. A good example is the *canzonetta*, from Rossi's *intermedio* for Guarini's *L'Idropica*, beginning 'Pingono in varii canti | I forsennati amanti | Quel che serbano in sen rinchiuso ardore'.[77] Using this poem as a model, one might surmise theatrical connections for one or more of Rossi's madrigals with musical vocabulary. They range from texts with *canto* (or *cantar*) stated once or several times[78] to a whole battery of melic images, as in the following poem by Guarini:

> Oh, 'tis useless for you to ask
> To *hear*, fair *siren*, my *song*!
> If you are deaf, I am dumb.
> At the *sound* of your *accents*
> I lost my *voice*; the only *sound* in my heart
> Is the *harmony* of my sighs and complaints.
> If your severity
> Removes their *sound* from you, behold my weeping,
> For my tears are my *song*.[79]

In another poem, by Marino, 'voices' are enhanced by 'instruments':

> Here, oh Thyrsis, fair Chloris laughed;
> Here she turned to me the two stars of Love;
> Here, to adorn my hair with the fairest flowers,
> She gathered an armful at the *sound* of my *pipes*.
> Here she released her angelic *voice* in *notes*
> That would shame the proudest bulls.[80]
>
> *(eight lines follow)*

The dedication piece to Vincenzo and Leonora ('Voi due terrestri numi'), probably intended to mark their anniversary, could have been performed as an *intermedio*. Stanzas 2–4 have their share of joyful music:

> The fair Mincio,
> Where the *muses* of Helicon lodge,
> *Resounds* your proud name,
> Worthy of sacred and glorious dominion.
>
> May the consecrated heroes rise
> To join us here in *singing*, happily,
> Your full praises,
> As may Mantuan and Ferrarese Homers.

[77] 'Let delirious lovers | Depict, in varied *songs*, | That ardour they keep shut in their breast', etc. For the setting of this madrigal (in four stanzas) as a chorus of nymphs, see above.

[78] Stated once: Cte: 12, M4: 7; and four times: Bk 4: 17.

[79] Bk 1: 5 ('Deh com'invan chiedete | D'*udir*, bella *Sirena*, il *canto* mio!', etc.).

[80] Bk 5: 16 ('Qui rise, o Tirsi, e qui ver' me rivolse | Le due stelle d'Amor la bella Clori', etc.; of the remaining eight lines, Rossi only set two).

Hearing such gentle *accents*,
The gods look on attentively in joy and mirth
While the heavens repeatedly *intone* the words
'May Vincenzo and Leonora live happily'.[81]

When dancing is added to the musical imagery, the likelihood of a staged presentation increases, as in a sonnet by Rinuccini ('Zeffiro torna'), familiar to most readers from its setting by Monteverdi (in his *Libro nono*):

Zephyr returns; it makes the air pleasant
With sweet fragrances and races its foot over the waves;
Murmuring through the green bushes,
It makes the flowers *dance* on the fields to its beautiful *sounds*.
With their hair wreathed in garlands, Phyllis and Chloris
Blend their dear and joyful *notes* of love,
While from the mountains and from the deepest and lowest valleys
The *songful* caverns increase their *harmony*.[82]

(six lines follow)

Theatrical Implications in the Music

Turning from the lyrics to the music, one might signal four kinds of evidence as providing possible leads to theatrical usage:

1. *Works based on strophic poetry, with the stanzas separated by an instrumental* ritornello. As a model, of course, there is 'Spazziam pronte' from *La Maddalena* (see above). Two other works are *madrigaletti*—their poetry, with its irregular verse lengths, has already been signalled under textual evidence.[83] The question is to what extent a *ritornello* points to a staged performance. *Ritornelli* are well known from the early opera, but they also occur in the madrigal literature. In Monteverdi's *Scherzi musicali* (1607), for example, the initial 'ritornelli are to be played at the end of every stanza, with two violins for the soprano parts and, for the bass, a chitarrone or harpsichord or some such similar instrument'.[84] Whether these and kindred works were employed in staged entertainments cannot be determined.

The same may be said of Rossi's two works with *ritornelli*, for which the assumption of theatrical functions rests on circumstantial evidence: the composer's presumably strong connections with the Jewish theatre; and the exceptional character, for Rossi at least, of the two *madrigaletti* in question (both in their poetry and in their having a *ritornello*). One of them is

---

[81] Cte: 1 ('Il bel Mincio *risuona*, | Ov'albergan' le *Muse* d'Helicona', etc.). For the first stanza, see Ch. 2.

[82] Mti: 18 ('Zeffiro torna e di soavi odori | L'aer fa grato', etc.).

[83] 'Gradita libertà' (Mti: 13); 'Vo' fuggir lontan da te' (Mti: 15). See above.

[84] From the original *Avvertimenti* to the collection (cf. Monteverdi, *Tutte le opere*, ed. Malipiero, x); the scoring recalls Rossi's for his instrumental collections.

particularly dancelike in the trochaic rhythms of its verses:[85] was it employed as a staged *balletto*?

2. *Works composed as* balletti.   Beyond 'Spazziam pronte', the only other *balletto* that Rossi composed, and so designated, is a 'fragment of a *balletto*', appended to his first book of instrumental works (Ex. 6.3).

In dealing with this *balletto*, various questions might be asked, from the least important, what is a 'fragment of a *balletto*', to the most important, what is the relation of *balletti* to the theatre? The first question may be

Ex. 6.3   Rossi, *Passeggio d'un balletto* 5/3 v. (Book 1, no. 27; third and fourth voices *si placet*)

[85] The poetry, with its changing verse lengths, should not be scanned by line, which would disrupt the trochaic metre, but be read as prose sentences (lines 1–3, then 4–8) having a continuous succession of longs plus shorts: 'Vō' fŭggīr lŏntāṇ dă tē, | Dŏnnā crŭdēl | Più d'ūnă fēra al mĭō pĕnār. | [*hiatus*] Più lănguīr sĕnzā mĕrcĕ̄, | Più nōn vŏ' sōspĭrār | Sĕnzā pĭetā̄ | L'ĕmpiā bĕltā̄ | D'ŭn'īnfĕdēl' (three stanzas follow).

quickly dismissed: the work, in its eight bars, appears to be the first section of a *balletto*. Its second section, no longer extant, might have totalled anywhere from eight to, probably, sixteen bars, if other short works of the composer (from among his *canzonette* and *sinfonie*) as well as Gastoldi's *balletti* are taken as exemplars.[86]

To answer the second question, one must know what a *balletto* is: the word refers to various possibilities, from a *balletto* of the Gastoldi type, with its particular structural and stylistic characteristics, to any work that was danced, hence *balletto* in the sense of *ballo*. Still another possibility is a *balletto* as a choreographed pantomime or, as it is usually referred to, a ballet. So conceived, it could have been performed in the theatre as a separate work or as part of a larger work (an opera, a *sacra rappresentazione*).[87]

Rossi's five-voice *balletto* resembles examples by Gastoldi, for the same number of voices,[88] in its trio texture, homophony, and strong rhythmic profile. It differs from them in being instrumental, though it could well have had a text, which, in order for the example to be included in a book of *sinfonie*, was omitted. But even it were textless, Gastoldi recognized the possibility of performing *balletti* vocally and instrumentally. He described his collections of *balletti*, for three and five voices, as suitable 'for singing, playing, and dancing'.[89] The same three manners of performance could apply to Rossi's 'fragment of a *balletto*'.

There remains the question, however, whether the piece was staged. The fact that *balletti* were danced, as Gastoldi acknowledged, would suggest the possibility of a theatrical performance, as in the many dances designed for

[86] Though referring here to a portion of a *balletto*, the word *passeggio* may also refer to a particular succession of dance steps forming a complete unit: cf. Caroso, *Il ballarino* (1581), fos. 8, 148, *passim*. Seven *canzonette* (out of 19 in Rossi's first publication) have an 8-bar first part (or *passeggio*), and of these, two have a second part in 8 bars, one in 11, one in 14, two in 15, and one in 16. Three *sinfonie* (out of 15 *a* 3 in S1) have an 8-bar first part, and of these, one has a second part in 16 bars, another in 20, and the third in 30. In Gastoldi's book of 5-v. *balletti* (1591), five (out of 15) have an 8-bar first part, and of these, separate examples can be found for a second part in 8, 10–12, and 16 bars. In his book of 3-v. *balletti* (1594), only one of those in two parts (eight works altogether, another eight being in three parts) has an 8-bar first part (followed, moreover, by an 8-bar second part).

[87] Separate works, such as Monteverdi's *Ballo delle ingrate* (1608) and his *Tirsi e Clori* (1619); *balletti* within larger works, such as Rossi's for *L'Idropica* (the first number of his *intermedio* was a choral ballet) and *La Maddalena*, not to mention numerous examples by other composers.

[88] Gastoldi's *balletti* 5 v. are true 5-v. pieces (though reducible to a 3-v. skeleton), whereas Rossi's *balletto* was originally written for 3 v., to which two were added to be performed *ad libitum*.

[89] The formula 'per cantare, sonare, et ballare' appears in all editions of Gastoldi's two books of *balletti*; see Lesure and Sartori (comps.), *Il nuovo Vogel*, i. nos. 1062–1101[bis]. Preceding Gastoldi (whose *balletti* were first printed in the 1590s), Mainerio published, in 1578, a volume of 4-v. *balli*, textless pieces meant 'to be sung and played on any kind of instrument' (see *Il primo libro de balli*, ed. Schuler). Further corroboration for different performing possibilities is offered by Brunelli's third book of *Scherzi, arie, canzonette e madrigali* (1616; cf. Lesure and Sartori (comps.), *Il nuovo Vogel*, i. no. 435): its *balletto* beginning 'Del bell'Arno' is followed by 'il medesimo ballo per sonare solo senza cantare' (here *balletto* and *ballo* are used interchangeably); another two pieces are *balli* (i.e. *balletti*) written for instruments alone.

sixteenth- and seventeenth-century *intermedi*.[90] If it were danced, and chances are that it was, it could equally have formed part of a dramatic *intermedio* or of a simple court entertainment (without costumes or staging). Since Rossi's two 'known' examples of *balletti* were, indeed, put to dramatic usage (in the *intermedi* for *L'Idropica* and *La Maddalena*), it may be assumed, with good reason, that the 'fragment of a *balletto*', completed by its second section, was written for a theatrical *intermedio* that could have taken place any time from the 1590s to 1607, the year the piece was published.[91]

3. *Various other dance types.* Moving from *balletti* to the dances, or *balli*, which occupy about a third of Rossi's instrumental works, one faces the tricky question of differentiating between them: *balletti* and *balli* carried different meanings, but were often used synonymously. The *balletto*, as mentioned, can be narrowly construed as a specific poetic and musical form, from Gastoldi's *balletti* to Thomas Morley's balletts. But the term also indicates a mimetically performed theatrical dance, without limitations on its poetic or musical form, which means that, theoretically, a *balletto* could be any kind of 'dance' adapted to the theatre. The term *ballo*, by comparison, refers to something that was danced, be it a *balletto*, in the various senses just adduced, or what, today, would probably be called a social or ballroom dance, covering the various *gagliarde*, *correnti*, and *brandi* in Rossi's repertory.

Potentially, all kinds of dances could have been used in both theatrical diversions and 'ballroom' dancing.[92] Our concern here is with the former: how many of Rossi's *balli* were devised for the theatre? The only evidence for theatrical usage is, again, circumstantial. Isacchino Massarano, as mentioned, choreographed dances for the Jewish theatre and other theatrical companies;[93] it is reasonable to assume that some of Rossi's dances served as his raw material. One of Rossi's *gagliarde*, in fact, is dedicated to Massarano, or a member of his family, who perhaps took part in its original execution.[94] Another *gagliarda* is dedicated to someone in the Norsa family, a name well known within the Jewish community:[95] various Norsas are

[90] For examples of the *balletto* as a theatrical dance, see Solerti, *Gli albori del melodramma*, iii. 277 ff.

[91] S4 has, for Son. 7, a series of variations 'sopra l'Aria di un Balletto'. The tune might have been borrowed (as was the case in Son. 5 'sopra un'Aria francese' or, in S3, in Br. 2 on an 'aria' by G. F. Rubini).

[92] Not only at court, but also in Jewish circles: see Friedhaber, 'Hamaḥol bekehilot yehudei dukasut mantova bame'ot ha-17 veha-18'.

[93] His name appears in the same documents citing Rossi's in connection with the Jewish theatre (see above, also Ch. 2). His part in preparing the dances for Guarini's *Pastor fido* has already been mentioned.

[94] S1: Gagl. 3 *a* 5/3, 'detta la Massara'. Other members of the Massarano family were active in the Jewish theatrical troupe (e.g. Jacob, Lazaro, Leon, Simon), as were other members of the Rossi family (e.g. Agnolino, Angelo, Emanuel, Isaac; see Ch. 2); yet the names of the choreographer and composer were inscribed in succession (see Plate 5).

[95] S1: Gagl. [2] *a* 5/3 'detta la Norsina'. On the Norsa family, see the listings for its various members in the index to Simonsohn, *History of the Jews in the Duchy of Mantua*, and the general

listed among participants in productions of the Jewish theatre.[96] What about the *gagliarda* called 'la Turca': is it a reference to Andreini's comedy by this name, performed in Casale in 1608?[97]

Writing in *Le gratie d'amore* (1602), Cesare Negri mentions having devised three theatrical *brandi*, of which two belonged to a *mascherata* staged in 1574 and the third to Giovanni Battista Visconti's pastoral comedy *Arminia*, performed in 1599.[98] One wonders how many of Rossi's *brandi* were theatrically employed. The same question might be asked about his *correnti*.[99]

4. *Sinfonie.*   Of the various forms of Rossi's instrumental music, the *sinfonia*, as is clear from Chapter 4, was his favourite. Nor did the composer tire of its cultivation: his sixty-five *sinfonie* are spread over his four printed collections. Why so many? The answer may have to do with their form and function. Rossi's *sinfonie* are short works, too short, it would seem, to stand alone. Were they played as introductions to vocal pieces, or to dances, their brevity would have been justified by their preparative usage. *Sinfonie* of this kind occur, moreover, in the *intermedi* for the play *La Pellegrina*, where they preceded madrigals by Malvezzi and Marenzio.[100] Belonging to the same tradition is the *sinfonia* that opens the *intermedio* 'The Rape of Proserpine'.

Early critics recognized the scenographic advantages to be gained from the *sinfonia*: Guidotti, for one, noted that during the *sinfonia* 'the scenery can be changed to accord with the purpose of the *intermedio*'.[101] Modern scholars have followed suit, among them Franco Piperno, who wrote, most emphatically, that 'the job of the instrumental *sinfonia* occurring in an opera, an *intermedio*, or any other dramatic action with music is, above all, if not exclusively, that of accompanying a scenic event: from the entrance or exit of certain actors to a change of scenery and the movement of machines and scenic apparatus'.[102] On the subject of Rossi's *sinfonie*, he remarked that they constitute a vast repository of materials supplied to meet the needs of

monograph by a later descendant, Paolo Norsa, *Una famiglia di banchieri, la famiglia Norsa (1350–1950)*.

[96] At least three Norsas (Febro, Salomon, Samuel) participated in the play *Acessi de Amor*.

[97] S3: 16. Andreini's *La turca* (1620), a 'commedia boschareccia e marittima', has, in its list of 'personaggi' (on fo. [*10]ᵛ), the notation 'sonatori'. From the foreword it is clear that the comedy was originally performed 'con sontuoso apparecchio' (fo. *3). A dance may have been inserted in Act II, Scene 7, to follow up the words 'A la cetra de' venti | Danzan ne' prati i fiori', etc. (67-8).

[98] After the (unsigned) entry for *brando* in Sadie (ed.), *The New Grove Dictionary of Music and Musicians*, iii. 198. See Negri's *Nuove inventioni di balli* (1604), with descriptions, and music, of various *brandi* (152–5, 165–8, 291–6).

[99] Negri, for example, includes a 'Balletto a due detto la Corrente . . .' in his *Nuove inventioni di balli*, 265–6.

[100] See the *sinfonie* in *Les Fêtes du mariage de Ferdinand de Médicis et de Christine de Lorraine*, ed. Walker, 14–15, 36, 77–9, 93–7. The first *sinfonia*, composed by Malvezzi, connects with its vocal number by thematic similarities.

[101] From Guidotti's preface to Cavalieri's *La rappresentazione di Anima et di Corpo* (see above).

[102] Piperno, 'La sinfonia strumentale del primo Seicento—I', esp. 153.

composers writing theatrical *intermedi*.[103] What he did not stress, and this seems to be the crucial point, is that Rossi probably wrote his *sinfonie*, first and foremost, to meet his own needs. If the point can be sustained, and it seems reasonable in the light of Rossi's connections with the theatre, then a large part of Rossi's theatre music may probably be found among his *sinfonie*. It is less clear whether these *sinfonie* were paired with a similarly large part of his theatre music to be found, perhaps, among his vocal works. I would like to believe they were, and on this hopeful note I rest my case for the premiss that Rossi's theatre music may be lying within the confines of his printed collections.

Conclusions

At least five conclusions may be drawn. First, Salamone Rossi, on the basis of the material examined here, seems to have played a significant role in Mantuan theatrical life. In effect, the conclusion reverses that which might normally have been inferred from the almost total unavailability of his theatre music. But Rossi is not the only composer who wrote for the theatre, yet left few traces of his activity. The history of the sixteenth- and seventeenth-century *intermedio* is one in which more is conjectured than is actually known about its music.

A second conclusion is that Rossi's participation in the theatre seems to have taken two forms: as a contributor, for one, to works of the non-Jewish theatrical companies that paid frequent visits to the Mantuan court[104] and, for another, to productions of the Jewish theatrical troupe. In both capacities, Rossi probably composed *intermedi* that consisted of one or more instrumental or vocal items. True, no more than two examples (of which only one has its music) remain for the former and no more than three (documentary) notices for the latter. But they are enough to imply a more extensive activity.

A third conclusion is that, of the two forms of participation, Rossi probably directed the major part of his efforts to writing for the Jewish theatre. Since the Jewish theatre prepared one or more productions per year, and its most distinguished musician was Rossi, it seems likely for him to have been closely involved in its activities. Such an involvement might explain the holes in his biography, so far as his connections with the court are concerned. It might explain the allusion, in a letter of Alessandro Pico, to Rossi's 'concerto', a group of musicians, perhaps three instrumentalists, that could

---

[103] Ibid. 160 ('Rossi's *sinfonie* clearly represent the most conspicuous body of works of their kind composed in the first part of the 17th c. Thus it is legitimate to hypothesize that were it necessary to choose *sinfonie* for theatrical presentation...one could have turned to Rossi's collections').

[104] On the sojourns of different theatrical companies (the Accesi, Uniti, Gelosi, Fedeli, etc.) at the Mantuan court, see Lea, *Italian Popular Comedy*, ii. 271 ff., also Oreglia, *The Commedia dell'Arte*. On the brilliance of theatrical life under Vincenzo I, see Fenlon, *Music and Patronage in Sixteenth-Century Mantua*, i. 121–62, esp. 147 ff.

have performed the instrumental portions of his *intermedi*. It might explain the large number of *sinfonie*, mostly for three voices, in his printed collections: some, if not many, may have been provided for use, in his various *intermedi*, in conjunction with vocal works.

A fourth conclusion is that Rossi's music for the theatre, generally thought to be no longer existent, may, in fact, be preserved in his printed collections. His two known examples led to the search for additional works; they served as a springboard, in this chapter, for defining various kinds of textual and musical evidence for possible theatrical connections. Potentially, any number of works, among those extant, could have been put to dramatic usage, ranging from *canzonette* and madrigals to dances and *sinfonie*. That is not to say that these, in fact, are Rossi's theatre works. Yet enough evidence remains to suggest that some of them were.

A fifth, and final, conclusion is that in order to locate Rossi's repertory of theatre music, wherever it may be, one must first designate the areas within which theatrical associations could have evolved. Whole areas of knowledge, it turns out, are covered by shadows: in a search for the unknown, it became apparent how little we know about the known. The evidence adduced so far raises basic questions about the character, uses, and functions of music, textually and musically, within theatrical representations. We have not answered the questions, but, to a certain extent, defined them for further investigation.

7

'The Songs of Solomon'

'...souls that enter into wedlock
as a man with a maid'
'*Songs*', no. 33

ALL of Rossi's collections are interesting for one or another reason, but 'The Songs of Solomon' are unique for being the first known collection of polyphonic works set to Hebrew texts. That in itself lends them historical significance. They stand out, further, for having a multipartite introduction of a length and complexity rarely to be encountered in the sacred musical repertory of the sixteenth and seventeenth centuries. In effect, the collection is a composite of apologetics and music, in which the various historical, literary, social, religious, and liturgical problems addressed in the introduction bear directly on the musical contents.

The title page is followed by Rossi's dedication to his patron, Moses Sullam; two unsigned poems in the composer's praise; a foreword by Leon Modena, who, like Sullam, assisted Rossi in his enterprise; a third poem of praise, by Modena; a rabbinical *responsum*, again by Modena, to a question put to him, in 1605, about the legitimacy of art music in the synagogue;[1] five statements, prepared and signed in the same year by leading Venetian rabbis, in approbation of the *responsum*; and, at the end, a declaration of copyright privileges, one of the earliest of its kind.[2] All these documents were assembled to justify the 'Songs' as a musical artifact with religious functions. The idea was to support the novelty of the collection by appealing to ancient and modern authority, from the Bible to the Talmud and rabbinical writings, including the *responsum* of Modena and the pronouncements in its favour.

Rossi's collection was controversial from the start. Art music is not part of the older Hebrew liturgical tradition; and though evidence for the tentative beginnings of its practice in the Italian synagogue can be traced to the early seventeenth century, neither then nor now did it ever become integrated into the prayer services of the Italiani, that is, those who practise the 'Roman rite', as a regular component.[3] True, towards the end of the eighteenth

---

[1] London, BL MS Add. 27148, fos. 9–10ᵛ; cf. Modena, *She'elot utshuvot ziknei yehuda*, ed. Simonsohn, 15–20.

[2] See Gradenwitz, 'An Early Instance of Copyright—Venice, 1622'.

[3] On the place of music in the Italian liturgy, see Fiderer-Abramovicz, 'Mekoma shel hamusika baliturgya shel yehudei italya'.

century art music did penetrate the European synagogue to become customary for Sabbath and holiday prayers, but not necessarily in Italy, or at
least not among the Italiani, who, in contradistinction to the Ashkenazi and
Sephardi Jews, tended, and still tend today, to favour a simple melodic
presentation over artful display. In anticipation of protest, the composer
and his advisers hoped, through the materials in the introduction, to
demonstrate that what seemed new was actually old.

The recourse to ancient authority serves authors who, pretending to
novelty, come into conflict with time-honoured practices. It appears in
secular and sacred writings from both Christian and Hebrew spheres, and
in this they concur with humanist tendencies in Renaissance culture.[4]
Rossi's works were not only perceived as novel, but also so described. To
be accepted, they needed to be bolstered by ancient example.

The combined literary-musical apparatus is enough to turn the 'Songs'
into a socio-historical document of the first order. Their singularity is
emphasized by their title. Rossi, as advised probably by Modena, called
his sacred works the 'Songs of Solomon', in playful reference to the 'Song of
Songs of [King] Solomon'. It was not that he conceived his 'Songs' as a
newfangled 'Song of Songs', though the connection with the latter comes
out, at least allegorically, in the last work, a wedding hymn. Rather, Rossi,
like others, followed a well-established rabbinical convention, which was to
choose a striking biblical quotation for a title. One reason for this was to
perpetuate the author's name, which, after his death, was likely to be
forgotten. Thus Isaac Arama (d. 1494), writing a book of homilies on the
Pentateuch, first printed in 1522, called it 'Akedat yitshak, or 'the binding of
Isaac', after Genesis 22: 9; and Judah Moscato assembled a collection of his
sermons under the title Nefutsot yehuda, or 'the dispersed of Judah' (1588),
after Isaiah 11: 12. Another reason was to demonstrate erudition, without
necessarily intending to relate the work, in content, to the book or passage from
which its title was taken. Still another reason, especially valid for Rossi's
'Songs of Solomon', was to flaunt the writer's pedigree: in this case, Solomon
the son of David; David the legendary progenitor, as pointed out in Chapter 1,
of the Rossi family; and David, once again, the author, it was thought, of the
Book of Psalms, from which the composer drew the lion's share of his texts.
Rossi associated himself with an ancient musical tradition initiated by David
and, from the time of his son Solomon, practised in the venerable Temple
liturgy. The association lent weight and lustre to his 'Songs'.

The biblical Song of Songs occupies a special position within the
Hebrew tradition for being an outwardly secular book, though dealing,

---

[4] For the playwright Leone de' Sommi's attempts to justify his literary innovations, see
Harrán, 'Jewish Dramatists and Musicians in the Renaissance'. Like Rossi's Hebrew songs, so
Sommi's Hebrew play (extant in four manuscript copies) has introductory matter: a prologue by
'Wisdom', showing that the author renewed ancient learning after its disappearance during the
Dispersion (a theme that recurs in Rossi's work); and a confirmation by the rabbi Meshullam
Sullam (in one of the four copies).

metaphorically, with spiritual love. Over the ages it was subject to commentaries that led the reader to ascend gradually to higher recognition of God's ways and purposes.[5] In Modena's *responsum* we are told of the rabbinical prohibition against singing a verse from the Song of Songs when performed as a secular item: love songs about the Lord demand ritual propriety.[6] One such song is the last in Rossi's collection. It ostensibly fêtes a bride, yet can, and will, be read for its sacred overtones.[7]

Obstacles in the Way of Preparing the Collection

For Rossi to devise a sacred collection, he had to surmount at least three hurdles. One was the animosity, in certain religious circles, towards innovation in the synagogue liturgy. Another was the lack of an established Jewish art music tradition. A third was the technical problem of how to compose as well as print music to Hebrew words.

The rabbinate rose to considerable power in the later sixteenth and early seventeenth centuries, and any alteration in Jewish law or ritual required its sanction. There were different tendencies within contemporary Judaism, some of them inimical to change, others more liberal; their representatives inevitably came into conflict. Thus Azaria de' Rossi, who, by using a novel historical methodology in his *Me'or 'einayim*, or 'Light of One's Eyes' (1574), arrived at an unorthodox reading of Jewish history, found himself under attack from the traditionalists. Exponents of *halakha*, or the strict ordinances of Jewish ritual, were often in disagreement with the kabbalists, who espoused views that, to some, seemed to border on heterodoxy. The Counter Reformation, which one might think would have sharpened the reactionary tendencies among the Jews, in defence of their own patrimony, produced a double result. On the one hand, the Jews did, in fact, become further entrenched in orthodoxy; but on the other, they practised new forms of devotion, as fanned by Kabbala. The period was one in which established socio-religious structures were expanded to admit changes or accommodate differences.

The situation in the musical sphere was no exception. When, in 1605, some sort of part singing was introduced into the synagogue in Ferrara, it sparked a controversy. Leon Modena defended the innovation in a lengthy *responsum*. Since further opposition was anticipated for Rossi's 'Songs', the

---

[5] One such commentary, written towards the end of the 15th c. by Yohanan Alemanno, was entitled *Ḥeshek shelomo* ('Solomon's Craving'). On its musical aspects, see Idel, 'Haperush hamagi vehate'urgi shel hamusika betekstim yehudiyim mitkufat harenesans ve'ad haḥasidut', esp. 37–42.

[6] For the introductory matter, see Rossi, *Hashirim asher lishlomo*, ed. Rikko, iii (a new reading will appear in CW xiii, forthcoming). For notes to the Hebrew version, see Adler (ed.), *Hebrew Writings Concerning Music in Manuscripts and Printed Books from Geonic Times up to 1800*, esp. 212–21, 285–8.

[7] See, on this point, Harrán, ' "Dum recordaremur Sion" '.

responsum, probably at Modena's suggestion, was republished in their introduction.

The usual way of breaking down resistance in the Jewish apologetic
literature was to bypass present or earlier phases of Judaism to concentrate,
instead, on the biblical period, or, more specifically, the Ancient Temple.
Hebrew culture had reached the peak of its development in the glorious
ritual celebrations inaugurated in the First Temple under Solomon. Musically, the liturgy, as known from short references in the Hebrew Bible,
included music for voices and instruments in various numbers and combinations. There were no restrictions put on music-making in secular
and religious festivities, and the result seems to have been a rich practice
within the stylistic and cultural bounds of ancient Hebrew monody. This
music, in later times, became idealized to almost mythic proportions,
after the example, in humanist literature, of Athenian Greece and Imperial
Rome.

Typical, in this respect, is Abraham Portaleone, who, in 1612, raised the
Ancient Temple to idyllic heights in a massive treatise on its architecture
and ritual.[8] He familiarized its music, describing it by analogy with Renaissance vocal and instrumental song. The only other music Portaleone knew
was that practised in the synagogue, which, traditionally, centred around
biblical cantillation and prayer readings. Developed during the years of
dispersion that followed the destruction of the Second Temple, its sacred
portions were sung, monophonically, according to the modal or schematic
formulas developed for projecting the words in their accentual and syntactic
propriety. By comparison with art music it must have seemed, to the outside
listener, strange, even monotonous. One could not really call it music;
rather, it was an inflected form of recitation, sometimes simple, other
times more florid. Art music it was not.[9]

For Rossi to change the practice of music in the synagogue was to go
against tradition. Art music smacked of the profane or the heretical, for it
was identified with the secular and sacred music of the Gentiles.[10] For some
Jews the sounds of madrigal-like compositions in the synagogue must have
seemed just as sacrilegious as the mention of 'the sacred Diana' in a sermon
by David del Bene, whereby one rabbi called for his excommunication.[11]

---

[8] Portaleone, *Shiltei hagiborim* (1611/12).

[9] The dichotomy, in the Jewish liturgy, between music proper and what has been termed
'the dimension of sound' forms the cornerstone of the argument presented by Edwin Seroussi in
'"Sound" and "Music" in the Traditional Synagogue: New Perspectives' (I am grateful to the
author for providing me with a transcript of his remarks before their publication in the
proceedings of the Second International Conference on Jewish Music, City University of
London, April 1997).

[10] Speaking of Jewish aversion to what appeared to be non-Jewish, Bonfil formulated the
general rule that 'whatever was considered an exclusive characteristic of the Other became *ipso
facto* negative with respect to the definition of the Self': see his *Jewish Life in Renaissance Italy*, 103.

[11] After Simonsohn, *History of the Jews in the Duchy of Mantua*, 625. Del Bene was forced to
leave Mantua.

The only way to vindicate the 'new music' was to tie it to the Ancient Temple and build an argument for the Hebrews as the originators of art music. As the reasoning went, the Hebrews were first, the Christians followed them; thus if Jews in the early seventeenth century cultivated art music it was not in imitation of the Christians but in reversion to an indigenous practice. Modena wrote, after the fourteenth-century Immanuel Haromi ('the Roman'): 'What does the science of music say to others? "I was stolen out of the land of the Hebrews".'[12]

The change was several years in the making; or so it would seem from evidence in the introduction. But the evidence is equivocal. In the title, for example, Rossi's collection is hailed as 'something new in the land' (after Isaiah 31: 22) and its publication, consequently, as unprecedented ('there was no beginning like this ever before... [Rossi] begins something that..., in this form, did not exist in Israel').[13] Turning to his co-religionists, Modena says they should consider themselves blessed in being favoured with so promising a beginning. He warns against the reaction of 'those sanctimonious persons, who remove everything new and every example of learning in which they have no part'. The question is whether these polyphonic works to Hebrew texts were new for being written down; new for being printed; or new for being the first of their kind. That they were the earliest to be printed is undoubted; that they were the earliest to be formally composed, i.e. not improvised, seems to be implied.

Contrarily, Modena and two of those who endorsed his *responsum* suggest antecedents. Referring to the controversy in Ferrara (1605), Modena mentions six to eight singers, who, trained in 'the science of song, i.e. *musica* ..., lifted their voices and rejoiced in the synagogue in song, praises, and hymns... in honour of the Lord'.[14] Their rendition was marked by 'order and relation in the arrangement of the voices according to the aforementioned science'.[15]

On the face of it, the description is open: for each of its components, one could imagine varying possibilities. Of the six or eight voices, it is uncertain whether they sang their own parts or performed in unison. That the singers were 'knowledgeable' about 'the science of music' would imply some

---

[12] Modena, in his foreword to the 'Songs', after Immanuel's 'Notebooks' (*Mahberot 'imanuel*, vi. 341, itself after Gen. 40: 15), ed. Yarden, 120.

[13] This and next quotation from Modena's foreword.

[14] Among them, 'Ein keloheinu', ' 'Aleinu leshabeah', 'Yigdal', 'Adon 'olam'. Of these, Rossi composed music to the first, third, and fourth (Sgs: 26, 28–9).

[15] Further details are provided in a letter that Modena addressed to Judah Saltaro da Fano (see Modena, *Igrot rabi yehuda arye mimodena*, ed. Boksenboim, 110–11). There we learn that the incident occurred shortly after Modena settled in Ferrara. Wishing to 'put the study of music on a stronger basis', he hired a teacher who came, daily, to impart the rudiments, it appears, to those unfamiliar with it (Modena does not say what was taught: how to read notes? How to perform a single voice? How to co-ordinate in singing polyphony?). They 'lifted their voices in song' on the eve of Shabbat Nahamu (the special Sabbath following the Ninth of Av), to the virulent objection of Moses Coimbran.

familiarity with part music, though to what extent cannot be said: their training might have been limited to the rudiments. Nor can one tell whether the music the singers performed was composed or improvised. The expression 'lifted their voices and rejoiced' might indicate a spontaneous outpouring of music, perhaps by singing a traditional melody with some light embroidery in one or more voices.

The only certainty is that the singers performed 'with order and relation in the arrangement of voices', that is, presumably, with carefully measured rhythms and, if there were parts, a determinate sequence of consonances and dissonances. Yet their music could have been monophonic or homophonic, precomposed or improvised, drawn from old melodies or based on new ones.

Whatever was sung, it awakened protest from one listener, who rallied others to his cause. But it is not clear what he objected to. Was it that the singers performed 'measured music'? Or was it that they dared to sing joyfully, though, with the destruction of the Temple and exile of the Jews, there was only reason for lamentation?

Other references in the *responsum* and its statements of approbation are even less conclusive. Modena speaks of the practice, in traditional song, of the cantor being joined by two assistants, who add their voices 'without orderliness, but rather a[d] aria ['to a tune'])'. The practice, he confirms, is known from the Ashkenazi synagogues: it consists, to this day, of freely improvised interpolations in the cantorial chant, usually to round off a phrase.

Ben-Zion Zarfati, in his approbation, alluded to the custom of certain singers who, in mid-sixteenth-century Padua, adapted sacred texts to secular tunes heard 'outdoors and in the streets'.[16] Though the tunes were probably 'measured', they seem to have been monophonic, not to speak of their use as sacred *contrafacta*.

Ezra da Fano leaves a wider breach for one's imagination in remarking that it is commendable to sing praises to the Lord, using 'pleasant voices presented in metres and measures according to the conventions of music'. Since the words *voices* and *presented* can be read in different ways, the statement may refer, for one, to performance or, for another, to composition according to the metres and rhythms of measured music. Part music is a possibility, but not a certainty.

The major thrust of Modena's *responsum* was to silence the voices of the objectors. Yet, again, a close reading raises doubts about the kind of music being described. For all its detail and interest the *responsum*, written in 1605 and republished in 1622, only vaguely relates to art music as polyphony. Modena and the rabbis who approved his document talk about music that is measured and ordered, using the key words *mishkal, mida*, and *sh'eur* for

---

[16] The reference is to the period when he studied under Rabbi Meir Katzenellenbogen (c.1555–65).

'metre', 'duration', and 'proportion', and *seder, yaḥas*, and '*erekh* for 'order', 'relation', and 'arrangement'.[17] Yet the words occur so casually[18] as to be applicable not only to polyphony, but also to melodies, with the said characteristics, for a single voice.

More significant is the borrowed term *musika*, which Modena defines, in the *quaestio*, as 'the art of song' (*ḥokhmat hashir*).[19] Literally, it reads the 'science of song', but here 'science' seems to be used in the sense of *ars*, as in the *ars grammatica* or *ars musica*, the theory or knowledge of grammar or music. The 'art of song' seems to be set in juxtaposition to liturgical chant, as already mentioned. Modena's intention was not to replace liturgical chant, but only to supplement it on certain holidays or feast-days with other types, possibly, though not necessarily, polyphonic. His main concern in the *responsum* was not with part music in the prayer services. Rather, it was with the legitimacy, for one, of introducing into the synagogue any kind of music not sanctified by liturgical tradition and, for another, of performing it joyfully. What he tried to show and get the Venetian rabbis to approve is that singing to God, in any shape and form, is a *mitsva*, or pious act; that the destruction of the Temple did not impose on the Jewish people an everlasting injunction of lamentation; and that it really made no difference what kind of music was heard as long as the singers performed it with decorum and devotion.

To conclude: there is no way one can specifically, and exclusively, read polyphony into the *responsum* without stretching its words beyond their non-committal formulation. When Modena remarks that if the voice of one cantor is pleasant to hear, then how much more pleasant would it be if it sounded as many, it should be remembered that even if a hundred voices sing the same line it remains monophony. When he mentions occasional two-part interpolations in the cantorial song, again he is not speaking of polyphony, but of a rather modest form of intervallic embellishment. Nothing in the *responsum* would indicate music, in 1605, on a par, in complexity and artfulness, with Rossi's later 'Songs'. The references to 'art music' are too vague to be interpreted as anything more than measured, ordered music.

The only tangible piece of evidence for part music is an incomplete, anonymous manuscript of Hebrew songs, originally composed for eight voices, yet extant in one alone, from the first part of the seventeenth century.[20] Eric Werner assigned it to Leon Modena, treating it as a document

---

[17] An approximate translation: non-musical terms were pressed into service to describe 'music', for which Hebrew had no regular vocabulary.

[18] The first three twice in the approbations, the last three once each in the *quaestio* and the *responsum*.

[19] The portion 'art' occurs five times thereafter and its seeming equation with the 'conventions of music' (*darkhei hamusika*) once.

[20] Cincinnati, Hebrew Union College, MS Mus. 101: of its 21 prayers and *piyyutim*, five were also set by Rossi.

that testifies to musical practices in Venice in the early 1630s, when Modena is known to have run a music 'academy'.[21] There is nothing binding in such an attribution; indeed, the composer, whose writing differs from Rossi's in being more declamatory, still remains unidentified. Were the works composed by Modena, he would not have described Rossi's collection as 'new'. Were they by someone preceding Rossi, he would have known about it and, again, would not have used the epithet 'new'. Dating the collection is problematic, though in its oratorical style it probably succeeded Rossi's 'Songs'.

All this leaves very little to go on for establishing a tradition of Hebrew polyphony before the 'Songs'. Even if attempts at part singing were made from the early years of the seventeenth century, Rossi seems to have been the first to compose Hebrew works on a more than casual basis, which only strengthens Modena's claim that his music was 'new' and marked a 'beginning'. Rossi, himself, regarded his Hebrew works as different from his secular ones; the Lord, he says, 'put *new songs* in my mouth'.[22]

Rossi walked an arduous path from his ideas to their elaboration. 'I strove evermore to multiply and magnify the psalms of David, king of Israel, until I set bounds for many of them according to the conventions of music.'[23] More easily said than done: Moses Sullam encouraged the composer, perhaps even extended a firm commission. 'How many times at your command', Rossi declares, 'did I toil until I discovered and regulated the materials of my song with joyful lips.' Playing on the double meaning of the homonymns *kol*, 'voice', and *kol*, 'everything',[24] Rossi remarked that since both of them came from Sullam,[25] it was only right that 'he return what he received' by choosing him as dedicatee.

The collection, to judge from the introductory matter, underwent a slow process of gestation. As the final fruits of the composer's efforts, the 'Songs' were originally 'sown' and 'planted'. Rossi 'worked and laboured' to accommodate his knowledge of secular music to the demands of sacred composition. Gradually, over the course of, perhaps, eight or more years,[26]

---

[21] See Werner, 'The Eduard Birnbaum Collection of Jewish Music', esp. 407–17, and comments in Adler (comp.), *Hebrew Notated Manuscript Sources up to circa 1840*, i. 394–401. On the academy, see Roth, 'L'accademia musicale del ghetto veneziano'.

[22] From Rossi's dedication.

[23] Quotations in this paragraph again from the composer's dedication.

[24] The initial consonants are different: *kuf* for the first, *kaf* for the second. Were it not for the phonetic transcription, in this book, of both consonants as *k*, the two words could have been distinguished as *qol* versus *kol*. Rossi purposely marked *qol*, 'voice', with a dot to indicate the play on words.

[25] 'Voice', meaning the commission? Words of support? 'Everything', meaning the financing?

[26] The collection may have originated, in conception, around 1612, during which the Jews were relocated in the ghetto (see Ch. 1). It could be that with the intensification of religious life within the ghetto special stimulus was provided for its preparation. Rossi's and Modena's descriptions leave the impression of a gradual build-up over a number of years. The 'fruits' of the 'seeds' that were 'planted' took time to mature. Rossi speaks of his troubles in shaping the

he assembled a miscellany of songs, yet seems to have been uncertain about how they would be received. So he decided to try them out: the singers found them 'delightful', as did the listeners, who wished to 'hear more'. His friends urged him to publish them, he hesitated. Finally, he yielded to their pressure and 'chose' a number of them for publication[27] (the collection, therefore, contained more items than were published). All this suggests that Rossi worked fairly independently, forging a new tradition out of secular and sacred components and ascertaining that the works would find a favourable audience before making them known to a wider public. It also suggests that even if there were sporadic attempts at part music before the 'Songs', they were neither generally known nor influential.

As a model for the composition of the 'Songs', Modena refers, in his foreword, to music in the Ancient Temple. There it flourished along with other sciences and was the object of careful instruction. 'Who could ever forget King David as an old man and would still not remember the efforts he expended, in advance, on orderly instruction in music for all the sons of Asaph and Heman and Jedutun, as written in the [first] book of Chronicles [25: 6], in order to make them understand how to produce sounds? He allowed them to have instruments for use in instrumental and vocal music.' The situation prevailed, we are told, as long as the First and Second Temples 'remained on their site'. When the Hebrews were forced into exile, they ceased their musical activities; their dispersion 'made them forget all knowledge and lose all understanding' of ancient sciences. Only when Salamone Rossi came on the scene was music restored to its former grandeur. 'Let them praise the name of God! Salamone alone is exalted, nowadays, in this knowledge'. The same praise of *musica antica* can be read in one of the dedicatory poems, in which Rossi is regarded as the successor of David and his son Solomon:

Send / as a present / to the son of Jesse [David]
This composition / of songs / in music.

May it cause more rejoicing / and joyful song / in the depths of his heart
Than all / precious articles / or treasures.

There rose / in Israel, / may God be blessed!,
Someone named / after his son [Solomon] / and having great might.

With his music / he is accustomed / to appear before princes,
Singing it / before his own dukes / and nobles.

After / the splendour of the nation / was dimmed,
And everything ceased / for many days / and many years,

---

songs; Modena refers to a 'day by day' accumulation of examples, which one should probably read as a synecdoche for 'month by month' or 'year by year'.

[27] Each of the statements in this paragraph may be traced to various parts of the introductory material: poem 1; Modena's foreword; Rossi's dedication.

He restored / the crown [of music] / to its original state,
As in the days / of the Levites / on their platforms.[28]

The remaining obstacle towards preparing the collection was the technical one of how to write and print music with Hebrew text and assure the accuracy of its publication. Hebrew reads from right to left and music, of course, from left to right. The composer had to choose between contraries: should the music be written from right to left to correspond to the Hebrew?[29] Or should the Hebrew be written from left to right to correspond to the music? After consulting no doubt with Modena, Rossi resolved on a compromise whereby the music remained intact and the separate Hebrew words, though not their syllables, were reversed. Thus in the example 'Yitgadal veyitkadash shemeih raba', which in Hebrew would be written backwards as *abar hiemehs hsadaktiyev ladagtiy*, the words, but not their letters or syllables, are printed from left to right and it is for the singer to divide them into syllables ('lad-ag-tiy hsad-ak-tiy-ev hiem-ehs ab-ar').

Rossi must have agonized over the decision, but in the end was prompted by one consideration: ease of singing. 'In the eyes of the composer,' we learn from Modena, 'it seemed better for the readers to pronounce the letters backwards and read, in contrary order, the words of the song that are well known to all than to reverse the direction of the notes from what is customary and have the readers move their eyes, as we Jews are used to write, from right [to left], lest they lose their minds.'[30] To illustrate the procedure in English: instead of having the syllables *sa-cred com-po-si-tion* written backwards as *cred-sa tion-si-po-com*, which would make any English reader 'lose his mind', their order would be reversed (*com-po-si-tion sa-cred*), which is something that the English reader could, if he had to, get adjusted to.

The correspondence of the Hebrew and the notes was tricky, and Rossi felt he could not guarantee their accuracy in the manuscript and printed copy. So he asked his learned friend Modena to check the pieces before submitting them to the publisher and, once the copy was ready, to do the proof-reading as well. Modena hesitated, for he was grieving over the death of his son. Moreover, it was unseemly for him to deal with music within the year prescribed, by ritual law, for mourning. In order to ward off possible criticism on that account, Modena emphasized that, by editing the music, he was performing a 'pious act' (*mitsva*), in reference, it would seem, to the rabbinical sanction that 'he who performs a pious act is exempted from

---

[28] Poem 3, by Modena, vv. 1–6 (out of 19). Each verse forms a distich, with its lines divided into three cola (indicated here by virgules).

[29] As we find it e.g. in a short 4-v. insert in Reuchlin's treatise on biblical accents: *De accentibus, et orthographia, linguae hebraicae* (1518), after fo. lxxxiii; for the relevance of this treatise to Hebrew and Italian conceptions of music, see Harrán, *In Search of Harmony*, esp. chs. 1–3.

[30] Modena's foreword.

performing a [second] pious act'.[31] In the end he ceded to the composer's request,[32] though complained that the task was arduous:

He [the composer] asked me to prevent any mistake that might come to the composition, to prepare and arrange it for printing, and to proof-read it by keeping my eyes open for printing errors and defects. My lyre has turned to grief; I am a fountain of tears; the death of my lovely Zevulun weighs on my heart.... Still, I did not want to take this pious act lightly. As a reward for performing it, I said, God will take mercy on his [Zevulun's] soul and it will be a light and sign of joy to the rest of the Jews. Thus I stand by watching over the work and, in the gates, announce to the multitude that it is not easy, for there was no beginning like this from earlier or later times, thus mistakes become as gains.[33]

Surprisingly, there are few mistakes. The music was scrupulously prepared and proof-read. Modena drew on his Hebrew scholarship along with his knowledge of music and his skills in proof-reading Hebrew to assure satisfactory results. In both its content and its presentation the collection is a landmark in the history of Hebrew music and its typography. In the copyright one reads that 'Salamone Rossi has, by his painstaking labours, become the first man to print Hebrew music', to which one might add 'and the first to set a high standard for its accuracy'.

Another technical obstacle relates to the composition. Rossi had no experience in writing part music to Hebrew texts, nor could he, as far as is known, fall back on previous written examples. He had to resolve the problems of adapting the music to the accentual and syntactical demands of Hebrew prosody. This meant a modification of his working methods for Italian composition, which explains why he 'laboured', for an extended period, over finding the 'proper form' for his 'Songs'.[34]

Still another problem to be solved was accommodating the music to the technical capacities of the performers. It is difficult to determine the level of musical literacy among seventeenth-century Mantuan Jews or, for that matter, their proficiency in reading Hebrew. In order to get the 'Songs' performed, Rossi may have scaled them down to the abilities of those with minimal musical knowledge. Only in works for fewer voices does he indulge in more ornamental writing, probably knowing that he could rely on at least two or three qualified singers to meet his requirements. In general, though, the music strikes a different rhythmic and textural pose from that of the secular works. The style may have been the result of a complex of considerations: Hebrew prosody, the capabilities of the singers,

---

[31] Babylonian Talmud, Suka 25b.

[32] For a similar example from the secular literature, see Antonio Falcone's dedication to a book of madrigals a 5 (1603) by his son Achille, recently deceased; despite his grief, Antonio decided to go ahead with its publication ('io per la morte d'Achille mio figliuolo fui da così intenso dolore trafitto, che non credeva già mai scemar si dovesse', etc.).

[33] Modena's foreword.

[34] From Rossi's dedication.

and the need to invest the 'Songs' with the propriety expected of sacred music.

The Uses and Purposes of the 'Songs'

Did Rossi intend his 'Songs' for the synagogue? Were they, in fact, performed there? These and similar questions have often been asked and just as often differently answered. There are those who believe that 'art music' could not have been heard in the synagogue because nowhere does Jewish traditional law, or *halakha*, specifically make provision for it. That is precisely the criticism that flared in 1605 when some sort of 'art music' was performed in the synagogue in Ferrara; and that Modena tried to disprove, in his *responsum*, by marshalling a body of evidence from biblical, talmudic, and rabbinical sources to the effect that nowhere does *halakha* specifically prohibit it. The criticism seems to have continued as a distinct murmur in the background of all later performances of Jewish 'art music', including Rossi's 'Songs'.

The introductory matter furnishes clear answers to the three key questions that surround the uses and purposes of the 'Songs': where were they meant to be performed? On which occasions? And for what reasons? These questions should be separated from the historical ones of whether they were, in fact, so employed.

Rossi's 'Songs' could have been performed, depending on their content and suitability, in one of four different places: the synagogue, the study hall, the house of a bride and groom, and private homes. The synagogue is mentioned at least eight times as a venue for *musika*. 'How could anyone with a brain in his head question praising God in song in the synagogue?'[35] Good singing required practice, thus the need to rehearse music in the study hall. 'It is a religious duty for a man on earth to study' in order to sing confidently in the prayer services.[36] Sacred songs should rightly be performed as a ritual act in the house of the bride and groom[37] and in private homes. The eleventh-century talmudist Rabbi Isaac Alfasi is quoted as saying that 'words of songs and praises and the remembrance of the favours of the Holy One (blessed be He!) are not avoided by any man of Israel; and it is the custom of all Israel to deliver them in the houses of bridegrooms and in houses of feasting to the sound of songs and rejoicing, and we did not see anyone take objection'.[38]

When were they performed? On holidays, feast-days, festivals, the Sabbath, and 'special Sabbaths'; at weddings and circumcisions; in times

---

[35] Three references in *responsum* and one in *quaestio*; one in poem 2; and three in approbations.

[36] Approbation 2 (see, further, poem 2, and various references in *responsum*).

[37] *Responsum*.

[38] Ibid.

of rejoicing; and at private celebrations (banquets and other festive occasions).[39] Rossi is said to have composed music to be presented 'before the ark on the Sabbath and all feast-days and festivals; for all religious occasions and for the strength and gladness of the bridegroom, the bride, and the father of sons'.[40] Should anyone wish music for any of these, the passage continues, 'he will find songs and praises available'.

Special emphasis is placed on rejoicing, thus the suitability of song for the feast of Simḥat Tora, or 'Rejoicing in the Law'. 'On the day of Simḥat Tora there are cantors who dance in the synagogue, clasping the book of Tora to their bosom and exhibiting all kinds of mirth; nor did we see anyone protest on account of them, for it is good to praise God in every honourable and splendid way.'[41] Of the holy days, the Sabbath is linked to celebration as for a wedding, 'for every holy Sabbath is a bride among us, and we are obliged to adorn her and rejoice for her with all kinds of rejoicing'.

Why were they performed? Chiefly, to honour, praise, and thank the Lord.[42] The title to the collection describes its contents as suitable 'for thanking God and singing to His exalted name on all sacred occasions'. The singers are enjoined to 'give honour to the Lord and glorify the place of His Lesser Sanctuary [the synagogue] and the festivities of His commandments by singing them [the 'Songs'] each in its proper time'.[43] The purpose of the 'Songs' is, thus, to express joy, be it on holidays or on all occasions of performing pious acts. Such acts, or *mitsvot*, range from worshipping the Lord to carrying out His ordinances. We learn, in the introduction, about 'times of *mitsva*', 'acts of *mitsva*', 'returns of *mitsva*', and the 'happiness of *mitsva*'.[44] The 'Songs', or at least most of them, were thus relevant to all times of religious and secular rejoicing in the Lord and His bounty (notable exceptions are Psalms 137 and 82, on which more below).

---

[39] Different terms are used, some of them synonymous: *zemanim* or *devar mitsva* or *'itot bemitsva*, all for 'sacred occasions' (Rossi's dedication, there *zemanei sason*, meaning 'happy occasions'; poem 3; *responsum*); *ḥagim*, or 'feasts' (poem 2; *quaestio*); *moʿadim*, i.e. 'seasons', or, more particularly, the Three Pilgrim Festivals (Rossi's dedication; poem 2; Modena's foreword; *quaestio; responsum*); *yom tov*, or 'holiday' (poem 3; *responsum*; approbation 3). On the use of the 'Songs' on the Sabbath, see poem 3, *responsum* (twice), and approbation 3; on their use on special Sabbaths, viz. eleven Sabbaths named, in some cases, after an extra reading from the Pentateuch (thus 'Shabat Shekalim') or the prophetic portion for the day (thus 'Shabat Ḥazon'), see *responsum*. On their appropriateness for wedding celebrations and circumcisions, see, for the first, poem 3, *responsum* (11 references), and approbation 3, and, for the second, poem 3 and approbation 3.

[40] From poem 3.

[41] This and next quotation from *responsum*.

[42] Honour (Rossi's dedication; Modena's foreword; poem 3; *quaestio*; approbation 3); praise (Modena's foreword, 'to sing to His magnificence'; *quaestio*, three times; *responsum*, twice); thank/praise ('lehodot': title; *responsum*, twice).

[43] Modena's foreword.

[44] 'Times' (*responsum*); 'acts' (poems 1, 3; *responsum*, seven times); 'recurrences' and 'happiness' (Modena's foreword).

The purposes of the 'Songs' are at one with the motives that guided Rossi in their composition and his notions of how they should be performed. From the introductory material one can, in fact, derive his mode of composition and his ideal of performance. In composition, Rossi recognizes the role of inspiration, for he wrote the 'Songs' 'when the Spirit rested on him'.[45] But inspiration only stirred the imagination; it had to be completed by hard work. Rossi speaks of 'shaping' the 'Songs', of 'striving' and 'labouring' until he 'discovered' their proper musical form. His goal, as said, was to 'multiply and magnify the psalms of David', hence increase their rhetorical power by appropriate music. For music to be 'appropriate', the composer clarifies, it had to be well constructed and pleasant to hear. Its hallmarks, then, were order (*seder*) and sweetness ('*arevut*), as we know them from classic rhetorical theory and sixteenth-century music aesthetics.[46] 'I ordered the pillars of the songs' and 'I wove together melodies of various kinds in voices of sweetness'.[47] The end was to make them have 'greater strength over the ears of whoever tests words'.

From the mode of composition it is possible to go one step further and detail the mode of performance that the composer and others thought best suited to the content and character of the 'Songs'. Part of its requirements may be extrapolated from the mode of composition.[48] Thus, as a corollary, the singers were expected to sing with 'order' and 'sweetness'. The labours that the composer invested in the construction of the 'Songs' were to be paralleled by those invested in rehearsing and improving their performance. Eventually, a 'proper' rendition would emerge, doing justice to the 'Songs' by 'enhancing' their texts.

Turning to more specific comments, one may note at least five requirements for 'proper song'. One is that the singers receive orderly instruction (*seder limud*).[49] Rossi, too, is said to have enthusiastically trained them.[50]

A second requirement is that the singers have a 'pleasant voice' (to complement the pleasant sounds of the music).[51] Songs to God were to be 'pleasantly' performed: Rossi said that as a composer he 'delighted, from

---

[45] This and next two references are to Rossi's dedication.

[46] See Harrán, *In Search of Harmony*, where the compositional theory of Zarlino, as the most influential representative of the *prima pratica*, is traced for its rhetorical antecedents. Zarlino, too, strove to impart 'order' and 'sweetness', i.e. 'elegance'. See, further, Harrán, 'Elegance as a Concept in Sixteenth-Century Music Criticism'.

[47] These two and next quotation are from Rossi's dedication.

[48] For an attempt to devise *ex compositione* a methodology for performing early music at large, see Harrán, 'Toward a Rhetorical Code of Early Music Performance'.

[49] Modena's foreword (viz. the portion in reference to King David's systematic course of music instruction).

[50] 'He [Rossi] taught the singers with much delight' (from poem 2).

[51] Cf. Rossi's dedication; poem 1; Modena's foreword; *quaestio*; *responsum*, three references; approbations 2, 4.

the beginning, in taking every offering of the voice to praise the [heavenly] Rider in a voice of sweetness, rejoicing, and thankfulness, for it is for the voice of man to honour the Lord'.[52] His remarks describe, by analogy, the kind of performance he expected of the singers. Modena saw his task, in the *responsum*, as one of deciding between the 'voice of the objector' to music and 'a voice pleasant after its kind for praising God'.[53] He said of his deceased son Zevulun that he was a 'sweet psalmist with a pleasant voice'.[54] He required of 'every cantor that he make his voice as pleasant as possible in prayer'.[55]

A third requirement is that the singers have a strong voice. Commenting on the need for careful preparation of synagogue chant, one of the signatories to the *responsum* wrote that studying enables the singer 'to stand and serve in the Holy Temple in a voice of strength'.[56] Modena said of the same cantor who sang pleasantly that the more resonant he makes his voice, the better the result.[57]

A fourth requirement is that the music be sung 'joyfully'.[58] How could music meant for rejoicing in God be performed otherwise? The connection between composition and performance is clear from the description of Rossi's having 'composed music for the words of the psalms with joyful melodies, to be presented before the ark in happiness and joyful song'.[59] Modena was right, we are told in the first approbation, to advise that music be 'sung joyfully in joyful songs and prayers'.[60]

The fifth and last requirement is that for the words to be properly understood it was imperative for singers to observe the rules of proper accentuation and articulation. 'They should duly take care', Modena urges, 'to pronounce the words with their lips so as to do justice to the vowels, accents, and any other details that enhance the reading.'[61]

It remains to be said whether the 'Songs' were, in fact, employed for the purposes they were designed to meet. One might distinguish two phases in their utilization, the first before, the second after their publication. The first corresponds to the period in which the 'Songs' were being composed and tried out, but where? Uncertainty prevails about whether they were inserted, on occasion, into the regular synagogue prayer services or merely tested under private circumstances. It stands to reason that, whichever the case, the home of Moses Sullam was a natural choice for their performance. Sullam had his own private synagogue, as was customary among loan bankers of standing in the community (see Chapter 1 and below). Since Sullam's synagogue was open to persons of an obviously liberal musical persuasion, Rossi could have counted from the start on a sympathetic audience. On Rossi's visits to Venice, the 'Songs' might have been

---

[52] Rossi's dedication.   [53] *Quaestio*.   [54] Modena's foreword.
[55] *Responsum*.   [56] Approbation 2.   [57] *Responsum*.
[58] Poem 3; approbation 1.   [59] Poem 3.   [60] Approbation 1.
[61] Modena's foreword.

performed privately in the home of Sara Copio or publicly in the Scuola Italiana where Modena officiated as cantor.

More difficult are the questions that relate to the use of the 'Songs', in Mantua and elsewhere, after their publication. Modena believed that once the singers became familiar with them, their new style would catch on to establish a tradition of Hebrew polyphony. 'You shall teach them to your children', he said, 'in order for them to understand the art of music; he who understands will teach his students, as was said of the Levites.' Rossi's works would continue to be sung; others would be composed after their example. 'I am certain that from the day this collection is published the number of Jews who study music will increase and they will sing to the magnificence of our God by using the "Songs" and others like them.'[62]

They did seem to increase, for there is evidence of choral singing in the 'accademia di musica' that Modena founded, in the Venetian ghetto, in 1628, perhaps, though not necessarily, to accommodate musicians in flight from Mantua. The 'accademia' seems to have functioned until the later 1630s. At its height the members, both singers and instrumentalists, met for music-making twice a week.[63] Though instrumental music was performed at private celebrations, as, moreover, in the 'accademia', little, if anything, is known of the organ or other instruments in later sixteenth- or early seventeenth-century Jewish prayer services.[64]

Reference to choral singing in Senigallia, from 1642 on, occurs in a *responsum* of the rabbi Nathaniel Trabotto; he implies that such singing had become habitual in Northern Italian synagogues on feast-days. What kind of singing he had in mind (improvised, composed, for one or more voices, etc.) is unclear.[65]

For the diffusion of Rossi's 'Songs' one can point to certain annotations in one of their printed parts, testifying to their having reached Central and Eastern Europe in the seventeenth and eighteenth centuries.[66] Whether the parts were sung from or merely consulted remains to be said. The records are silent on both the performance of the 'Songs' and the composition of any others after their example. Beyond the cryptic MS Birnbaum already mentioned, there is little evidence for the continuation of a Jewish part music tradition in Italy beyond mid-century. Certain works to Hebrew texts were commissioned from Christian composers, for example, the 'Cantata ebraica

---

[62] Modena's foreword.

[63] Two particular evenings were signalled (on the feast-days Shemini 'Atseret and Simḥat Tora). Information on the 'accademia' derives from a later account of the convert Giulio Morosini, *Via della fede* (1683), ii. 789–90, and a letter of Modena (BL MS Or. 5395, fo. 23). For the place of the academy in the life and thought of Modena, see Harrán, ' "Dum recordaremur Sion" ' and 'Jewish Musical Culture in Early Modern Venice'.

[64] On the use of the organ, see Benayahu, 'Da'at ḥakhmei italya 'al hanegina be'ugav bitfila'.

[65] The evidence is gathered in Adler, 'The Rise of Art Music in the Italian Ghetto', esp. 350–3.

[66] The quinto part, now in Oxford, Bodleian Libr., MS Opp. 4° 1119: see Adler (comp.), *Hebrew Notated Manuscript Sources up to circa 1840*, 32–3.

in dialogo', by Carlo Grossi, performed in 1681 to mark an anniversary celebration of the Jewish religious confraternity Shomerim Laboker, on which more below. To all intents, Rossi's collection failed to establish the tradition of part music by Jewish composers that Modena hoped it would. It might have been used here and there for singing in the synagogue, as intimated by Trabotto's comment, but until the nineteenth century the Jews were not stirred to cultivate art music as a regular constituent of the ritual.

If not in the synagogue, there is a possibility that some of the 'Songs' were used for paraliturgical functions. At least one of the texts with no place in the standard books of the Italian, or Roman, rite can be found in a formulary, from 1612, of the Shomerim Laboker ('Morning Watchmen'). Like other kabbalistic confraternities, the Shomerim scheduled its services in the early morning hours and was committed to recalling the destruction of the Temple and implanting the messianic hope for a new era of joy and a return to the promised land. The text, a *piyyut* by the kabbalist Mordecai Dato, was, to all appearances, intended for use by the Shomerim,[67] along with twelve others that figure in the order of its prayers as well as in regular liturgical books.[68] They include Psalm 137 'On the rivers of Babylon', which, in its plaintive content, certainly has nothing to do with the 'joyful songs' advertised in the title and introductory material to Rossi's collection. It did have a fixed place, though, in the daily ritual of the Shomerim. The same may be said of the ominous Psalm 82, where evil judges are warned that unless they change their ways they will be duly punished.[69]

Still another text that played a paraliturgical role was 'Yesusum midbar' from Isaiah 35, of which Rossi set selected verses (by contrast with Psalms 137 and 82 it is unreservedly cheerful). Until now, it has been surmised that the text, unknown to the Italian rite, was sung during private festivities. Yet it turns up, with all its verses, in another book designed for early morning prayers, *Kenaf renanim* (1626).[70] Whether Rossi's music to this and the previous texts was in fact composed for or used in confraternity services cannot be established, but it stands as a reasonable possibility. By expanding the traditional ritual of synagogue prayer, the confraternities might have been a natural habitat for musical innovation.[71]

One might argue that since Rossi's seeming mentor was Leon Modena, and Modena eventually turned anti-kabbalistic in his views, it is hardly

---

[67] *Ashmoret haboker* (1624): 'Eftaḥ shir bisfatai', fo. 171ᵛ–2; cf. Sgs: 27.

[68] Sgs: 4–5, 9–10, 12–14, 18, 21, 24, 31–2, variously printed in *Ayelet hashaḥar* (1612) and *Ashmoret haboker* (1624): five in both, two in the first only, five in the second only.

[69] For Psalms 137 and 82, see section below, 'Textual Typology' (respectively nos. 5 and 4).

[70] *Sefer kenaf renanim* (1626), fo. 54.

[71] On the importance of the Jewish confraternities in later 16th- and early 17th-c. Italy, see Simonsohn, *History of the Jews in the Duchy of Mantua*, 553–5; Bonfil, *Rabbis and Jewish Communities in Renaissance Italy*, 318–20; id., *Jewish Life in Renaissance Italy*, 171–2, 195–7, 230–2; id., 'Halakhah, Kabbalah, and Society'; and several writings by Horowitz, among them 'Coffee, Coffeehouses, and the Nocturnal Rituals of Early Modern Jewry'.

likely for Rossi to have had connections with kabbalist circles. Yet neither Modena nor Rossi can be pigeonholed into one or another religious slot. Modena, before formally repudiating Kabbala in his *Ari nohem*, or 'Roaring Lion [= Leon]' (1640), penned numerous introductions, poems, and statements of approbation for works of patently kabbalistic orientation, including a poem for the same prayer book, from 1612, that contained many of the texts to Rossi's 'Songs'.[72] In the conflict between traditional and more liberal opinions on music in the synagogue, Modena justified 'art music' via certain stock concepts, among them the return to Zion or the renewal of past glories, that the kabbalists turned to redemptive purposes. There is no reason, then, why the 'Songs' could not have functioned in varied religious contexts, liturgical and paraliturgical, in the years that preceded and followed their publication.

The texts of the 'Songs' are as open in their content as in their possible uses. Many of them have fixed places in the liturgy, yet in their frequent reference to the mystery of God, His unity, omniscience, and eternity, or to an era of peace and prosperity, when, as Isaiah said, wolves will dwell with lambs (11: 6), they cut across *halakha* and Kabbala to become part of a larger *hebraica veritas*. Just as the texts are conceptually labile, so is their music, which is 'available to whoever wishes to use its songs and praises for the glory of the Lord'.[73]

Textual Typology

Five different literary types can be discerned, ranging from psalms (in twenty settings) and other portions of the Hebrew Bible (one from Leviticus, the other from Isaiah) to various texts of post-biblical origin: prayers in prose (five settings); *piyyutim*, i.e. hymns in verse (five settings); and an incidental lyric (a wedding ode). The mainstay of the collection is the psalms, and it is no wonder that one of the poems in the introductory matter mentions Rossi's book as honouring (the psalmist) David.[74]

Biblical psalmody is obviously quite different in its prosody from Italian verse. For one thing, it lacks rhyme schemes or fixed verse lengths; for another, it has no regular accentuation. Rossi was thus forced to treat his Hebrew psalm texts entirely differently from his madrigals, and the result is a music with a phraseology and a rhythmic and melodic character of its

---

[72] On Modena's wavering attitude to Kabbala, see the note (by Ravid and Adelman) to his autobiography *Ḥayei yehuda*, tr. Cohen, 233–4. The poem ('Yom ze yehi mishkal'), also included in Modena's *Divan* (ed. Bernstein, no. 197), is a penitential ode with strongly messianic overtones (the yearning for the return to Zion, the restoration of the Temple, the coming of the Messiah). Mystic and messianic ideas were variously received and implemented by the kabbalists: see Idel, 'Differing Conceptions of Kabbalah in the Early Seventeenth Century'; also id., 'Major Currents in Italian Kabbalah between 1560–1660'.

[73] From poem 3.

[74] Ibid.

own.[75] The psalmodic principle extends to other biblical selections, for example the passage from Isaiah (no. 19 in the collection): its verses have the *parallelismus membrorum* of psalms and its music, as a result, their structure. But even in texts that are not psalmodic, for example, the *piyyutim* and prose prayers, the composer tends to treat them in analogy to psalms, with one or more intermediate caesurae plus final cadence for marking off shorter and longer portions of 'verses'.

Prayers occur in the first half of the collection and *piyyutim* in the second.[76] Both are surrounded by psalm settings, of which the largest groupings are nos. 8–14 and 20–4.

Certain works are so located as to articulate the beginning, middle, and end of the collection. Nos. 1–2 emerge as key works, recurring in later settings. The first of them is the all-important Kaddish (specifically the Full Kaddish, in distinction to other varieties), of frequent liturgical usage. Its second setting is placed exactly in the middle of the book (no. 16), as if to mark the beginning of its second part. No. 2, Psalm 128, relates to the Kaddish in its content: the Kaddish enjoins the believer to praise the Lord, Psalm 128 declares that he who believes in the Lord will be blessed (the notion of blessing is reinforced in no. 3, the prayer 'Barekhu', or 'Bless the Lord'). Later settings of no. 2 are spaced at intervals of ten, then eight pieces (nos. 12, 20). The end of the collection is marked by a special work: a semi-sacred epithalamium, composed with echo effects. It relates to, and summarizes, the collection, as shall be stressed at the end of the chapter.

Thematically, the poetry may be grouped into eight different categories. Each text has a main theme with one or more variants, yet may suggest a number of subsidiary themes, as follows:

1. *The praise of God (or an injunction to praise Him)* (it appears as a main theme in ten examples and as a subsidiary theme in seven).[77] Variants are 'bless the Lord';[78] 'he who fears (or believes in) God will be blessed',[79] or, elsewhere, 'may you (or we) be blessed',[80] 'the Lord blessed and exalted man',[81] and 'the Lord saved us from destruction';[82] and 'thank the Lord' (the word *lehodot* meaning both 'to thank' and 'to praise').[83]

2. *Entreating God for His favour.* The theme of supplication occurs in at least four varieties. One is a 'plea for help (or protection)' or a 'plea for

---

[75] On the idiosyncrasies of the Hebrew songs, see, at length, Harrán, 'Salamone Rossi as a Composer of "Hebrew" Music'.

[76] Prayers: Sgs: 1, 3, 6–7, 15–16; *piyyutim*: Sgs: 19, 25–9, 33.

[77] Main theme: Sgs: 1/16, 7, 11, 13, 24, 26, 28–9, 31–2. Subsidiary theme: Sgs: variously within 9, 14–15, 21, 25, 27, 30.

[78] Sgs: 3, or as a subsidiary theme, variously within 26, 28.

[79] Sgs: 2/12/20 and 30, and as a subsidiary theme, variously within 23, 28, 32.

[80] Sgs: variously within 2/12/20 and 9.

[81] Sgs: variously within 11, 24, 31–2.

[82] Sgs: variously within 21–2.

[83] Sgs: 14, 22–3, and as a subsidiary theme, within 26.

guidance'.[84] Another is a confirmation that 'our help is in the Lord'.[85] A third is a 'plea for mercy', which, in one example, is turned around to become God's personal appeal to judges to be merciful in dealing with the poor and needy.[86] A fourth is a 'plea for salvation',[87] which also appears as a 'plea for acceptance of our prayers' or a 'plea to be restored from captivity' or a 'plea for peace and prosperity'.[88]

3. *The proclamation of a festival* (one example)[89]

4. *The wicked will be punished* (a main theme in one example and a subsidiary theme in five others).[90] As variants one finds 'let non-believers be punished' and 'those who destroy the enemy will be blessed'.[91] The latter forms a complement to 'he who fears (or believes in) God will be blessed' (theme 1 above).

5. *Mourning in exile over the destruction of the Temple* (one example)[92]

6. *Return from exile* (one example)[93]

7. *The vision of a future era of gladness and prosperity* (it appears as a main theme in three examples and as a subsidiary theme in two).[94] As a variant one finds a 'plea for peace and prosperity' (treated under theme 2).

8. *A wedding ode* (one example)[95]

Clearly, the majority of the examples belong to categories 1–2. With the exception of 4–5, the tone is joyous and sanguine.

The texts, and their musical settings, should be placed in the context of Mantuan Jewish religious practices at the end of the sixteenth and beginning of the seventeenth centuries. At the time of the Jewish expulsion in 1630 there were nine synagogues and twenty-four rabbis in the ghetto (and others in the Mantovano). Most of the synagogues belonged to the Italiani, who practised the Roman rite, and it is with this rite that Rossi seems to have been affiliated, in distinction to the Ashkenazi one, as practised by Jews of mainly German extraction. Unlike Venice, Mantua had no synagogues of the Sephardi rite, as practised by Jews originally from the Iberian peninsula.[96] Beyond the private synagogue of Moses Sullam

---

[84] 'Plea for help (or protection)': Sgs: 5, and as a subsidiary theme, variously within 7, 15, 25. 'Plea for guidance': Sgs: within 15.

[85] Sgs: 18, 21, and as a subsidiary theme, variously within 11, 29, 31.

[86] 'Plea for mercy': Sgs: 9; its reversal to God's appeal: within 4.

[87] Sgs: 8, and as a subsidiary theme, variously within 15, 25, 27.

[88] 'Plea for acceptance of our prayers': Sgs: within 1/16. 'Plea to be restored from captivity': Sgs: within 17 (see theme 6 below). 'Plea for peace and prosperity': Sgs: variously within 1/16, 2/12/20, 15.

[89] Sgs: 6.

[90] Main theme: Sgs: 4; subsidiary theme: variously within 5, 13, 28, 30, 32.

[91] 'Let non-believers be punished' (Sgs: within 10) and 'those who destroy the enemy will be blessed' (also within 10).

[92] Sgs: 10.   [93] Sgs: 17.

[94] Main theme: Sgs: 19, 25, 27; subsidiary theme: variously within 1/16, 28.

[95] Sgs: 33.

[96] On the expulsion in 1630, see Simonsohn, *History of the Jews in the Duchy of Mantua*, 55–6; on synagogues in Mantua, see ibid. 567–71. Sephardi Jewish communities were founded mainly

(founded in 1588), others of the Italiani were the Scuola Grande, or 'Great Synagogue', founded in 1529 and moved, in 1633, to the former palace of Felicita Gonzaga (to whom Rossi had dedicated his Book 2 *a* 5; the synagogue—see Plate 13—was destroyed in 1938); a private synagogue of the Cases family, founded in 1590; and the Norsa synagogue, founded in 1513 by an early member of the Norsa family and, of all Mantuan synagogues, the only one to survive, though no longer in its original location (it houses the archive of the Mantuan Jewish Community). Rossi may have had connections with all four plus others in Mantua and its outlying domains.

Rossi's association with the Roman rite may be established by comparing the prayers and *piyyutim* of the 'Songs' with their versions in the Italian liturgical books. The Roman rite differs from the Ashkenazi one in having portions of its own, namely the two *piyyutim* for opening the Ark ('Songs', 25, 27) or the three verses from Psalm 80 used for removing the second Tora scroll from the Ark mainly on the first day of the Three Pilgrim Festivals ('Songs', 8); and in having variants, of sundry kinds, relating to spelling,[97] word order,[98] and omissions or additions of one or more words[99] and, here and there, of entirely different words or verses.[100] In their texts, then, there is no doubt that the 'Songs' correspond to the Italian rite.

The question is whether, in their music, Rossi's polyphonic songs evidence a connection with Italian monophonic synagogue chants. The melodies of these chants have been preserved, in part, by oral tradition, and our knowledge of them derives from older and newer sound recordings;[101]

in coastal cities on the Tyrranean (for those Jews arriving directly from the Iberian peninsula) or on the Adriatic (for those coming from Asia Minor, Turkey, and the Balkan countries); the case of the Sephardi synagogue founded in Ferrara in 1493 is a noteworthy exception. The main synagogue of the Ashkenazi Jews in Mantua was the Porto synagogue, founded in 1540. Though Rossi's 'Songs' seem to have been written for Italiani synagogues in Mantua, some of them, as suggested above, may have been tried out in synagogues in Venice, to which Rossi repaired on various occasions (see Ch. 1; most likely the Italian synagogue where Modena presided as cantor). For general works on Jewish liturgy, see Elbogen, *Jewish Liturgy*, tr. Scheindlin; and Idelsohn, *Jewish Liturgy*. On the Roman rite, see Luzzatto, *Mavo lemaḥzor benei roma*, ed. Goldschmidt.

[97] Spelling, as where (in Sgs: 1/16) the Ashkenazi version (henceforth *A*) has *eh* for certain Aramaic words which, in the Italian version (henceforth *I*), appear with *eih* (*shemeih, khiruteih, malkhuteih*).

[98] Word order, as where (in Sgs: 7) *A* has 'bekhol yom tamid', which, in *I*, is transposed to 'tamid bekhol yom'.

[99] Omissions of conjunctives or one or more words, as where (in Sgs: 1/16) *A* has *birkhata veshirata*, which, in *I*, appears without *ve*; or where (in Sgs: 7, v. 5) *A* has 'mimkomo hu yifen beraḥamav veyaḥon 'am hameyaḥadim shemo', which, in *I*, appears without 'hu' and 'beraḥamav veyaḥon'. Additions of words, as where (in Sgs: 1/16) *A* has *le'eila* once (with one exception: the Ten Days of Penitence, from New Year's to the Day of Atonement) and *I* has it twice; or *A* has *dekhol yisra'el* and *I* interposes the word *beit*.

[100] Entirely different words or verses, as v. 1 and portions of vv. 2 and 6 in Sgs: 7; or portions of vv. 8–9 in Sgs: 15.

[101] Such as those held by the National Sound Archives, Jerusalem.

ancient notations of psalms and readings from the Tora and Prophets;[102] modern anthologies of synagogue chants;[103] and a small list of secondary writings.[104] Characteristics of the Italian tradition are its emphasis on syllabic declamation (in contrast to the often melismatic style practised in the Ashkenazi and Sephardi traditions); and the relative simplicity of its tunes, confined largely to a tetrachord and moving diatonically by conjunct seconds. Pentatonicism or augmented seconds are not typical of the Italian melodies whereas they are of certain Eastern (or Ashkenazi) traditions.

How does this square with the content and style of Rossi's compositions? Rossi does not seem to have used traditional melodies in his pieces, so far as may be discerned from the limited evidence available.[105] Yet he does seem to preserve the basic lineaments of Jewish (monophonic) chant, as practised, that is, in the Italian rite, in his melodically and rhythmically pared lines:[106] Rossi emphasizes a syllabic over a melismatic style, while relegating the melisma to a decorative function for word emphasis (see below); he writes diatonically, having the melodies move by step to form motifs covering a fourth or fifth; the presentation of the texts is clear, often declamatory, in a homophonic, homorhythmic style. For the time being, that is as much as can be said about the composer's debt to or affinity with the Italian musical tradition. He stayed within its bounds in mood and manner, yet exceeded them in writing his own melodies and arranging them polyphonically.

It is precisely because Rossi broke with the established (monophonic) tradition of synagogue chant that there has been so much controversy over whether he actually intended his 'Songs' for practical usage. That he did so intend them may be determined from three kinds of evidence, of which we already dealt with one: the comments on the 'Songs' in their introductory matter. The other two have to do with his choice of texts, or more specifically what was excluded from the texts in their composition; and the presence of the same texts in the liturgical and paraliturgical books.

Beyond textual ties with the Italian rite, the 'Songs' reveal their liturgical functions through the omission of certain portions that could only be supplied by the congregation. As printed, the music is explicit in its omissions:

---

[102] Psalms, such as those in Bottrigari's *Il Trimerone* (1599), fos. 97–8. Readings, such as those published by Bartolocci in his *Bibliotheca magna rabbinica de scriptoribus*, iv. 427–41.

[103] Such as *Canti liturgici ebraici di rito italiano*, ed. Piattelli (preserving a repertory of chants as practised in the Roman synagogue).

[104] Mainly by Leo Levi: see his 'Canti tradizionali e tradizioni liturgiche giudeo-italiane'; 'Italy'; 'Melodie tradizionali ebraico-italiane'.

[105] With one notable exception: Rossi's Sgs: 8, which shows clear melodic affinities with a version of the melody sung in Northern Italy and recorded, in 1956, by Leo Levi (now in Jerusalem, National Sound Archives; see Jacobson, 'A Possible Influence of Traditional Chant on a Synagogue Motet of Salamone Rossi'). Yet Rossi's melody could just as well have been the source of the later one.

[106] For stylistic comparison, see examples from the Italian Sephardi rite as practised towards the end of the 19th c. in Leghorn (*Sefer shirei yisra'el / Libro dei canti d'Israele*, ed. Consolo) and in our own time in Florence (*Canti liturgici di rito spagnolo del Tempio Israelitico di Firenze*, ed. Piattelli).

double bars are used to mark off the sung portions, between which one is left to assume the interpolation of congregational responses. In Kaddish, 'Barekhu', and the Kedusha (or, more specifically, the Great Kedusha, in distinction to other varieties) the sung portions are those traditionally carried by the cantor, who, in Rossi's setting, becomes as it were 'polyphonic'—in distant analogy to early European polyphony, where soloist portions of responsorial chants were treated in *organum*. Without the responses, the texts are incomplete and in the case of the Kedusha senseless. There is no reason Rossi would have composed these texts unless they were completed, in the prayer services, by a congregation.

The exact functions of the 'Songs' can be ascertained from their location in the Italian liturgical books. Some of the texts were used on a single occasion; others were multifunctional. Some of the texts belonged to one or more of the daily prayer services (morning, afternoon, and evening); others were performed on Festivals (the Feast of Tabernacles, Passover, Pentecost) or on Sabbaths or special holidays (the New Moon, Purim, Hosha'ana Raba, Simḥat Tora). Some were appropriate for opening the Ark, or removing the scrolls from it, or proceeding with them, or rolling them up (*gelila*), or returning them to the Ark; others were employed for weddings or circumcisions, or for private functions in the home, or in the prayer services of confraternities.

Music

1. *General characteristics.* Having thirty-three works, the 'Songs' are Rossi's largest vocal collection. In their 3,529 bars, moreover, they are equivalent to about four of his eight vocal books or three of his four instrumental ones. All in all, the 'Songs' constitute one-fifth of his music.

The 'Songs' range from a minimum of seventeen bars to a maximum of 182,[107] with an average length of about 107. Yet these figures do not reveal the disparities between works for different ensembles, indeed, there is a gradual increase, in length, from those for three voices to those for seven and eight. Three different (average) lengths may be discerned: the shortest pieces for three voices, those in the medium range for four to six, and the longest ones for seven and eight.[108] As such, they correspond to the increasing amounts of music for each ensemble.[109] The general principle behind the composition is thus the larger the ensemble, the more works written for it and their greater individual length.[110] It is clear that the collection

---

[107] Minimum: Sgs: 6; maximum: Sgs: 25, 33.

[108] Shortest, about 77 bars; medium-sized, about 100 bars; longest, 182 bars for the one work *a* 7, about 136 bars for those *a* 8.

[109] From 464 bars for those *a* 3 to 505 for those *a* 4, 793 for those *a* 5, and 1,088 for those *a* 8.

[110] The only exception is works *a* 6 (amounting to 497 bars). Sgs: 25, the one work *a* 7, should probably be grouped with those *a* 8, for like them it is treated as a dialogue for split choruses.

demonstrates a grand thrust towards its seven- and eight-voice works, forming the most noticeable, if not impressive ones in their length, their split choruses, and, taken together, their overall bulk.[111]

The length of the pieces is a function of their poetry. Different criteria bear on judging the size of the different prosodic types: prayers in prose, psalms, measured *piyyutim*. Given the influence of biblical psalmody on other portions, as has already been noted, it is possible to use the psalm verse as a general yardstick for measuring length. The psalm verse varies in size, though tends to average around eight (Hebrew) words.[112] By this standard, the extract from Leviticus (9 words) is equivalent to one psalm verse; that from Isaiah (62) to about eight verses; the Kaddish, in its sung portions (81), to about ten; the Kedusha, in its sung portions (55), to about seven; the *piyyut* 'Eftaḥ na sefatai' (with its six stanzas and various refrains, altogether 115 words) to about fourteen; and so on.

The following conclusions may be drawn: the length of the poetry (for all thirty-three works) ranges from one verse to nineteen; the preferred number of verses is around eight or nine;[113] different settings of the same text[114] tend to have the same length; and the more verses, the longer the work. When, however, the work is disproportionately longer than its number of verses, the reason is to be sought in its extensive use of melismas or its slower pacing[115] (remember: the number of verses in non-psalmodic works is approximate).

A comparison of the vocal ensembles in 'The Songs of Solomon' with those in the secular vocal repertory reveals different emphases. Where, in the latter, five-voice works were the norm, and eight-voice ones appeared as special items at ends of collections, both voice types dominate the 'Songs'.[116] Yet, in the 'Songs', Rossi clearly places greater weight on eight-voice ones, for they run about a quarter longer than those *a* 5.[117] Three-voice ones are similar to his *canzonette*, without having their light or frivolous character; and as it so happens they occupy about the same percentage among the Hebrew works as the *canzonette* among the Italian ones. Where there are no secular vocal or instrumental works for seven voices, and indeed such works are scarce in the literature at large,[118] the

---

[111] About 35% of the collection.

[112] Sgs: 2 might serve as example. It consists of six verses, in the order of 8, 7, 10, 7, 9, 6 words, or a total of 47 words, which, divided by the six verses, gives one an average of 7.83. Sgs: 4 confirms the tendency: it has eight verses, with a total of 61 words, yielding an average of 7.62.

[113] More specifically, eight verses (in 7 works), ten (in 6), six (in 5), and nine (in 3).

[114] Sgs: 1/16, 2/12/20.

[115] Melismas: see Sgs: 3, 8. Slower pacing: see Sgs: 25.

[116] Secular collections: 84 works *a* 5, or 57%; three works *a* 8. Sgs: the 5- and 8-v. works are each represented by eight examples (separately, 24%).

[117] In the secular repertory, there was a similar increment in length, from the average 5-v. work (51–61 bars) to the average 8-v. one (79).

[118] Like Rossi's 'Songs', Priuli's *Musiche concertate . . . lib. 4°* (1622) have a gradual increase in the number of voices (in this case, from two to nine, with two works *a* 7). See also Vecchi's *Madrigali* 6 v. (1583) and his *Dialoghi* 7–8 v. (1608), each with one work *a* 7. The model seems to

No. of verses	Number in collection (and bar count)	Average length
1	3 (38 bars), 6 (17)	27
3	8 (85)	85
5	14 (80)	80
6	2 (89), 12 (100), 17 (90), 20 (88), 26 (100)	93
7	7 (86), 15 (96)	91
8	4 (91), 9 (87), 18 (76), 19 (91), 21 (98), 22 (96), 23 (88)	89
9	5 (97), 10 (107), 29 (93)	99
10	1 (132), 11 (140), 13 (118), 16 (142), 30 (110), 31 (120)	127
11	24 (127)	127
13	28 (147)	147
14	25 (182)	182
16	32 (157)	157
17	33 (182)	182
19	27 (179)	179

'Songs' do have a single example, which the composer wrote to complete the series of voice ensembles from three to eight.

In general, the 'Songs' show a greater variety of voice types than do the secular vocal or instrumental works. Where the Italian ones were for more or less fixed ensembles (the madrigals for five voices, or less often four; the *canzonette* for three; the *madrigaletti* for duet plus *continuo*) and the instrumental ones mostly for three voices, the 'Songs' adhere to no single ensemble. Rather, the composer conceived them as suitable to any one he chose, though, as said, he tended towards five- and eight-voice groupings.

The secular vocal collections were usually supplied with a *continuo* part, yet, with some exceptions, could be presented with or without it.[119] Unlike them, the 'Songs' were printed without a *continuo* and, to all appearances, dispensed with it, at least when performed in the synagogue.

One final point: the 'Songs' are the only vocal collection to contain additional settings of a single text,[120] thus providing a basis for structural and stylistic comparison within one and the same book.[121]

2. *Metres.* Most works are written in duple metre (24). Eight have mixed metres, ranging from two to seven signs in succession. One work in triple metre (no. 16) is obviously exceptional.

have been Willaert's *Musica nova* (1559), where both motets and madrigals were arranged in ascending order from four to seven voices (the collection has three 7-v. madrigals).

[119] The exceptions are Cte and all but one work in Bk 3, which were neither supplied nor meant to be performed with a *continuo*; and Mti, where the *continuo* was compulsory. See Ch. 5.

[120] The text of Sgs: 1 was set twice and that of Sgs: 2 three times.

[121] Unlike the secular collections where additional settings of the same text occurred in different books.

Of the mixed metres, the composer prefers C/3/$\mathcal{C}$[122] or, in extended form, C/3/$\mathcal{C}$/3/$\mathcal{C}$.[123] Usually the 3 section (i.e. 3/2) is short, sometimes too short to warrant changing the metre: thus in nos. 1 and 7, the triple interpolations are effected through coloration.[124] In all the pieces with mixed metres, 3 is followed by $\mathcal{C}$, as is customary in the composer's secular vocal and instrumental works.[125] Writing $\mathcal{C}$ after 3 seems to have been a convention, yet in reality $\mathcal{C}$ could have been replaced by C, with which, to all appearances, it was identical (on the problematics of establishing their identity, see Chapter 5).

Mixed metres are frequent in the settings of non-psalmodic poetry, mostly prayers.[126] The portions in triple metre were meant to highlight words. Yet none of the settings needed to have its words stressed, and the decision to do so seems to have been the composer's for musical reasons. Not so the triple-metre insertions in the three settings of Psalm 128: there at the portion 'your sons will be olive shoots around your table', the composer reacted to 'around', writing 3/[2] to convey its circularity. In 'Adon 'olam' the words testifying to the essence of God ('And He was and He is | and He shall be in glory') and his soteriological relation to man ('And He is my God and my living redeemer, | a rock for my suffering in a day of distress') were surrounded by the halo as it were of triple metre.

Compared with the Italian vocal works, the 'Songs' show an increased tendency to use mixed metres.[127] If anything, a line may be traced to the instrumental repertory: the eight works in mixed metres out of the thirty-three 'Songs' are, percentagewise, equivalent to the thirty works in mixed metres out of the 130 instrumental compositions.[128] The one work under 3 (no. 16), a second setting of the Kaddish, is just as much an exception in the Hebrew 'Songs' as the *balletto* 'Spazziam pronte' in the Italian repertory.[129] In its bouncy rhythms it resembles a dance and is as far removed from the sober earlier Kaddish (no. 1) as 'Spazziam pronte' from his madrigals. But our notions of the Kaddish as a sombre text are unfounded (they probably derive from the version recited at burial or in mourning). The Full Kaddish, and that is the version that Rossi composed, is at root a joyous expression of praise to the Almighty, and Rossi's music is precisely that. To this day, the

---

[122] Sgs: 2, 12, 20, all composed to the same text, Ps. 128.

[123] Sgs: 1, 29, and, with a slight variation, 7: C/3/$\mathcal{C}$/C/3/$\mathcal{C}$/C, in which C and $\mathcal{C}$ appear to be equivalent (see Ch. 5).

[124] They recall similar passages in three of his *canzonette* (nos. 8, 12, 17).

[125] Of the seven Italian pieces with 3 followed by duple metre, three have the latter signed as $\mathcal{C}$. Of the twenty instrumental ones with 3 followed by duple metre, nineteen have the latter signed as $\mathcal{C}$ and one as C.

[126] Kaddish (Sgs: 1); the Kedusha (7); 'Hashkivenu' (15).

[127] Except for one special work at the end of Bk 2, none of the madrigals ventured beyond duple metre; the few examples of mixed metres occur in Cte and Mti.

[128] In each case, about 25%.

[129] Except for this *balletto* (under 3), there were no other triple-metered vocal works; the domain of triple metre is the composer's instrumental music (44 exs., mainly dances).

prayer, in European communities, is often sung by the cantor, on holidays, to different melodies, many of them lively and mirthful.

3. *Modes.* The leading mode in the collection is Dorian transposed to G. Other modes, in descending order, are Lydian (with B flat), Dorian (untransposed) and Aeolian, and, least frequently, Mixolydian.[130] The importance of 'Dorian' is clear from combining the pieces written in both its pure and its transposed forms (twenty in all, or 60 per cent of the collection). Dorian on G is the only mode used for the works *a 3* and, together with Dorian, is the preferred mode for setting psalms (fifteen out of twenty), the two extracts from other portions of the Bible, and prayers (Kaddish in its two settings, 'Barekhu'). Lydian is the preferred mode for *piyyutim* (four out of five) whereas Aeolian is associated with texts of special import: despair in exile (Psalm 137), thanksgiving (Psalm 100, joyfully praising the Lord in song, which as we know from the introductory matter is what the 'Songs of Solomon' are about), and the sanctity of the Sabbath (Psalm 92) and of matrimony (in the wedding ode, no. 33).

All in all, the collection stresses minor modes (Dorian, Aeolian) over major ones (Lydian, Mixolydian) by 24 to 9. Some modes are treated ambiguously, reinforcing the inclination towards minor: the Kedusha, in Lydian, begins with twenty-one bars (out of eighty-six) in Dorian on G; or even towards mixing major and minor: the prayer 'Hashkivenu', in Mixolydian in its first two cadences and final one, has six intermediate cadences on A (Aeolian) and two on D (Dorian), plus another four on C (Ionian). Another modally labile work is the second setting of the Kaddish (no. 16), in which each of its six 'strophes' begins in Aeolian, only to effect a jarring transfer to Dorian in their last phrase (Ex. 7.1).[131]

Compared with the secular vocal collections, the 'Songs' even more clearly emphasize Dorian on G and, concomitantly, (untransposed) Dorian.[132] While the secular works have a small number of works in Ionian (6), the 'Songs' have none. Other changes in the 'Songs' are the larger number of works in Lydian and the smaller number of those in Aeolian and, most noticeably, of those in Mixolydian.[133] With the clear preference for minor over major modes, the 'Songs' come closest to Book 1 *a* 4.[134] In the secular works at large the preference narrows to a small majority, as confirmed, moreover, by Book 5 *a* 5,[135] published in the same year as the 'Songs'. The 'Songs' are decidedly more 'minor' than the secular works.

---

[130] Dorian transposed to G: 16 works; Lydian (with B flat): 6; Dorian (untransposed) and Aeolian: each 4; Mixolydian: 3.

[131] 'Magnified and sanctified be His great name...speedily and shortly'.

[132] Dorian on G: 48% in Sgs vs. 32% in secular works; untransposed Dorian: 12% in Sgs vs. 4% in secular works.

[133] Lydian: 18% in Sgs vs. 13% in secular works; Aeolian: 12% vs. 18%; Mixolydian: 9% vs. 26%.

[134] Sgs: 72% (min.) to 27% (maj.). M4: 76% (min.) to 22% (maj.).

[135] Secular works: 55% (min.) to 44% (maj.). Bk 5: 57% (min.) to 42% (maj.).

Ex. 7.1 Kaddish ('Songs of Solomon', no. 16, bars 1–7, 25–32)

The single modes of the 'Songs' are corroborated by the large number of cadences on the *finalis*. Considering the thirty-three works for their principal cadences, i.e. at the ends of verses, out of a total of 279 there are, in a proportional diminution by around 50 per cent, 144 on the *finalis*, sixty on the fifth degree, and thirty-six on the fourth degree.[136] The 'non-tonal' degrees are far more sparsely represented.[137]

Yet these statistics must be reinterpreted in accordance with the three literary types, psalms, prayers, and *piyyutim*, which reveal subtle differences. The psalms and *piyyutim* (including the wedding ode, no. 33) have the greatest cadential variety, though the tendency to emphasize the *finalis* is increased in the *piyyutim* with a corresponding decrease in cadences on IV and V;[138] the *piyyutim*, moreover, have more cadences on the second and sixth degrees than do the psalms. The prayers (including no. 19), by contrast, have the least cadential variety; indeed, they emphasize the 'tonal' degrees of I, IV, and V, more or less according to the percentages obtained for the whole repertory, except that the tonic occurs even more frequently. All in all, the prayers seem to be simpler, more elemental in their cadential planning.[139]

So much for the findings for 'principal' cadences in the repertory. Were the cadences within phrases considered, a slightly different picture emerges, one in which it is clear that the composer achieves variety within phrases (by cadences on non-tonal degrees) while stabilizing the mode at the ends of phrases (by cadences mainly on tonal degrees). The setting of Psalm 82 (no. 4) might serve as an example. Its verse cadences are on the 'tonal' degrees of Dorian on G, its intermediate cadences mostly on the 'non-tonal' ones, as follows:

Verse:	1	2	3	4
Cadences:	VII, III, i	III, V	VII, i	IV, IV

Verse:	5	6	7	8
Cadences:	VII, III, i	VII, v	VII, IV	III, v, VII, i

No. 16 (Kaddish), as already mentioned, is modally unstable, moving from Aeolian to Dorian; the instability is reflected, moreover, in the cadences of the phrases within each strophe, as follows:[140] VII, V, (VII, V), III, V, (V), I. The works in Aeolian mode proper are special inasmuch as they usually have no cadences on V at the end of verses (nor, for that matter,

---

[136] 144 on the *finalis* (or 52%), 60 on the fifth degree (or 21%), and 36 on the fourth degree (or 13%).

[137] 13 cadences on the second degree, 11 on the seventh and 10 on the sixth degrees, and, least of all, 5 on the third degree.

[138] The emphasis on I ('tonic') is particularly noticeable in the two works with strophic refrains, Sgs: 25, 27.

[139] In Sgs: 1, 3, 6, and (but for one cadence) 7, all cadences at ends of 'verses' are on I and V (though either one may be varied by being 'harmonized' as major or minor).

[140] The cadences in parentheses are for phrases omitted in later strophes.

within verses). Of the thirty-two final cadences and thirty-eight intermediate ones of nos. 14, 32, and 33, for example, only one intermediate one is on
V.[141] Similarly, nos. 25 and 27, in Lydian with B flat, are unusual in their
insistent repetition of cadences on the *finalis*,[142] but it must be remembered
that these are the only two pieces with a recurring textual-musical refrain.
The effect here is of a new simplicity, quite unlike the more devious modality of the other 'Songs', not to speak of the composer's madrigals. With
their refrains, the two pieces project an even folklike character.

4. *Counterpoint, texture, style.* Rossi demonstrated his skills in writing for
all sizes of vocal ensemble. His model in the 'Songs', as in his madrigals,
was sixteenth-century counterpoint, with its regulated use of dissonance, its
prohibition of parallels, and its smooth part writing. Yet here and there
Homer nodded: the collection has thirty-nine consecutive parallels,[143] most
of them in the works *a 8*.[144] The composer thus seems to have taken greater
liberties with eight-voice writing.[145]

It is difficult to compare the 'Songs', in their consecutives, with other
vocal collections, for none had so many eight-voice works.[146] Since the
'Songs', in their length, are equivalent to about four secular collections,
that would mean that (dividing 39—see above—by 4) they average about
nine consecutives per collection, which is rather high.[147] It would appear,
then, that some of the 'Songs' were written rather in haste.

The basic principle that determines the texture is as follows: the smaller
the number of voices the more melismatic the writing; conversely, the larger
the number, the more homophonic the writing. Thus the melodically and
contrapuntally more complicated examples occur in the first part of the
collection. As the ensemble increases, so does the tendency towards chordality. The most patently homophonic/homorhythmic examples are those for
eight voices: there variety is achieved not through melodic ornament, but
through the alternation and combination of the two choruses in response to
the syntactical divisions of the poetry and the semantical weight of its
constituents (whole or half verses or even smaller units).

The plainly homophonic style is a new one for Rossi, yet similar to that
in other composers' collections of psalms, for example, Gastoldi's *Psalmi*

---

[141] For the first hemistich of Sgs: 32, v. 14. An exception is Sgs: 10 (Ps. 137) with two of its nine
final cadences, but none of its twelve intermediate cadences, on V.

[142] At the end of all but two (out of 30) final cadences.

[143] And, less reprehensibly, four interrupted parallels.

[144] Thirty, to be exact: see, particularly, Sgs: 26–8, 31–2 (29–30 have one example apiece, 33
has none).

[145] Of the other consecutives, one occurred in a piece *a 4*; one each in two works *a 5*; two in
one work, and one in another, *a 6*; and three in the single work *a 7*.

[146] The three dialogues *a 8* in his madrigal books did, in fact, have many examples of
parallels between the two basses.

[147] The only secular collection that had as many was Bk 4, the others having either none (Cte)
or one (M4), two (Mti), three (Bk 1), or six (Bks 2–3).

vespertini quinque vocibus. Similar, yes, but with two qualifications: one is that Rossi worked in Hebrew, with its special syntactic and accentual demands; the other is that psalm compositions by Gastoldi, Viadana, and others, are more four-square, more intentionally declamatory, than Rossi's 'Songs'.

Relation of Music to Poetry

1. *Peculiarities of Rossi's treatment of the texts.* It has been noted that not all the prayer texts were composed in full. The ends of verses, in some, are marked with a double bar (‖) to indicate that there the congregation responds with one or more words.[148] Thus in the two settings of the Kaddish, the music consists of six sections corresponding to six 'verses', each to be followed by a response. The prayer 'Barekhu' has two sections, in which the second one, with the response 'Barukh adonai hamevorakh le'olam va'ed' ('Blessed be the Lord who is blessed for ever and ever'), is first recited by the congregation, then sung by the choir (it would ordinarily have been entrusted to the cantor,[149] who, in line with Modena's conception—see above—of how much more pleasant it would be were he to expand from one to many, becomes 'polyphonic', in this case three voices). No. 7, a setting of the Kedusha, has six sections, likewise with responses to be inserted between the 'verses'. Lest it be thought, however, that all double bars mark the place for insertions, in no. 8 they serve another purpose: the text consists of three non-adjacent verses from Psalm 80, and by separating them the double bars highlight the elliptical construction.[150]

Rossi's treatment of the words is exemplary. Either his Hebrew was especially good or he received advice from Leon Modena or others on how to handle it. Whatever the case, it is amazing to see how carefully the words were followed in their proper Hebrew syllabification and accentuation. The only examples of lightly flawed, though by no means erroneous, syllabification are confined either to Aramaic words (*u-va-'u-te-hon*

[148] The responses may be culled from the full versions of the texts given in the prayer books of the Italian rite (except for 'Amen', whose insertions may be ascertained from oral practice). For the liturgical sources, see the four major *maḥzorim*, viz. prayer books according to the yearly cycle of holidays and festivals, of the Italian rite as celebrated in the 15th–17th centuries (Casal Maggiore, 1485/6–1486/7; Bologna, 1539/40; Mantua, 1556/7; and Venice, 1587/8, itself reprinted in 1606, 1615/16, 1625, and 1675/6). See also two *siddurim*, viz. daily prayer books (Mantua, 1563/4; Venice, 1588/9); and two prayer books of the religious confraternity Shomerim Laboker (*Ayelet hashaḥar*, 1612; *Ashmoret haboker*, 1624).

[149] In the Venetian *maḥzor* from 1606, one reads that after the verse 'Barekhu et adonai hamevorakh' the response is recited twice, first by the congregation, then by the cantor (fo. 25ᵛ).

[150] The work has already been mentioned under possible musical evidence for Rossi's borrowing from traditional song. Its three verses were recited on Sabbaths and feast-days upon the removal of the second scroll. See e.g. the *siddur* from Venice, 1588/9, where, under the first day of Passover, the text is preceded by the inscription 'when they remove the second book, we say...' (fos. 122ᵛ–123).

abbreviated to *u-va-'ut-hon*)[151] or to others where by speech habit an *e* is inserted, for convenience of pronunciation, between two consonants (thus *ye-va-rekh-kha* becomes *ye-va-re-khe-kha*,[152] *yih-ye* becomes *yi-he-ye*,[153] and *yih-yu* becomes *yi-he-yu*[154]). Yet Hebrew, to start with, leaves a certain latitude in their treatment. Less satisfactory is the obviously Italianate pronunciation of *she-ga-malt* as the same three syllables plus a terminal *e*, a charming indiscretion, yet one with serious consequences for the rhythmic construction (Ex. 7.2).[155]

Ex. 7.2   The word *shegamalt* ('you rewarded [us]') from ''Al naharot bavel' (no. 10, bars 93–4)

One has to look far and wide for examples of incorrect accentuation. The only glaring ones are *kulékhem* (for *kulekhém*) and *halélu* (for *halelú*). They must have been an oversight, for Rossi generally treats syllables with mobile *sheva* as weak.[156]

Elsewhere the accentuation is altered not because the composer misread the words but because he responded to the metrical stresses of the hymns or *piyyutim*. Thus in the setting of 'Yigdal' (no. 28) eight words are accentuated on the penultimate, though, normally, they would have been on the ultimate.[157] The same holds for three words in the setting of 'Adon 'olam' (no. 29):[158]

---

[151] In Sgs: 1, the Kaddish (bars 83–5); the word is fully syllabified in its second setting (Sgs: 16, bars 85–8).

[152] In the three settings of Ps. 128: Sgs: 2 (bars 56–7), 12 (bars 61–6), 20 (bars 52–6).

[153] In Sgs: 29–30, the first a setting of 'Adon 'olam' (bars 30–1), the second of Ps. 112 (bars 17–18).

[154] In Sgs: 32, a setting of Ps. 92 (bars 135–7).

[155] The terminal *e* turns a quiescent *sheva* into a mobile one. That Rossi so intended may be inferred from the two minims provided for *mal-t[e]* in three of the voices (though not in the tenor, where the syllable *malt* falls correctly on a single note). The reading could be 'emended' by extending *malt* over both halves.

[156] *Sheva* is a vowel with either a quiescent or, in this case, a mobile form (the *le* of *kulekhem* and *halelu*). The first occurs in Sgs: 4, a setting of Ps. 82 (bars 60–2, top voice only); the second in Sgs: 30, a setting of Ps. 112 (bar 1, tenor).

[157] *Elóhim* (bars 2–3); *ve'eíno* (26); *netáno* (54–5); *móshe* (65); *umábbit* (67–8); *le'ámo* (75–6); *mehákei* (118–19); *yeháye* (124–5).

[158] Cf. Sgs: 29, bars 9–13, 40–5, 86–93.

'Adon 'olam' (in iambic tetrameter)
    Stressed syllables are italicized and bracketed words are shown in their
    usual (non-metric) accentuation

From second distich   Le-'*et* na-'a-*sa* / be-*hef*-tso [be-hef-*tso*] *kol*
From fifth distich   Le-*ham*-shil [Le-ham-*shil*] *lo* / le-hah-*bi*-ra[159]
From tenth distich   A-*do*-nai [A-do-*nai*] *li* / ve-*lo* i-*ra*

Other alterations occur in the *piyyutim* nos. 25 and 27 and in the wedding
ode no. 33. But, again, here, as elsewhere, there is nothing wrong with
Rossi's setting; rather, its irregularities of accentuation resided in the texts
themselves. In treating words, Rossi usually read them in their prosodic
context, which means, in short, that where certain ones seem incorrectly
rhythmicized the reason is often to be found in the metrical schemes.[160] In
the case of no. 29, the metre outwardly scans as iambic tetrameter, yet in
effect it follows the long-short pattern for the Arabic Hazağ ($\smile$ – – – / $\smile$ – – –).
The latter neutralizes the qualitatively stressed iambs (*Adón 'olám / ashér
malákh* becomes *Ădōn 'ōlām / ăshēr mālākh*, etc.).[161] But matters are not so
simple: the text itself is prosodically ambiguous, and Rossi seems to have
read it as standing somewhere between qualitative and quantitative
rhythms. As the text, so the music.

The position of words in relation to notes was very carefully specified:
Leon Modena saw to that in preparing the music for printing and in
proof-reading the copy.[162] Yet the division of words can be difficult in
melismatic passages. There one knows no more than where the first syllable of the word begins (obviously the first note) and its last syllable
ends (obviously the last note). But no indication is given for the start of
the middle and last syllables. There are two possible solutions to the problem, one according to the dictates of Italian word placement, as observed
by Rossi in his madrigals, the other according to those of Hebrew
prosody.

Italian words are usually accented on the penultimate (and less often on
the antepenultimate), and by convention the melisma falls on the accented
syllable and, as a result, the last note of the phrase on the last syllable
(though exceptionally the last syllable suffers a terminal melisma).[163]

---

[159] Here Rossi softens the iambic accentuation (lehahbira) to accommodate the penultimate
word stress.

[160] Or in other textual peculiarities: e.g. the use of hyphens between two or more words,
thereby removing the accent from all but the last (*kol-afsei-árets*, in Ps. 67, set as Sgs: 9), as a
proclitic; or the rule of the recessive accent (*nasog ahor*), where a dissyllable stressed on the
penult affects the previous word, advancing its accent from the ultimate to the penult (*hamónei
má'la* and *kevútsei máta*, in the Great Kedusha, Sgs: 7), as an enclitic.

[161] As for 'Yigdal', it follows the scheme of a modified Rağaz.

[162] As we learn from Modena's foreword (see above).

[163] For the melisma on the accented syllable and the last syllable on the last note, cf. Zarlino,
Le istitutioni harmoniche (1558), 341. For a terminal melisma on the last syllable, cf. Stoquerus, *De
musica verbali libri duo* (c.1570), fo. 40. On these and other rules for text placement, see the
appendix to Harrán, *Word-Tone Relations in Musical Thought*, 360–460.

Hebrew words, by contrast, are usually accented on the ultimate (and far less often on the penultimate), and the question is whether the accented ultimate receives a melisma, as one would expect it to. The conflict between Italian and Hebrew ways of treating the melisma may be illustrated by the opening of no. 3 (the word *Barekhú*, accented, as marked here, on *khu*, yet having a secondary accent on *Ba*; Ex. 7.3).[164]

(1)
(2) Ba - re - khú——— ברכו [Barekhú]
(3) Ba -   -   -   re   -   khú

Ex. 7.3 The word *Barekhú* ('Bless') from the work so beginning (no. 3, canto, bars 1–7): (1) placement in musical source; (2) Hebrew realization; (3) Italian realization (with *re* at the start of the dotted figure, as a convention of word placement)

Either solution (Hebrew, Italian) is feasible, and without further information one cannot determine the composer's preference. In solutions 2 and 3 *Ba* is treated as a secondary accent and *re* is minimized, though not for the same reasons: in the Italian transcript *re* is simply a weak syllable; in Hebrew it is no syllable at all, for it falls on a mobile *sheva*, which, morphologically, connects with *khu* (*Ba-rekhú*).

Similar ambivalence concerns *bemo'adám* in no. 6, except that now, like the Hebrew ordering of the syllables, the Italian one, too, results in a terminal melisma on *dám* (for it was not customary to place a syllable on a final note preceded by quavers;[165] Ex. 7.4). The Hebrew and Italian agree in treating *mo* as a secondary accent, with the other portions unaccented; yet again Hebrew has its own logic: *be* and '*a* are not officially syllables, the *be* being a mobile *sheva* and the '*a* a semivowel, hence not suitable for emphasis.

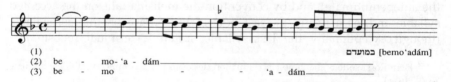

(1)
(2) be - mo-'a - dám——— במועדם [bemo'adám]
(3) be - mo   -   -   'a - dám———

Ex. 7.4 The word *bemo'adám* ('in their seasons') from 'Ele mo'adei adonai' (no. 6, canto, bars 10–15): (1) placement in musical source; (2) Hebrew realization; (3) Italian one

---

[164] For the rule specifying that in a dotted figure separate syllables are not to be assigned to the smaller note or notes after the dotted one, nor to the larger value that follows, see Zarlino, *Le istitutioni harmoniche*, 341.

[165] Cf. Stoquerus above on the terminal melisma, as well as his statement to the effect that in a series of crotchets or smaller values the syllable ought to be placed on the first note or on the larger one preceding it (*De musica verbali*, fo. 31ᵛ).

Altogether, about twenty-two problem cases can be spotted, mostly in the earlier, more melismatic part of the collection.[166] Their treatment may be determined in different ways. One is to save the melisma for the penulti-mate syllable when, in Hebrew, it is the accented syllable. Penultimately accented Hebrew syllables would be handled in the same way, then, as those in Italian (and, in both languages, the final syllable would thereby fall on the final note).

Another solution is to apply the usual rules for Italian text placement, whereby syllables are prevented from being sung on the first larger note after smaller ones or on the smaller ones themselves.[167] Thus, in Ex. 7.5, the proper Italian treatment might, on musical grounds, overrule the Hebrew deferment of the last syllable to the last note.

Ex 7.5   The word *shoveínu* ('our captors') from "Al naharot bavel' (no. 10, tenor, bars 24–6): (1) placement in musical source; (2) Hebrew realization (for accentual reasons); (3) realization after the conventions of Italian text placement

The burden of the evidence would seem to indicate that Rossi often favoured the Italian (and practical musical) approach over the Hebrew one. There are various instances of parts so written that they adapt naturally to Italian procedure. If not naturally, then under constraint: on the word *birnaná*, the melisma is forced *all'italiana* onto the antepenultimate and the last two syllables (because of repeated notes) onto the last two notes (Ex. 7.6).

Ex. 7.6   The word *birnaná* ('in joyous song') from 'Lamnatseah, 'al hagitit' (no. 14, canto, bars 19–23): (1) placement in musical source; (2) Italian realization

---

[166] Sgs: 3, bars 1–6 (canto, also alto and tenor); 6, bars 10–15 (canto, also alto and tenor); 7, bars 8–10 (bass), 18–20 (canto), 63–4 (tenor), 81–3 (tenor); 8, bars 1–7 (alto, also tenor), 8–14 (canto, also alto), 25–31 (canto, alto), 56–61 (canto, alto, tenor, bass); 10, bars 24–6 (tenor); 11, bars 15–17 (tenor); 12, bars 15–18 (alto); 14, bars 19–23 (canto); 16, bars 22–4 (canto), 33–6 (alto, quinto, tenor); 17, bars 4–7 (quinto); 19, bars 16–18 (quinto, also tenor); 20, bars 2–7 (bass), 75–7 (canto), 78–80 (alto); and 22, bars 5–8 (quinto).

[167] See Zarlino, *Le istitutioni harmoniche*, 341, also Lanfranco, *Scintille di musica* (1533), 69.

In solving the various problems of syllabic placement in melismas, the Italian approach, to summarize, was the one that Rossi tended to comply with, yet was not rigorous in enforcing. There are places where the Hebrew treatment works better musically or the music itself pointed the way to a solution, in which case the composer appears to have proceeded *ad rem*. Thus, in Ex. 7.7, the Hebrew one seems preferable for *yitenú* ('they will give') in the bass, as confirmed by the setting of the same word in the canto and tenor; and it seems preferable, again, for *kevútsei* ('crowds') in the canto, in order not to break the arched melody (even though having *tsei* on the final note violates the rule of Italian text placement that no syllable be sung to the longer note succeeding one or more short ones).[168] Yet the Italian treatment seems preferable for *aní* ('I') in the tenor (not only does it implement the same rule, but it has the tenor correspond to the other parts in placing *ni* on a downbeat).

(1) יתנו [yitenú]   קבוצי [kevútsei]   אני [aní]
(2) yi - te - nú   ke - vú - tsei_____   *a - ní_____
(3) *yi - te - nú__   *ke - vú - - tsei   a - ní_____

Ex. 7.7 Various words from 'Keter yitenu lakh' (no. 7, bass, bars 8–10; canto, 18–20; tenor, 63–4): (1) placement in musical source; (2) Italian realization; (3) Hebrew one (the preferred placement, in each instance, is marked by an asterisk)

A word of admonition before closing the discussion: the whole matter of Hebrew versus Italian accentuation becomes an academic issue without considering the conventions of oral tradition. After listening to sound recordings of prayers, psalms, and *piyyutim*,[169] as sung in the Italian rite, one comes away with the impression that what grammar demands is one thing, but what happens in practice is another.[170] Here and there mobile *shevas* receive tonic accents or short melismas and are either just as long as secondary accents or even longer. Judged from this standpoint, Rossi's setting of the Hebrew text in his 'Songs' is almost faultless; in fact, Rossi is considerably more meticulous in handling words than most practised cantors.

2. *Word painting*. The intrusion of Italian elements into the Hebrew 'Songs' may be detected, further, in examples of word painting. Though

---

[168] Yet it observes still another Italian injunction against splitting syllables of the same word by leaps; see Vicentino, *L'antica musica ridotta alla moderna prattica* (1555), fo. P iii.

[169] Among the recorded materials of the Italiani held in Jerusalem, National Sound Archives (with informants, for example, from Casale Monferrato, Turin, and Ferrara).

[170] That is exactly the tenor of the argument, to refer to a non-Hebraic subject, pursued by Jean Le Munerat in his theoretical tracts from the 1490s (see Harrán, *In Defence of Music*, esp. 53–77).

Rossi set the texts with a minimum of madrigalisms, still he reacted to words, here and there, for their illustrative or emotive qualities. In this he obviously departs from the conventions of synagogue song, which, in cantillation, for example, usually concern the division of the text into its syntactical components.

Rossi's main device for highlighting words is the melisma. Longer or shorter melismas are used to suggest movement (expansion, elevation, walking, proceeding, the flow of water; Ex. 7.8a–b),[171] music (song, to sing, psalm; Ex. 7.8c, also Plate 11),[172] and rejoicing (hallelujah, happiness, joy, prosperity; Ex. 7.8d).[173] Elsewhere they are used to emphasize momentous words (fear, blessing, and, especially, God).[174] Yet not always did the melisma fulfil a painterly function. Sometimes it adorned the end of a section or acted as a decorative feature within or at the conclusion of phrases.[175]

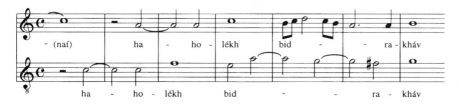

Ex. 7.8a   *Haholekh bidrakhav*, 'he walks in His ways' (no. 12 *a* 5, canto, alto, bars 12–18)

[171] Cf. (in order) Sgs: 1, bars 2–3 (*Yitgadal*, 'may [His great name] be magnified'); 33, bars 107–110, 111–13 (*beito rama*, '[over] his house will she be uplifted'); 2, bars 14–19, and 12, bars 10–18 (*haholekh bidrakhav*, 'he walks in His ways'); 4, bars 45–8 (*yithalakhu*, '[in darkness] will they walk'); 25, bars 11–13, 152–5, 175–9 (*binsoa' [ha'aron]*, 'during the procession [with the ark]'); 27, bars 171–5 (*binsoa' [ha'aron]*: not only are the words the same as those in no. 25, but the melismas on them are similar); and 10, bars 1–4 (*naharot*, 'rivers').

[172] Cf. (in order) Sgs: 2, bars 1–2; 17, bars 1–4; 18, bars 1–3; and 20, bars 1–7 (all but the last on the word *shir*, or 'song', with rising or falling scales to suggest the next word *hama'alot*, or 'of degrees'; in the last example, the scales are in fact deferred to *hama'alot*); 10, bars 34–6 ([*eikh*] *nashir*, '[how] will we sing'); 5, bars 6–8, and 9, bars 4–6 (*mizmor*, 'psalm', followed, in no. 9, by the word *shir*, 'song').

[173] Cf. (in order) Sgs: 7, bars 79–86 (*haleluyah*: extensive melismas plus word repeats); 19, bars 77–80 (*vesimha*, 'and happiness'); 9, bars 35–9 (*yismehu viranenu*, 'may they be happy and sing joyfully', with word repeats on *viranenu*); 14, bars 19–23 (*birnana*, 'with joyful song'); 17, bars 74–82 (*verina*, 'in joyous song', plus an extended melisma in the quinto on *alumotav*, 'his sheaves', bars 85–90, in accord with the joyful content); 32, bars 44–8 (*aranen*, 'I will rejoice'); 22, bars 71–6, 79–83, 86–91 (*nagila*, 'let us rejoice'); and 11, bars 70–2 (*betuv*, 'in the good').

[174] Cf. (in order) Sgs: 2, bars 9–11 (*yere*, 'who fears', followed by *adonai*, 'the Lord'); and 3, bars 1–7 (*barekhu*, 'may you bless'), 15–21 (*hamevorakh*, 'who is blessed'). For melismas on God, see Sgs: 4, bars 11–13 (*elohim*), 8 (florid melismas on *elohim hashivenu . . . venivashe'a*, 'God, restore us . . . and we shall be saved'; they gradually become more expansive from the first to the second and third verses); 7, bars 63–8 (*adonai eloheikhem*, '[I am] the Lord your God', also corresponding to the end of a section); 11, bars 45–7 (*adonai*); and 7, bars 1–7 (*keter*, 'crown', in the kabbalistic sense of godhead).

[175] For section endings, see Sgs: 1, bars 92–5, and 6, bars 10–17. For decorative purposes within phrases, see Sgs: 7, bars 8–11/15–21, and 23, bars 6–11; and at their end, Sgs: 33, bars 28–32 (plus echo 33–5).

Ex. 7.8b   *Naharot*, 'rivers' (no. 10 *a* 4, tenor, bass, bars 1–4)

Ex. 7.8c   *Shir*, 'song' (no. 17 *a* 5, bars 1–4, with rising or falling scales to suggest the next word *hama'alot*, 'of degrees')

Ex. 7.8d   *Nagila venismekha vo*, 'let us rejoice and be glad in it' (no. 22 *a* 6, bars 79–83)

Other devices used to depict words, though rather infrequently, are a particular rhythmic pattern for stagnation or destruction or, at the other extreme, rejoicing; harmonic alterations for weeping or strangeness; scalar motion for *ma'alot* ('steps'; see Ex. 7.8c); and repeats of words (anadiplosis) for greatness.[176]

To return to the melisma: notably exuberant ones occur in pieces for reduced ensembles (three or four voices). Of the words that are reinforced, the most salient category is those having to do with music and rejoicing, which are connected in the composer's mind as the twin fundaments of sacred devotion. Rossi appears to see music as a form of rejoicing and rejoicing, conversely, as appropriately and effectively conveyed through music (the words *rina* and *renana*, occurring often enough in the 'Songs', refer variously to joy, song, and prayer; see Ex. 7.6). The equivalent to the emphasis Rossi put on music and rejoicing in his 'Songs' is his use of melismas or faster figures in his madrigals on the words *canto, cantar, gioia, lieto, riso, ridi, amore, dolce*, etc.

Equating music with rejoicing, Rossi exploits the artifices of 'erudite music' (harmony, counterpoint, rhythmic variety, melodic interest, etc.) to communicate the joy of prayer and praise. Rejoicing in fact is the basic tenor of the collection, as is clear from the prefatory matter. In mourning, by contrast, 'music' in the sense of 'art music' is rejected.[177]

The main way to express sorrow is through monophony, after its practice in the synagogue. Rossi's setting of Psalm 137 (no. 10) may serve as an example of 'intoned speech', as befits its content: the sadness of exile. Taking his cue from the words, especially the portion 'How can we sing the song of the Lord in a foreign land?', the composer refrained from all melodic ornament, writing a starkly declamatory setting, as if words now took the place of melody. He scored the music for the more darkly coloured lower voices (alto, two tenors, and bass), and in this no. 10 is almost unique: Rossi rarely dispensed with the soprano, whether in Hebrew, instrumental, or Italian works.[178]

[176] For rhythm, see Sgs: 10, bars 6–8 ('there we sat'; lengthening); 24, bars 49–57 ('the Lord broke'; short rhythmic motif tossed back and forth between the voices); 11, bars 8–9/12–15 ('I will praise the Lord ... I will sing to my God ...'; crotchet motion); and 17, bars 73–5 ('will come back singing'; fast figure in tenor). For harmony, see Sgs: 10, bars 9–11 ('we wept'; B major chord, plus rhythmic lengthening), 40–3 ('in a foreign land'; B and E major chords). For scalar motion (on 'of degrees'), see Sgs: 2, bars 1–2; 17, bars 1–4; 18, bars 1–3; and 20, bars 1–7. For word repeats, see Sgs: 32, bars 47–53 ('how great are Your works'; stated first in the four lower voices, then in the four upper voices and, again, in the four lower ones, as if in a process of enlargement [great = big]).

[177] On the dichotomy of rejoicing and mourning in Rossi's Hebrew works, see Harrán, 'Psalms as Songs'.

[178] Soprano part, here referring to the voice notated in either a violin or a soprano clef. The exceptions, Mti: 9–12, 14, may have had pictorial reasons: no. 9 speaks of the lover being '*submerged* midst storms and dead', no. 11 of his 'face wrapped in a *pallid colour*', no. 12 of a grieving bird in the *dark of night* and *in winter*. No. 14 is a serenade (in which the lover pleads with his shepherdess, trying to break down her resistance).

The piece is special, too, in having a natural employed, pictorially, as a sharp. We know the device from Rossi's vocal and instrumental collections, and in the former, as was noted, it tended to be associated with evocative words, among them *finta* (= *ficta*, or *musica ficta*; see Chapter 5). In bar 42, F natural (*recte* sharp, in tenor) occurs against D sharp (in canto), on the words '*al admat nekhar* ('in a foreign land'), and in bar 83, F natural (*recte* sharp, in alto) occurs against D sharp (in tenor), now on the words '*aru 'ad hayesod bah* ('raze it to its foundations'). As was (usually) the case in the other collections, so here, too, the two sharps (on D and F, with the root B) function, to use tonal terminology, as a V or dominant chord in E minor.

Two principles are at work then: art music and its blandishments; and the would-be denial of art music through recitation. What is interesting is that towards the end of the collection Rossi seems to have achieved a compromise, in his eight-voice pieces, between the two: the music is pared of all melodic excrescence, it becomes more homorhythmic, more declamatory; yet as music, paradoxically, it becomes more dramatic, with its split choruses set in a vibrant *stile concertato*.

It is in the last work, or the wedding ode, that the true meaning of the 'Songs of Solomon' is revealed. Rossi's practice had always been to save unusual pieces for ends of collections, as a bonus to singers or prospective buyers—they would have found them musically interesting, yet not in any particular way textually edifying. In the wedding ode, replete with echo effects, Rossi not only wrote an unusual piece, but defined his motives in the collection: praise of God, rejoicing in Him; the groom and bride as an emblem for man and woman united in God.

The ode, 'one of the first examples of a Hebrew wedding cantata',[179] is preceded by a Sabbath hymn (Psalm 92), which relates to it by metaphor: the Sabbath, the holiest day of the week, is conceived as a bride. For all its secular allure, the wedding hymn is perhaps the most sacred item in the collection, for it touches on the essence of religious joy in the Jewish tradition: the union of Israel with God, in His emanation as *shekhina*.[180] Rossi moved from the outward act of matrimony according to *halakha*, or Jewish law, to its interpretation, in Kabbala, as an immersion in the divine. The music is transparent, as if to emphasize the special meaning of the words. They read, in the end, as an appeal for godly intervention. 'May You, God almighty, bless my friends, for ever, without cease, without end, for eternity'. The blessing on his friends should be read as a blessing on the Jewish

---

[179] Schirmann, 'Hate'atron vehamusika bishkhunot hayehudim be'italya bein hame'a ha-16 veha-18', esp. 97.

[180] Idel noted that Alemanno, in his commentary on the Song of Songs, *Heshek shelomo*, thought it possible to 'ascend, after the purification of the mind, the various stages of intellection and operations related to Kabbalistic mystical techniques and rituals, to the Eiyn Sof, the highest divine level according to the Kabbalists' ('The Anthropology of Yohanan Alemanno', 205). Thus the Song of Songs might be conceived as a catalyst for reaching higher forms of divine knowledge.

people for health and prosperity. Thus the collection comes full circle, for the first item, or Kaddish, concluded with the plea: 'May He who makes peace on His heights, make peace, in His mercy, for us and for all Israel, and say "amen".' The bridal pair celebrated in the 'Songs of Solomon' is, in the broadest sense, God and His people Israel.[181] Rossi thereby proclaims the affinity of his collection with the Song of Songs.

The play with different meanings is underlined by the echo effects. Each of the eleven stanzas concludes with a textual (and musical) echo. Textually, the point is to demonstrate how the two or three syllables that are echoed can be construed in either Hebrew or Italian. Thus the last word of the first stanza is *be'alma* ('with a maid'), of which the portion *'alma* is repeated: in Hebrew as *'al ma* ('what for?'), which in Italian reads as *alma* ('soul'); or the last word of the sixth stanza is *ne'elama* ('she is silent'), of which the portion *lama* is repeated: in Hebrew as *lama* ('why?'), which in Italian reads as *l'ama* ('he loves her'); and so on with other word games that the author, still unidentified, though probably Leon Modena,[182] plays with obvious glee. It is as if the author were telling us that however deep the chasm between Hebrew and Italian it can be breached through their homonyms.

Musically, the point is to demonstrate that different languages can be set to identical music without damaging their integrity. Rossi seems to be writing an epitaph to his own conception of Hebrew music as a blend of Italianism and Hebraism, not to speak of his own life story as a reconciliation of the separate cultures in which he moved.

---

[181] In a narrow sense, it is a couple of Rossi's and Modena's friends: I identified them (tentatively) as Rachel Copio (Sarah's sister) and Abraham Massarano. See Harrán, 'From Music to Matrimony'.

[182] Cf. Magid, 'Shir lo noda' me'et rav yehuda arye de modena'.

EPILOGUE

From Conflict to Consonance

T HE title of this book formed a proposition. But now we are faced with the question: can the predicate portion, 'Jewish musician in late Renaissance Mantua', be reconciled with the subject, 'Salamone Rossi'? Is it possible, that is, to synthesize the different elements in Rossi's biography and music into some kind of rational whole?

Any attempt to conceive Rossi's life and works as apodictically coherent would seem to be doomed, from the outset, by the disparity of their components: Jewish, Christian, Hebrew, Italian, Mantuan, vocal music, instrumental music, secular, sacred, liturgical, paraliturgical, the varying meanings of the term *Renaissance*—not to speak of its disputability as a historical or stylistic qualifier—in Italian and Jewish culture of the later sixteenth and early seventeenth centuries, music of the *prima pratica*, music of the *seconda*, music for the chamber, music for the theatre. Yet the components do, in fact, coalesce in the person of Salamone Rossi: he is the glue that holds them together, and the only sensible explanation for the amalgam is, obviously, that Rossi constitutes the sum total of his parts. The particular way they combine, in his actions and conceptions, to form a whole makes his story, as the stories of all other culturally vibrant composers, thoroughly unique in the annals of music history.

Rather than seek the ineffable reasons for cohesion, one might, more modestly, designate how the separate components operate to shape the lineaments of Rossi's biography and music into idiosyncratic constructs; that was the aim of the previous chapters. To sum up, two antithetical processes seem to be at work, one leading to differentiation, the other to fusion. At root, they exemplify an ontological binary wherein relevant historical and musical data may be construed according to their tendency, in one or another context, towards dissociation or unification. The way Rossi is 'read' thus depends on the vantage point from which he is examined. His multivalence is a function of the diverse influences to which he was subject and the diverse mutual adjustments he appears to have effected in real life and in the acts of performing and composing music.

Like consciously Jewish musicians in later times, Rossi confronted the problems of preserving his Jewish identity in a non-Jewish environment and of communicating, as a Jew, with Jews and Christians in such a manner as to be understood and esteemed by both. His solutions, biographically and artistically, were his own, but by illustrating the *paradoxe juif* they fall within the larger frame of Jewish–Christian relations in the Western Diaspora. There is a broad socio-cultural lesson to be learned from the way Rossi, doubtless more by instinct than by intent, accommodated to his surroundings.

Rossi, the man and musician, had his Jewish and Hebrew sides, as is evident from his connections with his family, with Jews in Mantua and Venice, and with the Mantuan Jewish communal institutions, to which one should add his spiritual commitment to the Hebrew tradition. He participated in productions of the Jewish theatrical troupe and was probably called upon to prepare or perform music for celebrations within the Jewish community; he might have been affiliated with one or more synagogues and perhaps confraternities in and even beyond Mantua.

At the same time, Rossi had his Mantuan and Italian sides. He was heavily involved in music-making for the Gonzagas and was occasionally invited to entertain guests at other courts (Mirandola, possibly Modena). He came into contact with the greater and lesser non-Jewish musicians who worked in or passed through Mantua, collaborating with them in composing, rehearsing, and often performing vocal and instrumental music for theatrical or private entertainments. He met with dukes, princes, and other worthies, receiving or soliciting commissions from them.

The outward dichotomy between Jewish and non-Jewish influences and motivations cuts through his production. Rossi supplied Hebrew compositions for services in the synagogue and possibly events in the community; he related to these compositions, so he intimated in the dedication to the published collection, as different from his Italian ones and demanding special efforts in their elaboration. He knew of an ancient Hebrew musical practice that flourished in the Temple, only to decline thereafter in the Exile; and he perceived himself, or at least was perceived by others, as playing a major role in its renascence. Leon Modena concluded that by writing Hebrew music Rossi both linked with an indigenous, though distant tradition and perpetuated it into the future. But before, during, and after pursuing his Hebrew inclinations, Rossi operated, with no less enthusiasm, within the constraints of an ongoing Italian musical tradition.

Rossi's Hebrew 'Songs' thus form the obverse side of a repertory which, otherwise, consists of works having historically and culturally different origins. His *canzonette* and madrigals are firmly rooted in Italian practice, as are his *canzoni*, dances, *sinfonie*, and sonatas. Here and there Rossi innovated within this practice, especially in his *sinfonie* and sonatas. Yet, in the main, he shaped the ideas for his non-Jewish works according to an inherently Italian, non-Jewish tradition of vocal and instrumental music.

What the Jewish and non-Jewish sides of Rossi's repertory have in common resides perhaps in their differentiation into *antico* and *moderno*. The *antico* in Jewish music is represented by its practice in the Ancient Temple and, from the Middle Ages on, by the cantillation of Scriptures and intonation of prayers in the synagogue. In effect, there was no *moderno* in Jewish music until Salamone Rossi composed his 'Songs', following the example, possibly, though not necessarily, of others, who, from the early seventeenth century, tried, with limited success, to introduce part music into prayer services. I say 'part music'—indeed, I have purposely been using the term, in earlier chapters, in referring to Hebrew art music in its pre-Rossian stage—because it is less committal than 'polyphony': part music is basically any music in parts, polyphony conjures up an image of learned counterpoint. The Jews might have practised some kind of 'part music', but whether it complied with the rules of counterpoint cannot be determined: 'part music' has the advantage of suggesting such a possibility without imposing it. Be that as it may, Rossi's 'Songs', hailed, by reason of their artful composition, as different from anything known among the Jews until their time, to paraphrase Modena, were perceived by some, it would seem, not as modern, but as foreign. To justify their novelty, they were explained, again by Modena, and whoever else prepared the prefatory material, as effecting a reconstitution of the mythically glorious Hebrew music that thrived in the Temple; thus the biblical *antico* became a conceptual source for Rossi's *moderno*.

The same split into *antico* and *moderno* may be detected in Rossi's non-Jewish works. Stylistically, his *canzonette* and four- and five-voice madrigals, as well as his dances, *canzoni*, and to a certain extent *sinfonie*, seem to exemplify a *prima pratica*, while his *madrigaletti* and sonatas, along with other *sinfonie*, do a *seconda*. It was Monteverdi who distinguished between works of the *prima pratica* as 'old' and those of the *seconda* as 'new'. Monteverdi's views may be questioned, but there is no denying that Rossi's repertory displays markedly contrasting stylistic tendencies, of ostensibly 'older' and 'newer' origin.

The division into *antico* and *moderno* seems to apply to the basic division, in Rossi's œuvre, into vocal and instrumental music. The madrigals, thereby, are 'old'; many *sinfonie* and the sonatas, 'new'. On another level, the same distinction can be reversed: the madrigals are 'new' because they are written to lyrics of the latest poets and, historically, because madrigals continue to be cultivated until well into the second decade of the seventeenth century; and *sinfonie* and sonatas are 'old' because they can be traced to earlier forms of composition, among them sixteenth-century *canzoni*.

On still another level, it is difficult to sustain the differentiation between Italian and Jewish sides of the repertory as illustrated by secular vocal and instrumental compositions versus Hebrew ones. Other principles might be invoked as causal explanations for Rossi's non-Jewish works. His Italian vocal ones seem to be posited on 'the word' as the determining factor of their composition. Words, of course, can be observed in widely contrasting ways, and Monteverdi's often highly dramatic madrigals from his later books are, musically, no less indebted to their verbal component than the much simpler, sometimes narrative madrigals of his earlier ones. The same holds for Rossi's later *madrigaletti*, so different from his madrigals, yet, for all that, no less verbally conditioned in their music.

Regard for the text usually translates, in the Italian works, into a relatively restrained melodic and rhythmic style, with emphasis on clear delivery and articulation of words and their syntactic units. Rossi might, in composition, have been bound to 'the word' by the force of the Hebrew *verbum sacrum*; yet he could equally have been word-conscious from humanistic currents in the sixteenth- and seventeenth-century madrigal. The primacy of the word, at any rate, narrows the distinction between whatever might be schematized as Hebrew and Italian forms of composition: they are at one in Rossi's conceptions and their realization.

Rossi's instrumental works may be posited on an opposite principle, the absence of words, with its implications for an inevitably distinctive mode of composition. Here the composer was freer to indulge his own preferences. Rossi was doubtless a virtuoso violinist, and in his instrumental music he did, eventually, give vent to his soloist inclinations. The result, all in all, was something quite different from his vocal music. Rossi was released from the constraints of words to impose his own ideas on instrumental composition, as determined by his stylistic biases and performing capacities. Where Rossi drew from verbal stimuli for his vocal works, he drew from himself for many of his instrumental ones: he is the measure of their form and content. In this, however, he is a man of his times, which, as we know, witnessed the gradual rise of the soloist in vocal and instrumental music. If Rossi did not follow through in his vocal works, it is because he worked in genres that were not particularly susceptible to soloistic penetration; the *canzonetta* and choral madrigal are not the habitat of the emerging soloist, whereas monody and dramatic music, which Rossi neglected, very much are.

Rossi could, in his mind's eye, fall back on the precedent of instrumental music among the ancient Hebrews; its wonders were common knowledge. In the biblical tales, familiar to, and recounted by, Jews and Christians alike, one reads, for example, of David, who, playing on his lyre, rid King Saul of his melancholy; or of the prophet Elisha, who asked to be brought a string player—'the hand of the Lord came over the player' and Elisha was inspired.[1] The tales were incorporated by the renowned Mantuan rabbi Judah Moscato into his impressive sermon on music entitled *Higayon bekhinor*, or 'Contemplations on the Lyre' (1588): there instrumental music is epitomized as an ideal vehicle for transmitting divine content (consonance, proportion, joy). Instrumental music, therefore, is very much part of the Hebrew tradition. For Rossi there was no problem in accepting it, unlike many of the rabbis who warned against it as unsuited to a people in mourning over the Destruction of the Temple. Rossi, in his person, appears

---

[1] David: 1 Sam. 16: 16, 23. Elisha: 2 Kgs. 3: 15.

to embody the achievements not only of singers but also of instrumentalists in the Ancient Temple: thus he was presented in the commentary to his sacred works and thus he proved himself in his vocal and instrumental repertory.

Yet there are forces tugging in the opposite direction, towards unification. In daily life Rossi moved between two cultures, combining, if not fusing them within his activities.[2] In this he seems to illustrate the possibility of breaking down civic and religious barriers, despite the increasing segregation of Jews from Christians in later sixteenth- and early seventeenth-century Mantua. Rossi was, of course, a privileged Jew, as were various Jewish doctors, loan bankers, and middlemen whose services were requested or required by Christians. They enjoyed favours denied their co-religionists, who felt the full burden of the social and economic restrictions imposed on the Jewish minority. Rossi's freedom of movement was facilitated by his exemption from wearing the yellow badge; as if, ironically, the only thing that separated Jews from Christians was the sign the Jews were forced to display on their clothing. True, with its removal, Rossi was protected, in his movements, from arrest or molestation. But it could not mend deep-rooted cultural divisions: the fate of Rossi, for all his privileges, lay with his people's.

More subtle and pervasive were the processes of unification that operate in Rossi's music. They may be detected in the apparent resolution of the conflict, already signalled, between the *antico* and *moderno* sides of his repertory; in the narrowing of the differences between instrumental and vocal genres; in the broadening of the audience towards which the composer directed his Hebrew works; in the notion of music, in both the Christian and the Jewish traditions, as harmony; in the elevation of 'song', in Hebrew music, to the rank of a category above specific media or styles; and in the conception of Hebrew music as the *primum mobile* of musical culture at large.

1. *Old versus new.* Rossi's music was both old and new when judged by the criterion of its usual texture. The larger part of his vocal and instrumental works lacked the more soloistic, hence 'newer' traits of his *madriga-letti* or sonatas. Yet homophony was thoroughly modern in serving the text for purposes of its elucidation. It hardly betokens a reactionary tendency in Rossi's music, in the sense of a reversion to older models of composition, from the middle or even early periods of the sixteenth-century madrigal. Rather, it emanated from his partiality to the fashionable *canzonetta*.

In a way, the simpler or seemingly more conservative side of Rossi's repertory was influenced by the *canzonetta*. Rossi was not the only one to yield to its charms, indeed, the *canzonetta* seems to have played a major role

---

[2] On processes of conceptual and stylistic consolidation, see Harrán, 'Cultural Fusions in Jewish Musical Thought of the Later Renaissance', and id., 'Tradition and Innovation in Jewish Music of the Later Renaissance'.

in forging Monteverdi's madrigals.[3] Its unpretentious style could be, and was, considered 'new' when measured by the yardstick of the more involuted madrigal from the 1550s on. Symptomatically, there is a *canzonetta* by Orazio Vecchi, from 1580, in which the poet declares that the *canzonetta*, without complicated rhythms ('black notes'), without dissonance or syncopation, exemplified the style that Orpheus used in Hades and that David used to calm Saul—one could not expect a more eloquent statement of humanistic and Hebraic cultural convergence:

Fa una canzone senza note nere	*Make a song without black notes,*
Se mai bramasti la mia gratia havere;	*If ever you crave to win my favour;*
Falla d'un tuono ch'invita al dormire,	*Make it in a mode that induces sleepiness,*
Dolcemente facendola finire.	*While making it end sweetly.*
Per entro non vi spargere durezze,	*Don't mix in dissonances,*
Chè le mie orecchie non vi sono avezze;	*For my ears are not accustomed to them;*
Falla...	*Make it in a mode...*
Non vi far cifra o segno contra segno,	*Don't write accidentals or counterpoint,*
Sopra ogni cosa quest'è 'l mio disegno:	*For my intention, above all, is the following:*
Falla...	*Make it in a mode...*
Con questo stile il fortunato Orfeo	*With this style the lucky Orpheus*
Proserpina la giù placar poteo;	*Was able to appease Proserpine down below;*
Questo è lo stile che quetar già feo	*This is the style that once assuaged*
Con dolcezza a Saul lo spirto reo![4]	*Saul's evil spirit with its sweetness.*

The simpler manner should be compared with the opposite type, said, in another item from the same collection, to be so unstable that few can sing or dance to it, to lack a firm tonality and a clear texture, and to show fancy, not thought.[5]

Thus the general orientation of Rossi's Italian works, inasmuch as they owe to the *canzonetta* for many of their traits, could be considered 'modern'. The same holds for his 'Songs', which, in their often unassuming homophony, might strike one as stylistically retrogressive. But, given the tendency of later sixteenth-century homophony towards declamation, connecting thereby with *seconda pratica* monody and recitative, the 'Songs' can be and, in their introductory matter, were in fact deemed a 'new music'. Here Rossi might be compared to the leading sixteenth-century Jewish dramatist Leone de' Sommi, author of the first known Hebrew play:[6] both

---

[3] See Ch. 3 and, as mentioned there, Ossi, 'Claudio Monteverdi's *Ordine novo, bello et gustevole*'.

[4] Vecchi, *Canzonette... lib. 2° 4 v.* (1580), 18; for music, see id., *The Four-Voice Canzonettas*, ed. DeFord, ii. 92–3 (my reading of the poetry, and its translation, is slightly different).

[5] 'Fammi una canzonetta capricciosa | Che nullo o pochi la sappian cantare, | E al tuon di quella si possi ballare. | Non ti curar di tuono o d'osservata, | Chè questo è meglio che tu possi fare. | ...Falla come ti dà la fantasia...': Vecchi, *Canzonette... lib. 2° 4 v.* (1580), 4; *The Four-Voice Canzonettas*, ed. DeFord, ii. 62–3.

[6] Sommi, *Tsaḥut bediḥuta dekidushin*, ed. Schirmann.

were innovators, and were so considered, within the Hebrew tradition. Like Rossi and his commentators, so Sommi emphasized the novelty of his achievement, conceiving his play as a combination of new and old ('behold and see the new which I filled with the old'). In Rossi's music the old is the texts, the new is the music composed to them; yet the new becomes the old in its being identified as a continuation of an ancient practice. Thus the old generates the new; and the new, for all its strangeness, refurbishes the old.

2. *Narrowing the 'generic' gap.* Despite its typologic diversity, Rossi's repertory coalesces through certain overall tendencies, deriving, again, from the *canzonetta*. They may be discerned, for one, in the predilection for bipartite or tripartite forms, either with repeats (in instrumental works and some *madrigaletti*) or without them (in madrigals), though even when there are no repeats the material tends clearly to be articulated, as in *canzonette*, into beginning, middle, and final sections; for another, in contrasts in texture and, within instrumental music, in metre, usually from section to section; and, for a third, in the patent simplicity of the material and its unaffected elaboration.

The *canzonetta* seems to provide a springboard for the development, in Rossi's works, of almost all types of musical expression. A tight network of connections emerges, starting, in Opus 1, with the *canzonetta* itself, which derives from the sixteenth-century vocal and instrumental *canzona*; and continuing, to speak of instrumental music, with the *sinfonia*, which, as treated by Rossi, often follows from the *canzonetta* in size, shape, and content. The *canzona*, too, is represented by a few examples in the composer's repertory, but, more importantly, it served as a model, in its reformulation as a *sinfonia*, for several of Rossi's sonatas. His dances (*gagliarda, corrente, brando*) bear resemblance to the *canzonetta* in their almost exclusively two-part form; their unweighted, often homophonic texture; and their outward artlessness. It is symptomatic that the dance suite of the Baroque evolved as a combination of two or more dances preceded by a *sinfonia* or similarly 'abstract' movement (prelude, overture), and it can be assumed that, as far as Rossi's works are concerned, the performers constructed such suites from the various *sinfonie* and dances available in his instrumental collections.[7]

The network spreads farther to embrace the composer's vocal works. His madrigals often seem to be modelled after his *canzonette*, and a direct stylistic and formal link between them can be established, within the *canzonetta* collection proper, in its last two works, which, to all appearances, are madrigals. Rossi never seems to have left the *canzonette* of his *primum opus* that far behind in his madrigals, which oscillate between madrigalesque poetry and its *canzonetta*-like musical treatment. Then, of course, there are the *madrigaletti*, which, in their own way, are, indeed, *canzonette*. As

---

[7] On individually constructed dance suites, see Harrán, 'From Mantua to Vienna'.

incongruous as it may seem, the Hebrew songs, too, derive from the *canzon-etta*, and this in their clarity of texture, their homeliness, and their straight-forward presentation. No. 16 bears an even more tangible relation to the *canzonetta* in its strophic form.

The *canzonetta*-madrigal, if one can call it such, is not restricted to Rossi's vocal collections. Rather, it seems to have been a favourite of many composers from Marenzio to Monteverdi. It introduced a breath of fresh air into the sometimes overly serious madrigal, offering an alternative approach to composition by virtue of its lighter texts, which, only naturally, invited comparably lighter music; the *villanesca* and *villanella* lurk on the sidelines.[8] The *canzonetta*-madrigal reflects a change of outlook in the later Renaissance, away from complication, heaviness, or density.

The *canzonetta*, in short, seems to set the foundation, in concept and practice, for a whole series of developments. They relate to the search, towards the end of the sixteenth century, for a more ingenuous form of musical expression. From this standpoint, Rossi's madrigals and his 'Songs', often thought of as 'conservative', are very much up to date; and his vocal and instrumental works, or, within the vocal ones alone, his Italian and Hebrew works, often thought of as intrinsically different from one another, are not so different after all. In the background stands the *canzonetta*: in penetrating the separate genres it acted to reduce the formal and stylistic distance between them.

3. *Broadening the audience.* Though the 'Songs', with their Hebrew texts, were intended for 'internal consumption', mainly as part of the Jewish prayer services, Rossi seems to have reached out, in their composition, to a broader audience. His was an attempt, to all appearances, to integrate his Jewish sacred works into the larger tradition of sacred music practised by Christians. The 'Songs' were shaped to appeal to their tastes; as much may be inferred from comments in the introduction, particularly those concerning the music customarily heard in the synagogue. Modena and, vicariously, Rossi had a low opinion of its artistic qualities: this was not the glorious music of ancient times, not even its faint echo. Foreign wanderings along with the trials and tribulations of survival made the Jews, so we were told, forget whatever they knew of it.[9] What evolved was—as it often appeared to the non-Jews—a sing-song rendition of the holy texts, less music than textual intonation. It became an object of parody, as much in music (the madrigal comedies, for example, of Orazio Vecchi and Adriano Banchieri) as in literature (the travel journals, for example, of Michel de Montaigne and Thomas Coryate).

---

[8] See DeFord, 'Musical Relationships between the Italian Madrigal and Light Genres in the Sixteenth Century'; Assenza, *Giovan Ferretti tra canzonetta e madrigale*; and, of course, the works themselves, e.g. Lasso's *villanelle*, in *Orlando di Lasso et alii*, ed. Cardamone.

[9] Modena's foreword, poem 3 (twice), and *responsum*.

Modena hoped, via Rossi's music, to remedy the situation. 'No more will bitter words about the Hebrew people be uttered, by its detractors, in a voice of scorn. They will see that full understanding is just as much its portion as theirs.'[10] What irked the detractors was not only the content of traditional chant but also the manner of its performance, which Modena bluntly described, after earlier examples from the Hebrew literature with parallels in patristic and later Christian writings, as a 'braying of asses'.[11] New principles were to be instituted for the music of the Jews, art music for one, a smooth and pleasant performance for another. Only then would Jewish music be restored to its ancient splendour and, as such, elicit the wonder of Christians.

Why this concern with the non-Jewish reaction? To minimize criticism: the point was to show that, in matters of music, as in other sciences, the Jews were, after all, not as boorish as usually depicted.

Duke Vincenzo was accustomed to visit one of the larger synagogues during Carnival, and the Jewish community honoured him by preparing a play, with musical interludes, and serving refreshments.[12] But the synagogues in Mantua and elsewhere attracted the curious on other occasions. Modena wrote, of his years in Venice, that when he delivered sermons, 'many esteemed friars, priests, and noblemen came to listen'; in 1629, for example, he preached in a Sephardi synagogue to an audience that included 'the brother of the king of France, various French noblemen, and five eminent Christian preachers'. Modena appears to have risen to the occasion ('God put such learned words into my mouth that all were very pleased, including many other Christians who were present').[13]

It was important to impress the audience with learning, but above all to demonstrate the rhetorical skills essential to good style and good presentation. Like Modena, so Rossi, in preparing his music for the synagogue, might have thought of how it would strike Christians. His intention was ostensibly to awaken the duke's and other visitors' admiration with his well-constructed, pleasant-sounding, and properly performed 'Songs'. He seems, in his sacred music, to have envisioned a mixed audience of Jewish habitués and, on occasion, inquisitive Christians. His motives, then, were twofold: the Jews needed to be won over to the idea of polyphony after the Christian model; the Christians needed to be shown that Jewish art music was no less advanced and its performance no less refined than their own. There would be no reason, then, to ridicule the Jews for musical ineptitude.

---

[10] Poem 3.

[11] *Responsum*. For Christian examples, see references in Harrán, *In Defence of Music*, 50–1.

[12] These visits began in 1588. Cf. Simonsohn, *History of the Jews in the Duchy of Mantua*, 662–3, also 666–7 n.

[13] Modena, *Ḥayei yehuda*, tr. Cohen, 96, 131; also 117 (for Christians who attended the festivities marking the completion of studying a certain Talmudic tractate), 128 (for 'Christian friars' present at a sermon Modena preached in Mantua, 1623).

The general policy, ever since the Counter Reformation, was, as stressed in earlier chapters, to separate Jews from Christians. Concrete measures were taken to ensure its implementation, among them, in Mantua, the institution of the ghetto under Duke Francesco. The consequence was a new emphasis on internal affairs: the Jews turned inward, socially, economically, spiritually. It was precisely in those years of increasing isolation that Rossi prepared his collection of 'Songs', in which he seemed to be working, musically, towards a contrary goal: to demolish the physical barriers between Jews and Christians. His music was not the traditional synagogue chant that characterized the Jews as 'different', hence alien, but a new music that, in its counterpoint, its sonorities, drew the Jews out of their own and into a non-Jewish orbit, hence revealed them as 'compatible' with their neighbours.

Separation from the outside usually leads to its reinforcement, as a countermeasure, from the inside. In the Mantuan ghetto, the Jews, after 1612, consolidated as a social and religious entity; though protected from external dangers by walls, they sought further protection by immuring themselves in their own tradition. Part of this tradition was synagogue chant, distinct from all other forms of sacred music, hence intrinsically 'Jewish' in its physiognomy. Rossi rebelled against traditional chant as the only acceptable form of Jewish liturgical music. In this he seems to break down the pat scheme, just outlined, whereby confinement leads to further estrangement. The 'Songs' are not the consequence of a closing-in of the Jewish people, in the sense that by being sung to Hebrew words and integrated into specifically Jewish prayer services they, too, close in upon themselves; rather, if anything, in their style and structure they contravene the process of reclusion. They were written with a mind to returning the Jews, musically, to the larger world. The problem with traditional chant was that it maintained social and religious barriers. Rossi sought to remove them: the keynote of his 'Songs' is harmony.

4. *Music as harmony.* The notion that music stands above, and can reconcile, cultural discrepancies is an old one; Rossi and his commentators seem to build on it to vindicate the 'Songs'. It rests on the equation of music with harmony.[14] Were it not for the differences in language and the concomitant differences in accommodating notes to words, the 'Songs', in Hebrew, could be compared, stylistically, to, say, the Mantuan composer Gastoldi's Latin psalms.[15] Both exhibit a preference for homophony and choral declamation; for semibreves and minims as their basic rhythmic units, with crotchets sparsely used for animation. Thus different languages and liturgies are neutralized by musical resemblances.

---

[14] On the implications of this equation for 16th-c. musical thought, see Harrán, *In Search of Harmony.*

[15] See e.g. Gastoldi, *Salmi per tutto l'anno a cinque voci* (1673); and, in general, Nagan, 'Giovanni Giacomo Gastoldi's Liturgical Compositions'.

The common denominator between Rossi's works and those, similarly composed, of his Christian contemporaries is their basic realization as *falsobordone*. Simple choral settings in *falsobordone* for the Church have been treated as 'a means of fulfilling Tridentine dictates about verbal intelligibility'.[16] Jewish music was also concerned with 'verbal intelligibility', both in the Italian Jewish traditional chant, with its modestly embellished readings of the sacred texts, and in Rossi's 'Songs', with their textures of such transparency as to permit every word to be distinctly heard and understood.[17] The 'Songs' were portrayed, in the introductory matter, as exhibiting *yaḥas* and *'erekh*, 'relation' and 'regulation'.

A third term comes into play, *haskama*, or 'agreement'. Judah Moscato employed it in his sermon on 'music', which he defines as 'harmony'.[18] The *falsobordone*, in its diverse Christian and Jewish applications, would seem to correspond to what Moscato meant by *yaḥasim niguniyim*, or 'musical harmony': agreement between different voices, in their composition, so as to be consonant; agreement between the music and the words, in their accommodation, so as to be accentually and syntactically concordant.

Moscato squeezed the word *harmony* for its full philosophical and theosophical implications: order, proportion, symmetry, consonance. He treats cosmological and anthropomorphic notions of harmony; he discourses on 'divine harmony', whose essence is God in His diverse emanations. Man relates to God, in the Judeo-Christian tradition, through the premisses of the biblical verse 'God fashioned man after His own image'.[19] God is perfect harmony, represented by the octave, or 2: 1. In Hebrew, the sign for God is the letter *yud*, whose numerological value is ten, for the ten *sefirot*, though ten are one. When calculated for its three letters, *yud* equals twenty, or, divided by ten, two; it is written as a double *yud*, i.e. two half circles, which, when joined, form a whole, or again 2: 1. The simpler the harmonies, the closer their approximation to empyreal concord.

What Moscato implied was a *falsobordone*, in which the intervals of the octave, unison, fifth, fourth, and third worked together to produce musical consonance. Yet it is a pale reflection of divine consonance, which, according to Moscato, was currently absent from the world. Its recreation must await the coming of the Messiah: then the world will resound in perfect harmony, as in the period before the Fall.

Messianic notions of harmony have already been detected in the introductory matter to Rossi's 'Songs'. The same 'Songs' were described there as inaugurating a new era, when together men 'will sing for joy, for they will

[16] See Roche, *North Italian Church Music in the Age of Monteverdi*, 36–7; and further on the Renaissance and Baroque *falsobordone*, Bradshaw, *The Falsobordone*.

[17] On the *falsobordone* as a form of choral monody, see Bettley, 'North Italian *Falsobordone* and its Relevance to the Early *Stile recitativo*'.

[18] For Hebrew, see Adler (ed.), *Hebrew Writings Concerning Music in Manuscripts and Printed Books from Geonic Times up to 1800*, 221–39, esp. 224.

[19] Gen. 1: 26–7.

see, eye to eye, the return of the Lord to Zion, in all haste, amen!'[20] In their texts, the 'Songs' emphasize the quintessential attributes of God, His unity, His consonance. 'One is He and no unity is like His unity...there is no end to His Oneness' (no. 28); 'from His place may He turn to His people who proclaim the unity of His name in the evening and in the morning, regularly, every day; twice out of love, while saying: "Hear Israel, the Lord is our God, the Lord is One"' (no. 7);[21] and 'He is One and there is no second to be compared to Him in likeness' (no. 29). The texts speak of His greatness and glory,[22] His mysteriousness,[23] and His omniscience. 'He watches and knows our secrets; He beholds the end of a thing at its origin'.[24]

The 'Songs' thus enter different worlds of harmonic agreement, from music on the lowest level of vocal sound production to the consummate proportions, on the highest, of the cosmos and heavens. They fall within the traditional categories of Boethian harmonic theory, as known from its three levels of musical relation (*instrumentalis*, *humana*, and *mundana*). The interpretation of the 'Songs' can be conducted from different vantage points, all of them combining to form a dense web of human, psychic-corporeal, and spiritual correspondences. These are, conceptually, what the 'Songs' are about.

5. *Song as a category above style or genre.* The tendency to draw Rossi's 'Songs' into wider circles of contextual significance, all of them representing different degrees of 'harmony', is paralleled in the tendency to view them as one among several possible 'harmonies' for Jewish sacred music. In the prefatory commentary to them, an attempt was made to define the essence of sacred song as inherent not in its form or style, but in its motivation and presentation. We read there that the 'Songs' were written for eulogizing God and, to this end, were to be delivered joyfully.

Thus conceived, Jewish sacred music allows various realizations. Indeed, in its later development, it branched out in diverse directions, all of them congruent, stylistically, with period conventions. One finds Hebrew cantatas from the seventeenth and eighteenth centuries or Hebrew sacred services or psalms from the nineteenth and twentieth written according to the dictates of one or another compositional practice. Though they differ in their styles, they unite in the reverential treatment of the texts, imposing on the singers the obligation, concomitantly, of their reverential delivery.

It follows that Song, with a capital S, is a broader category of Hebrew music than the 'Songs'. Rossi's Hebrew songs are manifestations of *musika*, or Jewish art music, within the frame of which any number of stylistic and

---

[20] End of Modena's foreword.

[21] The Trisagion was not set by Rossi, rather it was intoned by the congregation.

[22] Cf. Sgs: variously within nos. 1/6 (Kaddish), 7 (Kedusha), 13 (Ps. 8), 17 (Ps. 126), 19 (Isa. 35), 24 (Ps. 29), 28 ('Yigdal'), 29 ('Adon 'olam').

[23] Sgs: within no. 28 ('Yigdal'; viz. 'He is hidden...').

[24] Sgs: within no. 28 ('Yigdal').

idiomatic realizations are feasible. We know this from his non-Jewish works. Where Rossi's detractors, real or merely anticipated, would have been stubbornly single-minded in their conceptions of what should be performed in the synagogue, Rossi, through his mentor Modena, seems to have recognized the possibility of different varieties of music, hence was amenable to innovation.

Jewish music, as Song, ranks as a genus inclusive of varying species. Rossi and his spokesman Modena deny absolute value to traditional synagogue chant, treating it as relative to a certain cultural-historical framework, namely, the period of Jewish wanderings in the Diaspora. Yet in longing for a renewal of ancient Hebrew culture, and in setting their sights on a messianic era, they acknowledge other historical kinds of song that range on an extended time scale from songs of old to new songs and songs to come. Thus synagogue chant is divested of its seemingly universal validity, or as much as was ascribed to it by rabbinical custom, to become one among several expressions of Jewish melos. The polyphonic song that, via the 'Songs of Solomon', supplemented it—notice that I did not say 'replaced it', for Rossi's intention was not to reform, but to expand the synagogue repertory—is not regarded, in the commentary, as the ultimate song. Though it may be referred or compared to ancient music in its learning, i.e. its compositional literacy and artistic refinement, it does not mark the end of a development. Rather it is designated a 'beginning', hence by definition cannot be an end.

6.   *Hebrew music as the original music.*   The links between present and past widen still further with the conception of Hebrew music, in its practice by the Levites, as the oldest form of Song. It combined voices and instruments in smaller and greater numbers; it thus established the basic categories of *zimra defuma* and *zimra demana*, or vocal and instrumental music, as primordial forms of musical expression, which eventually narrowed, in the synagogue, to *zimra defuma*. More importantly, this music, so rich in its practice, caught the eye and ear of the Gentiles, or so the story goes, and they imitated it. In time, Hebrew music ceased, and what remained was incorporated into their works. Moscato traced the beginnings of philosophy and other sciences to the Hebrews, claiming that all the great thinkers of classical times were, intellectually, disciples of the ancient prophets; as for music, he traced its beginnings not to Pythagoras, but to Jubal. The perfect musician he identified not with Orpheus, but with Moses; and the perfect music he identified not with the New Testament, but with the Old. The erstwhile greatness of the Jews was tarnished by their sad history. It had to be renewed by assiduous scholarly and artistic efforts.

The glorification of the Ancient Temple, in Hebrew and rabbinical writings, is parallel, in the Christian Renaissance, to the glorification of Graeco-Roman antiquity. Both examples serve as a source of pride in one's heritage and as a stimulus to its renewal. Yet in the Jewish writings, particularly the medieval ones, the reference to the Ancient Temple performed another function: to consolidate the Jewish people in an era of dispersion. Despite their dissemination over the globe, the Jews could look back to an illustrious early history, where they were a single people united by a single purpose, the worship of God and the observance of His laws. The thought that there was once a glorious past acted to alleviate the hardships of the present. So did the thought that the redemption of the Jewish people was imminent. 'Return us to You, God, and we shall return; renew our days as of old' (Lamentations 5: 21).

Rossi was described, in the introductory matter to his 'Songs', as reviving ancient music and setting it at the cornerstone of a new Jewish tradition. His music outwardly appears to follow the modes and styles of musical expression cultivated by Christians. Yet the same modes and styles were, we are reminded, originally those of the Hebrews. In recovering them Rossi not only underscores basic unities in the Judeo-Christian heritage, but furnishes the premisses for a rich and varied conception of music, both Jewish and non-Jewish, in the future. His story expands its time to become a parable for renewal, by ideational association with a national, religious, or cultural patrimony, within the Western European art music tradition at large.

APPENDIX
Works

I. COLLECTIONS

Volume references (in roman numerals) are to the *Complete Works* edition (see Bibliography). For each collection, as summarized below, the first number indicates the item, the second (after the virgule) its equivalent in the Individual Listing.

Secular Italian

1589   *Canzonette* 3 v. (Cte)   vi
1/147, 2/56, 3/142, 4/10, 5/133, 6/113, 7/111, 8/145, 9/19, 10/114, 11/37, 12/78, 13/59, 14/64, 15/30, 16/3, 17/112, 18/71, 19/116

1600   Madrigals 5 v., Bk 1 (1603^2, 1607^3, 1612^4, 1618^5) (Bk 1)   i
1/105, 2/43, 3/121, 4/20, 5/31, 6/83, 7/14, 8/86, 9/110, 10/34, 11/119, 12/87, 13/28, 14/12, 15/138, 16/132, 17/94, 18/84, 19/7

1602   Madrigals 5 v., Bk 2 (1605^2, 1610^3) (Bk 2)   ii
1/49, 2/117, 3/9, 4/54, 5/97, 6/123, 7/125, 8/139, 9/68, 10/36, 11/18, 12/27, 13/41, 14/81, 15/100, 16/38, 17/82, 18/4, 19/91

1603   Madrigals 5 v., Bk 3 (1620^2) (Bk 3)   iii
1/60, 2/128, 3/8, 4/143, 5/67, 6/149, 7/40, 8/63, 9/50, 10/22, 11/120, 12/115, 13/79, 14/108

1610   Madrigals 5 v., Bk 4 (1613^2) (Bk 4)   iv
1/46, 2/25, 3/39, 4/136, 5/99, 6/61, 7/72, 8/135, 9/90, 10/103, 11/62, 12/44, 13/124, 14/106, 15/80, 16/66, 17/26, 18/23, 19/73

1614   Madrigals 4 v. (M4)   vii
1/101, 2/89, 3/129, 4/24, 5/88, 6/137, 7/57, 8/5, 9/75, 10/85, 11/140, 12/70, 13/35, 14/29, 15/1, 16/42, 17/11

1622   Madrigals 5 v., Bk 5 (Bk 5)   v
1/33, 2/77, 3/96, 4/74, 5/52, 6/98, 7/51, 8/118, 9/92, 10/17, 11/130, 12/65, 13/45, 14/127, 15/13, 16/107, 17/32, 18/15, 19/47

1628   *Madrigaletti* 2–3 v. (Mti)   viii
1/131, 2/109, 3/148, 4/104, 5/55, 6/76, 7/122, 8/6, 9/69, 10/2, 11/146, 12/141, 13/53, 14/93, 15/144, 16/134, 17/48, 18/150

Instrumental

1607	*Sinfonie, gagliarde*, etc., 3–5 v., Bk 1 (S1)	ix
	1/196, 2/197, 3/198, 4/199, 5/200, 6/201, 7/202, 8/203,	
	9/204, 10/205, 11/206, 12/207, 13/208, 14/209, 15/210,	
	16/247, 17/248, 18/189, 19/190, 20/279, 21/253, 22/254,	
	23/192, 24/255, 25/193, 26/194, 27/151	
1608	*Sinfonie, gagliarde*, etc., 3–5 v., Bk 2 (S2)	x
	1/211, 2/212, 3/213, 4/214, 5/215, 6/216, 7/217, 8/218,	
	9/219, 10/220, 11/221, 12/222, 13/223, 14/224, 15/225,	
	16/226, 17/227, 18/228, 19/229, 20/230, 21/231, 22/249,	
	23/250, 24/191, 25/251, 26/252, 27/256, 28/257, 29/258,	
	30/259, 31/260, 32/195, 33/157, 34/158, 35/159	
1613	*Sonate, sinfonie, gagliarde*, etc., 3 v., Bk 3 (16??[2], 1623[3], 1638[4])	xi
	(S3)	
	1/261, 2/262, 3/263, 4/264, 5/265, 6/266, 7/232, 8/233,	
	9/234, 10/235, 11/236, 12/237, 13/238, 14/239, 15/240,	
	16/173, 17/174, 18/175, 19/176, 20/177, 21/178, 22/179,	
	23/180, 24/152, 25/153, 26/154, 27/160, 28/161, 29/162,	
	30/163, 31/164, 32/165, 33/166	
1622	*Sonate, sinfonie, gagliarde*, etc., 3 v., Bk 4 (1642[2]) (S4)	xii
	1/267, 2/268, 3/269, 4/270, 5/271, 6/272, 7/273, 8/274,	
	9/275, 10/276, 11/277, 12/278, 13/241, 14/242, 15/243,	
	16/244, 17/245, 18/246, 19/181, 20/182, 21/183, 22/184,	
	23/185, 24/186, 25/187, 26/171, 27/188, 28/155, 29/156,	
	30/280	

Sacred Hebrew

1622/3	'The Songs of Solomon' (*Hashirim asher lishlomo*) 3–8 v. (Sgs)	xiii
	1/312, 2/304, 3/283, 4/299, 5/296, 6/288, 7/294, 8/289,	
	9/297, 10/282, 11/291, 12/305, 13/295, 14/301, 15/293,	
	16/313, 17/307, 18/309, 19/310, 20/306, 21/308, 22/303,	
	23/284, 24/300, 25/285, 26/287, 27/286, 28/311, 29/281,	
	30/290, 31/292, 32/302, 33/298	

II. INDIVIDUAL LISTING

Secular Works in Italian (150)

Text incipit (voices)[1]	Poet	Type (lines)[2]	Volume/no.

[1] The number of voices is exclusive of *basso seguente* parts.
[2] Abbreviations: B, *ballata*; B^to, *balletto*; B-M, *ballata*-madrigal; C, *canzone*; C^ta, *canzonetta*; C-M, *canzone*-madrigal; M, *madrigal*; S, *sonnet*. In strophic works, the number of lines is multiplied by the number of stanzas (e.g. 4 × 4).

1	Ah dolente partita (*4 v.*)	Guarini	M (8)	vii. 15
2	Ahi, ben ti veggio, ingrata (*2 v./Bc*)		M (9)	viii. 10
3	Ahi chi mi tien il core? (*3 v.*)		C^ta (4 × 4)	vi. 16
4	Ahi m'è forz'il partire (*5 v.*)		M (8)	ii. 18
5	Ahi, tu parti, o mia luce (*4 v.*)		M (6)	vii. 8
6	Alma de l'alma mia (*2 v./Bc*)		M (8)	viii. 8
7	Al partir del mio sole (*6 v.*)	Guarini	B-M (9)	i. 19
8	Amarilli crudele (*5 v.*)		C-M (9)	iii. 3
9	Amarillide mia (*5 v.*)	Rinuccini	M (9)	ii. 3
10	Amor, fa' quanto vuoi (*3 v.*)		C (4 × 3)	vi. 4
11	Amor, se pur degg'io (*8 v.*)		M (8)	vii. 17
12	Anima del cor mio (*5 v.; 1 v./chit.*)		M (8)	i. 14
13	Ardo, ma non ardisco (*5 v.*)	Marino	S (8)	v. 15
14	Arsi un temp'ed amai (*5 v.*)	Guarini	M (9)	i. 7
15	Arsi un tempo [ed amai] (*5 v.*)	—	—	v. 18
16	Asciuga i pianti (*text only*)	Chiabrera	M (14)	viii. app. 2: 4
17	Aura che per lo Ciel (*5 v.*) *2nd pt.*: Vanne, nuntia cortese	Marino	S (8 + 6)	v. 10
18	Ben può fortuna aversa (*5 v.*)		B-M (9)	ii. 11
	Canzon de' baci (in eight parts): see *O baci aventurosi*			
19	Cercai fuggir Amore (*3 v.*)		C^ta (4 × 4)	vi. 9
20	Che non fai, che non pensi (*5 v.*)	Rinaldi	M (7)	i. 4
21	Chi negherà corona (*text only*)	Chiabrera	B (10)	viii. app. 2: 2
22	Ch'io mora? oimè, ch'io mora? (*5 v.*)	Marino	B (11)	iii. 10
23	Clori mia, Clori bella (*5 v.*)		M (7)	iv. 18
24	Com'è dolc'il gioire (*4 v.*) *2nd pt.*: Sentir che la tua donna	Guarini	M (7 + 10)	vii. 4
25	Come il ferir sia poco (*5 v.*)	Marino	B (9)	iv. 2
26	Con la luce e col canto (*5 v.*)		M (9)	iv. 17
27	Con la sua forz'in mar (*5 v.*) *2nd pt.*: Fortunate campagne		M (8 + 6)	ii. 12
28	Cor mio, deh non languire (*5 v.; 1 v./chit.*)	Guarini	M (8)	i. 13
29	Cor mio, mentr'io vi miro (*4 v.*)	Guarini	C-M (8)	vii. 14
30	Correte, Amanti (*3 v.*)		C^ta (4 × 4)	vi. 15

	Text incipit (voices)	Poet	Type (lines)	Volume/no.
31	Deh com'invan chiedete (*5 v.*)	Guarini	M (9)	i. 5
	Deh taci, o lingua sciocca:			
	8th pt. of O *baci aventurosi*			
32	De la vaga mia Cintia (*5 v.*)	Marino	S (8)	v. 17
33	Di marmo siete voi (*5 v.*)	Marino	M (8)	v. 1
34	Dirmi che più non ardo? (*5 v.*)	Rinaldi	M (9)	i. 10
35	Dolcemente dormiva (*4 v.*)	Tasso	C-M (10)	vii. 13
36	Dolcissimo sospiro (*5 v.*)	Rinuccini	B-M (9)	ii. 10
	Dolori amari e soli:			
	2nd pt. of *Silvia, s'al suon*			
37	Donna, il vostro bel viso (*3 v.*)		C^{ta} (4 × 4)	vi. 11
	Donna priva di fè:			
	3rd pt. of *Gradita libertà*			
38	Dove, misero, mai (*5 v.*)	Chiabrera	M (6)	ii. 16
39	Dovrò dunque morire (*5 v.*)	Rinuccini	M (7)	iv. 3
40	Ecco l'hora, ecco ch'io (*5 v.*)	Marino	C (9)	iii. 7
41	E così pur languendo (*5 v.*)	Guarini	B-M (9)	ii. 13
42	Ed è pur ver ch'io parta (*4 v.*)		M (8)	vii. 16
43	Felice chi vi mira (*5 v.*)	Guarini	M (8)	i. 2
	Felicissimo dì:			
	2nd pt. of *Gradita libertà*			
44	Feritevi, ferite (*5 v.*)	Marino	B (9)	iv. 12
45	Ferma il piè (*5 v.*)	Marino	S (8)	v. 13
46	Filli, ai baci m'inviti (*5 v.*)	Marino	S (8 + 6)	iv. 1
	2nd pt.: Temi non forse			
47	Filli, ai baci m'inviti (*8 v.*)	—	—	v. 19
	2nd pt.: Temi non forse			
48	Fillide vuol ch'io viva (*3 v./Bc*)			viii. 17
49	Filli, mirando il cielo (*5 v.*)	Rinuccini	B-M (11)	ii. 1
	Fortunate campagne:			
	2nd pt. of *Con la sua forz'in mar*			
50	Fortunato augellino (*5 v.*)	Rinuccini	C (11)	iii. 9
51	Fuggi, fuggi, o mio core (*5 v.*)	Marino	M (8)	v. 7
52	Fuggì quel disleale (*5 v.*)	Marino	M (9)	v. 5
	Già del volto in sè stesso:			
	2nd pt. of *Ornasti, il veggio*			
53	Gradita libertà (*2 v./Bc + rit. 3 v.*)		C^{ta} (10 × 3)	viii. 13
	2nd pt.: Felicissimo dì			
	3rd pt.: Donna priva di fè			
54	Hor che lunge da voi (*5 v.*)	Chiabrera	M (8)	ii. 4
	Hor tepid'aura e leve:			
	4th pt. of *O baci aventurosi*			
55	Ho sì nell'alma impresso (*2 v./Bc*)		M (7)	viii. 5
56	I bei ligustri e rose (*3 v.*)		C^{ta} (4 × 4)	vi. 2
57	In dolci lacci (*4 v.*)		M (6)	vii. 7

Text incipit (voices)	Poet	Type (lines)	Volume/no.
58 In qual alpe, in qual selva (*text only*)	Chiabrera	B (9)	viii. app. 2: 3
59 Io mi sento morire (*3 v.*)		C^{ta} (4 × 3)	vi. 13
60 Io moro, ecco ch'io moro! (*5 v.*)	Marino	M (7)	iii. 1
Io non so se le parti:			
2nd pt. of *Vago augelletto*			
61 Io parlai, Filli tacque (*5 v.*)	Rinaldi	M (8)	iv. 6
62 Io parto, amati lumi (*5 v.*)	Rinuccini	C^{ta} (6)	iv. 11
63 Io rido, io rido, amanti (*5 v.*)	Marino	M (8)	iii. 8
64 L'alma vostra beltade (*3 v.*)		C^{ta} (4 × 4)	vi. 14
L'asciutto è caro al core:			
5th pt. of *O baci aventurosi*			
65 Lidia, i' ti veggio pur (*5 v.*)	Marino	S (8)	v. 12
66 Lidia, ti lasso (ahi lasso!) (*5 v.*)	Marino	M (10)	iv. 16
67 Lieve il morir mi fia (*5 v.*)	Marino	B (8)	iii. 5
68 Lumi miei, cari lumi (*5 v.*)	Guarini	M (11)	ii. 9
69 Messaggier di speranza (*2 v./Bc*)	Chiabrera	B (10)	viii. 9
70 Mia vita, s'egli è vero (*4 v.*)		M (8)	vii. 12
71 Mirate che mi fa (*3 v.*)		C^{ta} (4)	vi. 18
Miro, rimiro ed ardo:			
6th pt. of *O baci aventurosi*			
72 Mori, mi dici (*5 v.*)	Marino	M (8)	iv. 7
73 Movetevi a pietà (*6 v.*)		M (6)	iv. 19
74 Ne le guancie di rose (*5 v.*)		M (10)	v. 4
75 Nel tuo bel sen si strugge (*4 v.*)		M (11)	vii. 9
76 Non è quest'il ben mio? (*2 v./Bc*)		M (7)	viii. 6
77 Non ti bastava (*5 v.*)	Gatti	M (9)	v. 2
78 Non voglio più servire (*3 v.*)		C^{ta} (5 × 4)	vi. 12
79 O baci aventurosi ('Canzon de'	Marino	C (14 × 7 + 4)	iii. 13
baci'; *5 v.*)			
2nd pt.: Una bocc'homicida			
3rd pt.: Tranquilla guerra e cara			
4th pt.: Hor tepid'aura e leve			
5th pt.: L'asciutto è caro al core			
6th pt.: Miro, rimiro ed ardo			
7th pt.: Vinta all'hor dal diletto			
8th pt.: Deh taci, o lingua sciocca			
80 Occhi miei, se quel Sole (*5 v.*)		M (7)	iv. 15
81 Occhi, quella pietà (*5 v.*)	Celiano	M (11)	ii. 14
82 Occhi, voi sospirate (*5 v.*)	Chiabrera	C (7)	ii. 17
83 O com'è gran martire (*5 v.*)	Guarini	M (10)	i. 6
84 O dolc'[e] anima mia (*6 v.*)	Guarini	M (12)	i. 18
85 O dolcezz'amarissime (*4 v.*)	Guarini	M (12+10+6)	vii. 10
2nd pt.: Qui pur vedroll'al suon			
3rd pt.: O lungamente sospirato			
86 O donna troppo cruda (*5 v.*)	Guarini	M (7)	i. 8

Text incipit (voices)	Poet	Type (lines)	Volume/no.
87 Ohimè, se tanto amate (*5 v.; 1 v./chit.*)	Guarini	M (8)	i. 12
O lungamente sospirato:			
3rd pt. of *O dolcezz'amarissime*			
88 O Mirtillo, Mirtillo (*4 v.*)	Guarini	M (13)	vii. 5
Ond'ei, di morte:			
2nd pt. of *Rimanti in pace*			
89 O quante volt'invan (*4 v.*)		C-M (7)	vii. 2
90 Ornasti, il veggio (*5 v.*)	Marino	S (8 + 6)	iv. 9
2nd pt.: Già del volto in sè stesso			
91 O tu che vinci l'alba (*8 v.*)	Rinaldi	C (9)	ii. 19
92 Pallidetto mio sole (*5 v.*)	Marino	M (10)	v. 9
93 Pargoletta che non sai (*2 v./Bc*)		C^{ta} (9 × 5)	viii. 14
2nd pt.: Non è vero?			
3rd pt.: Non lo senti?			
4th pt.: Non t'intendo?			
5th pt.: Ahi che cieca e sorda sei			
94 Parlo, misero, o taccio? (*5 v.; 1 v./chit.*)	Guarini	M (9)	i. 17
95 Partirò da te (*1 v./[Bc]*)		C^{ta} (10)	viii. app. 1
Arrangement of no. 231			
96 Parto da te (*5 v.*)		M (9)	v. 3
97 Perchè fuggirmi, ahi lasso (*5 v.*)	Guarini	M (7)	ii. 5
98 Per far nova rapina (*5 v.*)	Marino	M (7)	v. 6
99 Perla che 'l mar produce (*5 v.*)	Chiabrera	C^{ta} (12)	iv. 5
100 Per non mi dir ch'io moia (*5 v.*)	Rinaldi	C-M (9)	ii. 15
101 Piangete, occhi miei lassi (*4 v.*)		M (7)	vii. 1
102 Pingono in varii canti (*text only*)	Chiabrera	C^{ta} (6 × 4)	viii. app. 2: 1
103 Poichè 'mori' dicesti (*5 v.*)	Marino	M (8)	iv. 10
104 Poichè 'mori' dicesti (*2 v./Bc*)	—	—	viii. 4
105 Pur venisti, cor mio (*5 v.*)	Guarini	M (7)	i. 1
106 Queste lagrime amare (*5 v.*)		M (12)	iv. 14
Qui pur vedroll'al suon:			
2nd pt. of *O dolcezz'amarissime*			
107 Qui rise, o Tirsi (*5 v.*)	Marino	S (8)	v. 16
108 Riede la primavera (*6 v.*)	Marino	M (10)	iii. 14
109 Riede la Primavera (*2 v./Bc*)	—	—	viii. 2
110 Rimanti in pace (*5 v.*)	Celiano	S (8 + 6)	i. 9
2nd pt.: Ond'ei, di morte			
111 Rose, gigli e viole (*3 v.*)		C^{ta} (4 × 4)	vi. 7
112 Scherzan intorno (*3 v.*)		C^{ta} (3 × 4)	vi. 17
113 Se gl'amorosi sguardi (*3 v.*)		C^{ta} (5 × 4)	vi. 6
114 Seguit'Amor (*3 v.*)		C^{ta} (3 × 4)	vi. 10
115 Se la doglia e 'l martire (*5 v.*)	Marino	M (9)	iii. 12
116 Se 'l Leoncorno corre (*3 v.*)		C^{ta} (4)	vi. 19
Sentir che la tua donna:			
2nd pt. of *Com'è dolc'il gioire*			
117 Sfogava con le stelle (*5 v.*)	Rinuccini	M (14)	ii. 2

Text incipit (voices)	Poet	Type (lines)	Volume/no.
118 Sì ch'io t'amai, crudele (5 v.)		M (11)	v. 8
119 Silvia, s'al suon (5 v.)		M (10 + 5)	i. 11
2nd pt.: Dolori amari e soli			
120 S'in me potesse morte (5 v.)		M (7)	iii. 11
121 S'io miro in te, m'uccidi (5 v.)	Rinaldi	M (8)	i. 3
122 S'io paleso il mio foco (2 v./Bc)		M (9)	viii. 7
123 Soave libertate (5 v.)	Chiabrera	C^{ta} (14)	ii. 6
124 Soavissimi baci (5 v.)	Marino	M (10)	iv. 13
Sorge più vaga in Ciel:			
2nd pt. of Zeffiro torna			
125 Spasmo s'io non ti veggio (5 v.)	Rinaldi	M (9)	ii. 7
126 Spazziam pronte (3 v. + rit. 3 v.)	Andreini	B^{to} (4 × 4)	viii. app. 3: 5
127 Tace la notte (5 v.)	Marino	S (8)	v. 14
128 Taci, bocca, deh taci (5 v.)	Marino	B (9)	iii. 2
129 Tanto è 'l martir d'amore (4 v.)	Stigliani	M (10)	vii. 3
130 Temer, Donna, non dei (5 v.)	Marino	M (8)	v. 11
131 Temer, Donna, non dei (2 v./Bc)	—	—	viii. 1
Temi non forse:			
2nd pt. of Filli, ai baci m'inviti			
132 Tirsi mio, caro Tirsi (5 v.; 1 v./chit.)	Guarini	M (12)	i. 16
133 Torna dolce, il mio amore (3 v.)		C^{ta} (5 × 4)	vi. 5
134 Tra mill'e mille belle (3 v./Bc)		M (9)	viii. 16
Tranquilla guerra e cara:			
3rd pt. of O baci aventurosi			
135 Troppo ben può (5 v.)	Guarini	B (11)	iv. 8
136 Tu parti, ahi lasso (5 v.)	Marino	M (9)	iv. 4
137 Tu parti a pena giunto (4 v.)	Guarini	M (7)	vii. 6
138 Udite, lacrimosi (5 v.; 1 v./chit.)	Guarini	M (13)	i. 15
Una bocc'homicida:			
2nd pt. of O baci aventurosi			
139 Un sguardo, un sguardo no (5 v.)	Chiabrera	C (7)	ii. 8
140 Vaghe luci amorose (4 v.)		M (9)	vii. 11
141 Vago Augelletto (2 v./Bc)	Petrarch	S (8 + 6)	viii. 12
2nd pt.: Io non so se le parti			
Vanne, nuntia cortese:			
2nd pt. of Aura che per lo Ciel			
142 Vattene pur da me (3 v.)		C^{ta} (4 × 4)	vi. 3
143 Vedrò 'l mio sol (5 v.)	A. Guarini	B (10)	iii. 4
Vinta all'hor dal diletto:			
7th pt. of O baci aventurosi			
144 Vo' fuggir lontan da te (2 v./Bc + rit. 3 v.)		C^{ta} (8 × 4)	viii. 15
145 Voi che seguite (3 v.)		C^{ta} (3 × 3)	vi. 8
146 Voi dite ch'io son giaccio (2 v./Bc)		M (7)	viii. 11
147 Voi due terrestri numi (3 v.)		C^{ta} (4 × 4)	vi. 1
148 Volò ne' tuoi begl'occhi (2 v./Bc)	Marino	M (10)	viii. 3

Text incipit (voices)	Poet	Type (lines)	Volume/no.
149 Vorrei baciarti, o Filli (*5 v.*)	Marino	B-M (11)	iii. 6
150 Zeffiro torna (*2 or 3 v./Bc*)	Rinuccini	S (8 + 6)	viii. 18
2nd pt.: Sorge più vaga in Ciel			

Instrumental Works (130)

Type	Volume/no.
BALLETTO (*for five or three voices*)	
151 Passeggio d'un balletto a 5 et a 3 si placet	ix. 27
BRANDO (*for three voices*)[3]	
152 Brando primo	xi. 24
153 Brando secondo ('Aria di Gio. Francesco Rubini. Fabricate le parti da l'autore')	xi. 25
154 Brando terzo ('Aria del medesmo. Fabricate le parti da l'autore')	xi. 26
155 Brando primo	xii. 28
156 Brando secondo	xii. 29
CANZONA (*for four voices*)	
157 Canzon [prima] per sonar	x. 33
158 Canzon [seconda] per sonar	x. 34
159 Canzon [terza] per sonar	x. 35
CORRENTE (*for three voices*)[4]	
160 Corrente prima	xi. 27
161 Corrente seconda	xi. 28
162 Corrente terza	xi. 29
163 Corrente quarta	xi. 30
164 Corrente quinta ('Va sonata una voce più alta de l'ordinario')	xi. 31
165 Corrente sesta	xi. 32
166 Corrente settima ('Aria di Gioan Battista Rubini. Fabricate le parti da l'autore')	xi. 33
167 [Corrente prima] *paired with Gagliarda seconda as* 'La sua Corrente'	xii. 20
168 [Corrente seconda] *paired with Gagliarda terza as* 'La sua Corrente'	xii. 21
169 [Corrente terza] *paired with Gagliarda quarta as* 'La sua Corrente'	xii. 22
170 [Corrente quarta] *paired with Gagliarda quinta as* 'La sua Corrente'	xii. 23
171 Corrente quinta (*misnumbered* 'sesta')	xii. 26
172 [Corrente sesta] *paired with Gagliarda ottava as* 'La sua Corrente'	xii. 27

[3] Nos. 152–4 from Bk 3, 155–6 from Bk 4.
[4] Nos. 160–6 from Bk 3, 167–72 from Bk 4.

Type	Volume/no.

GAGLIARDA[5]
For three voices

173	Gagliarda prima detta la Turca ('Va sonata a la quarta bassa')	xi. 16
174	Gagliarda seconda detta l'Incognita ('Va sonata una terza più bassa di quello si sona all'alta')	xi. 17
175	Gagliarda terza detta la Silvia	xi. 18
176	Gagliarda quarta detta la Disperata	xi. 19
177	Gagliarda quinta detta Amor perfetto	xi. 20
178	Gagliarda sesta detta la Turanina	xi. 21
179	Gagliarda settima detta l'Herba	xi. 22
180	Gagliarda ottava detta il Verdugale	xi. 23
181	Gagliarda prima detta la Sconsolata	xii. 19
182	Gagliarda seconda detta la Gratiosa (*plus* 'La sua Corrente [prima]')	xii. 20
183	Gagliarda terza detta la Favorita (*plus* 'La sua Corrente [seconda]')	xii. 21
184	Gagliarda quarta detta la Giustiniana (*plus* 'La sua Corrente [terza]')	xii. 22
185	Gagliarda quinta detta la Cavagliera (*plus* 'La sua Corrente [quarta]')	xii. 23
186	Gagliarda sesta detta la Corombona	xii. 24
187	Gagliarda settima detta l'Ingrata	xii. 25
188	Gagliarda ottava detta la Soriana (*plus* 'La sua Corrente [sesta]')	xii. 27

For four voices

189	Gagliarda [prima] a 4 detta Venturino	ix. 18
190	Gagliarda [seconda] a 4 detta Marchesino	ix. 19

For four or three voices

191	Gagliarda a 4 et a 3 si placet, detta la Zambalina	x. 24

For five or three voices[6]

192	Gagliarda [prima] a 5 et a 3 si placet, detta l'Andreasina	ix. 23
193	Gagliarda [seconda] a 5 et a 3 si placet, detta la Norsina	ix. 25
194	Gagliarda [terza] a 5 [et a 3 si placet], detta la Massara	ix. 26
195	Gagliarda a 5 et a 3 si placet, detta Narciso	x. 32

SINFONIA
For three voices[7]

196	Sinfonia prima ('Va sonata alla quarta alta')	ix. 1
197	Sinfonia seconda	ix. 2
198	Sinfonia tertia	ix. 3
199	Sinfonia quarta	ix. 4

---

[5] Nos. 173–80 from Bk 3, 181–8 from Bk 4.
[6] Nos. 192–4 from Bk 1, no. 195 from Bk 2.
[7] Nos. 196–210 from Bk 1, 211–31 from Bk 2, 232–40 from Bk 3, 241–6 from Bk 4.

Type		Volume/no.
200	Sinfonia quinta	ix. 5
201	Sinfonia sesta	ix. 6
202	Sinfonia settima	ix. 7
203	Sinfonia ottava	ix. 8
204	Sinfonia nona	ix. 9
205	Sinfonia decima ('Va sonata alla quarta alta')	ix. 10
206	Sinfonia undecima	ix. 11
207	Sinfonia duodecima	ix. 12
208	Sinfonia tertiadecima	ix. 13
209	Sinfonia quartadecima	ix. 14
210	Sinfonia quintadecima	ix. 15
211	Sinfonia prima	x. 1
212	Sinfonia seconda	x. 2
213	Sinfonia terza	x. 3
214	Sinfonia quarta	x. 4
215	Sinfonia quinta	x. 5
216	Sinfonia sesta	x. 6
217	Sinfonia settima	x. 7
218	Sinfonia ottava	x. 8
219	Sinfonia nona	x. 9
220	Sinfonia decima	x. 10
221	Sinfonia undecima	x. 11
222	Sinfonia duodecima	x. 12
223	Sinfonia terzadecima	x. 13
224	Sinfonia quartadecima	x. 14
225	Sinfonia quintadecima	x. 15
226	Sinfonia sestadecima	x. 16
227	Sinfonia settimadecima	x. 17
228	Sinfonia ottavadecima	x. 18
229	Sinfonia nonadecima	x. 19
230	Sinfonia ventesima	x. 20
231	Sinfonia ventunesima (*for vocal arrangement, see no. 95 above*)	x. 21
232	Sinfonia prima	xi. 7
233	Sinfonia seconda detta la Emiglia	xi. 8
234	Sinfonia terza detta la Cecchina	xi. 9
235	Sinfonia quarta	xi. 10
236	Sinfonia quinta	xi. 11
237	Sinfonia sesta	xi. 12
238	Sinfonia settima	xi. 13
239	Sinfonia ottava	xi. 14
240	Sinfonia nona	xi. 15
241	Sinfonia prima	xii. 13
242	Sinfonia seconda	xii. 14
243	Sinfonia terza	xii. 15
244	Sinfonia quarta	xii. 16

Type	Volume/no.
245 Sinfonia quinta	xii. 17
246 Sinfonia sesta	xii. 18

For four voices

247 Sinfonia [prima] a 4	ix. 16
248 Sinfonia [seconda] a 4 ('Alla quarta alta')	ix. 17

For four or three voices

249 Sinfonia [prima] a 4 et a 3 si placet	x. 22
(*for three-voice version, see, also, no. 213 above*)	
250 Sinfonia [seconda] a 4 et a 3 si placet	x. 23
(*for three-voice version, see, also, no. 215 above*)	
251 Sinfonia [terza] a 4 et a 3 si placet	x. 25
(*for three-voice version, see, also, no. 218 above*)	
252 Sinfonia [quarta] a 4 et a 3 si placet	x. 26
(*for three-voice version, see, also, no. 226 above*)	

For five or three voices[8]

253 Sinfonia [prima] a 5 et a 3 si placet ('Con doi soprani et il chittarrone')	ix. 21
254 Sinfonia [seconda] grave a 5 [et a 3 si placet]	ix. 22
255 Sinfonia [terza] a 5 et a 3 si placet	ix. 24
256 Sinfonia [prima] a 5 et a 3 si placet	x. 27
(*for three-voice version, see, also, no. 214 above*)	
257 Sinfonia [seconda] a 5 et a 3 si placet	x. 28
(*for three-voice version, see, also, no. 219 above*)	
258 Sinfonia [terza] a 5 et a 3 si placet	x. 29
(*for three-voice version, see, also, no. 228 above*)	
259 Sinfonia [quarta] a 5 et a 3 si placet	x. 30
(*for three-voice version, see, also, no. 224 above*)	
260 Sinfonia [quinta] a 5 et a 3 si placet	x. 31
(*for three-voice version, see, also, no. 212 above*)	

SONATA

For three voices[9]

261 Sonata prima detta la Moderna	xi. 1
262 Sonata seconda detta la Casalasca	xi. 2
263 Sonata [terza] sopra l'Aria della Romanesca	xi. 3
264 Sonata [quarta] sopra l'Aria di Ruggiero	xi. 4
265 Sonata [quinta] sopra Porto celato il mio nobil pensiero	xi. 5
266 Sonata [sesta] in dialogo detta la Viena	xi. 6
267 Sonata prima	xii. 1
268 Sonata seconda	xii. 2
269 Sonata terza	xii. 3
270 Sonata quarta	xii. 4

[8] Nos. 253–5 from Bk 1, 256–60 from Bk 2.
[9] Nos. 261–6 from Bk 3, 267–78 from Bk 4.

Type		Volume/no.
271	Sonata quinta sopra un'Aria francese	xii. 5
272	Sonata sesta sopra l'Aria di Tordiglione	xii. 6
273	Sonata settima sopra l'Aria di un Balletto	xii. 7
274	Sonata ottava sopra l'Aria 'È tanto tempo hormai'	xii. 8
275	Sonata nona sopra l'Aria del Tenor di Napoli	xii. 9
276	Sonata decima sopra l'Aria della Romanesca	xii. 10
277	Sonata undecima detta la Scatola	xii. 11
278	Sonata duodecima sopra la Bergamasca	xii. 12
For four voices		
279	Sonata [*recte* ricercare] a 4	ix. 20
For six voices		
280	Sonata a quattro violini e doi chitarroni	xii. 30

Sacred Works in Hebrew (33)

Text incipit (voices)		Source or type/author	Volume/no.
281	Adon 'olam (*8 v.*)	*Piyyut*	xiii. 29
282	'Al naharot bavel (*4 v.*)	Psalm 137	xiii. 10
283	Barekhu (*3 v.*)	*Prayer*	xiii. 3
284	Barukh haba beshem adonai (*6 v.*)	Psalm 118: 26–9	xiii. 23
285	Eftaḥ na sefatai (*7 v.*)	*Piyyut* by Matthew, son of Isaac of Bologna	xiii. 25
286	Eftaḥ shir bisfatai (*8 v.*)	*Piyyut* by Mordecai Dato	xiii. 27
287	Ein keloheinu (*8 v.*)	*Piyyut*	xiii. 26
288	Ele mo'adei adonai (*3 v.*)	Leviticus 23: 4	xiii. 6
289	Elohim, hashivenu (*4 v.*)	Psalm 80: 4, 8, 20	xiii. 8
290	Haleluyah. Ashrei ish (*8 v.*)	Psalm 112	xiii. 30
291	Haleluyah. Haleli, nafshi (*4 v.*)	Psalm 146	xiii. 11
292	Haleluyah. Ode adonai (*8 v.*)	Psalm 111	xiii. 31
293	Hashkivenu (*5 v.*)	*Prayer*	xiii. 15
	Kaddish: see *Yitgadal veyitkadash*		
	Kedusha: see *Keter yitenu lakh*		
294	Keter yitenu lakh (*4 v.*)	Great Kedusha	xiii. 7
295	Lamnatseaḥ, 'al hagitit (*5 v.*)	Psalm 8	xiii. 13
296	Lamnatseaḥ, 'al hasheminit (*3 v.*)	Psalm 12	xiii. 5
297	Lamnatseaḥ, binginot (*3 or 4 v.*)	Psalm 67	xiii. 9
298	Lemi eḥpots (*8 v.*)	*Wedding ode*	xiii. 33
299	Mizmor le'asaf. Elohim nitsav (*3 v.*)	Psalm 82	xiii. 4
300	Mizmor ledavid. Havu ladonai (*6 v.*)	Psalm 29	xiii. 24
301	Mizmor letoda (*5 v.*)	Psalm 100	xiii. 14
302	Mizmor shir leyom hashabat (*8 v.*)	Psalm 92	xiii. 32
303	Odekha ki 'anitani (*6 v.*)	Psalm 118: 21–4	xiii. 22

Text incipit (voices)	Source or type/author	Volume/no.
304 Shir hama'alot. Ashrei kol yere adonai (3 v.)	Psalm 128	xiii. 2
305 Shir hama'alot. Ashrei kol yere adonai (5 v.)	Psalm 128	xiii. 12
306 Shir hama'alot. Ashrei kol yere adonai (6 v.)	Psalm 128	xiii. 20
307 Shir hama'alot. Beshuv adonai (5 v.)	Psalm 126	xiii. 17
308 Shir hama'alot ledavid. Lulei adonai (6 v.)	Psalm 124	xiii. 21
309 Shir lama'alot. Esa 'einai (5 v.)	Psalm 121	xiii. 18
310 Yesusum midbar vetsiya (5 v.)	Isaiah 35: 1–2, 5–6, 10	xiii. 19
311 Yigdal elohim ḥai (8 v.)	*Piyyut*	xiii. 28
312 Yitgadal veyitkadash (3 v.)	Full Kaddish	xiii. 1
313 Yitgadal veyitkadash (5 v.)	Full Kaddish	xiii. 16

GLOSSARY OF MUSICAL TERMS
FOR THE GENERAL READER

Accidental a sign that indicates a pitch alteration by a SEMITONE (sharp for raising pitch, thus F becomes F sharp; flat for lowering it, thus E becomes E flat; natural for cancelling an alteration, thus E flat becomes E). *See also* CAUTIONARY ACCIDENTAL, REDUNDANT ACCIDENTAL.

Aeolian an older scale (or MODE) running from A to A an OCTAVE higher.

Alteration *see* ACCIDENTAL.

Antiphony/antiphonal alternate singing (or playing) by different voices of an ensemble.

Archlute an instrument resembling the CHITARRONE, yet smaller (and with a different tuning).

Augmented (interval) an INTERVAL expanded by a SEMITONE (thus a second, from C to D, would, when augmented, read from C to D sharp).

Ballata (*pl.* **ballate)** one of the verse types to be found in the Italian MADRIGAL; consists of a *ripresa*, two *piedi*, and a *volta* (as, for example, in the scheme abb/cdcd/da).

Ballata-madrigal a hybrid poetic type found in the Italian MADRIGAL.

Balletto (*pl.* **balletti)** often used in the sense of *ballo*, or 'dance'; also refers to a lighter, more popular vocal-instrumental type from the later sixteenth century.

Bar (*Amer.* **measure)** a group of beats marked off from similar groups by a barline (cf. BEAT).

Basso continuo (*or merely* **continuo)** a bass part played by one or more instruments as an accompaniment to an upper part or parts (vocal, instrumental, or both); it may or may not have 'figures', i.e. numbers or signs, to indicate the pitches to be added to the bass for filling out ('realizing') the harmony (*see* FIGURE, ACCIDENTAL, REALIZATION).

Basso ostinato a single melodic pattern set in the bass and constantly repeated; *see* GROUND BASS.

Basso seguente a CONTINUO part that, as written, duplicates the notes of the vocal bass.

Bass string one of the lower added strings on a CHITARRONE (it is UNSTOPPED, i.e. its pitch cannot be altered).

B durum in HEXACHORDAL theory there are two kinds of Bs, one unaltered, or *durum* (elsewhere *quadratum*), equivalent to B natural, the other lowered, or *molle* (elsewhere *rotundum*), equivalent to B flat; *see also* ACCIDENTAL.

Beat basic unit of time, as specified by the METRE (thus in duple metre there are two beats to a BAR, in triple metre there are three; the first of the two or three beats is known as a 'downbeat' and the portion—one or more beats—that precedes it as an 'upbeat').

Binary mensuration sign indicates the measurement of music in units of two (*see* MENSURATION).

B molle *see under* B DURUM.

Boethian in reference to the music theory of the Roman philosopher and statesman Anicius Manlius Severinus Boethius (d. 524).

Brando (*pl.* **brandi**) Italian dance, variant of French BRANLE.

Branle French dance, of which twenty-six varieties were enumerated in Thoinot Arbeau's *Orchésographie*, 1588.

Cadence the close of a musical phrase, marked by a particular melodic or harmonic formation (a cadence on F, for example, denotes a close on the pitch F); of the various degrees of cadentiality, a 'half cadence' is (obviously) less conclusive than a 'full cadence'.

Canto the top voice, or soprano.

Canzona (*pl.* **canzoni**) an instrumental work in two or more sections, often with different metres and contents.

Canzona da sonar/canzona per sonar a CANZONA meant to be played (not sung, as might be implied by *canzona*, 'song').

Canzona motif a rhythmic-melodic figure, characteristic of the CANZONA, in DACTYLIC RHYTHM and usually with repeated notes.

Canzona-sonata a SONATA that has the structural/stylistic characteristics of a CANZONA; often referred to, in the literature, as 'free sonata'.

Canzone (*pl.* **canzoni**) one of the verse types to be found in the Italian MADRIGAL.

Canzone-madrigal a hybrid poetic type found in the Italian MADRIGAL.

Canzonetta (*pl.* **canzonette**) a lighter, more popular variety of the Italian MADRIGAL.

Canzone-villanesca (*or simply* **villanesca**) a lighter, more popular variety of the Italian MADRIGAL (along with the CANZONETTA and the VILLANELLA).

Capoverso the first verse of a poem, to be distinguished from its INCIPIT, or opening words (by which vocal compositions are usually identified).

Cappella a group of musicians (singers, instrumentalists) serving, regularly, at a court or in a church.

Cautionary accidental a sign that forewarns against raising or lowering a pitch in places where, according to MUSICA FICTA, it might otherwise be altered (thus a sharp on B would prevent it from being read as B flat); cf. ACCIDENTAL.

Chanson a secular vocal type from which the instrumental CANZONA seems to have derived.

Chapel master same as *maestro di cappella*, or the person in charge of a CAPPELLA.

Chiavette an unaccustomed choice or arrangement of clefs, thought to indicate TRANSPOSITION (*see also* CLEF).

Chitarrone (*pl.* **chitarroni**) a large double-necked lute (sometimes referred to as *theorbo*).

Choral monody *see under* MONODY.

Choral recitation/recitative *see under* RECITATIVE.

Chordal progression a succession of two or more chords.

Chordal style different voices so written as to sound together fairly simultaneously; often synonymous with HOMOPHONY.

Chromatic/chromaticism music employing sharps and flats (cf. ACCIDENTAL) instead of the regular DIATONIC pitches of a scale (thus, for example, C–C sharp–D–G–A flat–G instead of C–D–G–A–G); linear chromaticism refers to a progression by step (F–F sharp–G) as against one by leap (C–A flat).

Clavicembalo harpsichord.

Clef the sign placed at the beginning of a STAFF to indicate the 'pitches' (*see under* SIGNS/SYMBOLS), also known as clef SIGNATURE; the clefs have different names (treble or violin, soprano, mezzo-soprano, alto, tenor, baritone, bass).

Coda 'tail', one or more bars added on to the end of a composition.

Codetta a short CODA.

Colon (*pl.* cola) member of a verse, as for example the two or sometimes three portions of a psalm verse.

Concertato music with alternating or contrasting voices or instruments in different groupings.

Concertato madrigal a MADRIGAL written in CONCERTATO style.

Concerto (*pl.* concerti) an ensemble of voices or instruments or both; also the kind of music (often in CONCERTATO style) played by it or a specific work so entitled.

Concerto delle donne 'the ladies' ensemble'; at least two performing groups of female singers are known to have been active in later Renaissance Italy, one at the court of Ferrara, the other, modelled after it, at the court of Mantua.

Conflicting signatures the indication, at the beginning of STAVES, of different accidentals for two or more voices, thus, for example, one flat in the soprano and tenor, two in the bass, and none in the alto; cf. ACCIDENTAL, SIGNATURE.

Conjunct melody a MELODY that proceeds by stepwise motion.

Consecutive intervals/consecutives two parts moving in parallel unisons, fifths, or octaves (*see* INTERVAL), all of which are forbidden in traditional COUNTER-POINT; also known as parallels.

Continuo *see* BASSO CONTINUO.

Contrafactum (*pl.* contrafacta) a vocal piece in which a new text (often sacred) is substituted for the original one (often secular).

Contralto appears to refer, in one of Rossi's instrumental books, to what, today, would be termed a viola.

Contrast motifs two different musical ideas set in juxtaposition (a typically Baroque device).

Corelli clash parallel seconds (*see* INTERVAL) at the CADENCE, often found in the works of Corelli.

Cori spezzati 'split choruses', referring to the division of an ensemble into alternating voice groups; cf. ANTIPHONY.

Cornett (*Ital.* cornetto) hybrid wind instrument, made out of wood and usually curved, with cupped mouthpiece; sounds somewhat like a trumpet.

Corrente (*pl.* correnti) an Italian dance.

Counterpoint/contrapuntal the artful vertical combination of two or more individual melodies to form a congruous whole.

Courante French variety of the CORRENTE.

Course refers to each of the six strings on a lute or a CHITARRONE (apart from its lower added strings; *see* BASS STRING); the strings appear singly or are doubled (and when doubled may be tuned either to a unison or an octave; cf. INTERVAL).

Cromorno Italian for crumhorn, a curved reed-capped instrument.

Crotchet (*Amer.* quarter note/quarter) a note whose duration is a quarter of a SEMIBREVE.

Dactylic rhythm in poetry, a long and two shorts (– ◡◡); in music, their rhythmic equivalent (for example, one crotchet and two quavers; cf. NOTES).

Diatonic the use of the natural tones of a SCALE, thus CHROMATIC or altered tones are excluded.

Diminished fifth the contraction of the INTERVAL of a fifth by a SEMITONE, thus, for example, the pitches E–B become E–B flat.

Distich two lines paired to form a couplet.

Divided chorus smaller divisions of the chorus, as distinct from the full-voice ensemble; cf. ANTIPHONY.

Dominant the fifth degree of the SCALE (also the chord built on it).

Dorian an older scale (or MODE) running from D to D an octave higher.

Downbeat see under BEAT.

Duple mensuration the measurement of music in units of two (also binary MENSURATION).

Duple metre two beats to a BAR (cf. BEAT, METRE).

Dynamics refers to the degree of sound volume, from, say, soft (*piano*) to loud (*forte*).

Echo the immediate repetition of a phrase, sometimes its concluding notes only and with a reduced ensemble (hence at a lower dynamic level).

Endecasillabo (*Eng.* **hendecasyllable**) an eleven-syllable line.

Envoi a short stanza appended to a strophic poem, as for example in Marino's *Canzone de' baci*, with seven stanzas and an envoi.

Falso bordone a style of writing in which a melody (often for a psalm) is presented in simple four-part harmony; *see* HARMONY.

Figur (*pl.* **Figuren**) a musical motif with a specific shape (rhythmic, melodic, textural, semantic), as explained mainly in seventeenth- and eighteenth-century German writings on the *Figurenlehre*, or 'doctrine of figures'.

Figure/figured (bass) one or more signs (either a number or an ACCIDENTAL) affixed to a note in the BASSO CONTINUO to indicate the INTERVAL or chord to be added to it.

Finalis the chief or central note of a MODE, also the one on which a melody in any one mode should end (thus in Dorian the *finalis* is D, in Phrygian E, and so on).

First-inversion triad a chord so arranged that its root appears not as the lowest note, but at the top (thus, for example, g–b–d' becomes b–d'–g'); as opposed to a 'second-inversion triad', when the root appears in the middle (d'–g'–b').

Foundation instrument (*Ital.* **istromento/strumento da corpo**) an instrument providing lower support for an ensemble (as opposed to a MELODY INSTRUMENT); usually refers to the instrument(s) used for realizing the BASSO CONTINUO.

Fugue/fugal a mode of composition whereby the motif or melody of one part occurs, imitatively, in the others (cf. IMITATION).

Full-voice chorus all voices perform, as against a 'divided chorus', with only half or some of its voices (cf. ANTIPHONY).

Gagliarda (*pl.* **gagliarde**) an Italian dance.

Gamba refers to VIOLA DA GAMBA, or 'bass viol', played on or between the knees.

Gigue lively species of dance.

Ground bass a pattern of notes stated over and again in the bass, with changing melodies or harmonies in the upper parts; largely synonymous with BASSO OSTINATO.

Harmony/harmonic the practices of chordal construction and CHORDAL PROGRESSION, also the simultaneous-sounding pitches that result.

Hemiola the change, in a melody, from one kind of rhythmic measurement to another, as when six CROTCHETS divide, in one BAR, as three groups of two and, in the next, as two groups of three.

Hemistich half of a poetic verse, marked by a caesura.

Hendecasyllable/hendecasyllabic *see* ENDECASILLABO.

Heptasyllabic *see* SETTENARIO.

Hexachord/hexachordal a series of six consecutive 'pitches' (cf. under SIGNS/SYMBOLS), starting from C, F, or G, whereby three different hexachords are defined; the three constitute the basis of medieval and early Renaissance solmization (i.e. the pedagogic scheme for learning to sing melodies and identify their pitches).

Homophony/homophonic two or more voices written in a fairly CHORDAL STYLE; in 'animated homophony' one or another voice has added RHYTHMIC interest.

Homorhythm/homorhythmic two or more voices moving together in identical RHYTHM.

Iambic metre in poetry, an iambic foot consists of a short and a long ($\smile$ –); an 'iambic tetrameter' has four such feet.

Imitation/imitative counterpoint/imitative style the repetition of a motif or theme in different voices with or without modification (cf. POINT OF IMITATION).

Incipit the initial words of the first verse of a poem (textual incipit) or the initial pitches of a melody (melodic incipit).

Instrumentation the instruments used or designated for performing ensemble music or, more specifically, for performing its basso continuo.

Intabulation the arrangement of vocal music for performance on the keyboard, lute, or various stringed instruments (cf. TABLATURE).

Intermedio (*pl.* **intermedi)** a vocal or instrumental interlude performed between or, sometimes, within the acts of a comedy or tragedy.

Interrupted parallels two CONSECUTIVE INTERVALS separated by a rest.

Interval/intervallic the pitch difference between two successive or simultaneous tones (referred to, in ascending order, as unison or prime, second, third, fourth, fifth, sixth, seventh, octave, plus compounds).

Intonazione a short organ prelude.

Inversion melodic, when a motif or theme has its intervals reversed (thus a fourth descending from g to d would become a fourth ascending from g to c'); harmonic, when the basic arrangement of pitches in a chord is altered (thus the lowest pitch becomes the middle or top one; *see under* FIRST-INVERSION TRIAD).

Ionian an older scale (or MODE) running from C to C an octave higher.

Lira a fifteenth- and sixteenth-century string instrument.

Lirone larger variety of LIRA.

Lydian an older scale (or MODE) running from F to F an octave higher.

Lydian with B flat LYDIAN does not have B flat in its SCALE, yet, for practical reasons (one of them the avoidance of dissonance) a flat is often added to B, in which case Lydian, in its succession of semitones and whole tones, resembles IONIAN (cf. SEMITONE, WHOLE TONE).

Madrigal (Italian) a lyric form known from poetry and music, in one species, of the fourteenth century and, in another, of the sixteenth and seventeenth centuries.

Madrigal comedy a play constructed from a series of madrigals.

Madrigal cycle a work comprising various madrigals in succession.

Madrigaletto a shorter variety of MADRIGAL.

Madrigalism composers of madrigals tended to 'describe' words through comparable musical devices (*see* WORD PAINTING); an instance of musical depiction is often referred to, in the literature, as a 'madrigalism'.

Maestro di cappella same as chapel master, or the person in charge of the CAPPELLA.

Major mode a MODE with a SEMITONE between its third and fourth degrees (as in Lydian when B has a flat, Mixolydian, and Ionian).

Major scale a SCALE that has a SEMITONE between its third and fourth degrees and between its seventh and eighth degrees.

Major third an INTERVAL consisting of two whole tones (*see* WHOLE TONE).

Mascherata a piece of music presented as or for a masked entertainment.

Melisma/melismatic in vocal music, an ornamental melodic figure of three or more notes sung to one syllable.

Melodic inversion *see under* INVERSION.

Melody/melodic a succession of tones that are shaped, in their pitches and rhythms, to form a coherent entity.

Melody instrument an instrument used for the upper voices of an ensemble, as against a FOUNDATION INSTRUMENT.

Mensuration the measurement of music according to signs indicating its division into groups of, basically, two or three units (duple or binary mensuration, often under C or ₵; triple or ternary mensuration, often under 3, which itself denotes either 3/1 or 3/2, according to context).

Metre the grouping of beats, as indicated by the SIGNATURE, into bars; includes the varieties of measurement described under MENSURATION.

Metrical change a change, within a piece, from one METRE to another.

Minim (*Amer.* **half note**) a note whose duration is half a SEMIBREVE.

Minor mode a MODE that has a WHOLE TONE step between its third and fourth degrees and between its seventh and eighth degrees (as in Dorian, Phrygian, and Aeolian).

Minor scale a SCALE that has a WHOLE TONE between its third and fourth degrees and, optionally, between its seventh and eighth degrees.

Minor third an INTERVAL consisting of a WHOLE TONE plus SEMITONE (as distinguished from a 'major third', with two whole tones).

Mixed metres as in a piece having two or more metres in succession (e.g., C/3/₵; cf. METRICAL CHANGE).

Mixolydian an older scale (MODE) running from G to G an octave higher.

Modal writing/modality musical composition according to modal scales (*see* MODE).

Mode a successive arrangement of the DIATONIC tones of the OCTAVE, with a different order of whole tones and semitones depending upon the initial pitch (see WHOLE TONE, SEMITONE); older scales, often known as 'church modes', include the Dorian, Phrygian, Lydian, Mixolydian, and, from the sixteenth century on, the Aeolian and Ionian (as distinguished from later major and minor scales).

Monody accompanied solo song, inaugurated in the early Baroque in contrast to sixteenth-century polyphony; 'choral monody' refers to three or more voices singing in monodic style.

Monophony/monophonic a single melodic line without accompaniment.

Monostrophic poem a poem having a single stanza (as the basis of musical composition).

Motet a vocal composition, usually on a sacred text, in POLYPHONIC style.

Multistrophic poem a poem having several stanzas (as the basis of musical composition).

Multistrophic work a musical composition having, for its text, a multistrophic poem.

Musica antica roughly the 'older' musical style of the sixteenth century.

Musica ficta the practice of altering pitches of the HEXACHORD by adding sharps or flats to them (*see* ACCIDENTAL).

Musica moderna roughly the 'newer' music inaugurated in the seventeenth century.

Musicus in BOETHIAN sense, a person capable of judging music (in its varying components of composition, performance, and intellection).

Natural a sign (ACCIDENTAL) that cancels a previous alteration.

Notes the signs by which pitches of different lengths are indicated, as follows (from longest to shortest): long, breve, semibreve, minim, crotchet, quaver, semiquaver.

Octave the first eight lines of a SONNET (hence sonnet octave); in music, an INTERVAL measuring eight DIATONIC degrees (as from c to c′).

Opus number a number assigned to a composer's works, in order of publication.

Organum early variety of POLYPHONY (from ninth to twelfth century), more specifically a style of writing whereby, for each single note of the lower voice, the upper one (or *vox organalis*) has ornamental figures of several notes (in what is termed 'florid' or, loosely, MELISMATIC style).

Parallel consecutives or merely parallels; *see* CONSECUTIVES.

Parallel fifths/octaves/seconds/unisons *see* CONSECUTIVES.

Parallelismus membrorum the division of a psalm verse into complementary portions (or 'members').

Pars (*pl.* **partes**) section of work (**prima pars**, *Ital.* **prima parte**, 'first part'; **secunda pars**, *Ital.* **seconda parte**, 'second part'; etc.); to be distinguished from 'part' in the sense of one voice of a composition, e.g. soprano, alto, tenor, bass (to be either sung or played; *see* PART MUSIC).

Partbook a book that contains the music for a single 'part', i.e. voice (thus, in MADRIGAL prints, one book was printed for the soprano, another for the alto, and so on).

Partenza a poem whose theme is leave-taking.

Part music music written for different voices, the word *part* here meaning 'voice'; usually synonymous with POLYPHONY.

Part song a piece of PART MUSIC specifically for vocal performance (as distinct from part music for instruments).

Passaggio (*pl.* **passaggi**) a generic term for an ornament, written or improvised.

Pastourelle a poem whose theme is, generally, the encounter between a knight and a shepherdess.

Pavan a slow dance in duple METRE.

Pentasyllable verse of five syllables.

Pentatonicism music based on a SCALE having five tones to an OCTAVE.

Phrygian an older scale (MODE) from E to E an octave higher.

Piyyut (*pl.* **piyyutim**) Hebrew for a post-biblical religious poem.

Poesia per musica poetry written especially for music, usually without literary pretension and often vapid.

Point of imitation theme or motif treated in IMITATIVE COUNTERPOINT.

Polychoral for two or more choruses.

Polyphony/polyphonic music having two or more 'parts', i.e. voices, usually in CONTRAPUNTAL style.

Preludium (*pl.* **preludia**) introductory instrumental piece.

Prima pars (*Ital.* **parte**) first part, i.e. section, of a work; *see under* PARS.

Prima pratica 'first practice'; term coined by Monteverdi in reference to sixteenth-century COUNTERPOINT, as against what he called the SECONDA PRATICA, or the new practices in music of his own era (roughly equivalent to MUSICA ANTICA vs. MUSICA MODERNA).

Proparoxytone a word or verse with an accent on the antepenultimate (as in the word *Dominus* or in a VERSO SDRUCCIOLO).

Psaltery an ancient plucked stringed instrument known until the seventeenth century.

Pseudo-imitation music in a quasi-IMITATIVE STYLE.

Pseudo-madrigal a MADRIGAL scaled down from four or more voices, as it was originally written, to an arrangement for, usually, a single voice plus instrumental accompaniment.

Pseudo-monody a MADRIGAL so written as to resemble MONODY, i.e. the top voice tends to be emphasized while the lower voice or voices serve as support.

Qualitative stress poetry, or the music set to it, with stressed or accented syllables.

Quantitative stress poetry, or the music set to it, with longer or shorter durations for its syllables.

Quaver (*Amer.* **eighth note/eighth**) note whose duration is one-eighth of a SEMIBREVE.

Quinto designates a fifth voice in music written for five or more voices.

Realize/realization adding harmonies to the bass line of a CONTINUO, the result being a 'realization'.

Recitative in vocal music, a declamatory mode of writing introduced in early opera; when music is so written as for two or three singers to perform in this style, it is sometimes dubbed 'choral recitative'.

Recorder an end-blown flute having a 'whistle' mouthpiece.

Redundant accidental a sharp or flat on notes of the same pitch in a single BAR, where, by modern convention, one ACCIDENTAL suffices.

Register the high, low, or middle areas of sound production by a voice or an instrument.

Responsorial in performance, the alternation of solo and choral portions, the latter as it were in 'response'.

Rhythm/rhythmic the patterns of long and short note durations on which melodies are based. In a 'dotted rhythm' the first of two or more NOTES has an added dot, which increases its duration by a half.

Ricercare (*pl.* **ricercari**) a POLYPHONIC instrumental form of the sixteenth and seventeenth centuries, often resembling, in structure and style, a (vocal) MOTET.

Ripresa the opening lines of a BALLATA.

Ritornello (*pl.* **ritornelli**) an instrumental section that variously may precede, follow, and conclude vocal portions in seventeenth-century sacred and secular works.

Romanesca a melodic scheme, with definite harmonic implications, used by many composers as a GROUND BASS.

Saltarello an Italian dance usually in TRIPLE METRE.

Scale a series of adjacent tones arranged, in a MODE or a MAJOR or MINOR SCALE, according to semitones and whole tones.

Scherzo (*pl.* **scherzi**) a poetic and musical subcategory of the CANZONETTA.

Scordatura a special tuning used for stringed instruments (whereby one or more strings are tuned up or down from their normal pitch).

Scoring the designation of specific instruments for different parts, i.e. voices; or, more generally, the composition of music for a certain arrangement of voices.

Seconda parte/secunda pars second part, i.e. section, of a work; *see under* PARS.

Seconda pratica *see under* PRIMA PRATICA.

Semibreve (*Amer.* whole note) a basic time unit, in relation to which other note values are measured (minim, crotchet, quaver, semiquaver); *see* NOTES.

Semiquaver (*Amer.* sixteenth note/sixteenth) a note whose duration is a sixteenth of a SEMIBREVE.

Semitone the interval of a second divides into two semitones, which together, form a whole tone; thus D to E, for example, comprises the semitones D to D sharp and D sharp to E.

Sequence the repetition of a melodic pattern at successively higher or lower intervals.

Sesquialtera 3/2, 'sesqui' referring, in fractions, to a numerator one half larger than the denominator (*see* MENSURATION *and under* SIGNS/SYMBOLS).

Sestet the last six lines of a sonnet.

Settenario (*Eng.* **heptasyllable**) a seven-syllable, or heptasyllabic, verse.

Sheva in Hebrew, a half-vowel with either a 'mobile' or a 'quiescent' form, as reflected, morever, in the way syllables are set to music: 'mobile' *sheva* is pronounced (e.g. *kulEkhem*), 'quiescent' *sheva* is silent (thus not *yigEdal*, but *yigdal*).

Sign synonymous with a sharp, flat, or natural (*see* ACCIDENTAL).

Signature short for various signs placed at the beginning of a piece or its individual STAVES, to indicate the MENSURATION (or METRE), the clefs, and, if it has them throughout, flats or sharps (*see* CLEF, ACCIDENTAL).

Signs/symbols

Harmony   I, II, III, IV, V, VI, VII: the different SCALE degrees on which chords are built. **6/4 chords:** three pitches so arranged as for the two outer ones to form a sixth and the lower and middle ones to form a fourth (*see* INTERVAL; also known as 'second-inversion triad': *see under* FIRST-INVERSION TRIAD).

Metre   C, ₵: two signs for duple METRE or binary MENSURATION. **3/2, ₵3/2:** sesquialteral mensuration. **3:** triple mensuration (often meaning 3/2). **3/1, 3/4, 6/2, 6/4:** various signs for triple metre (simple, compound). **12/2, 12/4:** signs for compound duple metre.

Number of voices   *a 3, a 4, a 5*: for three voices, for four, for five (or elsewhere 3 v., 4 v., 5 v.), etc. **5/3 voices, 4/3 voices:** can be performed in alternative versions for either five or three voices or, in other works, for either four or three voices (the term 'voices' referring, in instrumental music, to 'instruments' of course).

Pitches   **C, D, E, F, G, A, B**: successive pitch degrees of SCALE; where necessary, they have been differentiated according to the octave in which they occur, thus, for the one pitch C, from lower to higher octaves: C, c, c', c'', c''', etc.

Sinfonia (*pl.* **sinfonie**) as developed by Rossi, a short instrumental piece for three voices, though sometimes four or five, of an introductory character.

Si placet (*Ital.* **se piace**) refers to the possibility of performing a composition in one way or another, as when a *gagliarda*, for example, carries the indication 'for either four or three voices *as you choose*' ('gagliarda a 4 et a 3 si placet').

Sixth an INTERVAL measuring six DIATONIC degrees (as from C to A).

Sonata an instrumental form that, in Rossi's works, exhibited three species: the CANZONA-SONATA, the VARIATION SONATA, and the 'special sonata', i.e. explicable in relation to its own structure and content.

Sonata da camera a succession of various dance movements, usually preceded by a slow introduction (examples in the works of Corelli).

Sonata da chiesa a composition in four or more movements, usually in contrasting metres and styles (for possible use in the church; examples in the works of Corelli).

Sonnet one of the poetic types to be found in the Italian madrigal; consists of an octave plus sestet.

Sonnet octave the first eight lines of a sonnet.

Sonnet sestet the last six lines of a sonnet.

Spinet a keyboard instrument, similar to, though usually smaller than, a harpsichord.

Split choruses *see* CORI SPEZZATI.

Staff (*pl.* **staves**) the five horizontal and parallel lines, on and between which the NOTES are written.

Stile concertato music in CONCERTATO style.

Stile rappresentativo music in an appropriately theatrical (dramatic) style.

Stile recitativo music in a declamatory style (RECITATIVE).

Strophic poem poem with two or more stanzas (hence MULTISTROPHIC).

Suite (dance suite) a succession of dances assembled to form a single work; cf. SONATA DA CAMERA.

Supertonic the 'pitch above the TONIC', hence the second degree of a scale (or the chord built on it).

Suspension denotes a pitch retained from a previous chord, where it was consonant, yet now is temporarily 'suspended' over another pitch as a dissonance.

Syncopation stress placed, within a BAR, on a weak BEAT or one of its parts.

Tablature special notation used for the INTABULATION of vocal music for keyboard or certain string instruments.

Tactus basic unit of measure for beating (or dividing) music.

Tavola 'table of contents', as in printed madrigal or instrumental collections.

Tempo the speed of music, as sometimes marked (in Rossi's works) by the performing instructions 'adagio' (slow), 'presto' (fast), 'più presto' (faster).

Tetrachord a series of four notes spanning a fourth (as, for example, from D to G); *see* INTERVAL.

Texture/textural the particular way different voices are combined to form a musical 'fabric' (*see under* MONODY, MONOPHONY, HOMOPHONY, POLYPHONY, TRIO-SONATA TEXTURE).

Theorbo loosely, another term for CHITARRONE.

Third an INTERVAL measuring three DIATONIC degrees (as from G to B).

Thirdless chord a chord without its usual third, hence consisting of a fifth or octave or both (*see* INTERVAL); the result is an 'open', i.e. rather hollow, sound.

Through-composed music composed without noticeable repetitions of material.

Tonal compass the distance between the highest and lowest pitches of a melody, voice, or instrument; otherwise known as 'range'.

Tonal degree the SCALE degrees that, in a TONAL SYSTEM, are fundamental for establishing major and minor scales, namely, the first (or TONIC), the fourth (or subdominant), and the fifth (or DOMINANT).

Tonality music constructed according to major and minor scales and gravitating around their central tone, otherwise known as TONIC, or first degree; in a TONAL SYSTEM the other scale degrees bear specific functional relations to the tonic.

Tonal system a mode of composition based on major and minor scales and the operations of their separate degrees.

Tonic the first degree of a major or minor scale and the chord built on it.

Tonic accent a pitch that, because of being higher than its surrounding ones, stands out, hence receives an 'accent'.

Tonic cadence CADENCE on the TONIC.

Topos (*pl.* **topoi)** in poetry or prose, a stock idea or subject.

Transposed transferred from one set of pitches to another (as, for example, when a piece is played a fourth higher than its written pitches; *see* INTERVAL); in contrast to 'untransposed', or performed as written.

Transposition the transfer from one set of pitches to another (*see* TRANSPOSED).

Triad a chord consisting of three tones (root, third, fifth; *see* INTERVAL).

Trio-sonata texture duet plus accompaniment, as inaugurated in instrumental chamber music of the early Baroque.

Trio sonata a sonata characterized by TRIO-SONATA TEXTURE.

Triple metre a sign that indicates three beats to a BAR.

Trochaic octosyllables eight syllables in trochaic metre, i.e. four units of long plus short (– ◡).

Ultimate the last syllable of a word or verse (preceded by the penultimate, or next to last syllable, and the antepenultimate, or third from last syllable).

Unstopped in reference to an added (bass) string on a large lute, or CHITARRONE, with a fixed pitch (the upper strings can be 'stopped', i.e. pressed in different places, thus altering their pitch).

Upbeat *see under* BEAT.

Variation sonata a sonata constructed, usually, on a GROUND BASS.

Verso sdrucciolo a verse of twelve syllables with its terminal accent not on the penultimate (as in an ENDECASILLABO), but on the antepenultimate.

Villanella (*pl.* **villanelle)** a cognate form of VILLANESCA.

Villanesca (*pl.* **villanesche**) or CANZONE-VILLANESCA; a lighter, more popular variety of the MADRIGAL.

Viol *see* VIOLA.

Viola (*pl.* **viole**) refers to a violin or member of the violin family or, on the other hand, to a viol or member of the viol family; *viola*, then, seems to have been a general designation, in Rossi's time, for a stringed instrument of either family.

Viola da braccio an 'arm viol', or smaller-sized viol, held against the shoulder; also possibly a violin.

Viola da gamba a 'leg viol', or the bass member of the viol family, played on or between the legs.

Viol consort an ensemble of viols.

Voice leading in CONTRAPUNTAL music, the way the voices are joined in greater or lesser adherence to the principles of variety, smooth melodic progression, and the avoidance of dissonance and CONSECUTIVES.

Volta a dance of the later sixteenth century; also the concluding verse or verses in a BALLATA.

Whole tone comprises two semitones; together they form the INTERVAL of a second.

Word painting the 'portrayal' of words by seemingly analogous music (thus ascent by rising lines, flight by quick rhythms, etc.; cf. MADRIGALISM).

Word placement the relation of notes and syllables, as indicated in the source or realized in performance; often referred to as 'text placement' or 'text underlay'.

Zarlinian refers to Gioseffo Zarlino, a major sixteenth-century music theorist (pt. 3 of his *Istitutioni harmoniche*, 1558, was an extensive treatment of COUNTERPOINT).

Zimra defuma Hebrew, or more correctly Aramaic, for vocal music.

Zimra demana Hebrew, or more correctly Aramaic, for instrumental music.

BIBLIOGRAPHY

ADELMAN, HOWARD, 'Success and Failure in the Seventeenth-Century Ghetto of Venice: The Life and Thought of Leon Modena, 1571–1648', Ph.D. diss. (2 vols.; Brandeis University, 1985).

ADEMOLLO, ALESSANDRO, *La bell'Adriana ed altre virtuose del suo tempo alla corte di Mantova* (Città del Castello, 1888).

ADLER, ISRAEL, 'Les Chants synagogaux notés au XIIe siècle par Abdias, le prosélyte normand', *Revue de musicologie*, 51 (1965), 19–51.

—— *La Pratique musicale savante dans quelques communautés juives en Europe aux XVIIe–XVIIIe siècles* (2 vols.; Paris-La Haye, 1966).

—— 'The Rise of Art Music in the Italian Ghetto', in Alexander Altmann (ed.), *Jewish Medieval and Renaissance Studies* (Cambridge, Mass, 1967), 321–64.

—— (comp.), *Hebrew Notated Manuscript Sources up to circa 1840* (2 vols.; Munich, 1989).

—— (ed.), *Hebrew Writings Concerning Music in Manuscripts and Printed Books from Geonic Times up to 1800* (Munich, 1975).

AGAZZARI, AGOSTINO, *Del sonare sopra il basso con tutti li stromenti e dell'uso loro nel conserto* (Siena, 1607), tr. Oliver Strunk in his anthology of *Source Readings in Music History* (New York, 1950), 424–31.

ALDRICH, PUTNAM, *Rhythm in Seventeenth-Century Italian Monody* (New York, 1966).

ALLSOP, PETER, *The Italian 'Trio' Sonata: From its Origins until Corelli* (Oxford, 1992).

AMADEI, FEDERIGO, *Cronaca universale della città di Mantova*, ed. Giuseppe Amadei *et al.* (5 vols.; Mantua, 1954–7).

AMADEI, GIUSEPPE, 'Note sul teatro a Mantova nel Rinascimento', *Civiltà mantovana*, 9 (1975), 256–66 (also in *Mantova e i Gonzaga* (1977), 155–9).

AMRAM, DAVID WERNER, *The Makers of Hebrew Books in Italy: Being Chapters in the History of the Hebrew Printing Press* (Philadelphia, 1909).

ANDREINI, GIOVAN BATTISTA, *Lo schiavetto* (Milan, 1612).

—— *La Maddalena, sacra rappresentazione* (Mantua, 1617); and rev. edn., *La Maddalena lasciva, e penitente, azzione drammatica, e divota* (Milan, 1652).

—— *La turca, commedia boschareccia e marittima* (Venice, 1620).

—— *La centaura* (Paris, 1622).

—— *Lelio bandito* (Venice, 1624).

APEL, WILLI, *Die italienische Violinmusik im 17. Jahrhundert* (Wiesbaden, 1983).

ARBEAU, THOINOT, *Orchésographie* (Langres, 1588; fac. repr. of 1596 edn., New York, 1969).

Ashmoret haboker ['Morning Watch'] (Mantua, 1624).

ASSENZA, CONCETTA, *Giovan Ferretti tra canzonetta e madrigale* (Florence, 1989).

AUGERER, MANFRED, *et al.* (eds.), *Festschrift Othmar Wessely zum 60. Geburtstag* (Tutzing, 1982).

AVENARY, HANOCH, 'Jewish Music' (after Second Temple), in *Encyclopaedia judaica* (1972), xii. 566–663.

Ayelet hashahar ['The Deer's Dawn'] (Mantua, 1612).

BANCHIERI, ANDREA, *Conclusioni nel suono dell'organo* (Bologna, 1609; fac. repr. Milan, 1934).

BARBIERI, PATRIZIO, '"Chiavette" and Modal Transposition in Italian Practice (*c*.1500–1837)', *Recercare*, 3 (1991), 5–79.

BARTOLOCCI, GIULIO, *Bibliotheca magna rabbinica de scriptoribus* (4 vols.; Rome, 1675–94).

BARUCHSON, ZIPORA, 'Hasifriyot haperatiyot shel yehudei tsefon italya beshilhei harenesans' ['Private Libraries of Northern Italian Jews at the Close of the Renaissance'], Ph.D. diss. (Bar Ilan University, 1985).

BELKIN, AHUVA (ed.), *Leone de' Sommi and the Performing Arts* (Tel Aviv, 1997).

BELLONCI, MARIA, *Segreti dei Gonzaga*, 3rd edn. (Milan, 1963).

BENAYAHU, MEIR, *Haskama urshut bidfusei venetsya: hasefer ha'ivri me'et hava'ato lidfus ve'ad tseto la'or* ['Approbation and Approval in the Venetian Hebrew Press: The Hebrew Book from Printing to Publication'] (Jerusalem, 1971).

—— 'Da'at ḥakhmei italya 'al hanegina be'ugav bitfila' ['The Opinion of Italian Sages on Playing the Organ during Prayers'], *Asufot, sefer shana lemada'ei hayahadut*, 1 (1987), 265–318.

BERNARDI, STEFANO, *Madrigaletti a due et a tre voci con alcune sonate a 3 per due violini overo cornetti, et un chitarrone, trombone, overo fagotto. . . . Opera duodecima . . . libro secondo* (Venice, 1626).

BERNSTEIN, JANE A., 'Financial Arrangements and the Role of Printer and Composer in Sixteenth-Century Italian Music Printing', *Acta musicologica*, 63 (1991), 39–56.

BERTAZZOLO, GABRIELE, *Breve relatione dello sposalitio fatto dalla Serenissima Principessa Eleonora Gonzaga con la Sacra Cesarea Maestà di Ferdinando II* (Mantua, 1622).

BERTOLOTTI, ANTONIO, *Muzio Manfredi e Passi Giuseppe: letterati in relazione col duca di Mantova* (Rome, 1888).

—— *Musici alla corte dei Gonzaga in Mantova dal secolo XV al XVIII* (Milan, 1890; repr. Bologna, 1969).

BETTLEY, JOHN, 'North Italian Falsobordone and its Relevance to the Early *Stile recitativo*', *Proceedings of the Royal Musical Association*, 103 (1976–7), 1–18.

BEVILACQUA, ENRICO, 'Giambattista Andreini e la compagnia dei Fedeli', *Giornale storico della letteratura italiana*, 23 (1894), 76–155; 24 (1895), 82–165.

BIANCONI, LORENZO, *Music in the Seventeenth Century* (Cambridge, 1987).

BIRNBAUM, EDUARD, *Jüdische Musiker am Hofe von Mantua von 1542–1628* (Vienna, 1893; rev. and tr. into Italian by Vittore Colorni as 'Musici ebrei alla corte di Mantova dal 1542 al 1628: presentazione e aggiornamento', *Civiltà mantovana*, 2 (1967), 185–216, and after Colorni's version, tr. into Hebrew, then into English (as *Jewish Musicians at the Court of the Mantuan Dukes [1542–1628]*) by Judith Cohen (Tel Aviv, resp. 1975, 1978).

BOCCATO, CARLA, 'Lettere di Ansaldo Cebà, genovese, a Sara Copio Sullam, poetessa del ghetto di Venezia', *La rassegna mensile di Israel*, 3rd ser., 40 (1974), 169–91.

BONFIL, REUVEN [Robert, Roberto], 'Halakha, Kabbalah, and Society: Some Insights into Menahem Azaria da Fano's Inner World', in Twersky and Septimus (eds.), *Jewish Thought in the Seventeenth Century* (1987), 39–61.

—— 'Change in the Cultural Patterns of a Jewish Society in Crisis: Italian Jewry at the Close of the Sixteenth Century', *Jewish History*, 3 (1988), 11–30 (repr. in Ruderman (ed.), *Essential Papers on Jewish Culture* (1992), 401–25).

—— *Rabbis and Jewish Communities in Renaissance Italy*, tr. Jonathan Chipman (Oxford, 1990), originally *Harabanut be'italya bitkufat harenesans* (Jerusalem, 1979).

—— *Jewish Life in Renaissance Italy*, tr. Anthony Oldcorn (Berkeley, 1994), originally *Gli ebrei in Italia nell'epoca del Rinascimento* (Florence, 1991).

BORGIR, THARALD, *The Performance of the Basso Continuo in Italian Baroque Music* (Ann Arbor, 1987).

BOTTRIGARI, ERCOLE, *Il Trimerone de' fondamenti musicali*. Bologna, Civico Museo Bibliografico Musicale, MS B 44.

BOWERS, ROGER, 'Some Reflection upon Notation and Proportion in Monteverdi's Mass and Vespers of 1610', *Music & Letters*, 73 (1992), 347–98; with a response by Jeffrey Kurtzman and counterresponse by Bowers in *Music & Letters*, 74 (1993), 487–95.

BRADSHAW, MURRAY C., *The Falsobordone: A Study in Renaissance and Baroque Music* (n.p., 1978).

Brescia, Biblioteca Queriniana, MS L. IV. 99.

BRINTON, SELWYN, *The Gonzaga—Lords of Mantua* (London, 1927).

BROWN, HOWARD MAYER (comp.), *Instrumental Music Printed before 1600: A Bibliography* (Cambridge, Mass., 1965).

BRUNELLI, ANTONIO, *Regole utilissime per il scolaro* (Florence, 1606).

BUETENS, STANLEY, 'Theorbo Accompaniments of Early Seventeenth-Century Italian Monody', *Journal of the Lute Society of America*, 6 (1973), 37–45.

BURKE, PETER, *The Italian Renaissance, Culture and Society in Italy* (Princeton, 1987).

CACCINI, GIULIO, *Le nuove musiche* (Florence, 1601; fac. edn. New York, 1973), ed. H. Wiley Hitchcock (Madison, 1970).

CAIMO, GIOSEPPE, *Madrigali and Canzoni for Four and Five Voices*, ed. Leta E. Miller (Madison, 1990).

CANAL, PIETRO, 'Della musica in Mantova: notizie tratte principalmente dall'archivio Gonzaga', *Memorie del R. Istituto Veneto di Scienze, Lettere ed Arte*, 21 (1879), 655–774 (repr. Geneva, 1978).

CANALE, FLORIANO, *Canzoni da sonare a quattro, et otto voci . . . libro primo* (1600), ed. James Ladewig (New York, 1988).

Canti liturgici di rito spagnolo del Tempio Israelitico di Firenze, ed. Elio Piattelli (Florence, 1992).

Canti liturgici ebraici di rito italiano, ed. Elio Piattelli (Rome, 1967).

CARNEVALE, LUIGI, *Il ghetto di Mantova* (Mantua, 1884).

CAROSO, FABRITIO, *Il ballarino* (Venice, 1581; fac. repr. New York, 1967).

CARVER, ANTHONY F., *Cori spezzati* (Cambridge, 1988).

CASTELLO, DARIO, *Selected Ensemble Sonatas*, ed. Eleanor Selfridge-Field (2 vols.; Madison, 1976).

Il catalogo delle più onorate cortigiane di Venezia nel Cinquecento (Venice, Museo Correr, Miscellanea Cicogna, MS 2483, itself copied from an apparently sixteenth-century print; fac. repr. Venice, 1956).

CHATER, JAMES, 'Castelletti's "Stravaganze d'Amore" (1585): A Comedy with Interludes', *Studi musicali*, 8 (1979), 85–148.

CHIABRERA, GABRIELLO, *Opere* (4 vols.; Venice, 1730–1).

Cincinnati, Hebrew Union College, MS Birnbaum, Mus. 101.

CIPOLLA, CARLO, *Money, Prices, and Civilization in the Mediterranean World* (Princeton, 1956).

COHEN, JUDITH, 'Thomas Weelkes's Borrowings from Salamone Rossi', *Music & Letters*, 66 (1985), 110–17.

—— 'Salamone Rossi's Madrigal Style: Observations and Conjectures', *Orbis musicae*, 9 (1986), 150–63.

COLORNI, VITTORE, 'La corrispondenza fra nomi ebraici e nomi locali nella prassi dell'ebraismo italiano', in *Italia judaica* (Rome, 1983), 67–86, first section of full study published in his *Judaica minora* (Milan, 1983), 661–825.

—— 'Cognomi ebraici italiani a base toponomastica straniera', in *Italia judaica* (Rome, 1989), 31–47, repr. in his *Judaica minora: nuove ricerche* (Milan, 1991), 65–83.

—— 'Una correzzione necessaria a proposito di Anselmo Rossi, musico mantovano del Seicento', *Civiltà mantovana*, 28–9 (1990), 201–4.

CONFORTO, GIOVANNI LUCA, *Breve e facile maniera d'essercitarsi a far passaggi* (Rome, 1593; fac. edn. with German tr. by Johannes Wolf, Berlin, 1922).

CONIGLIO, GIUSEPPE, *I Gonzaga* (Varese, 1967).

—— *et al.* (eds.), *Mantova: la storia, le lettere, le arti* (9 vols. in 11; Mantua, 1958–65).

COOPERMAN, BERNARD (ed.), *Jewish Thought in the Sixteenth Century* (Cambridge, Mass., 1983).

CORDERO DI PAMPARATO, STANISLAO, 'I musici alla corte di Carlo Emanuele I di Savoia', *Biblioteca della Società Storica Subalpina*, 121 (1930), 84–93.

COZZI, GAETANO (ed.), *Gli ebrei a Venezia, secoli XIV–XVIII* (Milan, 1987).

CROCKER, EUNICE CHANDLER, 'An Introductory Study of the Italian Canzona for Instrumental Ensembles and its Influence upon the Baroque Sonata', Ph.D. diss. (Radcliffe College, 1943).

DAHLHAUS, CARL, *Studies on the Origin of Harmonic Tonality*, tr. Robert O. Gjerdingen (Princeton, 1990).

D'ANCONA, ALESSANDRO, 'Il teatro mantovano nel secolo XVI', *Giornale storico della letteratura italiana*, 5 (1886), 1–52; 6 (1886), 313–51; 7 (1886), 48–93. Repr. in his *Origini del teatro italiano*, ii. 398–575.

—— *Origini del teatro italiano*, 2nd edn. (2 vols.; Turin, 1891). On Jewish theatre, see ii. 398–429 ('Gli ebrei di Mantova e il teatro').

DAVARI, STEFANO, *La musica a Mantova* (Mantua, 1975; repr. after *Rivista storica mantovana*, 1 (1885), 79–183).

DAVERIO, JOHN, 'In Search of the Sonata da camera before Corelli', *Acta musicologica*, 57 (1985), 195–214.

DEFORD, RUTH I., 'The Evolution of Rhythmic Style in Italian Secular Music of the Late Sixteenth Century', *Studi musicali*, 10 (1981), 43–74.

—— 'Musical Relationships between the Italian Madrigal and Light Genres in the Sixteenth Century', *Musica disciplina*, 39 (1985), 107–68.

DOLET, ÉTIENNE, *Commentariorum linguae latinae tomus secundus* (Lyons, 1538).

EHRMANN, SABINE, *Claudio Monteverdi: Die Grundbegriffe seines musiktheoretischen Denkens* (Pfaffenweiler, 1989).

ELBOGEN, ISMAR, *Jewish Liturgy: A Comprehensive History*, tr. Raymond P. Scheindlin (Philadelphia, 1993).

ELWERT, W. THEODOR, *La poesia lirica italiana del Seicento: studio sullo stile barocco* (Florence, 1967).

Encyclopaedia judaica (16 vols.; Jerusalem, 1972).

ERRANTE, VINCENZO. ' "Forse che sì, forse che no": la terza spedizione del duca Vincenzo Gonzaga in Ungheria alla guerra contro il turco (1601) studiata su documenti inediti', *Archivio storico lombardo*, 5th ser., 42 (1915), 15–114.

FABBRI, PAOLO, *Gusto scenico a Mantova nel tardo Rinascimento* (Padua, 1974).

——'Tasso, Guarini e il "Divino Claudio": componenti manieristi nella poetica di Monteverdi', *Studi musicali*, 3 (1974), 233–54.

——*Monteverdi*, tr. Tim Carter (Cambridge, 1994).

FENLON, IAIN, *Music and Patronage in Sixteenth-Century Mantua* (2 vols.; Cambridge, 1980–2).

——'*In destructione turcharum*: The Victory of Lepanto in Sixteenth-Century Music and Letters', in Francesco Degrada (ed.), *Andrea Gabrieli e il suo tempo* (Florence, 1987), 293–317.

FERRARI, DANIELA (ed.), *Mantova nelle stampe: trentottanta carte, piante, e vedute del territorio mantovano* (Brescia, 1985)

Les Fêtes du mariage de Ferdinand de Médicis et de Christine de Lorraine (Florence, 1589), ed. D. P. Walker (Paris, 1963).

FIDERER-ABRAMOVICZ, ADRIANA, 'Mekoma shel hamusika baliturgya shel yehudei italya: hemshekhiyut veshinui' ['The Place of Music in the Liturgy of the Italian Jews: Continuity and Change'], MA thesis (Tel Aviv University, 1987).

FIGINO, GREGORIO COMANINI, *Il Figino, overo del fine della pittura* (Mantua, 1591).

FLANDERS, PETER, 'The Madrigals of Benedetto Pallavicino', Ph.D. diss. (New York University, 1971).

FOA, SALVATORE, *Gli ebrei nel Monferrato nei secoli XVI e XVII* (Alessandria, 1914; repr. Bologna, 1965).

——*La politica economica della casa savoia: gli ebrei dal secolo XVI fino alla rivoluzione francese* (Rome, 1961).

FOCHESSATI, GIUSEPPE, *I Gonzaga di Mantova e l'ultima duca*, 2nd edn. (Milan, 1930).

FOLLINO, FEDERICO, *Compendio delle sontuose feste fatte l'anno M.DC.VIII nella città di Mantova per le reali nozze del Serenissimo Prencipe D. Francesco Gonzaga con la Serenissima Infanta Margherita di Savoia* (Mantua, 1608; repr. in Solerti, *Gli albori*, iii. [205]–34, also in Chiabrera, *Opere*, iv. 107–40).

FORTUNE, NIGEL, 'Italian Secular Monody from 1600 to 1635: An Introductory Study', *Musical Quarterly*, 39 (1953), 171–95.

FRIEDHABER, ZVI, 'Hamaḥol bekehilot yehudei dukasut mantova bame'ot ha-17 veha-18' ['Dance in the Jewish Communities of the Duchy of Mantua in the Seventeenth and Eighteenth Centuries'], *Pe'amim*, 37 (1988), 67–77.

GAFFURIO, FRANCHINO, *De harmonia musicorum instrumentorum opus* (Milan, 1518; fac. repr. Bologna, 1972), tr. Clement Miller (Neuhausen-Stuttgart, 1977).

GANASSI, SILVESTRO DI, *Opera intitulata Fontegara* (Venice, 1535), English tr. Hildemarie Peter (Berlin-Lichterfelds, 1956).

GASTOLDI, GIOVANNI GIACOMO, *Balletti a cinque voci con li suoi versi per cantare, sonare & ballare* (1591), ed. Michel Sanvoisin (Paris, 1968).

——*Balletti a 3* (1594), ed. Daniel Benkö (Budapest, 1981).

——*Salmi per tutto l'anno a cinque voci, col suo basso continuo a beneplacito* (Bologna, 1673).

GHIRARDINI, GHERARDO, 'Salamone Rossi, musico alla corte dei Gonzaga: studio biografico', *La rassegna mensile di Israel*, 51 (1985), 96–103.

GHISI, FEDERICO, 'Le musiche per "Il ballo di donne turche" di Marco da Gagliano', *Rivista italiana di musicologia*, 1 (1966), 20–31.

GIUSTINIANI, VINCENZO, *Discorso sopra la musica de' suoi tempi* (1628; Lucca, Biblioteca Comunale, MS O49), tr. Carol MacClintock (n.p., 1962).

GMEINWIESER, SIEGFRIED, *et al.* (eds.), *Musicologia humana: Studies in Honour of Warren and Ursula Kirkendale* (Florence, 1994).

GRADENWITZ, PETER, 'An Early Instance of Copyright—Venice, 1622', *Music & Letters*, 27 (1946), 185–6.

Grande dizionario della lingua italiana (14 [A–R] vols.; Turin, 1960–   ).

GUSSAGO, CESARIO, *Sonate a quattro, sei et otto, con alcuni concerti a otto* (1608), ed. Andrew Dell'Antonio (New York, 1994).

HAAR, JAMES, 'The "Madrigale arioso": A Mid-Century Development in the Cinquecento Madrigal', *Studi musicali*, 12 (1983), 203–19.

HAMESSLEY, LYDIA RIGMOR, 'The Reception of the Italian Madrigal in England: A Repertorial Study of Manuscript Anthologies, ca. 1580–1620', Ph.D. diss. (2 vols.; University of Minnesota, 1989).

HANSELL, KATHLEEN KUZMICK, 'The Origins of the Italian Trio Sonata', MA thesis (University of Illinois, 1969).

HARRÁN, DON, 'Verse Types in the Early Madrigal', *Journal of the American Musicological Society*, 22 (1969), 27–53 (repr. in Ellen Rosand (ed.), *The Garland Library of the History of Western Music* (14 vols.; New York, 1985), iii. 287–313; and, in an Italian tr. as 'Tipologie metriche e formali del madrigale ai suoi esordi', in Paolo Fabbri (ed.), *Il madrigale tra Cinque e Seicento* (Bologna, 1988), 95–122).

—— *Word-Tone Relations in Musical Thought: From Antiquity to the Seventeenth Century* (Neuhausen-Stuttgart, 1986).

—— 'Salamone Rossi as a Composer of Theatre Music', *Studi musicali*, 16 (1987), 95–131.

—— 'Salamone Rossi, Jewish Musician in Renaissance Italy', *Acta musicologica*, 59 (1987), 46–64.

—— *In Search of Harmony: Hebrew and Humanist Elements in Sixteenth-Century Musical Thought* (Neuhausen-Stuttgart, 1988).

—— 'Elegance as a Concept in Sixteenth-Century Music Criticism', *Renaissance Quarterly*, 41 (1988), 413–38.

—— *In Defence of Music: The Case for Music as Argued by a Singer and Scholar of the Late Fifteenth Century* (Lincoln, Nebr., 1989).

—— 'Cultural Fusions in Jewish Musical Thought of the Later Renaissance', in Fabrizio Della Seta and Franco Piperno (eds.), *In cantu et in sermone: For Nino Pirrotta on his 80th Birthday* (Florence, 1989), 141–54.

—— 'Tradition and Innovation in Jewish Music of the Later Renaissance', *Journal of Musicology*, 7 (1989), 107–30 (repr. in Ruderman (ed.), *Essential Papers on Jewish Culture* (1992), 474–501).

—— 'Allegro Porto, an Early Jewish Composer on the Verge of Christianity', *Italia: studi e ricerche sulla storia, la cultura e la letteratura degli ebrei d'Italia*, 10 (1993), 19–57.

—— 'Jewish Dramatists and Musicians in the Renaissance: Separate Activities, Common Aspirations', in Gmeinwieser *et al.* (eds.), *Musicologia humana* (1994), 291–304; also in Belkin (ed.), *Leone de' Sommi and the Performing Arts* (1997), 27–47.

—— 'Madama Europa, Jewish Singer in Late Renaissance Mantua', in Thomas J. Mathiesen and Benito V. Rivera (eds.), *Festa musicologica: Essays in Honour of George J. Buelow* (Stuyvesant, NY, 1995), 197–231.

—— 'Doubly Tainted, Doubly Talented: The Jewish Poet Sara Copio (d. 1641) as a Heroic Singer', in Irene Alm *et al.* (eds.), *Musica franca: Essays in Honour of Frank A. D'Accone* (Stuyvesant, NY, 1996), 367–422.

—— 'Research into Music of the Renaissance: New Perspectives, New Objectives', *Israel Studies in Musicology*, 6 (1996), 81–98.

—— 'The Fixed and the Changeable in the Problematic of Stylistic Definition', in Kristine Pfarr (ed.), *Festschrift Christoph-Hellmut Mahling zum 65. Geburtstag* (Mainz, 1997), 489–500.

—— 'Toward a Rhetorical Code of Early Music Performance', *Journal of Musicology*, 15 (1997), 19–42.

—— '"Dum recordaremur Sion": Music in the Life and Thought of the Venetian Rabbi Leon Modena (1571–1648)', *Association for Jewish Studies Review*, 23 (1998), 17–61.

—— 'Jewish Musical Culture in Early Modern Venice', in Robert C. Davis and Benjamin Ravid (eds.), *The Jews of Venice: A Unique Renaissance Community* (Baltimore, forthcoming).

—— 'From Mantua to Vienna: A New Approach to the Origins of the Dance Suite', in Walter Kreyszig (ed.), *Austria, 996–1996: Music in a Changing Society* (3 vols.; Vienna, forthcoming).

—— 'Psalms as Songs: The "Psalms of David" in Salamone Rossi's "Songs of Solomon"', in *Musica antiqua europae orientalis, Bydgoszcz 1994* (forthcoming).

—— 'Salamone Rossi as a Composer of "Hebrew" Music', in Edwin Seroussi and Eliyahu Schleifer (eds.), *Festschrift in Honour of Israel Adler* (Jerusalem, forthcoming).

—— 'From Music to Matrimony: The Wedding Odes of Rabbi Leon Modena (1571–1648)', in *Proceedings of the Twelfth World Congress of Jewish Studies, Jerusalem, 1997* (Jerusalem, forthcoming).

—— (ed.), *Fragmenta polyphonica judaica* (including works by Civita, Porto, and Sacerdote; in preparation for the Jewish Music Research Centre, Hebrew University, Jerusalem).

—— (*olim* Donald Hersh), 'Verdelot and the Early Madrigal', Ph.D. diss. (2 vols.; University of California at Berkeley, 1963).

HARTMANN, ARNOLD, Jr., 'Battista Guarini and *Il pastor fido*', *Musical Quarterly*, 39 (1953), 415–25.

HODGKINSON, C. C., 'Terminology, Performance, and Structure of the "Bass" in Few-Voiced Seventeenth-Century Italian Instrumental Music', Ph.D. thesis (Sheffield University, 1978).

HOLMAN, PETER, *Four and Twenty Fiddlers: The Violin at the English Court, 1540–1690* (Oxford, 1993).

HOROWITZ, ELLIOTT, 'Coffee, Coffeehouses, and the Nocturnal Rituals of Early Modern Jewry', *Association for Jewish Studies Review*, 14 (1989), 17–46.

HUGHES, D. OWEN, 'Sumptuary Law and Social Relations in Renaissance Italy', in John Bossy (ed.), *Disputes and Settlements: Law and Human Relations in the West* (Cambridge, 1983), 69–79.

IDEL, MOSHE, 'Haperush hamagi vehate'urgi shel hamusika betekstim yehudiyim mitkufat harenesans ve'ad haḥasidut' ['The Magical and Theurgic Interpretation of Music in Jewish Texts from the Renaissance until Hassidism'], in *Yuval: Studies of the Jewish Music Research Centre* (Hebrew University), 4 (1982), 33–63 (Hebr. section).

—— 'Major Currents in Italian Kabbalah between 1560–1660', in *Italia judaica: gli ebrei in Italia tra Rinascimento ed età barocca* (Rome, 1986), 243–62 (repr. in Ruderman (ed.), *Essential Papers on Jewish Culture* (1992), 345–68).

—— 'Differing Conceptions of Kabbalah in the Early Seventeenth Century', in Twersky and Septimus (eds.), *Jewish Thought in the Seventeenth Century* (1987), 137–200.

—— 'The Anthropology of Yohanan Alemanno: Sources and Influences', *Topoi*, 7 (1988), 201–10.

IDELSOHN, ABRAHAM ZVI, *Jewish Liturgy and its Development* (New York, 1932).

IMMANUEL HAROMI ('the Roman'; d. 1335), *Maḥbarot* ['Notebooks'], ed. Dov Yarden (Jerusalem, 1957).

JACOBSON, JOSHUA R., 'A Possible Influence of Traditional Chant on a Synagogue Motet of Salamone Rossi', *Musica judaica*, 10 (1987/8), 52–8.

JENSEN, NIELS M., 'Solo Sonata, Duo Sonata, and Trio Sonata: Some Problems of Terminology and Genre in Seventeenth-Century Italian Instrumental Music', in Nils Schiørring *et al.* (eds.), *Festkrift Jens Peter Larsen* (Copenhagen, 1972), 73–101.

JOYCE, JOHN J., *The Monodies of Sigismondo d'India* (Ann Arbor, 1981).

KAMEN, HENRY ARTHUR FRANCIS, *The Iron Century: Social Change in Europe, 1550–1660* (London, 1971).

KIRKENDALE, WARREN, 'Alessandro Striggio und die Medici: Neue Briefe und Dokumente', in Augerer *et al.* (eds.), *Festschrift Othmar Wessely* (1982), 325–53.

—— 'Zur Biographie des ersten Orfeo, Francesco Rasi', in *Festschrift Reinhold Hammerstein zum 70. Geburtstag* (Laaber, 1986), 297–335.

—— *The Court Musicians in Florence during the Principate of the Medici: With a Reconstruction of the Artistic Establishment* (Florence, 1993).

KISCH, GUIDO, 'The Yellow Badge in History', *Historia judaica*, 19 (1957), 89–146.

KURTZMAN, JEFFREY, 'An Early Seventeenth-Century Manuscript of "Canzonette e Madrigaletti Spirituali"', *Studi musicali*, 8 (1979), 149–71.

LAKI, PETER G., 'The Madrigals of Giambattista Marino and their Settings for Solo Voice (1602–1640)', Ph.D. diss. (University of Pennsylvania, 1989).

LANFRANCO, GIOVANNI MARIA, *Scintille di musica* (Brescia, 1533; fac. repr. Bologna, 1970).

LASOCKI, DAVID, and PRIOR, ROGER, *The Bassanos: Venetian Musicians and Instrument Makers in England, 1531–1665* (Aldershot, Hants, 1995).

LEA, KATHLEEN M., *Italian Popular Comedy: A Study in the 'Commedia dell'arte'* (2 vols.; Oxford, 1934).

LEOPOLD, SILKE, *Monteverdi: Music in Transition*, tr. Anne Smith (Oxford, 1991), originally *Claudio Monteverdi und seine Zeit* (Laaber, 1986).

LESURE, FRANÇOIS, and SARTORI, CLAUDIO (comps.), *Il nuovo Vogel* (3 vols.; Pomezia, 1977).

LEVI, BONAJUTO ISAC, *Indice-repertorio dell'Archivio della Comunità israelitica di Mantova* (10 vols. in manuscript).

LEVI, LEO, 'Canti tradizionali e tradizioni liturgiche giudeo-italiane', *La rassegna mensile di Israel*, 23 (1957), 403–11, 435–45.

——'Melodie tradizionali ebraico-italiane', in *Studi e ricerche 1948–1960* (Rome, 1961), 61–8.

——'Italy: Musical Tradition', in *Encyclopaedia judaica* (1972), ix. 1142–7.

LEWIS, EDGAR J., 'The Use of Wind Instruments in Seventeenth-Century Instrumental Music', Ph.D. diss. (University of Wisconsin, 1964).

LIEBSCHER, JULIA, *Das italienische Kammerduett (ca. 1670–1750)* (Tutzing, 1987).

London, British Library, MS Egerton 3665: The Tregian Manuscript (copied by Francis Tregian the Younger in London between 1613 and 1619), ed. Frank A. D'Accone (2 vols.; New York, 1988).

LUZIO, ALESSANDRO, and TORELLI, PIETRO (comps.), *L'archivio Gonzaga di Mantova* (2 vols.; Ostiglia and Verona, 1920–2).

LUZZATTO, SAMUEL DAVID, *Mavo lemaḥzor benei roma* ['Introduction to the Festival Prayer Book of the Roman Rite'], ed. Daniel Goldschmidt (Tel Aviv, 1966).

MACCLINTOCK, CAROL, *Giaches de Wert (1535–1596): Life and Works* (n.p., 1966).

MAGID, DAVID, 'Shir lo noda' me'et rav yehuda arye de modena' ['An Unknown Poem by Rabbi Leon Modena'], *'Alim lebibliografya vekorot yisra'el*, 2 (1935), 103–6.

MAINERIO, GIORGIO, *Il primo libro de balli* (1578), ed. Manfred Schuler (Mainz, 1961).

MANFREDI, MUZIO, *Madrigali* (Venice, 1605).

MANGSEN, SANDRA JOAN, 'Instrumental Duos and Trios in Printed Italian Sources, 1600–1675', Ph.D. diss. (2 vols.; Cornell University, 1989).

——'*Ad libitum* Procedures in Instrumental Duos and Trios', *Early Music*, 19 (1991), 29–40.

Mantova e i Gonzaga nella civiltà del Rinascimento (Mantua, 1977).

MARCHETTO DA PADUA, *Lucidarium* (between 1309 and 1318), ed. and tr. Jan W. Herlinger (Chicago, 1985).

——*Pomerium* (between 1318 and 1326), ed. Giuseppe Vecchi (n.p., 1961).

MARINI, BIAGIO, *Affetti musicali, opera prima* (1617), ed. Franco Piperno (Milan, 1990).

——*Madrigaletti a 1–4 voci . . . con il suo basso continuo, libro quinto, opera nona* (Venice, 1635).

MARINO, GIOVAN BATTISTA, *Le rime* (2 vols.; Venice, 1602), rev. edn. as *La lira* (Venice, 1608, and, with pt. 3 (verses written after 1602), 1614). For other verses, see Marino's collections *La sampogna* and *La galleria* (both 1620).

——*Lettere*, ed. Marziano Guglielminetti (Turin, 1966).

MASON, KEVIN BRUCE, *The Chitarrone and its Repertoire in Early Seventeenth-Century Italy* (Aberystwyth, 1989).

MASSARANO, ABRAMO, *Sefer hagalut vehapedut* ['The Book of Exile and Redemption'] (Venice, 1634; fac. edn. plus Italian tr. as *L'esilio e il riscatto: le vicende degli ebrei mantovani tra il 1627 e il 1631* [Bologna, 1977]).

MENGHINI, MARIO, *Tommaso Stigliani: contributo alla storia letteraria del secolo XVI* (Genoa, 1890).

MERULO, CLAUDIO, *Il primo libro de ricercari da cantare, a quattro voci* (1574); *Ricercari da cantare a quattro voci . . . libro secondo* (1607); *Ricercari da cantare a quattro voci . . . libro terzo* (1608) (altogether sixty ensemble ricercars), ed. James Ladewig (3 vols.; New York, 1987).

MILANO, ATTILIO, *Storia degli ebrei in Italia* (Turin, 1963).

MODENA, LEON, *Historia de riti hebraici* (Venice, 1638; fac. repr. of 1678 edn., Bologna, 1979).

—— *Divan*, ed. Simon Bernstein (Philadelphia, 1932).

—— *She'elot utshuvot ziknei yehuda* ['*Responsa* of the Elders of Judah'], ed. Shlomo Simonsohn (Jerusalem, 1955).

—— *Igrot rabi yehuda arye mimodena* ['Letters of Leon Modena'], ed. Jacob Boksenboim (Tel Aviv, 1984).

—— *Ḥayei yehuda* ['The Life of Judah'], ed. Daniel Carpi (Tel Aviv, 1985). For Engl. version, see *The Autobiography of a Seventeenth-Century Venetian Rabbi: Leon Modena's 'Life of Judah'*, tr. Mark R. Cohen, with historical notes by Howard Adelman and Benjamin Ravid (Princeton, 1988).

MOENS, KAREL, 'La "nascita" del violino nei Paesi Bassi del sud: alla storia di un luogo dove collocare l'inizio della storia del violino', in Marco Tielle (ed.), *Monteverdi: imperatore della musica (1567–1643)* (Rovereto, 1993), 84–131.

MOLIN, CRISTINA DAL, 'Recovery of Some Unedited Manuscripts by Leone de' Sommi at the National Library of Turin', in Belkin (ed.), *Leone de' Sommi and the Performing Arts* (1997), 101–17.

MONTEATH, KATHRYN BOSI, 'The Five-Part Madrigals of Benedetto Pallavicino', Ph.D. diss. (University of Otago, 1981).

MONTEVERDI, CLAUDIO, *Tutte le opere*, ed. G. Francesco Malipiero (16 vols.; Vienna, 1926–42).

—— *L'Orfeo, favola in musica*, ed. Denis Stevens (London, 1968).

—— *The Letters of Claudio Monteverdi*, tr. Denis Stevens (Cambridge, 1980).

MORLEY, THOMAS, *A Plain and Easy Introduction to Practical Music* (1595), ed. R. Alec Harman (London, 1952).

MOROSINI, GIULIO [*olim* Samuel Naḥmias], *Via della fede mostrata agli ebrei* (3 vols.; Rome, 1683).

MORTARA, MARCO, *Catalogo dei manoscritti della biblioteca della Comunità israelitica di Mantova* (Leghorn, 1878).

MORTARO, ANTONIO, *Primo libro de canzoni da sonare a quattro voci* (1600), ed. James Ladewig (New York, 1988).

MOSCATO, JUDAH, *Higayon bekhinor* ['Contemplations on a Lyre'], the first of his sermons published in *Sefer nefutsot yehuda* ['Book of the Dispersed of Judah'] (Venice, 1588/9). See Adler (ed.), *Hebrew Writings Concerning Music* (1975), 223–39; and for an annotated Germ. tr. by Herzl Shmueli, *Higgajon bechinnor: Betrachtungen zum Leierspiel des Jehudah . . . Moscato* (Tel Aviv, 1953).

Musiche de alcuni eccellentissimi musici composte per la Maddalena, sacra rappresentazione di Gio. Battista Andreini fiorentino (Venice, 1617).

NAGAN, ZVI HERBERT, 'Giovanni Giacomo Gastoldi's Liturgical Compositions: An Examination of his Psalms, Magnificats, Marian Antiphons, and Motets', MA thesis (Tel Aviv University, 1976).

NAGLER, ALOIS MARIA, *Theatre Festivals of the Medici, 1539–1637*, tr. George Hick-enlooper (New Haven, 1964).

NEGRI, CESARE, *Le gratie d'amore* (Milan, 1602; fac. repr. New York, 1969).

NERI, ACHILLE, 'Gli "intermezzi" del *Pastor fido*', *Giornale storico della letteratura italiana*, 11 (1888), 405–15.

—— 'Gabriele Chiabrera e la corte di Mantova', *Giornale storico della letteratura italiana*, 7 (1896), 317–44.

NETTL, PAUL, 'Giovanni Battista Buonamente', *Zeitschrift für Musikwissenschaft*, 9 (1926–7), 528–42.

—— 'Musicisti ebrei del Rinascimento italiano', *La rassegna mensile d'Israel*, 2 (1926/7), 59–71.

NEWMAN, JOEL, 'The Madrigals of Salamon de' Rossi', Ph.D. diss. (Columbia University, 1962).

NORSA, PAOLO, *Una famiglia di banchieri, la famiglia Norsa (1350–1950)* (2 vols.; Naples, 1953–9).

NORSA, UMBERTO, *Relazione sulle istitutioni di culto e beneficenza esistenti nella communità israelitica di Mantova* (Mantua, 1901).

NORTH, NIGEL, *Continuo Playing on the Lute, Archlute, and Theorbo: A Comprehensive Guide for Performers* (Bloomington, Ind., 1987).

Il nuovo Zingarelli: vocabolario della lingua italiana, 11th edn. (Bologna, 1983).

NUTTER, DAVID, 'The Italian Polyphonic Dialogue of the Sixteenth Century', Ph.D. thesis (University of Nottingham, 1978).

OREGLIA, GIACOMO, *The Commedia dell'Arte*, tr. Lovett F. Edwards (London, 1968).

Orlando di Lasso et alii: canzoni villanesche e villanelle, ed. Donna G. Cardamone (Madison, 1991).

OSSI, MASSIMO, 'Claudio Monteverdi's *Ordine novo, bello et gustevole*: The Canzonetta as Dramatic Module and Formal Archetype', *Journal of the American Musicological Society*, 45 (1992), 261–304.

OSTHOFF, WOLFGANG, *Theatergesang und darstellende Musik in der italienischen Renaissance* (2 vols.; Tutzing, 1969).

PACE, PIETRO, *Madrigali a quattro et a cinque voci con sinfonia se piace, e parte senza* (Venice, 1617).

PALESTRINA, GIOVANNI BATTISTA PIERLUIGI DA, *Werke*, ed. Franz Xaver Haberl *et al.* (33 vols.; Leipzig, 1862–1907, repr. Farnborough, 1968).

PALISCA, CLAUDE, '*Ut oratoria musica*: The Rhetorical Basis of Musical Mannerism', in Franklin W. Robinson and Stephen G. Nichols, Jr. (eds.), *The Meaning of Mannerism* (Hanover, NH, 1972), 37–65.

PALLAVICINO, BENEDETTO, *Opera omnia*, ed. Peter Flanders and Kathryn Bosi Monteath (7 vols.; Neuhausen-Stuttgart, 1982–96).

PARISI, SUSAN HELEN, 'Ducal Patronage of Music in Mantua, 1587–1627: An Archival Study', Ph.D. diss. (2 vols.; University of Illinois, 1989).

—— 'Musicians at the Court of Mantua during Monteverdi's Time: Evidence from the Payrolls', in Gmeinwieser *et al.* (eds.), *Musicologia humana* (1994), 183–208.

—— 'The Jewish Community and Carnival Entertainment at the Mantuan Court in the Early Baroque,' in Jessie Ann Owens and Anthony M. Cummings (eds.), *Music in Renaissance Cities and Courts: Studies in Honor of Lewis Lockwood* (Warren, Mich., 1997), 297–305.

PARKER, GEOFFREY, *Europe in Crisis, 1598–1648* (Ithaca, NY, 1979).

—— and SMITH, LESLIE M. (eds.), *The General Crisis of the Seventeenth Century* (London, 1978).

PARROTT, ANDREW, 'Transposition in Monteverdi's Vespers of 1610: An "Aberration" Defended', *Early Music*, 12 (1984), 490–516.

PENNA, LORENZO, *Li primi albori musicali per li principianti della musica figurata* (1672), 4th rev. edn. (Bologna, 1684; fac. repr. Bologna, 1969).

PETRACCI, PIETRO (ed.), *Ghirlanda dell'Aurora, scelta di madrigali de' più famosi autori di questo secolo* (Venice, 1608).

PETROBELLI, PIERLUIGI, '"Ah dolente partita": Marenzio, Wert, Monteverdi', in *Claudio Monteverdi e il suo tempo* (Verona, 1969), 361–76.

PIPERNO, FRANCO, 'La sinfonia strumentale del primo Seicento—I', *Studi musicali*, 4 (1975), 145–68.

—— 'I quattro libri di musica strumentale di Salamone Rossi', *Nuova rivista musicale italiana*, 13 (1979), 337–57.

—— ' "Concerto" e "concertato" nella musica strumentale italiana del secolo decimo settimo', *Recercare*, 3 (1991), 169–202.

PIRROTTA, NINO, 'Scelte poetiche di Monteverdi', *Nuova rivista musicale italiana*, 2 (1968), 10–42 (repr. in tr. as 'Monteverdi's Poetic Choices', in id., *Music and Culture in Italy from the Middle Ages to the Baroque: A Collection of Essays*, ed. Lewis Lockwood and Christoph Wolff (Cambridge, Mass., 1984), 271–316).

—— and POVOLEDO, ELENA, *Music and Theatre from Poliziano to Monteverdi*, tr. Karen Eales (Cambridge, 1982), originally *Li due Orfei: da Poliziano a Monteverdi*, 2nd edn. (Turin, 1975).

POLAK, EMIL J., *Medieval and Renaissance Letter Treatises and Form Letters* (2 vols.; Leiden, 1993–4).

POLIAKOV, LÉON, *Jewish Bankers and the Holy See from the Thirteenth to the Seventeenth Century*, tr. Miriam Kochan (London, 1977), originally *Les Banquiers juifs et le Saint-Siège du XIIIe au XVIIe siècle* (Paris, 1965).

PORTALEONE, ABRAHAM, *Shiltei hagiborim* ['Shields of Heroes'] (Mantua, 1611/12). Musical portions reprinted in Adler (ed.), *Hebrew Writings Concerning Music* (1975), 246–83. See also Daniel Sandlar, 'Pirkei hamusika besefer "Shiltei hagiborim"...' ['The Musical Chapters in the Book *Shiltei hagiborim*...'], Ph.D. diss. (Tel Aviv University, 1980).

PORTIOLI, ATTILIO, *Il matrimonio di Ferdinando Gonzaga con Catherina de' Medici* (Mantua, 1882).

PRAETORIUS, MICHAEL, *Syntagma musicum* (3 vols.; Wolfenbüttel, 1614–18, fac. repr. Kassel, 1958–9).

PRIOR, ROGER, 'Jewish Musicians at the Tudor Court', *Musical Quarterly*, 69 (1983), 253–65.

QUAZZA, ROMOLO, *Mantova e Monferrato nella politica europea alla vigilia della guerra per la successione (1624–7), da documenti inediti tratti dall'Archivio Gonzaga* (Mantua, 1922).

—— 'Ferdinando Gonzaga e Carlo Emanuele I (Dal trattato di Pavia all'accordo del 1624)', *Archivio storico lombardo*, 49 (1922), 29–118.

—— *La guerra per la successione di Mantova e del Monferrato (1628–31)* (Mantua, 1926).

QUONDAM, AMEDEO, *Le 'carte messaggiere': retorica e modelli di comunicazione epistolare (per un indice dei libri di lettere del Cinquecento)* (Rome, 1981).

RAVID, BENJAMIN, *Economics and Toleration in Seventeenth-Century Venice: The Background and Context of the* Discorso *of Simone Luzzatto* (Jerusalem, 1978).

—— 'Contra Judaeos in Seventeenth-Century Italy: Two Responses to the *Discorso* of Simone Luzzatto by Melchiore Palontrotti and Giulio Morosini', *Association for Jewish Studies Review*, 7–8 (1983), 301–51.

—— 'From Yellow to Red: On the Distinguishing Head-Covering of the Jews of Venice', *Jewish History*, 6 (1992), 179–210.

REINER, STEWART, 'La vag'Angioletta (and others)', *Analecta musicologica*, 14 (1974), 26–88.

A Renaissance Entertainment: Festivities for the Marriage of Cosimo I, Duke of Florence, in 1539, ed. Andrew C. Minor and Bonner Mitchell (Columbia, Mo., 1968).

REUCHLIN, JOHANNES, *De accentibus, et orthographia, linguae hebraicae* (Haguenau, 1518).

RINALDI, CESARE, *De' madrigali di Cesare Rinaldi bolognese prima, et seconda parte* (Bologna, 1588).

RIVOIRE, PIETRO, 'Contributo alla storia delle relazioni tra Carlo Emanuele I e Ferdinando Gonzaga', *Bollettino storico-bibliografico subalpino*, 4 (1899), 408–44.

ROCHE, JEROME, *North Italian Church Music in the Age of Monteverdi* (Oxford, 1984).

ROMANO, REMIGIO (comp.), *Prima raccolta di bellissime canzonette musicali e moderne di auttori gravissimi* (Vicenza, 1622).

ROMANSTEIN, STANLEY E., 'Giovanni Battista Buonamente and Instrumental Music of the Early Baroque', Ph.D. diss. (2 vols.; University of Cincinnati, 1990).

ROSSI, SALAMONE, *Complete Works*, ed. Don Harrán (Corpus Mensurabilis Musicae, 100, 13 vols. in 5; Neuhausen-Stuttgart, vols. i–xii, 1995, vol. xiii forthcoming).

—— *Hashirim asher lishlomo* ['The Songs of Solomon'], *psaumes, chants et hymnes* (in *Cantiques de Salomon Rossi hebreo*...), ed. Samuel Naumbourg (Paris, 1877; repr. New York, 1954—contains all but three pieces, edited separately by Eric Werner as *Three Hebrew Compositions for Mixed Chorus* (New York, 1956), viz. nos. 6, 18, 31). For a better, though far from faultless reading, see *Hashirim asher lishlomo, Thirty-Three Psalms, Songs, and Hymns*, ed. Fritz Rikko (3 vols.; New York, 1967–73). A new edition will appear as vol. xiii of Rossi's *Complete Works* (as above). For an annotated reading of the original prefatory matter, see Adler (ed.), *Hebrew Writings Concerning Music*, 212–21, 285–8.

ROTH, CECIL, 'L'accademia musicale del ghetto veneziano', *La rassegna mensile di Israel*, 3 (1927/8), 152–62.

—— *The History of the Jews of Italy* (Philadelphia, 1946).

—— *The Jews in the Renaissance* (Philadelphia, 1959).

RUDERMAN, DAVID (ed.), *Essential Papers on Jewish Culture in Renaissance and Baroque Italy* (New York, 1992).

Sacre rappresentazioni dei secoli XIV, XV e XVI raccolte e illustrate, ed. Alessandro D'Ancona (3 vols.; Florence, 1872).

SADIE, STANLEY (ed.), *The New Grove Dictionary of Music and Musicians* (20 vols.; London, 1980).

SALMEN, WALTER, '...*denn die Fiedel macht das Fest': Jüdische Musikanten und Tänzer vom 13. bis 20. Jahrhundert* (Innsbruck, 1991).

SCHAERF, SAMUELE, *I cognomi degli ebrei d'Italia con un'appendice su le famiglie nobili ebree d'Italia* (Florence, 1925).

SCHIRMANN, CHAIM, 'Hate'atron vehamusika bishkhunot hayehudim be'italya bein hame'a ha-16 veha-18' ['Theatre and Music in the Italian Ghettos between the Sixteenth and Seventeenth Centuries'], *Zion*, 29 (1964), 61–111 (repr. in id., *Studies in the History of Hebrew Poetry and Drama* (2 vols.; Jerusalem, 1979), ii. 44–94).

SCHRADE, LEO, *Monteverdi, Creator of Modern Music* (New York, 1950).

Sefer kenaf renanim ['The Book of the Songbird'] (Venice, 1626).

Sefer shirei yisra'el / Libro dei canti d'Israele: antichi canti liturgici del rito degli ebrei spagnoli, ed. Federico Consolo (Florence, 1892).

SEGARIZZI, ARNALDO (ed.), *Relazioni degli ambasciatori veneti al Senato* (4 vols.; Bari, 1912–16).

SEGRE, RENATA, *The Jews in Piedmont* (2 vols.; Jerusalem, 1988).

SELFRIDGE-FIELD, ELEANOR, *Venetian Instrumental Music from Gabrieli to Vivaldi*, 3rd rev. edn. (New York, 1994).

SHULVASS, MOSES AVIGDOR, *The Jews in the World of the Renaissance*, tr. Elvin I. Kose (Leiden and Chicago, 1973), originally *Ḥayei hayehudim be'italya bitkufat harenesans* (New York, 1955).

SIMON, R., and GIDROL, D., 'Appunti sulle relazioni tra l'opera poetica di G. B. Marino e la musica del suo tempo', *Studi secenteschi*, 14 (1973), 81–187.

SIMONSOHN, SHLOMO, 'Sefarim vesifriyot shel yehudei mantova, 1595' ['Books and Libraries of Mantuan Jews, 1595'], *Kiryat sefer*, 37 (1961/2), 103–22.

—— *History of the Jews in the Duchy of Mantua* (Jerusalem, 1977), tr. from *Toledot hayehudim bedukasut mantova* (2 vols.; Jerusalem, 1962–4).

—— *The Jews in the Duchy of Milan* (4 vols.; Jerusalem, 1982–6).

SLIM, H. COLIN, 'Gian and Gian Maria: Some Fifteenth- and Sixteenth-Century Namesakes', *Musical Quarterly*, 57 (1971), 562–72.

SOLERTI, ANGELO, *Le origini del melodramma: testimonianze dei contemporanei* (Turin, 1903; repr. Bologna, 1969).

—— 'Feste musicali alla corte di Savoia nella prima metà del secolo XVII', *Rivista musicale italiana*, 11 (1904), 675–724.

—— *Gli albori del melodramma* (3 vols.; Milan, 1905, repr. Hildesheim, 1969).

SOMMI, LEONE DE', *Tsaḥut bediḥuta dekidushin* ['A Comedy of Betrothal', from the 1550s], ed. Chaim Schirmann as *Hamaḥaze ha'ivri harishon* ['The First Hebrew Play'] (Jerusalem, 1945, 2nd edn. 1965).

—— *Quattro dialoghi in materia di rappresentazioni sceniche* (1565), ed. Ferruccio Marotti (Milan, 1968).

SPENCER, ROBERT, 'Chitarrone, Theorbo, and Archlute', *Early Music*, 4 (1976), 407–22.

STIGLIANI, TOMMASO, *Libro primo del Rimario nel qual si contiene il trattato del verso italiano composto in ventisei capitoli* (Bologna, 1693).

STOQUERUS, GASPAR, *De musica verbali libri duo* (Madrid, Biblioteca Nacional, MS 6486, c.1570).

STOW, KENNETH R., *Catholic Thought and Papal Jewry Policy, 1553–1593* (New York, 1977).

—— *The Jews in Rome*, i (Leiden, 1995).

TAGMANN, PIERRE, 'La cappella dei maestri cantori della basilica palatina di Santa Barbara a Mantova (1565–1630)', *Civiltà mantovana*, 4 (1969), 376–400.

TAMBORRA, ANGELO, *Gli stati italiani, l'Europa e il problema turco dopo Lepanto* (Florence, 1961).

TASSO, TORQUATO, *Canzone della coronatione del Serenissimo Sig. Don Vincenzo Gonzaga duca di Mantova et Monferrato, etc.* (Mantua, 1587).

A Thematic Index to the Works of Salamon Rossi, comp. Joel Newman and Fritz Rikko (Hackensack, NJ, 1972).

TOMLINSON, GARY, 'Music and the Claims of Text: Monteverdi, Rinuccini, and Marino', *Critical Inquiry*, 8 (1981–2), 565–89.

——*Monteverdi and the End of the Renaissance* (Berkeley, 1987).

TORREFRANCA, MASSIMO ACANFORA, ' "I canti di Salomone" di Salamone Rossi: un caso di confluenza fra tradizioni italiane ed ebraiche nel primo Seicento', unpublished *tesi di laurea* (University of Rome, 1986).

TOSCANO, RAFAELE, *L'edificazione di Mantova e l'origine dell'antichissima famiglia de' principi Gonzaghi e d'altre nobilissime familie di detta città* (Mantua, 1587).

TWERSKY, ISADORE, and SEPTIMUS, BERNARD (eds.), *Jewish Thought in the Seventeenth Century* (Cambridge, Mass., 1987).

VECCHI, ORAZIO, *The Four-Voice Canzonettas: With Original Texts and Contrafacta by Valentin Haussmann and Others*, ed. Ruth I. DeFord (2 vols.; Madison, 1993).

VICENTINO, NICOLA, *L'antica musica ridotta alla moderna prattica* (Rome, 1555; fac. repr. Kassel, 1959).

WERNER, ERIC, 'The Eduard Birnbaum Collection of Jewish Music' (in particular, MS 4. F. 71), *Hebrew Union College Annual*, 18 (1943/4), 397–428 (repr. under title 'Manuscripts of Jewish Music in the Eduard Birnbaum Collection of the Hebrew Union College Library' in id., *Three Ages of Musical Thought: Essays on Ethics and Aesthetics* (New York, 1981), 241–72).

——'The Oldest Sources of Synagogal Chants', *Proceedings of the American Academy of Jewish Research*, 16 (1947), 225–32.

WERT, GIACHES DE, *Opera omnia*, ed. Carol MacClintock and Melvin Bernstein (17 vols.; n.p., 1961–77).

WHENHAM, JOHN, *Duet and Dialogue in the Age of Monteverdi* (2 vols.; Ann Arbor, 1982).

ZARLINO, GIOSEFFO, *Le istitutioni harmoniche* (Venice, 1558; fac. repr. New York, 1965).

ZUCCARO, FEDERICO, *Il passaggio per l'Italia con la dimora di Parma* (Bologna, 1608; rev. edn., Rome, 1893).

INDEX